READER C(

What People Are Saying About
Q. David Bowers and
Grading Coins by Photographs

This groundbreaking work on coin grading has earned the respect of experts nationwide. Here are some reader comments.

"*Grading Coins by Photographs* is magnificent! A must-read for today's sophisticated collector. This will be the most important grading book in my numismatic library."

—*John Albanese, cofounder of PCGS, NGC, and CAC*

"Outstanding! *Grading Coins by Photographs* is a peerless guide—an essential reference for numismatists and collectors at all levels."

—*Mitchell A. Battino, numismatist and certified appraiser*

"*Grading Coins by Photographs* is by far the finest work ever produced on the subject of grading. I really like the Bowers approach to this difficult task. This new work will help everyone in the hobby take a fresh, and more accurate, look at grading."

—*Kenneth Bressett, numismatic author and researcher*

"*Grading Coins by Photographs* is an important addition to any numismatic library—a comprehensive, detailed, well-illustrated explanation of today's grading standards. In addition to excellent photographs of various grades, it explains useful nuances regarding striking, as well as characteristics unique to each series. These offer assistance to beginner and advanced collectors, as well as dealers, in the grading process."

—*Elizabeth Coggan, professional numismatist*

"Dave Bowers's text reveals the decades of experience he's accumulated dealing in rare coins. If a picture is worth a thousand words, readers will be rewarded by the millions with this landmark publication."

—*Jeff Garrett, numismatic author and coin dealer*

"Comprehensive and complete. The text alone makes this the finest detailed descriptive work ever done on grading, and the photos are as strong as the text. *Grading Coins by Photographs* will become the standard of the industry."

—*Ira Goldberg, numismatist, auctioneer, and author*

"*Grading Coins by Photographs* is a total delight, absolutely essential reading for all serious collectors. I always enjoy and learn from David Bowers's books. He has presented a tremendous amount of information on the critical issue of coin grading."

—*David Hall, cofounder of PCGS; president of Collectors Universe*

"This is a very useful book. Bowers's critiques of the illustrated coins are more instructive than the generalities about ideal coins found in most grading guides. This kind of 'real-world' grading is hard to impart to beginners."

—*David W. Lange, research director, NGC*

"Dave Bowers provides both collectors and dealers with an extremely useful resource. Not only does he thoroughly address the grading of every series in U.S. coinage (a matter that is of the utmost importance to anyone who spends their hard-earned money on American coins), he also cleverly interweaves both the idiosyncrasies and the history of each design wherever this information is most appropriate."

—*Scott Mitchell, professional numismatist, Stack's Rare Coins*

"All of Dave Bowers's books are highly regarded, and *Grading Coins by Photographs* is, without question, an essential part of any numismatist's library. Clear, concise, specific, and insightful, this guide takes much of the mystery out of grading coins."

—*Michael Savinelli, collector and numismatic researcher*

"Using this book will put you ahead of most collectors, right from the start. It's like having a grading expert at your side."

—*David M. Sundman, president, Littleton Coin Company*

"Time will tell, but I predict Dave Bowers's *Grading Coins by Photographs* will become an important—and well-worn—reference for hobbyists, regardless of whether they are new to the field or longtime, serious collectors."

—*James Taylor, president and CEO, ANACS*

"The text for circulated coins is fantastic—this book is without equal."

—*Scott Travers, numismatic consumer advocate and author*

"Dave Bowers has done it again. *Grading Coins by Photographs* is indispensable to new and seasoned numismatists alike. It is destined to be a dog-eared book that collectors and dealers carry with them to shows and auctions."

—*Dave Wnuck, co-owner, Coin Rarities Online*

GRADING COINS
BY
PHOTOGRAPHS
2ND EDITION

Q. David Bowers

Foreword by
David M. Sundman

Special Consultants
Kenneth Bressett and Bill Fivaz

Reviewed by
Leading Numismatic Grading Experts

Whitman
Publishing, LLC
PUBLISHING SINCE 1934

Pelham, Alabama

GRADING COINS
BY
PHOTOGRAPHS
2ND EDITION

© 2021 Whitman Publishing, LLC
1974 Chandalar Drive, Suite D, Pelham, AL 35124

Correspondence concerning this book may be directed to the publisher, Attn: Grading Coins by Photographs, at the address above.

ISBN: 0794836879
Printed in China

About the cover: Grading is very important whether you're buying coins or selling them. An MCMVII (1907) High Relief Saint-Gaudens $20 gold coin is worth about $13,000 in AU-55; its value nearly *doubles* to $25,000 in MS-63. Not knowing the difference can cost you thousands of dollars. The differential for other coins can be even more dramatic. For example, a single point in Mint State for the 1886-O Morgan dollar (from MS-64 to MS-65) can mean a price difference of $175,000 or more.

If you find *Grading Coins by Photographs* to be useful, we recommend the *Official American Numismatic Association Grading Standards for United States Coins,* also available from Whitman Publishing.

For a complete catalog of numismatic reference books, supplies, and storage products, visit Whitman Publishing online at www.whitman.com.

Whitman®

TABLE OF CONTENTS

About the Author vi

Foreword *by David M. Sundman* vii

Credits and Acknowledgments xi

Introduction *by Q. David Bowers* xii

Chapter 1: Importance of Grading 1

Chapter 2: History of Grading 7

Chapter 3: Expert Techniques in Grading 14

Chapter 4: Understanding the Surfaces of Coins 20

Chapter 5: Smart Grading and Buying 29

Chapter 6: How to Use This Book 38

Chapter 7: Grading U.S. Coins 40
        Half Cents 41
        Large Cents 59
        Small Cents 85
        Two-Cent Pieces 101
        Three-Cent Pieces 106
        Nickel 5-Cent Pieces 114
        Half Dimes 130
        Dimes 155
        Twenty-Cent Pieces 185
        Quarter Dollars 190
        Half Dollars 226
        Dollars 263
        Gold Dollars 300
        Gold Quarter Eagles 307
        Gold $3 Pieces 320
        Gold $4 Stellas 323
        Gold Half Eagles 326
        Gold Eagles 342
        Gold Double Eagles 354

ABOUT THE AUTHOR

Q. David Bowers has been a professional numismatist since he was a teenager in the early 1950s. He has served as president of the American Numismatic Association (1983–1985) and as president of the Professional Numismatists Guild (1977–1979); is a recipient of the ANA's Farran Zerbe Award; was the first ANA member to be named Numismatist of the Year (1995); in 2005 was given the ANA Lifetime Achievement Award; and has been inducted into the ANA Numismatic Hall of Fame. Bowers was awarded the highest honor  given by the Professional Numismatists Guild (the Founder's Award) and has received more "Book of the Year" awards and "Best Columnist" honors from the Numismatic Literary Guild than has any other writer. He is the author of more than 50 books, hundreds of auction and other catalogs, and several thousand numismatic articles. He has graded and cataloged many of the finest coin collections ever brought to the market.

Foreword writer David M. Sundman grew up in the family stamp-and-coin firm founded by his parents. Graduating from Gettysburg College in 1970 with a degree in history, he rejoined Littleton Coin Company in 1972; today he serves as its president. Sundman is a life fellow of the American Numismatic Society and a life member of the American Numismatic Association, and is a member of the Professional Numismatists Guild and many other numismatic and philatelic organizations. He is a frequent speaker at numismatic events and has mounted many exhibits.

Special consultant Kenneth Bressett has been involved in the hobby since the 1940s. He has written many numismatic articles and is author or editor of more than a dozen related books; a past governor, vice president, and president of the ANA; and a highly accomplished researcher. He has served for many years as the editor of *A Guide Book of United States Coins* (the "Red Book"); is a recipient of the NLG's Clemy Award; and is an inductee in the ANA Numismatic Hall of Fame.

Special consultant Bill Fivaz, who has collected coins since 1950, is one of today's best-known figures in numismatics. He has garnered every major honor the hobby community offers, including election to the ANA Hall of Fame, Numismatist of the Year, and the Farran Zerbe Award. A familiar instructor at the ANA Summer Seminar and other venues, Bill is also author of many articles and several books. He is a well-known consultant on matters involving grading, authentication, variety attribution, and other technical aspects of numismatics.

FOREWORD BY DAVID M. SUNDMAN

I am a principal of Littleton Coin Co., LLC, one of America's oldest and largest family-owned numismatic firms. For more than 60 years in numismatics, we've concentrated on serving the traditional date-and-mintmark collector of U.S. coins. My mother and father started our firm in a one-room office. Today our staff serves hundreds of thousands of customers from a modern 85,000-square-foot building, handling several millions of coins in the course of a year, through the mail and via our Web site. My brothers and I grew up in "the trade" (we worked cheap!). When I was around the age of 10, one of the early lessons my father Maynard Sundman instilled in me was the importance of conservative grading. He wanted to ensure customers were pleased and would want to come back. As our first coin buyer, he had learned that the way to ensure repeat customer orders was to be consistent and fair in his grading. At the same time, he pointed out you didn't want to undergrade, as you'd be hurting yourself.

Like so many young collectors who began in the 1950s, I concentrated on picking coins out of pocket change to put in my blue Whitman folders. Growing up in the business, and working for my father sorting lots of coins by date on the weekends, I had more opportunities than most kids to see old U.S. and world coins up close. In those days I couldn't afford to buy very much, as my allowance of a quarter (later a half dollar) a week wouldn't go very far. Supplemented by coins I could sell to the company from my circulation finds—such as better-date Lincoln cents, Buffalo nickels, and Mercury dimes—as the years went on, my financial picture improved.

One of my first collections that I had to pay more than face value for was my U.S. large cent collection. I couldn't afford many of the early (1793 to 1814) coins, except in the lowest conditions, what might be called About Good to Good, but the 1816 to 1857 coins were still fairly affordable. As these did not come from pocket change, I splurged $14 for a two-binder set of sturdy Wayte Raymond "National" album pages and covers to house the coins. This collection really took a leap forward when my father purchased a large lot of several thousand large cents from dealer Maurice Storck for a couple of dollars per coin. (Storck dealt in coins from the inexpensive to the rare, and was in the contingent of Americans who attended the Cairo sale of the King Farouk collection in 1954.)

Amazingly, in those days—when price spreads between grades were so much smaller—when you bought such a large group some of the very best coins would range from Extremely Fine to lustrous brown Uncirculated. My father allowed me to sort the coins in this lot by date and major variety, as listed in the *Guide Book of United States Coins* (the "Red Book"), and to pull out high-grade examples for my new collection. By the time I'd gone through thousand of cents, searching for the best example of a particular variety, I'd learned much about how to differentiate between weakly struck and well-struck examples. Years later when I was in college, I sold those choice large cents back to our firm to pay for a trip to Europe. The market prices for nice coins had advanced significantly since I'd bought them a decade earlier, and the profitable sale of the coins so carefully chosen confirmed that I had learned something about grading. It also confirmed to me that I wanted to be a coin dealer.

By the late 1950s, collecting Lincoln cents by date was at a fever pitch, fueled by the discovery of the 1955 Doubled Die. Key dates such as 1909-S V.D.B. and 1914-D were increasingly hard to find on the wholesale market, and only the luckiest person could spot one in pocket change. Even with our then-small coin business, my father could not keep up with customer requests for them. He ran "Wanted to Buy—Coins" classified advertisements in various publications around the country, offering to pay $15 each for 1909-S V.D.B. cents in Fine to Very Fine condition. Although that price seems incredibly low today, it was a very fair price back then. The *Guide Book* price for Fine was $17.50, and the next highest grade listed was Uncirculated, at $30. Shortly after the classified ad appeared, a lady from California sent my father a full roll of 50 coins. When the coins were shipped to us, and he opened the Registered Mail package, there was a problem. My dad wrote the lady and said, "I can't pay you $15 a coin. I'm advertising to pay $15 for Fine to Very Fine and your coins are much better than that; they are Uncirculated."

She wrote back, insisting he honor his buy price, and pay her the $15 a coin! Eventually he was able to make her understand they were worth more, and bought the roll. Today it's hard to imagine a full roll of 50 1909-S V.D.B. cents, all in brilliant Uncirculated condition! I remember Dad letting me examine the entire group spread out neatly in a line, all with the unusual light straw-golden color so characteristic of pristine examples of this variety. Today a roll of 50 would be worth $200,000 or more. The whole experience of that transaction drove home the point that accurate grading and fairness were one and the same, whether buying or selling, whether dealing with our essential suppliers, or with our valuable customers.

Maynard Sundman expected his suppliers to be fair, and treated them fairly in return. He learned the hard way. Not everyone was fair in their business practices, and especially in the coin-grading arena, but he soon learned to do most of his business with those who were—and he learned how to grade.

Several years later he added to his library a copy of the handbook *How to Be A Successful Coin Dealer,* by young Q. David Bowers. This helpful guide was offered by the weekly publication *Coin World* (still going strong today) as a premium to new advertisers, and was also sold separately, going through several editions. It still may be the only book ever published on the subject. One of Dave's maxims contained within was the following:

> When you are beginning your business (and after you have become established as well!) adopt a strict standard of grading. You may not make windfall profits this way, but you will build very, very loyal clientele. It is upon such a loyal clientele that any successful coin business is based. No dealer can rely upon one-time sales to buyers who quickly become disappointed with the material purchased.

This was advice my father agreed with wholeheartedly, and he became a fan of Dave's and, in time, a friend. They often corresponded. When my Dad would come across an interesting old publication or clipping on coins, he'd often send it to him. Like our own firm's experience, Dave's entire success was based on repeat business.

We concentrated on buying and selling coins that were right for the grade, perhaps the top third of the population within any category. Today, some dealers and collectors use the term "high end." These coins were worth more than the run-of-the-mill coins within a grade, as they were free from major scratches, nicks, and planchet problems. To ensure consistent grading by our own staff, we developed sample sets for review in combination with written and visual guidelines.

Through our extensive advertising in popular publications, we reached the average American, teaching him or her to collect coins in an organized fashion with albums and checklists, so progress could be monitored as additional pieces were acquired. Although many youngsters answered our advertisements over the years, the business was aimed at serving adult collectors. Many if not most of them were certainly tyros, youthful in their experience in the hobby and certainly new to concepts of coin grading. Maynard Sundman never wanted to unfairly take advantage of this. Littleton Coin specialized in taking a person at whatever level they were at in their hobby pursuit, and enrolling them in a coins-on-approval service. The advantage was that the customer could hold the coins in their hands, and see the quality for themselves, and make a decision to buy or not, at their leisure, without pressure. They could show them to friends and ask others' opinions.

In any good business, the goal is to keep customers for life. In the coin business, to achieve this, accurate grading was and still is an essential part of the success formula. Certainly many of our customers did not know how to grade coins when they began collecting, but we knew if they stuck with it, they'd learn. When that day arrived, we wanted them to always be able to look back on a coin they'd purchased from us, and be pleased with the grade. At the same time, what we considered to be select coins within each grade could not be the cheapest coins on the market. By and large, nearly all of our customers came to appreciate quality, often after they had tried "bargain" offers elsewhere.

In 1970, when James F. Ruddy's revolutionary *Photograde* book first came out, our firm quickly adopted it as a useful guide for training our staff. We added it to our catalog, and sold tens of thousands of copies over the years. At the time it was revolutionary for its clear descriptions and ease of study, with useful photographs, a real step forward.

It is always a major awakening when a collector first realizes that grading coins is not so easy, and that he has much to learn. Eventually, with careful study, a collector learns that a coin's characteristics can and often do vary by year and mint, and sometimes by die variety within a coin series. Discerning these differences, and how they affect grading, can take years of study. The author of the present Whitman Publishing book, *Grading Coins by Photographs,* has been in a unique position over the decades to survey a vast array of the rarest and most important coins from some of the finest collections ever assembled. He's worked with some of the keenest fellow students of numismatics. He is widely acknowledged for his splendidly detailed and accurate auction descriptions in the many catalogs and price lists he's published since the 1950s. While others have been accorded similar opportunities over the years, none has proven better at recording the experiences and sharing them in print with his fellow numismatists than Q. David Bowers.

This varied experience has greatly assisted the creation of *Grading Coins by Photographs.* It truly is a distillation of more than 55 years of numismatic study—careful one-by-one observation of more than a million rare coins—combined with discussion with experts such as Bill Fivaz, David W. Akers, Jeff Garrett, Kenneth Bressett, and many others, including graders at the leading certification services. The information on grading each U.S. series is superior and far more extensive than that in the *Official American Numismatic Association Grading Standards for United States Coins* and the earlier mentioned *Photograde.* What's more, it gives you a realistic picture of the highest grades for key dates that are most likely to be seen in a series. If you are a new collector embarked on putting together a very high-quality set, careful attention to this will save you from wasting time chasing coins in a quality that may be impossible to obtain. After all, the object is to *collect* coins. If someday you come across a better example, you can always upgrade. I make a regular practice of this in my own collecting activity. I know some collectors even put together a "Set #2" and a "Set #3" of coins they've since upgraded. Of course, you can also decide to sell, which can provide good feedback on your grading.

Within each coin series that particularly interests you, you'll find Bowers's extensive notes on striking characteristics by date and mintmark. These are facts mostly known to only the most sophisticated collectors and specialists, information that is not available elsewhere in a single book. Contributions by Bill Fivaz, probably *the* leading expert on die varieties and the idiosyncrasies of striking quality and a longtime authority on grading, are the icing on the cake.

For years I've recommended to our new customers that they pay attention to the actual coin when making a buying decision. Compare coins side by side—don't just compare prices. Really, prices don't mean very much if one coin is of high quality and the other low. The cheaper or "low-end" coin may be the worst buy, as Dave points out in this book. For the certified-coin buyer, he recommends that you ignore the grade on the holder—look at the coin. Don't collect *numbers*—collect nice-looking, conservatively graded *coins*.

I consider this the best grading guide *ever* published. *Grading Coins by Photographs*, with its extensive photographs and detailed notes on different coin types, including striking characteristics and availability, is a groundbreaking work that should be on every numismatist's bookshelf. Never has so much grading knowledge been so readily available in one volume.

With this book in your hands, and knowledge in your mind from having read it, you can embark on examining the coins themselves. Dave calls this "field" work, and it is absolutely necessary. No matter what grade level you decide to collect, it is important to become familiar with the entire spectrum of possibilities within the series—ranging from About Good or Good, through Extremely Fine, About Uncirculated, and Mint State. One can never know too much about grading!

While certified coins dominate some parts of the marketplace, there are still many "raw" coins available. In fact, dealers in early American coins such as copper half cents and cents often have the majority of their inventory housed in envelopes, and not certified. You can explore these and other possibilities, while many other buyers are handicapped by uncertainty and are limited to reviewing coins in "slabs."

An innovation in this book is the inclusion of clear color photos of high-grade Uncirculated and Proof coins, with accompanying notes. This will give you a good reference point, for comparison. These real-life descriptions are what some dealers call *market grading*, as opposed to strict *technical grading*. Coins do have differences, and many of these are nicely explained in the introductory chapters and in the grade descriptions.

As to an overview, here is why I think that *you* will find this book useful in your collecting:

While learning goes on for life, the key concepts to achieve grading competency can be learned with a few years of intensive study. Mistakes are also part of the process; you can't learn without making some along the way. A good guide such as this one can help you minimize them. Using this book will put you ahead of most collectors, right from the start. It's like having a grading expert at your side.

As you learn to grade coins accurately with the help of this book:

You will learn to look at the coin itself, ignoring the grading label on its holder.

You will learn to *cherrypick* coins that are exceptional specimens for your collection.

You will be a confident and more knowledgeable buyer.

You will have more fun, and build a collection you will cherish.

Thanks to Q. David Bowers for *Grading Coins by Photographs*. It is a great gift to numismatics.

David M. Sundman
Littleton, New Hampshire

CREDITS AND ACKNOWLEDGMENTS

These numismatists and organizations provided coins and/or coin photographs for this book.

David W. Akers
Jack Beymer
Doug Bird
Fonda Chase
Bill Fivaz
Jeff Garrett
Heritage Auctions
Gwyn Huston
Tom Hyland
Wayne Imbrogno
Jon Lerner

Littleton Coin Company
Harry Miller
Charles Moore
Dan Moore
Douglas Plasencia
Smithsonian Institution (National
   Numismatic Collection; Richard
   Doty and James Hughes)
Stack's Rare Coins
Ken and Stephanie Westover
Rich Uhrich

The following numismatic experts contributed a professional review of the grading text.

Gary Adkins
John Albanese
Jeff Ambio
Mitchell Battino
Kenneth Bressett
Elizabeth Coggan
Michael Fahey
Bill Fivaz
Jeff Garrett
Ira Goldberg
Larry Goldberg
Ken Goldman
John Grellman
Ron Guth
Jim Halperin
Brad Karoleff
David W. Lange

Julian Leidman
Denis Loring
J.P. Martin
Scott Mitchell
John Pack
Jim Reardon
Harry Salyards
Michael Savinelli
Rick Snow
Lawrence R. Stack
David M. Sundman
James Taylor
Scott Travers
Frank Van Valen
Doug Winter
David Wnuck

Wynn Bowers, Kenneth Bressett, Bill Fivaz, Patty Moore, and David M. Sundman reviewed the introductory chapters. Frank Van Valen assisted in attributing die varieties pictured in chapter 7.

Whitman Publishing and the author express appreciation to all of the preceding for their contributions to *Grading Coins by Photographs*.

INTRODUCTION BY Q. DAVID BOWERS

Welcome to the second edition of this book, which in a short time has become very popular. It has fulfilled the need for more detailed descriptions and appropriate color illustrations than can be found in most grading texts.

From the time I discovered numismatics in 1952 and began adding "pennies" to a Whitman folder, I realized the importance of grading. In 1953 I became a dealer on a small scale, and grading became even more important to me, as an offered coin could vary considerably in value depending on its state of preservation. There were no generally accepted guides to grading at the time, and everyone had his or her own interpretation. Sellers were always "testing" me to see what I would accept.

Generally, most of the dealers and collectors I came to know recognized when a coin was Uncirculated or Mint State, meaning that it had no visible wear. However, within that category there was little distinction. Similarly, one person's Very Fine could be another's Fine or Extremely Fine. Proofs were generally listed simply as *Proof* or *Brilliant Proof*, with no notation as to minute differences. My own catalogs of the 1950s, as well as nearly all priced and auction catalogs of other dealers, were similar.

A few connoisseurs sought out what might be called "gems"–Mint State and Proof coins with few problems. Bargain hunters didn't care. In the 1950s relatively few people were particular in this regard. I recall that John J. Pittman, Mrs. R. Henry Norweb, and Lester Merkin were very careful about quality, but they were among the rare exceptions. That changed as values increased, and by the early 1960s careful attention was paid to grading. Such terms as *gem, choice,* and the like were rarely used, and when they were they had no consistency in the marketplace. In time, starting in a large way in the coin-market boom of 1960 to 1964, these designations became common. Definitions remained lacking, however. Today, grading, if not actually sophisticated, appears to newcomers to be that way, with the proliferation of numbers including 11 different stages of Mint State.

I have always found the subject of grading to be interesting, and have written about it extensively. In 1969 and 1970 when my fine friend and associate James F. Ruddy was snapping pictures for use in the coin-grading book *Photograde,* I wrote some of the narrative (Jim did the grade descriptions). In the late 1970s, when the American Numismatic Association formulated its Official Grading Standards, I joined Abe Kosoff and Kenneth Bressett in the creation of the text. It fell to me to write the general introduction explaining the nuances of grading techniques and their application. Ken wrote the individual descriptions. Over a long period of time, I have written extensively on the subject of grading and have participated in various classes and seminars. I am still observing, still learning. Grading doesn't stand still. It is dynamic. Interpretations constantly evolve. Not too long ago, Ken and I assisted the ANA in updating the *Official American Numismatic Association Grading Standards for United States Coins* to its most recent edition.

The present book, *Grading Coins by Photographs,* is unique. It goes significantly beyond any texts currently in use. Rather than simply stating that, for example, early half dimes and dimes should be graded the same way, I study each type separately, pointing out the idiosyncrasies and also making due note of how die varieties and striking can be important in each series. One rule does not–can not–fit all. For example, among silver dollars of the 1795 to 1798 era with Draped Bust obverse and Small Eagle reverse, one particular "Small Letters" reverse die, used over a span of all of these years, was so shallow in its original relief, and the accompanying rim was so low, that a specimen can appear to be, say, Extremely Fine-40 on the obverse, while the reverse may not be any better than Fine-12 or Very Fine-20. This particular variety should be graded by the obverse only. For certain other varieties, the opposite is true. Morgan silver dollars (of 1878 to 1921) in Mint State are nearly always a point or two higher in grade on the reverse than on the obverse, even though we all use just a single number when grading them today.

One picture is worth a thousand words, so they say. Accordingly, the text is well illustrated in color, with narrative descriptions accompanying the designated grade in many instances. It is my hope that if you read carefully the information about the listed coins from the 1790s to date, you will appreciate and indeed learn what experienced dealers and collectors know. A numerical grade is one thing, but often there are other aspects involved in determining the market value of a coin. I believe that after you study this book and use it in the field, in the real-life marketplace, you will *think* like a grading expert!

Across the hobby, general interpretations have changed from time to time. Now, in the second decade of the 21st century, the interpretation of Uncirculated or Mint State is more liberal than it was 30 or 40 years ago. As an example, David W. Akers's studies of gold coins from the dollar to the double eagle, published from 1975 to 1982, analyze auction appearances and grades, and point out that many early issues are very rare or even unknown in Mint State. The $2.50 and $5 pieces of the Charlotte and Dahlonega mints are examples. Today, such coins that used to be graded as About Uncirculated (AU) are now often graded as MS-60, MS-61, and MS-62. It can be argued that a coin is either Uncirculated or it is not—black and white. However, that does not always seem to apply in today's marketplace. Many pieces incorrectly graded as lower-level Mint State show actual circulation wear (different from abrasions and contact marks from being jostled in bank bags). I make an effort to describe this in the text.

If I were to use old-time standards, then a definition of an early gold coin in MS-60 or 61 would be that *no* wear would be present. You as a reader would be very frustrated to find that MS-61 coins, including examples certified by the leading coin-grading services, did indeed show wear. At this point my text would become *theoretical* rather than practical. You'd ask, "Where the heck can I find those wear-free coins that Dave Bowers defines in *Grading Coins by Photographs?*" Ken Bressett and I faced the same problem in updating the *Official American Numismatic Association Grading Standards for United States Coins.* The strength of the word LIBERTY on certain copper, nickel, and silver coins was for generations a determinator as to grade. In some series, all of the letters needed to be present to be called *Fine* (today's F-12 or F-15). In recent times there has been a deterioration, or "gradeflation," as it is sometimes called, and some grading services suggest that not all letters have to be readable. Current certification-service practices and techniques in use in the early 20th century trump any idealism. Practicality intervenes, as it must, to make this book useful for you in the real-world marketplace. However, explanations of such changes are given, and I believe you will gain a keen understanding of today's grading philosophies.

The fact that grading is highly subjective, rather than objective—aesthetic, even as it strives to be scientific—gives you many opportunities when you buy. As one of many examples, if you were to examine 100 different Capped Bust half dollars certified as

MS-60 you would find many differences among them. Some would have obvious wear and be dull in appearance, perhaps better called AU-55 or 58. Others would be highly lustrous and would immediately seem to be "high end," perhaps a candidate to be called MS-62 or MS-63, but would have wear on the portrait. Such situations are very real in the marketplace. If you read this book carefully, combining it with extensive observation of coins themselves as well as illustrations in catalogs and elsewhere, you should become among the most expert of dealers and collectors. And, you will learn about those puzzling MS-60 Capped Bust halves, so you can make some really great buys. I daresay that a "high-end" MS-60 half dollar can be worth *twice as much* as a "low-end" example of the same grade.

As an interesting exercise, if you have access to a computer—and most readers do—go on line and seek pictures of Peace silver dollars dated 1921 and 1928-S that have been certified as, say, MS-64. In a very short time my above words will come to life! You will find the good, the bad, and the ugly.

Opportunities abound!

The object of this book is to illuminate the *art* of grading, and, together with some field work, enable you to grade as well as do long-established numismatists. You will go *beyond* numerical grades and learn of other aspects that can affect a coin's value, sometimes dramatically. Many of the opinions, insights, and comments in the first edition of this text had never appeared in any other reference book on grading.

As you review offered coins in all series you will be able to make better purchases, getting more for your money. This advantage is made possible by the somewhat illogical situation of the vast majority of buyers simply looking at the assigned grade, and not at the coin itself! Of course, if this is all you want to do, then you don't need this book. However, if you do read and employ the text, I believe this book will pay for itself many times over when you cherrypick for grade and overall quality. Indeed, its purchase price may be the best money you've ever spent in numismatics. Between its covers you will read what I have learned from a lifetime in the profession.

I thank David Sundman for his fine foreword to this book, and I am appreciative of the many people who have helped over the years in the creation of studies involving grading. Many people have played a part. The expert dealers and collectors who reviewed the text and made comments contributed much as well, and are acknowledged in the credits. Today, grading isn't *solved*, nor is it scientific. However, it is better *understood* than ever before.

Now, onward to one of the most fascinating, most important subjects in numismatics!

Q. David Bowers
Wolfeboro, New Hampshire

Chapter 1

The Importance of Grading

Grading as a Key to Value

"How rare is it?" "What is it worth?" These are the two usual questions that anyone who owns an old coin asks. Scarcely ever is there a question about how many were minted, who designed it, and what role the coin played in commerce. To be sure, many people do care about art, history, romance, and other aspects of coinage, and they are the foundation of our hobby. However, rarity and value make the wheels of numismatic commerce turn.

As to the market price of a coin, information abounds. Check the *Guide Book of United States Coins* (the annually issued "Red Book"). Or punch a few keys and look on the Internet, and you can find hundreds of offerings of popular coins—say an 1884-CC Morgan dollar, or a 1960 Small Date Lincoln cent, or an 1883 Without CENTS Liberty Head nickel.

Values are not precise, but for a specific coin in a given grade, say Mint State-63, market prices for a particular variety of Morgan dollar might range from $150 to $180, if they are certified (professionally graded and encapsulated) by the Professional Coin Grading Service (PCGS), the Numismatic Guaranty Corporation of America (NGC), or ANACS. There are other certification services, too, of course, but their business is not as extensive, and often the coins will not sell for the same levels to buyers who simply look at the labels on holders. To an educated buyer—perhaps *you* after you gain knowledge—the label will be unimportant, as will whether or not it is certified. That will change when time comes to *sell*, for certification increases the marketability of just about every coin. Moreover, the leading certification services guarantee the *authenticity* of each coin—an exceedingly valuable aspect that is often overlooked.

While pricing information is abundant, this is not so with useful information about grading. There are some fine guides in print, most notably the *Official American Numismatic Association Grading Standards for United States Coins*, *Photograde*, the *Official Guide to Coin Grading and Counterfeit Detection* (published by PCGS), the *NGC Grading Guide for U.S. Coins*, and a few others. However, a library of current titles on coin grading would occupy just a few inches of shelf space.

To reiterate, grading is perhaps the single most important factor affecting the price of a coin. Rarity is important, of course, and so is demand. However, for a given variety of large copper cent, or gold $20 double eagle, or Shield nickel, its value is affected dramatically by the grade it seems to be in. The word *seems* is appropriate, for grading is, always has been, and will forever admit of a generous proportion of, old-fashioned *opinion*. What is Gem Uncirculated or Mint State-65 to one expert can legitimately be viewed as a lower grade, MS-64, by another expert, and MS-66 by yet another. This is because grading is interpretive, not an exact science.

PRICES AND GRADES IN THE MARKETPLACE

As to the dramatic effect a grade can have on a coin, using a recent edition of the *Guide Book of United States Coins,* consider the the 1901 Philadelphia Mint Morgan dollar:

1901 Morgan silver dollar—VF-20: $50 • EF-40: $110 • AU-50: $450 • MS-60: $2,300 • MS-63: $18,000 • MS-64: $60,000 • MS-65: $250,000

How dramatic this is! A perfectly nice collectible VF-20 coin at $50 compared to $250,000 for an MS-65, a figure *5,000 times* as much! Stated another way, if it were possible to find them, you could own 5,000 1901 Morgan dollars in VF-20 grade for the price of a single MS-65 coin!

Also worth noting is that an MS-64 1901 dollar is valued at $60,000, while an MS-65 is valued at $250,000. The difference of $190,000 is not to be sneezed at, and is enough to buy you a nice Mercedes sports car, with a nice Jaguar to keep alongside it in your garage for your significant other, and with enough money left over to buy gas for—well, who can tell how long, these days! I don't mean to be overly dramatic here, but a small difference in grade can mean a great difference in price. The 1901 dollar is an extreme example, but there are countless other coins that show dramatic differences in value vis-à-vis grade. Consider this coin:

1793 copper half cent—AG-3: $1,200 • G-4: $2,200 • VG-8: $3,500 • F-12: $5,500 • VF-20: $9,000 • EF-40: $18,500 • AU-50: $27,500

While AG-3 (About Good-3; more will be said about grading numbers and abbreviations), is a rather minimal grade, describing a coin barely discernible as to the design type, there is no question that VF-20 at $9,000 or EF-40 at $18,500 can represent a truly excellent coin, and AU-50 at $27,500 can be superb. If you are in the marketplace, it certainly will pay you to know if a coin offered as EF-40 is a "nice" example, or if, perhaps,

1793 half cent certified as AU-50.

it is optimistically graded, and would more realistically be called VF-20. If you are contemplating bidding on an AU-50, you want to be sure that it is not only technically in that grade, but also has good eye appeal and other desirable features.

Without question, one of the most popular and desired of all 20th-century coins is the 1909-S V.D.B. Lincoln cent, a coin that Dave Sundman mentions in his foreword to this study. The Red Book lists these values, again showing wide price differences from one grade to the next:

1909-S V.D.B. Lincoln cent—G-4: $650 • VG-8: $750 • F-12: $850 • VF-20: $1,000 • EF-40: $1,200 • AU-50: $1,250 • MS-60: $1,400 • MS-63: $2,200

A beautiful Mint State 1909-S V.D.B. Lincoln cent.

In other instances, a small separation in grade does *not* necessarily mean a large difference in price. Take for example the 1936 Elgin (Illinois) Centennial commemorative half dollar. All of these were distributed as souvenirs, and buyers paid a premium for them. Accordingly, most were carefully saved by their buyers, and today Mint State coins are the rule, not the exception. The Red Book suggests these values:

1936 Elgin commemorative half dollar—AU-50: $220 • MS-60: $240 • MS-63: $270 • MS-65: $325

1936 Elgin commemorative half dollar certified as MS-65.

The difference of $30 is not apt to give you indigestion if as a beginning buyer you purchase an MS-63, only to find, upon gaining knowledge, that it really is an MS-60. A $30 error you can probably afford. However, for a 1909-S V.D.B. cent, or, if you have a well-endowed checkbook, a high-level 1901 Morgan dollar, such a difference can spoil your day!

CASE STUDY: THE 1884-CC DOLLAR

The 1884-CC Morgan dollar illustrates another interesting aspect of grading.

Back in 1884 the Carson City Mint struck 1,136,000 silver dollars. In comparison, the earlier-discussed 1901 Morgan dollar was produced in the prolific quantity of 6,982,000 pieces.

Nearly all of the 1901 dollars either were passed into circulation in or around that time and became well worn, or were melted down in a great destruction of dollars that took place in 1918. Just a handful have survived at the MS-65 level.

As to the 1884-CC, at the time they were minted, the Treasury Department had a glut of silver dollars. In 1878 Congress had passed the Bland-Allison Act, mandating that Uncle Sam buy millions of ounces of silver each year, to support the declining price of the metal and to help the economy in the American West. Silver dollars were not particularly needed; except for certain limited areas, nearly everyone used *paper* dollars to buy and sell goods and services. Accordingly, year by year after 1878, new silver dollars, stored in cloth bags of 1,000 each, piled up. In fact, the Philadelphia Mint had so many of them that they took over some space in the *Post Office* in that city, and, for good measure, had a special steel-walled building constructed in the interior courtyard of the Mint. Silver dollars were everywhere, and hardly anyone wanted them or knew what to do with the *tons* of coins that kept accumulating.

As scarcely anyone wanted 1884-CC dollars, they were stored at the Carson City Mint after being struck. In 1911, by which time that particular mint had not struck coins for 18 years, most of the stored 1884-CC dollars, still their original canvas bags, were shipped to the Treasury Building in Washington, D.C., where they were stored in vaults. Largely forgotten, these came to light in the early 1960s when there was a rush on silver dollars of all kinds (prompted by a rise in the international value of silver). Inventories were taken, and in March 1964 it was found that 962,638 coins, or 84.73% of the original mintage, still remained—nearly all of them in beautiful Mint State grade! In ensuing years these were packaged in holders and sold at a premium to the public. As these words are being written, PCGS, NGC, and ANACS combined have certified only 70,645 coins in MS-60 or finer grade—this out of nearly a million Mint State coins.

Today, many collectors and newer dealers feel that the rarity of a coin is determined by how many have been certified. The 1884-CC Morgan dollar—popular, valuable, and frequently traded—provides a reality check. As each of the 962,638 coins was sold at a premium to collectors and investors, all or nearly all still exist today. And yet, as noted above, only 70,645 coins—7% of those found—have been certified. Surprised? I bet you are! I do not mean to be iconoclastic, but simply want to give you a reality check on grading and related aspects. In numismatics, relatively few people do this. Along the way, this is a lesson for you to contemplate.

The Red Book lists these prices:

1884-CC Morgan dollar—VF-20: $160 • EF-40: $180 • AU-50: $210 • MS-60: $250 • MS-63: $285 • MS-64: $330 • MS-65: $550

1884-CC Morgan silver dollar certified as MS-67.

As relatively few 1884-CC dollars were ever circulated, today a Mint State coin is at least a hundred times more common than one in VF or EF grade! Using the same population reports, in AU-53 grade, only 8 such coins have been certified. In gem MS-65 the number is 13,671. It is correct to say that for every AU-53 that has been certified there have been 1,709 MS-65 coins. But, who cares? Rarity doesn't mean much in this instance, as just about everyone would prefer to have a Mint State coin.

By way of a related illustration, in 2003 at the Philadelphia Mint, First Flight Centennial commemorative silver dollars were struck, with 53,533 being distributed. The Red Book lists these at $40 in MS-67 grade. In practice, probably 99% of those in the marketplace grade from MS-67 to MS-70, the latter representing perfection. If someone were to come along and say they have a coin kept as a lucky pocket piece, and it had been worn down to EF-40 grade, and was the only one in existence at that low level, it's easy to see that this would be a non-event—you would not want to buy it, and I wouldn't either. The point of this, as an ancillary comment, is that while grade can determine price, rarity within a certain *lower* grade, as higher grades are more readily available, is meaningless, and, in many instances, actually represents coins with little market value.

Quality can be found within just about any grade, ranging from well worn to Mint State. Shown here are two Capped Bust half dollars, each certified as AU-50 by the same grading service. Which one would you pick to add to a type set?

Another leading grading service certified each of these dimes as VF-20—another demonstration of how *you* can evaluate graded coins and cherrypick for quality.

YOUR SECRET TO SUCCESS

Probably 80% to 90% of buyers in the marketplace, or perhaps even more, rely upon the grade that a dealer or certification service assigns to a coin. It does not make much difference to such people whether close examination might suggest a lower grade or, sometimes, a higher grade. A few years ago a dealer bought an About Uncirculated Draped Bust half dime for about $5,000. He stripped away the gray toning with a cleaner and then chemically recolored it with vivid iridescent hues. This recoloring masked the true surface of the coin, and upon examination it was very difficult for me to see that it had light wear. Certified as Mint State-63 by a leading service, it was sold for more than $30,000! This "coin doctor" was as proud as can be, noting that it was an ideal situation: he made a lot of money, the grading service earned a fee, and the new owner of the coin was delighted with its appearance and the number assigned to it.

Bill Fivaz, special consultant to this book, commented that in 2003 he consigned and sold at auction a 1916 Doubled Obverse Die Buffalo nickel from his collection, "properly graded by PCGS as AU-55," for $53,625. In 2008 that same coin, certified by a major grading service as MS-63 after having been "worked," was listed in the *Certified Coin Dealer Newsletter* at $110,000!

In 1999 I cataloged a double eagle attributed as the 1853, 3 Over 2, variety. It was from the SS *Central America* treasure of gold coins then being distributed. The coin was sent to a leading service and came back graded as AU-58. It was listed at auction and sold. The buyer, a dealer, immediately resubmitted it to the same service, and, presto, it was returned to him as "MS-62." A coin that was once thought to be circulated or lightly worn, the very definition of *About* Uncirculated, had not magically shed its wear, so to speak, but now it was stated to be clearly Mint State, not just slightly, but several numbers into that category. If you were to buy this coin today, would you consider it to be MS-62? Would you believe the holder label, or would you examine the coin closely and make an informed opinion?

What if someone told you the same coin was AU-58 a few weeks before it was changed by the same service to MS-62? Would this make a difference to you? If someone said that the coin, certified as MS-62, was *really* AU-58, would you believe him? As to the earlier-mentioned "MS-63" half dime, if you bought it and learned that it was a cleaned and recolored AU, would you be happy to own it? These are real questions, not rhetorical, and are worth contemplating. I do not have specific answers, and am not sure that any would be definitive. I am simply illustrating some of the complexities that swirl in the world of grading coins.

Your secret to success is knowledge. There is no question that the more you can learn about grading, the better buys you can make in the marketplace. This is called *cherry-picking*, a term popularized by Bill Fivaz and J.T. Stanton in the *Cherrypickers' Guide to Rare Die Varieties* and widely used in the hobby. The concept is this: review coins in the marketplace, already graded, and with your knowledge, pick out those that are exceptional values within those grades. Bill has commented, "Knowledge is power, but it is only relevant if you *use* it!"

Some years ago a motivational speech was titled "Acres of Diamonds." The thesis was that the business world offered countless "diamonds" of opportunity, but you need to recognize them and pick them up. The fact that grading is a matter of opinion, and that certified and other coins often differ widely in their quality, is an *advantage* for you! If grading were completely scientific, and all MS-63 coins were exactly the same, there would be no advantage at all, no profit opportunity for your knowledge. There would be no "acres of diamonds" waiting for you.

Chapter 2

HISTORY OF GRADING

GRADING IN THE EARLY DAYS

As part of learning to grade coins it may be interesting and informative for you to review the history of this art in numismatics—to learn what has been done by those collectors and dealers who have gone before us. How did different terms come about? What about all of those numbers? Is grading scientific? Or is it artistic? My comments are necessarily brief (I could write a *book* on the history of grading). Here goes.

The hobby of numismatics, at one time often called *numismatology,* began with a few scattered collectors, such as the Reverend William Bentley of Salem, Massachusetts, and Pierre Eugène Du Simitière, of Philadelphia, during the colonial period of American history. Coin collecting did not begin in a serious way in America, however, until 1857 and 1858. The old "large" copper cent was discontinued by the Act of February 21, 1857, and began to be withdrawn from circulation. These little mementos of life of yesteryear, childhood spending, and the like, all of a sudden became dear to the hearts of Americans, and a scramble ensued to save as many different dates from circulation as possible. In 1858, the American Numismatic Society was founded, with other organizations taking form around the same time and later. Coin auctions became serious business by 1859. The early 1860s saw a wide expansion of coin dealerships, auction offerings, and more, including the use of such popular references as Montroville W. Dickeson's *American Numismatical Manual* (1859), W.C. Prime's *Coins, Medals and Seals* (1861), and others. Newspapers and magazines carried popular articles on numismatics, with *Historical Magazine,* launched in 1857, being a particularly popular venue.

It is tempting to think nostalgistically about a simpler time in American numismatics, before the complex problems of today made their appearance. With grading, however, there never was such a simpler time. In 1860, George Jones wrote *The Coin Collectors Manual,* a sort of early combination of the Red Book and the *Coin Dealer Newsletter,* listing prices realized for coins sold at auction in New York and Philadelphia. Jones demonstrated that grading has been a matter of disagreement since the cradle days of the hobby, writing: "It is a matter of regret that there is such a diversity of opinion with regard to the condition of a coin. There must be an absence of prejudice and interest in the coin in question, in order to give a fair report of it, and at times, even experienced collectors and dealers will disagree."

Many of the disagreements Jones mentioned arose from sheer ambiguity. General terms such as *Good, Fine, Uncirculated,* and *Proof* were used. Sometimes intermediate steps such as *Nearly Fine* or *About Proof* were inserted. Today, one might find little sense in some of these, such as "About Proof" (either a coin is a Proof or it is not). It was a time of expansion and learning, and the hobby and its language were in a development stage.

Soon it became known that certain dealers and auction houses delivered "nice" coins when they were described as Uncirculated, while others might be selling pieces that were cleaned, or even counterfeit. There were no rules of engagement, and just about any-thing went. Buying through the mail was a hazardous procedure, as no catalogs offered photographs (such illustrations did not appear until 1869, and then only in a small way). The best protection was to place bids with W.E. Woodward, Edward Cogan, Henry Chapman, or some other dealer who attended the sales in person and could inspect the offered items. Before the event, coins were arrayed on long tables, and could be exam-ined. Sometimes, important coins were passed around on trays as the sale took place. The dealer would then bid for his client, adding a fee for representation, typically 5% (a figure still popular today). Connoisseurship, such as it was, was apt to vary widely.

T. Harrison Garrett, heir apparent to the Baltimore & Ohio Railroad fortune, began collecting coins while a student at Princeton in the 1860s, and by the mid-1880s he had the finest private holding in America. Second finest was that of Lorin G. Parmelee, a Bostonian who operated a business selling baked beans to hotels and restaurants. Both gentlemen had a keen eye for quality. Most others collected haphazardly, seeking a price advantage in lieu of quality. No published grading standards were in effect, although there was a continuous call for them.

GRADING TECHNIQUES DEVELOP

When the American Numismatic Association (ANA) was formed in 1891, collecting became more organized on a popular level. (In contrast, the venerable American Numismatic Society was more of a formal group, devoted to scholarship and collecting, but not with a wide membership, not holding conventions, etc.) The first technical dis-cussion of grading to appear in *The Numismatist* (still published today as the journal of the ANA) was part of the "Numismatic Foundation Stones" series by Joseph Hooper. "Coins are graded as to condition, and the following terms thereto apply," noted the writer, who then gave a list ordered by Roman numerals, as shown here:

I. Mint Brilliant Proofs, or rst strikes on planchets, especially prepared for numismatic purposes.

II. Mint Proofs, on ordinary prepared planchets. Brushing Proofs produces what is termed "hay marks" [today referred to as hairlines] and should never be adopted, the sale value being lowered.

III. Uncirculated, showing no abrasion or wearing of the reliefs, scratches, nicks or indentations. A coin may be Uncirculated and yet not have the sharp impres-sion of the rst strike as the dies tire, widen in sinkages, and lose their sharpness, gradually, in so much that the later impressions have often been mistaken for die varieties, more especially where the same dies have done long service for a large issue.

IV. Extremely Fine.

V. Very Fine.

VI. Fine. Below this condition, unless for extreme rarities, we would not recom-mend the bidding on at auction sales.

VII. Very Good.

VIII. Good. The latter conditions as described in the sales are often disappoint-ing, the terms applied misleading, until understood, being used by dealers to describe a certain state of preservation.

```
   IX. Very Fair.

    X. Fair.

   XI. Poor.

  XII. Very Poor.
```

While specimens in the lower order of conditions are better than none at all, still the aim of the collector should never be below VI or Fine. On account of distance, the large majority of collectors cannot attend sales, and have to be guided by descriptions as given in the sale catalogues, and for this reason, if no other, extreme care should be exercised by the cataloguer in making it a true description of the coins to be sold.

There we have it—numerical grading, albeit in Roman numerals, as early as 1892! Interestingly, Hooper's advice has stood the test of time, and still comprises sensible advice for coin collectors.

INTO THE 20TH CENTURY

In March 1913, collector/dealer H.O. Granberg, who had one of the greatest collections ever formed and who at one time was president of the ANA, shared his "Proposed Grading Standards," here excerpted.

A Uniform Standard of Grading (1913)

Many members have asked me to inaugurate some scheme for a uniform standard of classifying the condition of coins. It can be safely said that every member has some standard by which he judges the condition of coins, and it can be safely said that no two of these standards is exactly alike. Now, no two persons can think and see exactly alike in all respects, but if some standard were given the utmost publicity there is no reason why everyone concerned would not think nearer alike. My experience has been that the holder or owner of a coin is inclined to overestimate its condition, and the non-owner of a coin is apt to underestimate its condition. In other words, the condition of the coin varies if you own the coin or if someone else owns it. It is human nature. This will be the hardest phase to adjust, but if some descriptive standard was down in black and white, this variance of opinion could be reduced.

These remarks apply to collectors as well as dealers. My experience has been that no two dealers judge condition exactly alike, but I think the dealer holds to his standard more consistently than the collector who, to bid intelligently, has got to learn the standard of each dealer. This is another phase to be taken up. The condition of wear as "Fine," "Good," "Fair," etc., is not enough. Some qualifying word should be employed as well, such as "bright," "scratched," "tarnished," etc. A good many dealers object to calling attention to faults, defects, and other imperfections in coins, as the mentioning of these defects in cold type tends to make the coin appear worse than it really is. This is partly true, or rather has become so, for only marked defects are stated, and whenever a coin's bad points are mentioned, the general supposition is that the coin is pretty bad.

Another phase also must be borne in mind, the question of expense. Elaborate descriptions are not sought for, but fair descriptions, and a good deal can be said in a few words, if the right words are used. It is these right words in the right place that I want to bring before the meeting. I think it best to put the following suggestions before you for discussion. Possibly it will be best to read the suggestions as a whole and then take up each point by itself, and, if in the opinion of those present the final decision meets with approval, to adopt the same and give it the utmost publicity.

Proposed Grading Standards

Proof—Coins struck by a hand press from new and sharp dies that are polished. Any defects in striking, or imperfection in the planchet should be noted. If the coin has suffered since striking, the blemish should be mentioned. The word "Proof" should be qualified by such word as "brilliant," "dull," "tarnished," "haymarked," "finger-marked," "scratched," "rubbed," etc.

Uncirculated—Struck for circulation, but not worn in any way. Any defects, such as scratches, nicks, bruises, fingermarks, spots, tarnish, etc. should be mentioned, also poor striking and defects in planchet. Copper coins that have dulled or have changed color, but show no signs of wear, may be termed Uncirculated, but no corroded coin should be termed Uncirculated.

Very Fine—The condition but little below Uncirculated, with imperceptible wear, or showing only under close scrutiny. Lightly tarnished coins may be placed under this classification, but the fact should be mentioned. Badly tarnished coins should never be called Very Fine nor should coins marred in any way other than in a slight change of color.

Fine—Showing very slight traces of wear only in the parts in the highest relief. Any blemishes should be noted.

Very Good—A worn coin but every part distinct, nothing but very marked defects need be mentioned.

Good—Everything distinct but somewhat worn.

Fair—Much worn but all outlines showing.

Poor—Everything below Fair.

Grading Evolves Further

The first useful *book* on grading was *A Guide to the Grading of United States Coins*, by Martin R. Brown and John W. Dunn, published in 1958. This went through several editions, later ones of which were issued (beginning in 1964) by Whitman Publishing Company. In 1969 my business partner, James F. Ruddy, who had been an active dealer since the early 1950s, and who had a sharp eye for grading and was well respected, put his photographic and observational talents to use, and set about creating *Photograde*. For the first time, actual illustrations were given of different types in grades from very low, such as About Good, up through About Uncirculated. Uncirculated and Proof pieces were not illustrated. *Photograde* enjoyed immediately popularity. Reprints with essentially the same photographs were issued for years afterward, although neither Jim Ruddy nor I had any connection with later editions.

In the 1970s, the ANA grabbed the bull by the horns, and under the direction of dealer Abe Kosoff set about creating standards. Dealers and collectors were surveyed, ideas gathered, and a text prepared. Kenneth E. Bressett wrote the grading descriptions, Abe Kosoff wrote prefatory material, and I wrote the narrative and background about grading. Since then, Ken and I have cooperated on a number of later editions, the most recent being titled the *Official American Numismatic Association Grading Standards for*

United States Coins. Later editions of the ANA text have had illustrations for circulated grades, in black and white, following the lead of *Photograde.* Hundreds of articles and a number of other studies on grading have been published in recent decades, including in *Coin World* and *Numismatic News.*

Following the tradition of the early days, descriptive words have been used to describe coins. In order from the lowest grade upward, the adjectives have been Poor, Fair, Good, Very Good, Fine, Very Fine, Extremely Fine, About Uncirculated, and Uncirculated. These apply to circulation strikes. Proofs, derived from a special method of manufacture of coins for collectors, are described differently, simply as Proof, then with a description as to whether they are average, choice, or whatever.

For those who were familiar with the system, it was known that a "Good"-grade coin represented one that had seen extensive circulation, often with some of the letters worn away, and a rather minimal grade for many issues. It was not a "good" coin at all, in terms of being a "nice" coin. A newcomer, if asked, "Would you like to buy a Good example of a rare 1877 cent?" might logically think that "Good" meant "a very desirable, high-quality" example.

MODERN ALPHANUMERICAL GRADING

Although numerical grading (albeit in Roman numerals) had been proposed as early as 1892, as noted, it fell to Dr. William H. Sheldon to create the framework for the system we know today. The venue was his book, *Early American Cents,* published in 1949. Sheldon developed what was a *market formula*—a mechanical construct—for evaluating large cents of the era from 1793 to 1814. Reviewing the market as he saw it in 1949, he concluded that a coin at a minimal Uncirculated level, which he called Mint State–60 (MS-60), was worth about three times more than a Very Fine (VF-20) coin. Accordingly, 20 was given to Very Fine, compared to 60 to Mint State. A nicer Mint State, Choice, was called MS-65, and such pieces were worth a *slight* premium above MS-60 at the time. As amazing as it may seem today, there was no particular scramble to seek the finest grade, and most collectors of early copper cents were perfectly satisfied to obtain a Very Fine or Extremely Fine. Few if anyone having a minimal Uncirculated-grade (MS-60) cent of, say, a variety of 1794, would walk a mile to upgrade to MS-65.

As part of the Sheldon market-price system, a *basal value* was assigned to each die variety. This concept is not used today, but was employed for a few years after Sheldon's book appeared. A particular variety might have been assigned a basal value of $2 if it was scarce. By means of the formula, a VF-20 cent variety with basal value of $2 would be worth 20 times $2, or $40, whereas a Mint State coin would be worth 60 times $2, or $120. A Good (G-4) cent would be worth $8. And so the system went. While it accurately predicted auction prices for a short time after it was developed, the growth of the rare-coin marketplace rapidly caused it to become obsolete, and it was not used after the early 1950s. Indeed, few people used it even at the beginning. While basal values faded away, the numerical system remained.

In 1949 Sheldon suggested that a large copper cent in MS-60 grade would have a market value of twice what the same variety would bring in VF-30 preservation. Such a ratio soon proved to be unrealistic. (1807 cent, Sheldon-275 variety. MS-60.)

Stripped of basal values and no longer used as a formula, the numbers gradually were adopted by collectors of other coins beyond copper cents of 1793 to 1814, including cents of later dates, colonials, copper half cents, and then other series. It was not that numbers had any particular magic. They were simply *shorthand* that made grading easy to understand. In a wink, even a newcomer could understand that a Good coin described as G-4 was nowhere near as nice as a Fine (F-12) and was far short of an Extremely Fine (EF-40).

As to the *logic* of the numbers, there never was one, other than the failed market formula. It will be seen that the range for Very Fine begins at VF-20 and stops short of EF-40, and covers 20 numbers. On the other hand, the entire range of About Uncirculated, from AU-50 to just short of MS-60, covers 10 numbers, and Mint State covers 11 numbers, all tightly spaced, from MS-60 to 70. The ANA grading standards have many more numbers than Sheldon ever contemplated, and in the real-world marketplace and within certification-service policies, still other grades have been added.

If today you were to buy a coin certified as VF-35, and careful study by advanced collectors and dealers convinced you that it had been overgraded by 15 points, and was just VF-20, you probably wouldn't lose much sleep. In fact, it might not bother you at all. On the other hand, if you purchased a coin as MS-65 and were later convinced it was AU-50, also a difference of 15 points, you might lose interest in numismatics altogether. Can you imagine how terrible it would be if a lottery winner interested in coins had paid $225,000 for an MS-65 silver dollar of 1901 (an earlier example cited), and learned that it was really AU-50 and worth perhaps $450? Eek! My gosh! All heck might break loose!

With this understanding, you now know that a mathematical formula is not part of the system, but that its numbers are simply shorthand. They cannot be added, subtracted, divided, or multiplied with any mathematical logic.

CERTIFICATION SERVICES

In the late 1970s the ANA launched the American Numismatic Association Certification Service, known as ANACS (later the ANA sold it, and today ANACS is owned privately). For a fee, the graders at ANA headquarters in Colorado Springs would review a coin and, after ascertaining its authenticity, would assign separate obverse and reverse grades (such as MS-63/65) and return it to the sender, along with a certificate and photograph. Coins poured in, and profits to the ANA were immense. Counterfeits were endemic in the marketplace, and ANACS was the major force in the hobby in combating them. In fact, fakes were so prevalent that John J. Ford Jr. reported that more than 50% of the 1916-D Mercury dimes he had seen at a recent convention were phony. Today we all benefit from the work ANACS did.

While the ANA graders might not have been completely consistent (nor was or is anyone else), there was some comfort in having a disinterested third party (other than buyer or seller) review the grade and certainly the authenticity. A buyer of a 1793 half cent graded EF-40 would find comfort if the ANA designated it at that grade or close. If it was called F-15, then the owner would probably take his future coin-buying business elsewhere. Dealers and collectors soon learned that ANACS certification added value. A 1901 Morgan silver dollar graded by ANACS as MS-63 was readily saleable at that price level. The same coin, if graded by John Doe's Coin Shop in Centerville—well, we're not so sure. There might be doubts.

In 1986 David Hall and a group of dealers launched the Professional Coin Grading Service (PCGS), which graded coins for a fee and hermetically sealed them in plastic holders, complete with an interior label. By this time there had been some problems with the switching and even the buying and selling separately of ANACS photographic certificates. Sometimes certificates for coins in higher grades were combined with look-alike lower-grade coins, creating a fraud. In 1987 John Albanese, who had been a founder of PCGS, initiated the Numismatic Guaranty Corporation of America (NGC), which offered a similar encapsulation service. These two firms both unconditionally guaranteed the authenticity of the coins they certified. From the 1970s to the present time there have been more than 100 different commercial services, some of which were simply marketing tools of coin dealers who owned them and had little cachet among knowledgeable numismatists. Some have had no guarantees of authenticity.

As grading was, is, and always will be more subjective than objective, more of an art than a science, the determinations of leading third-party services such as ANACS, PCGS, and NGC are often subjected to reconsideration by others, or even by the same services when individual coins are resubmitted for a second look. In a memorable instance, the Amon Carter specimen of the 1804 dollar was graded by a leading service as EF-45, then later regraded by the same service as AU-58. This practice of "resubmission" has earned millions of dollars in fees for the services. It seems to be a win-win situation. Owners of coins profit, the grading services profit, and almost everyone is smiling. However, the overall result is "gradeflation," or the lowering of quality standards of a coin grade over a period of time. For this reason, a coin certified by a leading service in 1990 as, say, MS-65, might be evaluated as MS-66 or even MS-67 by the same service today.

In 2008, John Albanese (who had sold his interest in NGC years earlier) formed the Collectors Acceptance Corporation (CAC), which endeavors to review the reviewers, so to speak. For a fee, coins certified by NGC and PCGS are reviewed as to whether they were, in the opinion of CAC, "on target," and also whether they are "nice" examples within the assigned grade—with decent eye appeal and the like. Stickers are applied to NGC and PCGS coins that pass muster. A notice sent by John Albanese to the hobby community included this:

> *The Problem:* A loss of accountability and "gradeflation" have conspired to dilute the quality of coins in the market; as a result, this is the first time that many coin prices are decreasing in spite of a bull market in precious metals.
>
> *The Solution:* Segregate and identify true premium coins and build a market based on that group.
>
> *Mission:* Restore credibility to the coin market by halting gradeflation and leveling the playing field for professional coin dealers and amateur collectors alike.

This was an immediate sensation, and CAC soon advertised that it was overwhelmed with business. No specific notation is made as to sharpness of strike, so it seems that you will still be able to cherrypick Full Details coins from among CAC-evaluated coins. It is always nice to leave *something* to the imagination!

Chapter 3

EXPERT TECHNIQUES
IN GRADING

GETTING STARTED

Can *you* become a grading expert? I believe you can!

Read this book. Study the techniques. Look at as many coins as you can, using the Internet, auction catalogs, and other sources for field work, so to speak. Take your time. Read, view coins of the type you read about, then read about them again. While practice might not make you or anyone else perfect, it will give you a broad knowledge.

This will take some time. How long? This is up to you. In my experience I have seen many newcomers become fairly adept at technical grading within a few weeks' time. Market grading, or the combining of technical factors with the realities of striking and other aspects of coins, takes longer.

Some numismatists have collected for years and still do not have the confidence to evaluate coins on their own. There is a large factor of plain, old-fashioned *laziness*. For most buyers it is easiest simply to rely on what coin sellers say about grades, or to read the labels on holders. For *you* it is great that others do this, for it gives you the opportunity for one-upmanship, to find *hidden value* that others do not see.

Pick a Favorite Series

For starters, do not try to become an expert on all coin types at the same time. Instead, pick a series that interests you—either because you collect those coins, or you find them attractive, or you simply want to use them as a focal point for study. Pick a series for which many coins can be found on the Internet and in catalogs. Flowing Hair half dollars of 1794 and 1795, as delightful as they may be, would not be a good study platform, for relatively few of them are around. Better would be a series such as Liberty Head nickels, Mercury dimes, or Lincoln cents. Morgan silver dollars are ideal, as they are old and traditional, and examples can be readily found in just about every grade from G-4 to Gem MS-67 or even higher.

By zeroing in on just one specialty, you can learn techniques more quickly and gain confidence. The variables are fewer. Start with certified coins, as you will then see what NGC, PCGS, and other services are calling MS-63 or MS-65 or whatever. You will soon see wide variables within these ranges.

Combine looking at pictures in catalogs and on the Internet with some time in the field—at coin shops and conventions. Regarding digital images of coins for sale: they are not completely foolproof, for they can easily be altered to eliminate problems that would be obvious if the coins were viewed first-hand.

On your own—no one will have to tell you—within a week or two of such activity, if you want to be in the fast lane, you will be able to look at certified Morgan dollars and determine which ones are "low end," or overgraded or assigned the grade in a minimum basis; which ones seem to be right on target; and which ones actually might be candidates for the next higher grade. On the other hand, if you want to be more casual about it, a month or two or three of less intense effort will accomplish the same thing.

At the left is the obverse of an 1891-O dollar certified as MS-65 that sold for $10,120 at auction. At the right is a similar coin, a slightly better strike (check the hair above the ear), but certified as MS-64 by the same service, that brought $690. Which is the better buy? As your grading expertise increases, you will benefit from being able to intelligently make such decisions. There are *many* such choices in the marketplace.

In the Morgan dollar series MS-64 is a good grade for such a test. If you examine dozens of different coins, you will find some that you would not want to purchase even if they were priced at the MS-62 or MS-61 levels. You will also find some that are every bit as nice as some certified as MS-65 (and thus more expensive, sometimes *much* more) by the same services. You will become excited. "Hey, there's an MS-65 coin I can buy at an MS-64 price!" That is precisely what many dealers and traders do: cherrypick for grade!

Sharpness of strike is important. Eye appeal is important, and that will come naturally as well. Soon you will be able to tell whether a Morgan dollar is beautiful, ugly, or somewhere in between. While art is in the eye of the beholder, most numismatists generally can tell the difference between a coin that is pretty and one that is not.

While others will see an 1891-O Morgan dollar in a holder marked MS-64, you will see more. You will know if it is well struck, or if some parts of the design are flat. You will know if it has too much friction to be a "nice" MS-64, and might better be designated MS-63, or if it is really gorgeous, relatively mark-free, and is just as nice as many MS-65 coins.

You will have an advantage. You will become a smart buyer.

Now, to the techniques and what to look for.

Viewing Coins for Grading

For the proper grading of coins a good source of illumination and a good magnifier are both needed. My favorite is an incandescent lightbulb of, say, 60 watts, placed within a foot or two of a coin. The surrounding room should not be brightly lighted. I like an incandescent lamp as it gives a nearly pinpoint light source at a distance and helps reveal hairlines and problems. Halogen lamps are used by some, but there have been warnings that they can be dangerous. As coins such as Proofs might reflect light into your eyes, I have avoided using this type of lamp, but they are in wide use at conventions and in coin shops. Fluorescent lamps are not recommended, but they are often used as well.

To examine a coin, a handheld magnifier is desirable. A level of magnification such as 4x, which can be doubled with a similar lens to be 8x, is ideal for most coins. A loupe giving higher magnification is desirable if details need to be checked. However, the narrower the field of vision and the higher the magnification, the more difficult it is to grade a coin, as you can literally get too close to the subject. (A microscope would be virtually useless.)

Take a coin and hold it by its edges, or by the edges of its container. Rotate it slowly, reflecting the light from the lamp to the surface of the coin, into your eye, at first without the use of a magnifier, to form an initial opinion of the grade. Then use a magnifying glass. This procedure will highlight the field and surfaces and will make hairlines and marks evident. You will quickly see that lines can appear and reappear as the coin is turned, depending on the orientation to the light. A tiny scratch viewed parallel to the light beam might become invisible, while if it is crosswise to the light beam it will be fully seen. Do this carefully as you view both sides of a coin. The edge, sometimes called the "third side" of a coin, should be checked as well, if the coin is not in a sealed holder.

Grading coins in a location with distant overhead lights, such as at a show or convention, or with distant table lamps, can be misleading, as coins often appear to be nicer than they actually are. For proper grading, a coin needs to be observed close up, and carefully.

Many "slabs" (plastic encapsulation cases) holding certified coins have become scuffed or have tiny lines and marks of their own. If you wiggle a slab slightly, any marks on the slab will move in relation to the coin inside. In contrast, hairlines or marks on the coin itself will not move.

After you view the coin with your eyes, then under 4x or higher magnification, you may wish to take a loupe or stronger glass to check the specifics of any nicks, scratches, spots, or other problem areas. Be sure also to examine the edge of the coin carefully if it is not sealed in a plastic holder.

A Helper Would Be Nice

As you are in a learning process, if you can have an experienced numismatist nearby while you do this—such as the helpful owner of a coin shop or a dealer setting up at a convention—so much the better. If you do this in a commercial venue, it is nice form to buy something as a courtesy—a book or two, or a coin on your "want list." Dealers are in business to make a profit, and in today's world expenses can be considerable. Many dealers are willing to help newcomers to the hobby. Ask around, and find one who does. You may also be able to find helpful mentors at a local coin club meeting.

With a helper on hand, as you see things on a coin's surface, ask him or her to comment on their significance. Is that spot trivial, or does it negatively affect the value? Are these light abrasions normal for the grade? Other questions will suggest themselves. Such mentoring will be very useful, if you can find someone to do it. Otherwise you are on your own, as, indeed, most collectors have been over the years.

Practice Your Skills

After you feel you have achieved a level of expertise with Morgan silver dollars or another series of your choice, keep at it. Continue to review Morgan dollars as you see them, perhaps not as intensely as before. The next step is to pick a different series, again one in which there are many coins that can be viewed in a combination of the Internet, catalogs, and in person at coin shops and conventions. You might select Barber silver coins—dimes, quarters, and half dollars—from 1892 to 1916. These can be studied in parallel, as all three denominations have the same basic grading characteristics on the obverse. You will quickly find that this time around the going will be easier. I dare say that within an hour or two of immersion in Barber coins you will be able to determine a low-end, medium, or high-end coin within a given grading designation. You will also appreciate that in comparison to Morgan silver dollars (if those were your first choice), Barber coins are much rarer in Mint State. Still, there are quite a few of them around. Among Barber quarters and half dollars, with the Heraldic Eagle reverse, you will see that on many coins the eagle's claws at the lower right are weakly struck, as are some of the arrows. More about this general subject is found elsewhere in this book. You may be surprised to notice that some coins are actually quite flatly struck in that area, but sell for the same prices and are described in the same general way as those with Full Details. While looking at Barber silver coins (or whatever other series you pick out for further practice), read the appropriate sections in chapter 7 of this book.

Before you know it, grading will become "instinctive," so to speak. This will enable you to make your first pass quickly. Then you can examine the coins in detail.

Before going further, take the two groups you have selected so far—say, Morgan dollars and Barber silver coins—and spend a few hours checking other grades. A good benchmark is EF-40, easy enough to find in Morgan dollars, quite scarce among Barber coins. Also try a higher-level Mint State, such as MS-66 or MS-67. For these the Internet and catalogs will not be as useful, as minute distinctions are often not observable. However, when you visit a coin shop or convention, you can check such pieces there. For good measure, examine some other grades as well, gaining familiarity all across the spectrum from well worn to gem.

Now that you have a working familiarity with two or more series, review the coins you already have in your collection. No doubt they are of different series. Perhaps when you were buying you simply did as most do: you reviewed the grade marked on an envelope or holder, considered the price, and made a purchase accordingly. Now you can view your coins with authority. If you are typical, you probably see some you would not have bought had you known then what you know now. This is part of growth.

EVERYBODY'S FAVORITE SUBJECT!

If I want to get mail from readers of my columns in *Coin World* or *The Numismatist*, all I need to do is write about grading! As the subject is artistic, not completely scientific, and admits of many different opinions and views, there is no end to the discussion. Perhaps in that regard it is not much different from religion, politics, what is "good" and what is "bad" art, or where is the best place to spend a vacation.

Sometimes the focus is narrowed, such as on a particular coin. I remember once having an example of a 1788 Vermont copper, the die variety known as Ryder-16 (Bressett 15-S).

These Vermont pieces were and still are a numismatic love of mine, and I enjoy studying and collecting them. This particular variety is quite curious. It was struck at a facility known as Machin's Mills, a private mint near Newburgh, New York, that is said to have employed a guard in a hideous mask to frighten off onlookers. Operations were conducted in secret, as the facility turn out thousands of mostly counterfeit copper coins imitating British halfpence as well as the coppers of Connecticut, New York, and other places. Vermont pieces were part of the production as well, although these were legitimate, as one of the partners of the enterprise actually had a contract with Vermont.

Vermont copper of 1788, die variety Ryder-16, struck from dies that were purposely made without detail, so the resultant coins would appear to be worn. A specialist graded this example as EF-45.

The object of Machin's Mills was to manufacture copper pieces that could be spent easily. Accordingly, dies were often made with lack of detail, so that the struck pieces would appear to be worn, thus suggesting that they had been readily used in circulation for quite some time. Likely, the coins were toned in some manner before they were put into circulation. I considered my 1788 Ryder-16 to be Mint State. Careful examination revealed brown luster on both sides, rather subtle, but not broken by any abrasions or marks. At quick glance, however, the coin appeared quite worn, perhaps one that had seen a generation of use. In passing this around for discussion, grades were all over the place, ranging from Very Fine to Uncirculated, and many levels in between.

In a somewhat similar situation, at an ANA convention in 1990, Barry Cutler, then an attorney for the Federal Trade Commission, was part of a program discussing the professional grading and encapsulation of coins. The general thrust was whether such grading was precise. As part of the test, he picked a 1908 Saint-Gaudens double eagle, variety Without Motto. This particular issue can be very difficult to grade, as most are somewhat lightly struck on the obverse. The sample coin was shown to a number of expert graders employed by certification services. Their professional opinions ranged from AU-58 all the way to MS-64.

If you want to try a similar exercise on your own, you might enjoy doing it, and it will furnish a reality check as to the present discussion of art versus science. I will deliberately pick coins that are a bit tricky. Find a 1908 double eagle that is certified as, say, MS-62. Find an Indian Head half eagle from 1908 to 1916, certified as MS-62 or 63. Find a Standing Liberty quarter dated in the 1920s, certified as MS-64 Full Head. Put some masking tape around both sides of the top of the holder, so as to conceal the grade on the front and the grade coding on the back. Then, at a coin club meeting or a gathering of collectors and dealers, pass the pieces around and ask the viewers to put down their opinions on a slip of paper. Compare the results. I absolutely guarantee that some grades will be quite different from the others, even if the people in your audience have been numismatists for a decade or more.

The object here is simply to illustrate that different people can grade coins in different ways. The reality is that if you buy a coin graded by an expert or several experts at a specific number, for some series the chances are very good that coins graded by others will be higher or lower. Equipped with this knowledge, you will be a very smart buyer (the subject of chapter 5).

Is this 1908 Without Motto double eagle AU-58 or MS-64? Or is it in some other grade? Professional opinions can and do vary, often widely. This piece has quite a few marks, a cut on the skirt of Miss Liberty, and a carbon-streak planchet defect at the top of the left leg. It was certified as MS-64.

Chapter 4

Understanding the Surfaces of Coins

The Nature of Metals

Understanding how different coins react with the atmosphere, liquids, heat, chemicals, and the world in which they exist is the key to understanding why their surfaces have changed since they left the coining press. This is an advanced concept beyond basic grading, but is essential for full understanding of what makes a coin desirable or otherwise.

Among American coins, the main metallic alloys and their properties are as follows.

Copper and Bronze. Copper of varying degrees of purity was used to produce half cents and large cents from 1793 to 1857. As the metal was obtained from many sources (including roofing, ship bottoms, and miscellaneous scrap) in the early days, impurities were often present. In some instances, freshly minted coins, rather than being bright orange-red, may have been dark or irregular.

For most years, however, the quality of planchets used to create these early coppers was excellent. Sources often included outside suppliers such as Boulton & Watt in England and various companies in the United States. Later, beginning in 1864, bronze Indian Head cents and two-cent pieces, and, still later, Lincoln cents were generally made of high-quality metal, although the composition could vary slightly. As an example, bronze used in San Francisco in 1908 and 1909 to make Indian Head cents and Lincoln cents had a light yellow cast to it, or at least this developed on coins as they naturally toned over a period of time. In contrast, Philadelphia Mint pieces did not develop this tint.

Copper is a very chemically active metal, and immediately after striking, a copper or bronze piece begins to acquire toning. Over a period of years, this generally develops into a light brown, which mutes the original brilliance, and can be very attractive. Flecks and spots, often seen today, are caused by holding a coin improperly, or looking at it while talking or breathing (during which processes small bits of moisture fall on the surface). Fingerprints and moisture remain latent for a long time, sometimes years, then later develop into brown toning or even gray or black discoloration.

Copper coins are affected by industrial and other fumes containing sulfur, and tend to tone brown in such environments. The visual effect can be quite pleasing. In seaside areas there are traces of salt in the air, detrimental to the surfaces of copper coins, sometimes resulting in minute green or black spotting. Years ago it was often a rule of thumb that collectors living near the coast should not collect copper! The same was said of people living in other high-humidity areas. Today, the matter is not as serious, due to protection afforded by certain Lucite holders, certified-coin holders, Koin-Tain holders, and the like. However, it would be bad practice to leave a brilliant bronze coin out in the open at a summer cottage in Wildwood Crest on the Jersey shore.

Nickel Alloy. The metal used for three-cent pieces of 1865 to 1889 and for nickel five-cent pieces for most years since 1866 is an alloy composed of 75% copper and 25% nickel. This is a very durable metal—one that resists wear and discoloration. Over a period of time, nickel coins tend to tone lightly, often with a hint of blue, gray, or yellow. On Proofs, the surface will acquire a slight haze. Clad coins of various denominations from 1965 to date have nickel-alloy faces and react similarly.

Silver. Silver coins are composed of an alloy that since 1837 has consisted of 90% silver, with 10% copper (and traces of other metals) added for strength. Over time, silver will tone golden brown, then gray, then black, sometimes with nuances of iridescence. Precisely the same thing happens to sterling-silver tableware over a period of time.

Industrial fumes, vapors from coal and gas furnaces, and other elements in the air can affect toning of a coin, more so with silver than with other coinage metals. Some years ago my firm had occasion to auction the coin collection formed by the New York Public Library. For decades the pieces had been kept face up in coin cabinets, the obverses exposed to the air. New York City traffic exhaust being what it was and is, combined with other essences of the metropolis, the obverses of earlier silver pieces had turned dark gray, often coal black, while the reverses usually remained bright.

Silver coins can gain attractive delicate iridescent toning if stored in Raymond "National" and certain cardboard holders with sulfur content. Morgan and Peace dollars stored in cloth bags often acquired colorful toning if one side of the coin came into contact with the cloth.

Gold. Gold coins are composed of 90% gold, with 10% copper (and traces of other metals) added for strength. Some gold coins have significant amounts of silver as an "impurity," such being the case for many struck from California gold. These tend to have a lighter color. Over a period of time gold coins will tone a warm yellow-orange, this being from the copper part of the alloy. This is desirable, and the record shows that in the days of the California Gold Rush, one leading producer of gold coins, Wass, Molitor & Company, actually roasted its gold coins before passing them out in circulation, to give them a pleasing color.

General Information. Further affecting the surface of a coin and the development of toning is heat. Kept in warm surroundings, the chemical activity of copper, nickel, and silver coins is increased, and toning takes place at a rapid pace. This process is often used to artificially tone coins. Dampness promotes toning, often spotting or staining.

Coins that actively circulated developed a different pattern of toning and oxidation than did stored coins. Copper large cents, Indian Head cents, and Lincoln cents passed from hand to hand received light friction, toning from handling, and the like, and generally turned light to medium brown. Coins that survive today with oxidized surfaces or deep-gray or black surfaces were either subjected to some other circumstance, such as being stored in a damp place or buried, or else were made with imperfect copper. Nickel and silver coins in circulation tended to become a pleasing light gray.

Improper mixing of alloys and the presence of impurities can result in carbon inclusions, or small black spots, on silver and gold coins. Incompletely mixed copper in a gold coin can cause tiny brown stains or spots. You need to find these by your own inspection, as grading numbers do not reveal them. The improper mixing of alloy in bronze cents, especially those of the late 19th century, resulted in a "woodgrain" effect as the pieces toned—a streaked mixture of lighter and darker hues. In contrast to most other improper mixes, this can be very *attractive*. In fact, Rick Snow, a well-known authority on Indian Head cents, once illustrated a woodgrain-toned 1873 Doubled Die cent as the cover coin on a book.

Albums, Panels, and Folders

Beginning in 1928, cardboard album pages with clear cellulose acetate slides were marketed by M.L. Beistle of Shippensburg, Pennsylvania. Distribution was later given to Wayte Raymond, who marketed album pages under the Raymond, National, and other labels. The cardboard part of the holders, which touched the edges of the coins, contained sulfur, which reacted with copper to gently tone the edges and sometimes the rims. Kept in such a holder, a coin would be well preserved, but would gradually acquire toning over a period of time, darkest near the cardboard, lighter toward the center. Today, this is sometimes called "album" or "halo" toning. The slides on these pages, if in contact with the coins, often imparted microscopic scratches. Particularly vulnerable were Proof Barber silver coins and Morgan dollars, although other series were affected as well. Today these scratches are called "slide marks" and can be seen under a low-power magnifier.

Beginning in 1934, several varieties of "penny boards," or coin panels, were marketed by various companies. These consisted of cardboard with a paper backing, with holes in which coins could be inserted. It became a popular pastime to look through circulation and retrieve Indian Head cents, Liberty Head nickels, and the like. Often, these were pressed into the spaces with a thumb or finger, years later causing a visible fingerprint. On some, the instructions suggested the coins be cleaned with salt and vinegar to make them brighter. In any event, the coins were exposed face upward, and toned over a period of time.

Other coin-storage and display products were marketed. Beginning in the 1950s, Lucite holders became popular. These provided a new level of protection for coins. Pieces carefully placed in these holders tended to remain unchanged for long periods of time.

In earlier times, other methods of storing coins included wooden cabinets with sliding drawers, popular from the 19th century to the early 20th. In such an arrangement, coins were placed face up in shallow drawers with a wood bottom or perhaps lined with felt or paper. The exposed side tended to tone over a period of time, and sometimes the reverse did as well.

Small paper envelopes such as used for holding medical pills became standard for collectors and dealers to store coins before putting them in a holder or a cabinet. These eventually standardized into the dimension of 2 by 2 inches, enabling them to be conveniently placed in long cardboard boxes originally made to store player-piano rolls. The 2-by-2 size is still used today, although player-piano rolls are an anachronism. These paper envelopes, which contained sulfur, tended to gently tone coins over a period of time.

At the turn of the 20th century, the Mint packaged Proof coins by wrapping them in thin tissue. This seemed to have a particularly large amount of sulfur and other reactive ingredients, with the result that bronze coins in particular toned quickly, to a rich brown or brown with traces of blue, often very attractive. Silver Proofs acquired vivid iridescence.

In 1936, when the Mint resumed issuing Proof coins after a long lapse, they were put up in cellophane holders with glued seams. The glue in the seams often reacted with the coins, causing dark toning lines. In the late 20th century, clear flexible plastic envelopes containing polyvinyl chloride (PVC) came on the market and were almost universally used in place of paper envelopes. These were clear, and permitted a coin to be seen easily. These were among a class of transparent holders popularly known as "flips." Generally unknown until a later time, the PVC had a negative effect on coins stored within. Tiny beads of green "goo" tended to form on copper, nickel, and silver coins, although gold was largely unaffected. The effects on nickel coins in particular were unfortunate, and after prolonged storage the gooey substance actually ate into and etched the surface. Today, PVC coin flips are commonly used to display auction lots prior to a sale, as the coins can be seen clearly without patrons' actually touching their surface. However, it is advised that *immediately* upon acquiring such coins, they be removed and put into better holders.

At the same time PVC holders were being popularized, little snap-together capsules called Koin-Tains were marketed, as they still are today. These are made of slightly flexible hard plastic, round, a little larger than the coin itself. They seem to be a very good way to preserve coins from atmospheric effects. I have never seen any evidence to the contrary. Some museums use them.

Most hard plastic holders used by PCGS, NGC, ANACS, and other certification services tend to preserve coins well. However, they are not completely airtight, and colors can change. Also, a coin that has been carelessly dipped or that has latent fingerprints or moisture will change color in a certified holder as chemical action takes place. In one notable instance, a superb Gem Proof Lincoln cent certified as virtually perfect by a leading service sold for a record price. Within months, the piece turned stained and blotchy, as the latent effects of dipping took their toll. The particular certification firm gave a refund, earning admiration in the process, but most if not all firms are careful to state they are not responsible for such changes.

Dipped and Cleaned Coins

The vast majority of "brilliant" U.S. coins dated in the 19th century and earlier, in numismatic hands, have been dipped, cleaned, or subjected to some treatment in the course of their lives. Exceptions are certain gold coins and Morgan silver dollars. Otherwise, bronze coins and silver coins that are fully brilliant, including the edges, virtually certainly have been dipped, and many have been cleaned.

Beginning in the 19th century, and continuing for generations afterward, the chorus in numismatics was "brilliant is best." Lotions and potions were advertised in *The Numismatist, The Numismatic Scrapbook,* and later in *Coin World* and *Numismatic News,* offering to make coins brilliant. Some of these simply were silver or jewelry dips, fine if used carefully and not often. Others were pastes, or corrosive substances, which actually damaged coins. As recently as the 1980s, if a Proof silver coin, or commemorative, or nickel was not bright and brilliant, the market for it generally was very limited. Few people wanted toned coins. In fact, the term *BU* (for "Brilliant Uncirculated") was generally used in advertisements. To make coins saleable, dealers and collectors bringing pieces to market would often clean them, after which they would be sold. Then they would tone again, and be cleaned again. Over a period of years *The Numismatist* included quite a bit of absolutely terrible advice. Three samples from a large file:

> *Rub with baking soda:* "There is no use of coin collectors having tarnished silver coins in their collection any longer, as they can safely remove the tarnish discoloration from an Uncirculated or Proof coin by using the following instructions without any possible danger of injuring the coin whatsoever: Lay

1880 Liberty Seated half dollar certified as PF-68 Cameo. Presumed to have been dipped, for otherwise it would have toning.

1870-CC Liberty Seated half dollar certified as PF-64. Halo toning from being encased in an album page with the edge of the coin touching sulfur-content cardboard.

1877 Liberty Seated half dollar certified as MS-66. Combination of halo and mottled toning; some fingerprints on the obverse.

All coins on this page shown enlarged.

1862 Liberty Seated half dollar certified as PF-62. Dipped and cleaned multiple times, giving many hairlines and defining the grade. Retoned to what most would agree is a pleasing appearance.

the coin on a small piece of cotton flannel in a saucer. Squeeze lemon juice on the coin, then apply common baking soda on a wad of cotton batting and gently rub the coin. Add lemon juice and soda until the tarnish is removed. Then dip the coin in boiling water and wipe off with a cotton flannel cloth, and you again have a brilliant coin." ("Cleaning Coins," by J. Henri Ripstra, then-president of the ANA, April 1939)

Use a wire brush: "Bronze coins that are dirty or slightly corroded should be treated with a very fine steel brush, followed by the use of a fine wire brush." Then there was this piece of bad advice: "Clean coins with lemon juice, later using baking soda." ("Cleaning and Care of Coins," by Alan Sutherland, May 1947)

For making silver coins bright: "First cyanide, then a good silver polish, applied with an old tooth-brush and, if necessary, a final rub with chamois leather and rouge." ("Let's Keep It Clean," by G.R.L. Potter, January 1949)

Dipping? Cleaning? There is a difference in numismatic distinction. Dipping can be beneficial, but improperly done, or done multiple times, it can be harmful. Cleaning is always harmful.

Dipping refers to the immersing of a coin in a liquid, perhaps letting it remain there for some time, or gently swishing the liquid around so it will interact with the surface. When removed, the coin will be brighter. While repeated or improper dipping can be very harmful to a coin and negatively impact its value, careful dipping once or twice can enhance its appearance and possibly the value.

In contrast, *cleaning* generally refers to using an acidic substance that etches the surface of the coin, or a polish or substance that is applied with pressure or friction. This brightens the coin, but creates hairlines or minute porosity.

Historically, when struck, every Proof coin made by the U.S. Mint had a hairline-free surface. However, with some handling and light polishing, combined with dipping, hairlines developed. Today, the vast majority of pre-1936 Proof coins show hairlines under magnification. This means unequivocally that the pieces have been cleaned at one time or another. Repeated cleaning generated repeated hairlines. Otherwise, every Proof would be lightly toned and would be called a Gem, say PF-66, PF-67, or higher. There would be no such thing as PF-62, 63, or similar pieces.

With all of the preceding stated, you can see that the typical early American coin, whether in the hands of a numismatist or stored in a safe deposit box or bureau drawer, tended to naturally tone over a period of time. If dipped or cleaned, it would retone.

I suggest that both dipping and cleaning are a dangerous business, as their effects cannot be reversed. But it seems that to experiment with these processes is part of numismatic human nature. An admonition such as "Don't do it!" is likely to have little effect, as curiosity will prevail. If this is so with you, by all means practice with pocket change or coins of little value that you can spend afterward. Do not work with scarce, rare, or numismatically important pieces.

There is also a code of silence regarding dipping and cleaning. A Proof 1914 half dollar that has hairlines in the field acquired them by being cleaned with an abrasive, such as silver polish, or by being rubbed. However, in numismatic nomenclature it will be referred to as, for example, "Proof-63" or, if bright, "Proof-63, brilliant." A full and more accurate description would be: "Proof-63 with hairlines from cleaning." An 1834 Capped Bust half dollar certified as MS-65 and with brilliant surfaces would more fully be described as, "MS-65, dipped to make it brilliant." A leading dealer recently commented, "My customers want brilliant coins, but they don't want to be told they have been cleaned or dipped."

The preceding is stated simply to give understanding, not to be controversial. So long as collectors, dealers, and professional graders like the system, it will be continued, although collectors are often not as aware.

Popular Procedures

Again, cleaning and dipping coins is not recommended. Conservation should be left to the experts. However, if you feel compelled to do this, do not use any polish or abrasive substance. Don't even *think* of wiping a Proof with a soft cloth. These procedures will simply add hairlines to the surface of the coin, most notably on Proofs. The process is irreversible.

Similarly, do not use any acidic substance. Years ago, potassium cyanide, a deadly substance, was commonly used to clean silver coins. It etched away a few microns of surface, effectively removing friction and rubbing, dulling the mint luster somewhat, but still improving the surface of the coin. The fumes, if inhaled, are lethal, and one leading numismatist, collector Sanford Saltus, died while cleaning silver coins in his hotel room, when he mistook a glass of potassium cyanide for a nearby glass of ginger ale. In Saltus's obituary in *The Numismatist*, August 1922, was this comment: "Potassium cyanide, although one of the most deadly poisons, is frequently used by collectors in cleaning coins, as it will have the desired effect when other methods fail."

In the 1950s, James F. Kelly, the Dayton, Ohio, dealer, cleaned coins with cyanide, and once gave me a demonstration. "It removes rubbing from silver coins," he said, "and makes them look Uncirculated." Today, a Liberty Seated silver coin, for example, with a minutely matte surface in the fields and the higher parts, and in higher grade, is apt to have been cyanided years ago. (I have never tried it myself and do not plan to.) The same is true of many copper coins that have an unnaturally bright orange color. In recent times, I am not aware that cyanide has been used, but who knows?

Placing silver coins in an aluminum pan with baking soda dissolved in boiling water will brighten them by galvanic or electrolytic action, a procedure that has been recommended now and then. Aluminum metal, such as foil, attached to one pole of a battery, and a silver coin to the other, in a solution of baking soda or washing soda, accomplishes the same thing. This removes minute traces of surface metal and will cause dullness, but will not add hairlines.

As to dipping, there are a number of commercial solvents available from jewelers and even coin-supply houses. To use such dip, pour it in a glass dish. Immerse the coin, perhaps swirling the dish so that the liquid comes into contact with the surface. After a time, the coin will become brilliant. Then, carefully remove the coin, and rinse it extensively under a stream of cold water. Then carefully pat it dry (do not rub it) with a soft cloth. The result will be a bright coin, but one with a very chemically active surface. Immediately, it is a candidate to begin toning all over again. If the dip is not removed entirely, it will cause iridescent streaking, staining, or blotching on a bronze or copper coin, staining on a nickel coin, and irregular toning on a silver coin. Gold coins are not affected as much. Dipping makes them bright, and removes any warm yellow-orange color acquired over a period of time.

Susan L. Maltby, in *Coin World*, April 28, 2008, in an article, "Silver Cleaning Techniques," included this information:

The most common silver corrosion product is silver sulfide. Silver sulfide is also referred to as either "toning" or "tarnish." . . . The thickness of the silver sulfide layer on the surface of the coin defines the color we see. A thicker film appears darker in color. Silver-cleaning products and techniques remove the silver sulfide layer electrolytically; chemically or with an abrasive.

It is important to keep in mind that toning is corrosion. Corrosion converts a small amount of metal on the surface of a coin to a corrosion product. This conversion process is irreversible. Once corroded, the surface of the metal can never again be Mint State. Toning can hide serious problems. Although cleaning a heavily toned coin can be rewarding, it can also be very disappointing.

As silver dip removes oxidation and toning (numismatists usually avoid the term *tarnish*) from the surface of the coin, it also removes very minute traces of metal itself. A Proof, if dipped once or even twice, might not show this, but if a Proof is carefully dipped a half a dozen or a dozen times it will become dull and lifeless, devoid of all of its *original* surface.

Restoring Cleaned Coins

Again, this is a subject perhaps left to the experts. In his book, *Early American Cents* (1949),William H. Sheldon recognized that more than just a few copper large cents had been unfortunately cleaned. He gave instructions for retoning them, such as by brushing them with sulfur powder. In the late 1940s John J. Ford Jr. acquired a 1793 Chain cent that was bright orange, from having been cleaned. Desiring to have it tone naturally, he placed it on a windowsill on his house in a suburb of New York City. Some days went by, and painters came to redo the outside. As you might imagine, John had forgotten about the cent, and when he looked for it, it was no longer there.

The use of a camel-hair brush, with light hairs, to rub over the surface of a circulated large cent, is a well-known way to remove dirt and film, and to give it a lustrous appearance. This was often practiced by the American Numismatic Society's curators and perhaps still is. It is not recommended for Proof coins, however, as any friction is apt to develop hairlines.

Certain types of grease used to treat leather can be effective in removing green or other spots of oxidation from copper, if such pieces are placed in grease and left there for a few days. However, the chemical nature of such substances is apt to vary, and such a process should be tried experimentally with low-value coins first.

Heating will tone a copper coin. A dipped Indian Head or Lincoln cent placed carefully on top of a low-wattage light bulb and left there for a time, or left in a dish near an oil or coal furnace, will gain a darker color. Blotching and staining can result as an unintended consequence, as can unnatural vivid toning, although the latter sometimes attracts buyers who are unaware of how the color developed.

Silver coins can be toned any number of different ways. One dealer told me that frying them in a pan would turn them gray, more or less approximating natural toning. A more inventive entrepreneur came up with the idea of putting silver coins in Raymond "National" holders, and subjecting them to unnatural warmth. This might accelerate the pleasing "album" toning that holders such as these generated. If the doctoring didn't work out, the coin was simply re-dipped, and the process was started over again. Combinations of heat and chemicals have been used to impart rainbow toning to Morgan dollars, sharply enhancing their resale value, as well as to tone other silver coins. There is no end to innovation, so it seems. "Better coins through chemistry," a wag once commented.

Worthwhile Conservation

Now you are aware of the seldom-discussed aspects of coin dipping, cleaning, and restoring. Other processes can be mentioned.

Conservation (as opposed to cleaning), if done carefully so as not to remove metal from a coin's surface, can enhance the value of a coin. Bill Fivaz gives this explanation: "If the *original luster* of the coin has been preserved during the process, it may be considered *conserved*. If the original luster has been disturbed, it should be considered *cleaned*." Nice explanation that seems to be right on target.

The Numismatic Conservation Service, affiliated with NGC, has accomplished much in this regard, including restoring coins from the wrecks of the SS *Republic* and the SS *New York*. The recovered gold treasure from the SS *Central America* (lost at sea in 1857, found in the late 20th century) was carefully curated by Bob Evans, one of the discoverers, with careful rinses and processes, removing from the coins rust particles (from iron in the ship), scale, and grime, and making Uncirculated pieces appear virtually as new, with original luster intact.

1857-S double eagle recovered from the wreck of the SS *Central America*. Conserved by Bob Evans. Certified as MS-67.

Plain soap and water can remove grease and grime from coins without harming them, providing no friction is used. Acetone, a volatile commercial solvent that must be used with care (it is inflammable, the fumes should not be inhaled, and skin contact should be avoided), will de-grease coins. Ammonia will remove haze and grease, but will sometimes give copper (in particular) and nickel coins a bluish hue. Acetone and ammonia both strip the surface of any protective oils and may serve to accelerate toning.

Professional conservators are few and far between, while amateurs are numerous. I would leave conservation up to the experts. However, if you must experiment, again I recommend you use coins from pocket change.

SUMMARY

The test of the success or failure of a dipping, cleaning, or conservation process is in the appearance and true nature of the coin, as viewed and studied under high magnification. If you do *nothing* with a coin, the subject can always be reconsidered. Dipping and cleaning are irreversible and can be harmful. Were it not for these efforts to "improve" coins, nearly all Proofs would be superb gems!

Mere words cannot possibly cover this complex subject, but this discussion gives you a general idea of some of the intricacies involved.

Chapter 5

Smart Grading and Buying

The Risk of Becoming Spoiled!

"A little knowledge is a dangerous thing," it has been said. However, a lot of knowledge can be very beneficial. If you read this text carefully, and combine this with some field work examining coins in person, you will know that a coin graded by someone else as EF-40, or MS-65, or some other number, may have features far beyond the number indicated.

One of the key issues among Buffalo nickels from 1916 to 1938 is the 1926-S. Examples in true Mint State are very rare. An early-2008 issue of *Coin World's Coin Values* suggested that in MS-64 grade an example is valued at $20,000. However, one notch higher, in MS-65, it is valued at $110,000. If you were to find a certified 1926-S in the marketplace, it would simply be marked MS-64 or MS-65. As a smart buyer, you will look at it carefully. How would you feel if the $100,000 coin were lightly struck at the center of the obverse, and on the reverse had little or no fur on the head of the bison, and the fur on the shoulder was indistinct? Then, suppose that the MS-64 coin at $20,000 had Full Details, and was needle sharp. Further suppose that the MS-65 piece was rather dullish in appearance, lacking eye appeal, while the MS-64 was richly lustrous and virtually said, "Buy me!" Although I might be wrong, I suggest that the MS-64 would be your object of desire, and you might not want the MS-65 at all, not even at half price (unless you could sell it to someone).

Many coins have *wide differences* in striking sharpness, with market prices often unrelated to this aspect of quality. Once more, lucky you! With knowledge, you can tell the difference. Most other buyers would have no clue as to the items just discussed. Indeed, the popular Registry Set competitions, in which owners of coins try to outdo each other with the highest numerical grades, would give honors to the unattractive, weakly struck MS-65, but not to the gorgeous MS-64!

This means that in the real world you need to be a contrarian, you need to think for yourself. Do this, and I doubt that you will ever look at a coin the same way again. You will have become spoiled, so to speak. But not really; a better description is that you will have become a *true connoisseur.*

Choices, choices. Two 1926-S Buffalo nickels, each certified as MS-64 by the same leading service. The one on the left is flatly struck on the leg, above the leg, and on most of the head, and sold for $17,250 in March 2007. The one on the right is close to Full Details, has a much sharper strike, and sold for $16,560 in October 2006. Which would you rather have? There are many such choices in the real world. With knowledge you can often gain an advantage.

BEYOND THE GRADE

As noted, numerical grade can be one thing and numismatic desirability for a connoisseur (but not necessarily for the average buyer) can be something else entirely. What are the other aspects to look for?

Sharpness of strike is one, and is further discussed in the following pages. The presence or absence of planchet adjustment marks and planchet defects is another, also treated below. The quality of the dies can be important. Some coins were struck from dies that were simply worn out, and that should have been retired from production earlier. This is often seen among coins made in large quantities, such as Morgan and Peace silver dollars. Coins that grade MS-65 or higher can have grainy, streaky fields, rather than deeply lustrous surfaces, from "tired dies." Sometimes during striking dies came together without a planchet between them, causing them to "blank" or "clash," leaving marks of injury on both.

All of these factors combined enable you to determine that a coin within a certain assigned grade is either "high end"—and thus a prime candidate to purchase for your collection or resale—or average, or "low end." The latter are to be avoided if at all possible. The market will not suffer, as such pieces, if priced slightly lower, will attract many buyers. Price is *everything* to the majority of coin buyers. In contrast, *quality* is a fuzzy concept, difficult for most people to understand. You, of course, will be an exception.

At the same time, added to the above needs to be knowledge as to the nature of a given coin at the time of striking, characteristics of the dies, and what to expect. Earlier I mentioned a 1788 Vermont copper, the variety known as Ryder-16, which was made from dies that were deliberately weak in the details. There is no such thing as a Full Details piece of this particular variety. Among U.S. silver dollars, the first year of issue, 1794, always comes with the stars at the lower-left obverse somewhat lightly struck, and with the corresponding part of the reverse weak as well. It seems that the die faces were not completely parallel in the press, and, beyond that, the press was of inadequate strength (for which reason the production of dollars was discontinued, and not resumed until the summer of 1795 when a larger-capacity press was on hand). If, as a collector of silver dollars, you desire a 1794, you will need to acquire one that has this lightness of strike. A Full Details coin does not exist—or, if it does, no one is known to have ever seen it.

At the other end of the spectrum, there are many coins that approach perfection and are easy to find. Just about all modern Proof sets and commemoratives sold by the U.S. Mint are in grades that can be called PF-68 to 70. A 2005-S Proof set graded PF-70 would generate nothing more than an unstifled yawn from a specialist. Again, many buyers are clueless, and a lot of very *common* Mint products are packaged in holders marked PF-69 or 70 and sold to unsuspecting buyers, who have heard that these grades are wonderful, and think that they are buying *rarities*, not realizing that anything *lower* than PF-69 or 70 is rare!

In summary, examination of a particular coin in combination with knowledge of minting and other characteristics will make you a very smart buyer—with an expertise which few others have.

WHERE THE MONEY IS!

In a few limited areas of American numismatics, if a coin is recognized as being especially well struck, it can command a premium—sometimes a huge premium. The curious thing is that these coins do not have to have Full Details, meaning that *everything* is needle-sharp. All they have to do is qualify for sharpness in one particular area of a coin, and even that can be loosely interpreted. Widely used are these designations:

Full Steps (FS) Jefferson Nickels

What does this mean? The answer is that on the reverse the center of the Monticello building has six steps. Depending on the standards used, either five of those steps must be complete and distinct, or all six of them. They cannot be broken by nicks or abrasions. If the steps are sharp, then the rest of the coin usually is as well. However, some FS coins can be weakly struck in other areas, such as the back of Jefferson's head. Consider these selected prices from *Coin World's Coin Values*, April 2008 (also the source of the other values quoted here):

Detail of a 1973-D Jefferson nickel with four (out of six) steps complete. Relatively few Jefferson nickels were ever struck with six Full Steps, but those that qualify can sell for very high prices.

> *1941-D Jefferson nickel*—MS-65: $10 • MS-65 FS: $40 • MS-66: $35 • MS-66 FS: $80
>
> *1953-D Jefferson nickel*—MS-65: $23 • MS-65 FS: $400 • MS-66: $42 • MS-66 FS: $3,000

Full Bands (FB) Mercury Dimes.

What does this mean? The answer is that the horizontal bands on the reverse need to be fully separated, or split, with each band made up of two horizontal elements. This primarily applies to the center set, as the bands at the top (three horizontal elements) and bottom (two horizontal elements) of the fasces are usually well defined, being away from the center of the design. No nicks or abrasions are allowed

Left: Detail of a 1942-D Mercury dime with Full Bands (FB) showing a split between the two horizontal elements. Right: Detail of a 1936 dime with the bands merged together.

to interrupt or bridge the separation. *Not* considered is the sharpness, or lack thereof, for the rest of the coin. The date might be weak on the obverse, or the hair to the right of Miss Liberty's face can be weak, or the border indistinct, and yet it can still be assigned the FB designation. Bill Fivaz suggests that weakness on the obverse may have happened when a fresh reverse die was put into a coining press, but a well-used obverse die was not replaced at the same time. No matter. It is only the bands that count!

> *1925-D Mercury dime*—MS-65: $1,800 • MS-65 FB: $4,000 • MS-66: $2,500 • MS-66 FB: $5,000
>
> *1945 Mercury dime*—MS-65: $25 • MS-65 FB: $8,000 • MS-66: $40 • MS-66 FB: $16,000

Full Head (FH) Standing Liberty Quarters. What does this mean? The answer is that the highest details on the head of Miss Liberty should be full. Bill Fivaz uses these criteria: (1) A *full unbroken* hairline from brow to neck, this being the most important; (2) All three leaves clearly visible; and (3) The ear hole visible. *Not* considered is the sharpness, or lack thereof, for the rest of the coin,

Left: Overall view of a 1917, Type I, quarter with true Full Head (FH) and with sharp rivets in the shield and Full Details overall. Right: Detail of a 1920 quarter certified as FH, which the head *nearly* is, but notice the lower-left rivets on the shield are missing.

such as the two lower-left shield rivets and the decoration at the center of the shield, which can be weak or missing on a "FH" coin! Moreover, the head is often no more than 80% full on coins designated "FH" by the grading services. No matter. It is only information printed on a certified holder that seems to count!

> *1920 Standing Liberty quarter*—MS-65: $600 • MS-65 FH: $2,200 • MS-66: $1,100 • MS-66 FH: $5,000

> *1926-D Standing Liberty quarter*—MS-65: $600 • MS-65 FH: $25,000 • MS-66: $2,500 • MS-66 FH: $50,000

Full Bell Lines (FBL) Franklin Half Dollars. What does this mean? The answer is that the lowest horizontal lines at the bottom of the bell on the reverse need to be complete—fully struck and not broken by nicks or abrasions. In actuality, it is often difficult to figure out whether they are complete or not, especially the incuse lines near the crack on the bell.

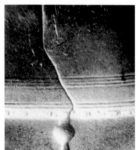 

Left: Detail of a Full Bell Lines (FBL) Franklin half dollar. Notice the lower lines are complete, including on both sides of the crack. Right: Detail (with larger area overall) of a Franklin half dollar with partial bell lines.

> *1948-D Franklin half dollar*—MS-65: $140 • MS-65 FBL: $275 • MS-66: $1,000 • MS-66 FBL: $1,300

> *1953-S Franklin half dollar*—MS-65: $75 • MS-65 FBL: $18,000 • MS-66: $550 • MS-66 FBL: Unpriced

Where the Money Could Be for You!

The preceding prices are interesting to study, and many others can be contemplated as well. I have never seen a 1926-D Standing Liberty quarter with Full Details, and perhaps none exists. However, coins certified as Full Head (FH) are not hard to find. For my money I'd hold out for one with Full Details, or I'd save a lot and simply buy a regular MS-65 or 66 without an FH label.

Perhaps most dramatic is the 1945 Mercury dime in MS-66 grade, said to be worth $40 if a usual strike, but $16,000 if with Full Bands (FB). If you had been a collector in the 1950s, few people would have known of this, and simply by looking you might have found an FB coin for a regular price.

The good news is that nearly all other types of coins come in different degrees of sharpness. Buffalo nickels of 1913 to 1938 are *usually* weakly struck, but no consideration is given to this. Liberty Walking half dollars of 1916 to 1946 are *usually* weakly struck, but no consideration is given to this.

 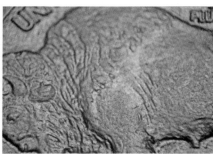

Left: Detail of braid ribbon on a Buffalo nickel with Full Details. Right: Detail of the fur on the bison's head and back on a Buffalo nickel with Full Details.

You, yes *you*, can learn about this (and more will be found in chapter 7) and, if opportunities present themselves, buy Full Details coins for no more than flat strikes! Amazing, but true. Acres of numismatic diamonds await your picking them up!

"You can see a lot by just looking," commented famous baseball player and manager Yogi Berra. When it comes to Full Details or lack thereof, all you need to do is *look*. On the facing page is a gallery of photographs illustrating points to look for on certain coins.

BILL FIVAZ COMMENTS

As to why many coins are weakly struck, Bill Fivaz wrote this for inclusion in the present book:

> When dies for any coin are designed, every effort is taken not to have deep parts of the die(s), which create the high portions on a finished coin, directly opposite each other. A classic example of design flaw is the 1921 Peace silver dollar. Struck in high relief, the central portion of both the obverse and reverse dies of this coin were opposite each other. That is why you will virtually never find a fully struck coin of this date. There will always be a weakness in the central portion of Liberty's hair on the obverse and the leading or outer part of the eagle's wing on the reverse. When a coin is struck, the central areas of the die(s) are the last to fill, and if they are the deepest parts of the die(s), there is simply not enough metal in the planchet to adequately strike up the full design in those areas. This is also true on the Buffalo nickel. The area surrounding the tie on the braid is the central point on the obverse, and directly opposite this on the reverse is the "line" of raised fur on the bison's back and the upper portion of the left leg. Thus, on a coin that is not fully struck, a weakness of varying clarity will manifest itself in these areas.
>
> This design flaw, while not as severe as on the 1921 Peace dollar (which prompted a design change in 1922 to a much lower relief), is the reason only an extremely small percentage of the Buffalo series can be found with what may be considered a "full" strike. If I were to guess, I'd say that less than 2% of the entire mintage would be

Left: Flatly struck stars on the obverse of a 1901 Liberty Head nickel. As coins with Full Details exist, there is no need to buy a coin like this. Right: Flat stars to each side of the head of Miss Liberty on an 1858 half dollar. Again, no need to compromise, as other coins with Full Details exist.

A pair of 1926-D Standing Liberty quarters, each certified as MS-64 FH (Full Head) by a leading service. The one on the left, with the shield rivets missing at the lower left, sold for $16,100 in August 2006. The one on the right, with better details overall and a full set of shield rivets, commanded $9,660 at auction in February 2008. Which would you rather have?

Left: 1901-S Barber half dollar certified as gem MS-65. *However,* the upper right of the shield and nearby wing are weakly struck, as are the eagle's claws below. Right: 1810 half dollar with flatly struck top of wing and with black carbon streaks in the planchet, certified as MS-64.

Left: 1923-S Liberty walking half dollar certified as MS-64. Flatly struck, with no details on the head or her left hand. Right: 1921 Peace silver dollar with flatly struck hair. Both of these coins usually come poorly struck, and for either one a Full Details example may not exist. The goal is to find as sharp of a strike as you can, which for each of these varieties will be sharper than the illustrated coins.

considered Full Details or completely detailed strikes; possibly 15 to 20% would fall into the "sharp" category (where the groove above the tie on the braid is easily visible); about 50% would be "typical," and the remaining 30% would be "weak" strikes.

There are some dates that are exceptions to the above, due to fresh hubs and/or dies or a design change. The initial mintages of the 1913 Buffalo nickels are generally better strikes because of the newness of the hubs (a positive) and dies (a negative image). The 1921 Philadelphia and San Francisco Buffalo nickel mintages were struck by redesigned dies and are usually either sharp or Full Details. For some reason the Mint reverted to the pre-1921 design after that one year.

It's also good to keep in mind that the strike factor in the grading formula is an important component in determining the overall desirability of a coin, while it is not considered in arriving at a grade in technical grading. A connoisseur will often consider multiple factors such as luster, contact marks, and sharpness of strike, all of which combine to determine eye appeal.

ADJUSTMENT MARKS AND PLANCHETS

Quality of the original planchet (the metal disk from which a coin is struck), while not generally affecting commercial and certified grading, can be a factor in the value of a coin, especially for smart buyers who are connoisseurs. Silver and gold coins of the 1790s and early-19th century often have planchet adjustment marks, sometimes severe. These were caused at the Mint when a planchet was found to be slightly overweight, then filed down by hand to the correct specification prior to striking. It was simpler to intentionally make the planchet slightly heavier than need be, and then remove excess metal. Light planchets were destroyed (except for a few scattered known instances in 1795; see notation under Flowing Hair silver dollars of this date).

It is not at all unusual to see coins graded MS-65, or even higher, with significant adjustment marks. If you are seeking the best coin for the price paid, you will want to look for examples that are on *perfect* planchets. It is hard to imagine a coin with significant adjustment marks being anything other than "low end" within its grade category.

Left: Severe vertical planchet adjustment marks at the date of a 1795 Flowing Hair silver dollar, variety BB-27, graded MS-65. Right: Severe adjustment marks on the reverse of a 1795 Draped Bust silver dollar, variety BB-52, graded EF-40.

HIGH END AND LOW END

To reiterate the concept of "high end" and "low end": within any grade classification there are coins that barely make it, and coins that are so nice that perhaps they should be assigned a higher grade. By cherrypicking for quality within a grade you will get the cream of the crop, not the dregs. Sellers, whether they are collectors disposing of duplicates or their main holdings, or dealers with auction or fixed-price offerings, almost never mention or imply "low end." In descriptions of coins for sale, such terms as *low-end, tarnish,* and *overgraded* are as rare as a five-leaf clover. It is up to *you* and you alone to make these determinations.

It seems to me that a high-end coin should be conservatively graded within its category. If there is a chance of obtaining a coin with Full Details, a high-end coin should be such. Remember, there are many coins that do not exist with needle-sharp definition of all aspects of the design. A short list includes dozens of different Jefferson nickels, most Standing Liberty quarters and Liberty Walking half dollars of the 1920s, several different varieties of Buffalo nickels, and many colonials (remember the 1788 Ryder-16 Vermont I mentioned in chapter 3, as an example).

The planchet on a high-end coin should be of high quality, with no copper stains, carbon flecks, laminations, or any other problems. The coin should be struck from fresh dies or those that have seen just moderate use, not from worn or "tired" dies. The coin should have no planchet adjustment marks. If in Mint State, it should have crisp luster, not be dull or grainy. If in a circulated grade, the coin should be free from cuts, edge bumps, or other problems. A silver coin should range from medium-toned to brilliant, not dark gray or black.

In addition to all of these technical considerations, *none* of which are a part of the ANA alphanumerical grading system, the coin should be pretty to view. Eye appeal is very important. If in explaining a coin you have to add the word *but,* then be careful.

Now enters the aspect of *practicality.* You need to know the territory, what to expect, and what does not exist. This will involve some pleasant study apart from the basics given in this book. If you collect modern commemorative coins from 1982 to date, it is important for you to know that a PF-69 or PF-70 coin is not unusual. Such coins are the rule, not the exception, for many issues. If you collect early half cents, you will want to know that most dated 1794 are on rough planchets, as are those of 1797, but half cents of 1793, 1795, and 1796 (a rarity) are on smooth, attractive planchets.

Read, observe, read some more, contemplate what you have learned, and enjoy your numismatic future. Remember those numismatic diamonds. You, as a knowledgeable buyer, can profit immensely. Opportunities abound!

An Ideal Holder?

Sometimes I am an idealist in a non-ideal world. Because the world is not ideal, many opportunities exist. Perhaps from the aspect of cherrypicking it is best that the following does *not* exist!

In my view, the ideal certified coin holder would include this information:

1. The opinion of grade, EF-40, MS-66, or whatever, as established by recognized experts—still with the realization that such is a matter of opinion.
2. Information as to the quality of strike, such as Full Details, or 60% Full Head, or similar.
3. An opinion as to the quality of eye appeal—as evidenced by a person who is identified as a critic and recognized as such. The appeal could be rated from 1 to 10, 1 being ugly and 10 being gorgeous. Of course, this would be a matter of opinion, as is the assigning of a grading number. However, critics would become known for their taste, as is widely accepted and very

true today for reviewers of books, critics of concerts and movies, and tasters of wine.

4. A hologram record would be kept of each coin (similar to what the Gemological Institute of America does now for diamonds), to prevent switching, resubmissions, etc., and to serve as an identification of this particular specimen. In that way, it could be determined that this coin was graded as, say, MS-65, by PCGS on October 18, 2007, or whenever. This would also be beneficial as a security measure in case a coin were to be stolen.

It can be argued that numbers 1 and 3 are matters of opinion, but that is no different than today, when we have only number 1, which is certainly a matter of opinion. To my mind, number 3 could become very valuable, depending upon the reviewer identified. For example, if the late Lester Merkin were alive today and were such a reviewer, a holder with his opinion given would have great meaning to me.

The above features would not eliminate the human element, but I know that if I saw a coin described as MS-65, with Full Details, and rated as a 9 or 10 in eye appeal by a critic I respect, I would have every reason to believe that this, indeed, was a worthwhile consideration for purchase.

Chapter 6

How to Use This Book

Chapter 7 lists federal circulating coins by design types, beginning with the earliest half cent and ending with the latest double eagle. In between, all the different types are discussed. To grade a coin, particularly at the circulated levels, match it to the picture, and you will either be in the ballpark or close. Then read the description. Keep in mind that opinions differ, and within a given type there can be differences as well. One rule does not fit all. If you would like verification of this, just compare the descriptions and photographs in this book with *Photograde* and the *Official American Numismatic Association Grading Standards for United States Coins*. In some instances, all three pictures will be slightly different. However, general rules are useful, and you should be able to do quite well, given some practice.

Coins are illustrated in three enlarged sizes, to give a general sense of their relative diameters. Small coins (such as trimes and Indian Head cents) have been enlarged to 23 mm; bigger coins (such as half cents and quarter dollars) have been enlarged to 30 mm; and the largest-sized coins (e.g., half dollars and double eagles) have been enlarged to the size of a silver dollar, 38.1 mm. Silver dollars are shown at actual size. The Mint State coins illustrated for each type have been enlarged slightly more than other grades.

Proof coins for each type, as appropriate, are discussed and illustrated after the type's circulation-strike grades.

The photographs shown are of actual coins in the marketplace, the majority of them attributed by PCGS and NGC. There are no composite photographs. In each case the obverse and reverse illustrations are from the same specimen. While a picture is worth a thousand words, so they say, the text has value as well. Each picture is accompanied by an explanation, sometimes a little narrative, which you may find useful. To get an even broader view, I reiterate that it is useful to go on the Internet and seek out similar coins in similar grades from the leading services, to verify what is shown here and also to give some ideas as to differences that can occur within a given grade. Do "field" work by visiting coin shops and shows.

It is important to grade to a fixed standard, such as by the guidelines outlined here, and then endeavor to relate coins in the marketplace to these standards. Otherwise, you might see a dozen overgraded coins marked "EF-40" and assume that the coins are right and that the standards are wrong, or you might forget the standards in the enthusiasm to acquire coins.

Jim Reardon, a longtime buyer for Littleton Coin Company and a leader of classes on grading, gives this advice:

> When we are training staff members, we caution them to learn to grade to a fixed standard, and not grade to the sample in front of them. The tendency for anyone working on a large lot of coins is to grade to the group—and not to a standard. Many beginners rank them in context to other coins within the lot.

The result can be to overgrade coins in some instances and to undergrade them in others. If some dealer puts a double-row box in front of you, with every coin having a small problem, the natural tendency might be to pick the best coins from the box to buy for stock. However, while the selected coins might be the best of a group of terrible coins, on an absolute basis *none* should be bought. If the same coins were graded against a fixed standard, they would each prove to be unacceptable.

Undergrading can also take place. If a group of original 1,000-coin bags of Morgan dollars were offered, and these were quality coins that had not been tossed around in a vault over the years, instead of realizing they were nearly all of high quality, it would be natural to downgrade many, as a bag of dollars "should" contain many sub-par pieces along with nice ones. In actually, perhaps nearly all are in higher grades.

It time, grading of a Lincoln cent or Morgan dollar becomes almost intuitive and can be done quickly for starters, then reviewed or "finalized" later. Meanwhile, before you gain this level of expertise it is important to go slowly and carefully.

In the following pages each section has an introduction giving a thumbnail history, plus, and especially important, what to look for in sharp striking. While it can be argued that sharpness of strike is one thing and grade is another, both combine in real life to make a given coin desirable or undesirable. Grade alone will not do it. Accordingly, reading these guidelines is strongly suggested.

You would do well to remember that there is quality *within every grade*. Not all EF-45, MS-65, or other-grade coins are equal. There will be high-end coins within every grade as well as midrange and low-end pieces. As a connoisseur you may find a high-end MS-64 coin to be a better purchase than a low-end MS-66. To reiterate a theme, you will be able to cherrypick for grade. You will buy better coins, often paying little or no more for the opportunity, and the value of your collection will be significantly higher.

Congratulations!

Chapter 7

GRADING U.S. COINS

A NOTE ON EARLY COPPER COINS

Collectors should know that early copper coins of all kinds may exhibit "tooling" (engraving done outside the Mint in order to simulate worn-away or weakly struck details). Sometimes these coins have also been burnished to smooth out porous areas. Learn to recognize the signs of these alterations. They are considered to be damage, and significantly decrease the coin's value.

DIE-VARIETY ATTRIBUTIONS

The attributions of specific die varieties can be found in the following references:

half cents—Walter Breen, *Walter Breen's Encyclopedia of United States Half Cents 1793–1857* (1983), source for Breen **(B)** numbers; Roger S. Cohen Jr., *American Half Cents—The "Little Half Sisters,"* second edition (1982), source for Cohen **(C)** numbers; and Ronald P. Manley, *The Half Cent Die State Book, 1793–1857* (1998)

large cents—*Walter Breen's Encyclopedia of Early U.S. Cents 1793–1814* (2001) (extensive revision of the Sheldon texts); J.R. Grellman, *Attribution Guide for United States Large Cents 1840–1857,* third edition (2002); Howard R. Newcomb, *United States Copper Cents 1816–1857* (1944, reprinted), source for Newcomb **(N)** numbers; William C. Noyes, *United States Large Cents 1793–1814* (1991), and *United States Large Cents 1816–1839* (1991); William H. Sheldon, *Early American Cents* (1949) and its successor, *Penny Whimsy (1793–1814)* (1958), source for Sheldon **(S)** numbers; and John D. Wright, *The Cent Book 1816–1839* (1992)

half dimes—Russell Logan and John McCloskey, *Federal Half Dimes 1792–1837* (1998), source for Logan-McCloskey **(LM)** numbers

dimes—David Davis, Russell Logan, Allen Lovejoy, John McCloskey, and William Subjack, *Early United States Dimes 1796–1837* (1984), source for **JR** numbers (named after early U.S. Mint engraver John Reich)

quarter dollars—A.W. Browning, *The Early Quarter Dollars of the United States 1796–1838* (1925, reprinted and updated), source for Browning **(B)** numbers

half dollars—Al C. Overton, *Early Half Dollar Die Varieties 1794–1836* (1967; third edition, 1990), source for Overton numbers

silver dollars—M.H. Bolender, *The United States Early Silver Dollars from 1794 to 1803,* third edition (1982, since updated), source for Bolender **(B)** numbers; Q. David. Bowers, *Silver Dollars and Trade Dollars of the United States: A Complete Encyclopedia* (1993), source for Bowers-Borckardt **(BB)** numbers

gold $2.50, $5, and $10 pieces—John W. Dannreuther, from the notes of Harry W. Bass Jr., *Early U.S. Gold Coin Varieties: A Study of Die States, 1795–1834* (2006), for Bass-Dannreuther **(BD)** numbers

gold $4 pieces—Stellas, like all pattern coins, are cataloged by their Judd numbers, which are assigned in the standard reference, *United States Pattern Coins.*

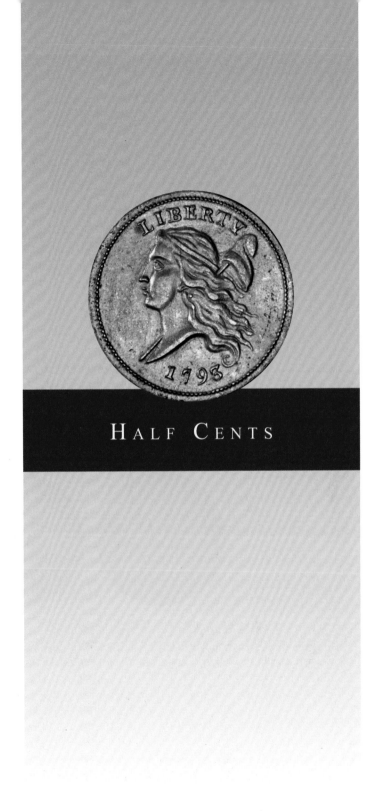

HALF CENTS

HALF CENTS, 1793–1857

1793 LIBERTY CAP, HEAD FACING LEFT

History. The 1793 half cent is distinctive as the only year of its design type. The design was adapted from Augustin Dupré's Libertas Americana medal created in Paris in 1782 by commission from Benjamin Franklin. The Liberty Cap dies are attributed to Joseph Wright, a talented artist who also cut the dies for the 1793 Liberty Cap cent. Unfortunately for numismatic posterity, Wright died of yellow fever in September 1793.

Striking and Sharpness. Half cents of this type are often light brown and on fairly smooth planchets, indicating a good quality of copper used. Borders on both sides are raised beads, an unusual feature not later used in the series. Sometimes certain beads can be weak, but this is the exception, not the rule. Certain varieties are lightly defined at HALF CENT on the reverse, due to a combination of striking and shallow depth of letters in the die. On some coins, up to and including VG-8, these words may be completely missing. Accordingly, this feature cannot be used in assigning a grade.

Availability. Half cents of this date are usually seen in lower grades, AG-3 to F-12 or so. Extremely Fine and About Uncirculated examples are rare, and Mint State coins are very rare. When encountered, which is rarely, Mint State coins are apt to be in ranges from MS-60 to 63. Within a given grade the quality is usually quite satisfactory. In the marketplace, grading is often liberal. Early American Coppers Club (EAC) interpretations are often lower than are certification service interpretations, this being true for all copper half cents and large cents.

MS-60 to 65 (Mint State)

Illustrated coin: 1793, Breen 3, Cohen 3. MS-60 BN.

Well struck and nicely centered on the planchet, this example shows no sign of wear. Its color is a rich orange-brown overall, with a bit of darker gray-brown on the lower right edge and field of the obverse. The faint roughness on the obverse is a flaw of the original planchet, and is not related to wear.

Note: Abbreviations used in die-variety attributions, along with the reference works on which the attributions are based, are discussed on the first page of this chapter. All coins are shown enlarged, for clarity.

Obverse. In the lower ranges, MS-60 and 61, some slight abrasions can be seen on the higher areas of the portrait. Luster in the field is incomplete, particularly in the center of the open areas. At the MS-63 level, luster should be complete, with no abrasions evident. In higher levels, the luster is deeper, and some original mint color may be seen.

Reverse. In the lower ranges some abrasions are seen on the higher areas of the leaves. Generally, luster is complete in all ranges, as the open areas are protected by the lettering and wreath. Otherwise, same comments apply as for the obverse.

AU-50, 53, 55, 58 (About Uncirculated)

Obverse. Friction is seen on the higher parts, particularly on the rounded cheek and on the higher strands of the hair. Friction and scattered marks are in the field, ranging from extensive at AU-50 to minimal at AU-58. Luster may be seen in protected areas, minimal at AU-50, but sometimes extensive on an AU-58 coin. Border beads, if well struck, are separate and boldly defined.

Illustrated coin: 1793, B-3, C-3. AU-50.
This grade would probably be viewed as conservative by many. A well-struck coin with excellent detail in most areas, but with the beads light on the right obverse rim. Light wear is seen on the higher areas.

Reverse. Friction is seen on the higher wreath leaves and (not as easy to discern) on the letters. The fields, protected by the designs, show friction, but not as noticeably as on the obverse. At AU-55 and 58 little if any friction is seen. The reverse may have original luster, toned brown, minimal on lower About Uncirculated grades, sometimes extensive at AU-58. Border beads, if well struck, are separate and boldly defined. Grading at the About Uncirculated level is mainly done by viewing the *obverse*.

EF-40, 45 (Extremely Fine)

Obverse. Wear is seen on the portrait overall, with reduction or elimination of some separation of hair strands on the highest part. The cheek is ever so slightly flat on the highest part. Some leaves will retain some detail, especially where they join the stems. Luster is minimal or non-existent at EF-40 and may survive in traces in protected areas at EF-45.

Illustrated coin: 1793, B-2, C-2. EF-40, perhaps conservatively graded.
The coin has decent strike on both sides except for some blending of border beads, not unusual at this level.

Reverse. Wear is seen on the highest wreath and ribbon areas and the letters. Luster is minimal, but likely more noticeable than on the obverse, as the fields are protected by the designs and lettering.

VF-20, 30 (Very Fine)

Obverse. Wear on the portrait has reduced the hair detail to indistinct or flat at the center on a VF-20 coin, with slightly more detail at VF-30. The thin, horizontal (more or less) ribbon near the top of the hair is distinct. The border beads are blended together, with many blurred or missing. No luster is seen.

Illustrated coin: 1793, B-1, C-1. VF-30.
A sharp coin, with lightly granular surfaces. HALF CENT is weak on the reverse due to striking, not to wear.

Reverse. The leaf details are nearly completely worn away at VF-20, and with slight detail at VF-30. The border beads are blended together, with many indistinct. Some berries in the sprays may be worn away, depending on the strike (on strong strikes they can be seen down into Very Good and Good grades). No luster is seen. HALF CENT may be weak, but is fully readable, on certain coins (such as B-1, C-1) in which this feature was shallowly cut into the dies.

F-12, 15 (Fine)

Obverse. The hair details are mostly worn away, with about one-third visible, mainly at the edges. Border beads are weak or worn away in areas. F-15 shows slightly more detail.

Reverse. The wreath leaves are worn flat, but their edges are distinct. HALF CENT may be missing on variety B-1, C-1 (also true of lower grades given below). Border beads are weak or worn away in areas. F-15 shows slightly more detail.

Illustrated coin: 1793, B-2, C-2. F-15.
Scattered planchet flaws from the strip-rolling process are not unusual, but must be mentioned. The reverse, if graded alone, might be considered a VF.

VG-8, 10 (Very Good)

Obverse. The portrait is well worn, although the eye can be seen, and the hair tips at the right show separation. Border beads are worn away, and the border blends into the field in most if not all of the periphery. LIBERTY and 1793 are bold. VG-10, not an official ANA grading designation, is sometimes applied to especially nice Very Good coins.

Reverse. The wreath, bow, and lettering are seen in outline form, and some leaves and letters may be indistinct in parts. Border beads are worn away, and the border blends into the field in most if not all of the periphery.

Illustrated coin: 1793, B-2, C-2. VG-8.
Raised rim beads are gone, and rim blends into the field in areas. The outside areas of the letters are worn.

G-4, 6 (Good)

Obverse. The portrait is worn smooth and is seen only in outline form, although the eye position can be discerned. LIBERTY and 1793 are complete, although the date may be weak.

Reverse. Extensive wear is seen overall. From half to two-thirds of the letters in UNITED STATES OF AMERICA and the fraction numerals are worn away. The reverse shows more evidence of wear than does the obverse, and is key in assigning this grade. G-6 is often assigned to finer examples in this category.

Illustrated coin: 1793, C-6. G-6.
A well-worn example, but one showing the portrait, LIBERTY, and date very clearly. The reverse shows fewer details.

AG-3 (About Good)

Obverse. Wear is more extensive than on the preceding. The portrait is visible only in outline. LIBERTY is weak but usually fully discernible. 1793 is weak, and the bottoms of the digits may be worn away.

Reverse. Parts of the wreath are visible in outline form, and all but a few letters are gone. Grading of AG-3 is usually done by the reverse.

Illustrated coin: 1793, B-2, C-2. AG-3.
This is a well-worn and somewhat porous example.

Fair-2 (Fair)

Obverse. Worn nearly smooth. Date is partly visible, not necessarily clearly. Head of Miss Liberty is in outline form. Some letters of LIBERTY are discernible.

Reverse. Worn nearly smooth. Peripheral letters are nearly all gone, with only vestiges remaining. Wreath is in outline form. HALF CENT ranges from readable to missing (the latter on certain die varieties as struck).

Illustrated coin: 1793. Fair-2.
This coin is well worn and granular, but identifiable as to date and distinctive type.

1794–1797 LIBERTY CAP

History. Half cents of this type were struck in 1794 with Large Head and Medium Head portrait styles and in 1795 and 1796 with Small Head.

Striking and Sharpness. Half cents of 1794 are usually on dark planchets with rough surfaces, usually of low aesthetic quality overall. Most 1795s are on high-quality planchets, smooth and attractive, this being more true of the later plain-edge type rather than the early thick-planchet issue. Striking can be weak in areas, and often the dentils are incomplete on one or both sides. Many Small Head coins, particularly of 1795 to 1797, have very little detail on the hair, even in higher grades. Half cents of 1796 are great rarities; quality varies, but higher-grade pieces are usually attractive. Half cents of 1797 are usually seen in low grades and on poor planchets; striking varies widely, but is usually weak in areas. Dentils can be weak or can be prominent in various circulated grades, down to the lowest; on certain varieties of 1795 they are prominent even on well-worn coins.

Care must be taken in the assigning of any grade, combining knowledge of a given die variety and its relief or sharpness in the die, with observations of actual wear. Because this admits of differences of opinion among experts, grades of certified coins can vary widely in their interpretations. The astute buyer must take die-variety idiosyncrasies into consideration. As confirmation of this, the PCGS *Official Guide to Coin Grading* notes that for Very Fine grades "high relief coins have approximately 30% to 70% of the hair visible. Regular relief coins usually have less than half the hair distinct." This spells O-P-P-O-R-T-U-N-I-T-Y for the astute buyer. Generally, grading guidelines follow those of the half cent of 1793, but more expertise is required

Availability. As a general type, this issue is scarce, but available. Most are in lower grades, but Very Fine and Extremely Fine coins come on the market with regularity. About Uncirculated and the occasionally seen Mint State coins are usually very attractive.

MS-60 to 70 (Mint State)

Illustrated coin: 1794, Breen 9, Cohen 9. MS-65.
A spectacular coin of a year seldom seen in Mint State. Both sides have rich brown surfaces. On the obverse the luster is light, while on the reverse it is not as noticeable. Note that the obverse die is in very high relief and of the Large Head style, while the reverse is in shallower relief.

Note: Abbreviations used in die-variety attributions, along with the reference works on which the attributions are based, are discussed on the first page of this chapter. All coins are shown enlarged, for clarity.

Obverse. On MS-60 and 61 coins there are some traces of abrasion on the higher areas of the portrait. Luster in the field is incomplete, particularly in the center of the open areas. At MS-63, luster should be complete, and no abrasion is evident. At higher levels, the luster is deeper, and some original mint color may be seen. At MS-65 there are some scattered contact marks and possibly some traces of fingerprints or discoloration, but these should be minimal and not at all distracting. Above MS-65, a coin should approach perfection.

Reverse. In the lower ranges some abrasions are seen on the higher areas of the leaves. Generally, luster is complete in all ranges, as the open areas are protected by the lettering and wreath. Otherwise, the same comments apply as for the obverse.

AU-50, 53, 55, 58 (About Uncirculated)

Obverse. Friction is seen on the higher parts, particularly the center of the portrait. Friction and scattered marks are in the field, ranging from extensive at AU-50 to minimal at AU-58. To reiterate: knowledge of the die variety is important. For certain shallow-relief dies (such as 1797) an About Uncirculated coin may appear to be in a lower grade. Luster may be seen in protected areas, minimal at AU-50, but sometimes extensive on an AU-58 coin.

Illustrated coin: 1797, 1 Over 1; B-1, C-1. AU-58.
This coin has lustrous light-brown surfaces. It was struck from a buckled and cracked obverse die. A decent strike overall, with excellent eye appeal—rare for this date, although this particular variety is often seen nicer than most others of the year.

Reverse. Friction is seen on the higher wreath leaves and (not as easy to discern) on the letters. The fields, protected by the designs, show friction, but not as noticeably as on the obverse. At AU-55 and 58 little if any friction is seen. The reverse may have original luster, toned brown, minimal on lower About Uncirculated grades, sometimes extensive on higher. Grading at the About Uncirculated level is mainly done by viewing the *obverse*.

EF-40, 45 (Extremely Fine)

Obverse. Wear is seen on the portrait overall, with reduction or elimination of some separation of hair strands on the highest part. This varies by die variety, as some are better delineated than others. The cheek shows light wear. Luster is minimal or nonexistent at EF-40, and may survive in traces in protected areas (such as between the letters) at EF-45.

Illustrated coin: 1794, B-1a, C-1a. EF-45.
This coin's dies were cut in shallow relief and with low rims. This makes the coin much less sharp overall than the one illustrated for Mint State.

Reverse. Wear is seen on the highest wreath and ribbon areas and the letters. Luster is minimal, but likely more noticeable than on the obverse, as the fields are protected by the designs and lettering. Sharpness will vary depending on the die variety. Expect certain issues of 1794 and 1797 to be lighter.

VF-20, 30 (Very Fine)

Obverse. Wear on the portrait has reduced the hair detail to indistinct or flat at the center. The border dentils are blended together, with many indistinct. No luster is seen. Again, knowing details of the die variety is important. A VF-20 or 30 1797 is very different in appearance from a 1794 Large Head in the same grade.

Illustrated coin: 1795, B-4, C-4; date punctuated as "1,795" due to a die flaw; plain edge. VF-20.
The dentils are prominent on the left side of the obverse, from light to missing at the right side. The center of HALF CENT is slightly light due to the die, not to wear. The die is sunken at ER (AMERICA), as made.

Reverse. The leaf details are nearly completely worn away at VF-20, with slight detail at VF-30. The border dentils are blended together, with many indistinct. No luster is seen. The sharpness of details depends on the die variety. Half cents of 1797 require special care in their study.

F-12, 15 (Fine)

Obverse. The hair details are mostly worn away, with about one-third visible, mainly at the edges. Border dentils are weak or worn away in areas. F-15 shows slightly more detail.

Reverse. The wreath leaves are worn flat, but their edges are distinct. Border dentils are weak or worn away in areas. F-15 shows slightly more detail.

Illustrated coin: 1795, Punctuated Date. F-15.

VG-8, 10 (Very Good)

Obverse. The portrait is well worn, although the eye can be seen, and the hair tips at the left show separation. Border dentils are worn away on some issues (not as much for 1795 coins), and the border blends into the field in most if not all of the periphery. LIBERTY and the date are bold. VG-10, not an official ANA grading designation, is sometimes applied to especially nice Very Good coins.

Reverse. The wreath, bow, and lettering are seen in outline form, and some leaves and letters may be indistinct in parts. Border dentils are worn away, and the border blends into the field in most if not all of the periphery. In certain die varieties and die states, especially of 1797, some letters may be very weak or missing.

Illustrated coin: 1794, B-2a, C-2b. VG-10. This coin has fairly strong features overall for the grade, and some granularity.

G-4, 6 (Good)

Obverse. The portrait is worn smooth and is seen only in outline form, although the eye position can be discerned. LIBERTY and the date are complete, although the date may be weak. Dentils are gone on some, but not all, die varieties.

Reverse. Extensive wear is seen overall. From half to two-thirds of the letters in UNITED STATES OF AMERICA, and the fraction numerals, are worn away. Certain shallow-relief dies may have letters missing. G-6 is often assigned to finer examples in this category.

Illustrated coin: 1795, B-1, C-1. G-4. This coin shows smooth, even wear. It was struck on a dark planchet. HALF CENT is light due to being shallowly cut in the die.

AG-3 (About Good)

Obverse. Wear is more extensive than on the preceding. The portrait is visible only in outline. LIBERTY is weak but usually fully discernible. The date is weak, and the bottoms of the digits may be worn away.

Reverse. Parts of the wreath are visible in outline form, and all but a few letters are gone. Grading of AG-3 is usually done by the reverse, as the obverse typically appears to be in a slightly higher grade. If split grading were used, more than just a few half cents of this type could be designated as G-4 / AG-3 or even G-6 / AG-3.

Illustrated coin: 1795, B-4, C-6; date punctuated as "1,795." AG-3.

The obverse, if graded separately, would be a clear G-4 or even G-6, but with some light scratches. The reverse is worn down to AG-3.

1800–1808 DRAPED BUST

History. By the time the Draped Bust motif was used for half cents in 1800, it was already a familiar sight on U.S. cents and silver coins. The design was discontinued after 1808.

Striking and Sharpness. Striking varies. Weakness is often seen at the center of the obverse and on the wreath leaves on the reverse. Planchet quality is often porous and dark for 1802, 1803, 1807, and 1808 due to the copper stock used, but it is not described on the labels of certified coins. Here is another cherrypicker's delight, made possible by the fact that certified holders only list the alphanumerical grade.

Availability. As a type, Draped Bust half cents are available in any grade desired, up to and including Mint State, the latter usually dated 1806 (occasionally 1800 and, less often, 1804), by virtue of old-time hoards. The year 1804 includes many different die varieties and die states. Apart from aspects of strike, cherrypicking for planchet quality is essential for 1802, 1803, 1807, and 1808.

MS-60 to 70 (Mint State)

Illustrated coin: 1804, Crosslet 4, Stems to Wreath; Breen 1539, Cohen 10. MS-63 RB.
This is a nice example, with a generous amount of Mint red on the obverse and traces of red on the reverse. There is a spot in the area below the chin and in front of neck.

Note: Abbreviations used in die-variety attributions, along with the reference works on which the attributions are based, are discussed on the first page of this chapter. All coins are shown enlarged, for clarity.

Obverse. In the lower grades, MS-60 and 61, some slight abrasions can be seen on the higher areas of the portrait. Luster in the field is incomplete, particularly in the center of the open areas, which on this type are very extensive. At the MS-63 level, luster should be nearly complete, and no abrasions evident. In higher levels, the luster is complete and deeper and some original mint color may be seen. MS-64 coins may have some slight discoloration or scattered contact marks. A well-graded MS-65 or higher coin has full, rich luster; no marks visible except under magnification; and a blend of brown toning or nicely mixed (not stained or blotchy) mint color and natural brown toning.

Reverse. In the lower Mint State ranges some abrasions are seen on the higher areas of the leaves. Generally, luster is complete in all ranges, as the open areas are protected by the lettering and wreath. Sharpness of the leaves can vary by die variety, so check this aspect. Otherwise, the same comments apply as for the obverse.

AU-50, 53, 55, 58 (About Uncirculated)

Obverse. Friction is seen on the higher parts, particularly the hair of Miss Liberty. Friction and scattered marks are in the field, ranging from extensive at AU-50 to minimal at AU-58. Luster may be seen in protected areas, minimal at AU-50, with more at AU-58. At AU-58 the field may retain some luster, as well. In all instances, the luster is lesser in area and in "depth" than on the reverse of this type.

Illustrated coin: 1806, B-4. C-4. Large 6, Stems. AU-58.

Reverse. Friction is evident on the higher wreath leaves and (not as easy to discern) on the letters. Again, the die variety should be checked. The fields, protected by the designs, show friction, but not as noticeably as on the obverse. At AU-55 and 58, little if any friction is seen. The reverse may have original luster, toned brown, minimal on lower About Uncirculated grades, often extensive at AU-58.

EF-40, 45 (Extremely Fine)

Obverse. Wear is seen on the portrait overall, with reduction or elimination of some separation of hair strands on the highest part. The cheek shows light wear. Luster is minimal or nonexistent at EF-40, and may survive among the letters of LIBERTY at EF-45.

Reverse. Wear is seen on the highest wreath and ribbon areas, and the letters. Luster is minimal, but likely more noticeable than on the obverse, as the fields are protected by the designs and lettering.

Illustrated coin: 1804, B-12, C-11. Plain (not Crosslet) 4 in date, Stems to Wreath on reverse. EF-45.
Probably lightly cleaned years ago, this coin's obverse has a slightly orange hue.

VF-20, 30 (Very Fine)

Obverse. Wear on the portrait has reduced the hair detail to indistinct or flat at the center. The border dentils are blended together, with many indistinct. No luster is seen.

Reverse. The leaf details are nearly completely worn away at VF-20, and with slight detail at VF-30. The border dentils are blended together, with many indistinct. No luster is seen.

Illustrated coin: 1804, B-7, C-8. VF-20.

F-12, 15 (Fine)

Obverse. The hair details are mostly worn away, with about one-third visible, mainly at the edges. Border dentils are weak or worn away in areas. F-15 shows slightly more detail.

Reverse. The wreath leaves are worn flat, but their edges are distinct. HALF CENT may be missing on variety B-1, C-1 (also true of lower grades given below). Border dentils are weak or worn away in areas. F-15 shows slightly more detail.

Illustrated coin: 1804. F-15.
This is the "Spiked Chin" variety, so called because of a thornlike projection from the chin. The variety does not affect the grade.

VG-8, 10 (Very Good)

Obverse. The portrait is well worn, although the eye can be seen, as can hints of hair detail (some at the left shows separation). Curls now appear as mostly solid blobs. Border dentils are worn away on most varieties, and the rim, although usually present, begins to blend into the field. LIBERTY and the date are bold. VG-10, not an official ANA grading designation, is sometimes applied to especially nice Very Good coins.

Reverse. The wreath, bow, and lettering are seen in outline form, and some leaves and letters may be indistinct in parts. The border may blend into the field on some of the periphery.

Illustrated coin: 1805, Small 5, Stems; B-3, C-3. VG-8.
This coin has smooth, even wear. The obverse die has the usual bulge in the right field seen on this variety.

G-4, 6 (Good)

Obverse. The portrait is worn smooth and is seen only in outline form, although the eye position can be discerned. LIBERTY and the date are complete, although the date may be weak. The border blends into the field more extensively than on the preceding, but significant areas are still seen.

Reverse. Extensive wear is seen overall. From half to two-thirds of the letters in UNITED STATES OF AMERICA and the fraction numerals are worn away. G-6 is often assigned to finer examples in this category.

Illustrated coin: 1805, Small 5, Stems; B-3, C-2. G-4 (NCS).
The coin shows much wear, but the key features for G-4 are present. The surfaces are dark and lightly porous and should be described as such in a listing.

AG-3 (About Good)

Obverse. Wear is more extensive than on the preceding. The portrait is visible only in outline. LIBERTY is weak but usually discernible. The date is weak, and the bottoms of the digits may be worn away, but must be identifiable.

Reverse. Parts of the wreath are visible in outline form, and all but a few letters are gone.

Illustrated coin: 1802, 2 Over 0. AG-3.
The obverse is clearly G-4 or so, but the overall grade is defined by the reverse, which is AG-3.

1809–1836 Classic Head

History. This design by Mint engraver John Reich was first used in 1809, a year after it was adopted on the copper cent. It was continued through 1836. Essentially the same head of Miss Liberty was used on Classic Head $5 gold coins of the 1830s. Half cents were not popular in commerce, and mintage quantities diminished sharply after 1809.

Striking and Sharpness. Coins of 1809 to 1811 usually have areas of light or incomplete striking. Grading coins of the early years requires special care and expertise. Sometimes coins as high as Mint State appear "blurry" in areas, due to the dies and striking. Those of later years are often found well struck and are easier to grade. Areas to check include the dentils and rims on both sides, the star centers and hair detail on the obverse, and the leaf detail on the reverse.

Availability. As a type this issue is easily enough found, although 1811 is scarce and 1831 and 1836 are notable rarities. Mint State coins from old hoards exist for certain of the later dates, particularly 1828, 1833, and 1835, but often have spotting, and many seen in the marketplace are cleaned or recolored. Care is advised. Although 1809–1811 half cents are often seen with extensive wear, those of the 1820s and 1830s are not often seen less than Very Fine, as they did not circulate extensively.

MS-60 to 70 (Mint State)

Illustrated coin: 1835. MS-63 BN.
This example has lustrous brown surfaces and nice eye appeal.

Note: Abbreviations used in die-variety attributions, along with the reference works on which the attributions are based, are discussed on the first page of this chapter. All coins are shown enlarged, for clarity.

Obverse. In the lower grades, MS-60 and 61, some slight abrasions can be seen on the portrait, most evident on the cheek, as the hair details are complex on this type. Luster in the field is complete or nearly complete. At MS-63, luster should be complete, and no abrasions are evident. In higher levels, the luster is complete and deeper, and some original mint color may be seen. MS-64 coins may have some slight discoloration or scattered contact marks. A well-graded MS-65 or higher coin has full, rich luster, with no marks visible except under magnification, and has a nice blend of brown toning or nicely mixed (not stained or blotchy) mint color and natural brown toning. Coins dated 1809 to 1811 may exhibit significant weakness of details due to striking (and/or, in the case of most 1811s, porous planchet stock).

Reverse. In the lower Mint State grades, some abrasions are seen on the higher areas of the leaves. Mint luster is complete in all Mint State grades, as the open areas are protected by the lettering and wreath. Sharpness of the leaves can vary by die variety, so check this aspect. Otherwise, the same comments apply as for the obverse. Coins dated 1809 to 1811 may exhibit significant weakness of details due to striking (and/or, in the case of most 1811s, porous planchet stock).

AU-50, 53, 55, 58 (About Uncirculated)

Obverse. Friction is seen on the higher parts, particularly the cheek and hair (under magnification) of Miss Liberty. Friction and scattered marks are in the field, ranging from extensive at AU-50 to minimal at AU-58. Luster may be seen in protected areas, minimal at the AU-50 level, with more showing at AU-58. At AU-58 the field may retain some luster as well.

Reverse. Friction is seen on the higher wreath leaves and (not as easy to discern) on the letters. Again, half cents of 1809 to 1811 require special attention. The fields, protected by the designs, show friction, but not as noticeably as on the obverse. At AU-55 and 58, little if any friction is seen. The reverse may have original luster, toned brown, minimal on lower About Uncirculated grades, often extensive at AU-58.

Illustrated coin: 1809, B-6, C-6. AU-58.
Here is a lovely specimen with rich, brown luster. Stars 1 to 5 on the left are weak, as struck, and the dentils are light in that area (not mentioned on third-party grading labels; such distinctions are up to the buyer to discover and evaluate). Otherwise, the striking is sharp.

EF-40, 45 (Extremely Fine)

Obverse. Wear is seen on the portrait overall, with reduction or elimination of some separation of hair strands. The cheek shows light wear. Luster is minimal or nonexistent at EF-40 but may survive among the letters of LIBERTY at EF-45.

Reverse. Wear is seen on the highest wreath and ribbon areas and the letters. Luster is minimal, but likely more noticeable than on the obverse, as the fields are protected by the designs and lettering.

Illustrated coin: 1811, B-2, C-2. EF-40.
This coin is of about typical strike, with some lightness at the star centers, although wear caused some of the lightness. The surfaces are lightly granular.

VF-20, 30 (Very Fine)

Obverse. Wear on the portrait has reduced the hair detail, but much can still be seen (in this respect the present type differs dramatically from earlier types).

Reverse. The wreath details, except for the edges of the leaves, are worn away at VF-20, and have slightly more detail at VF-30.

Illustrated coin: 1811, B-2, C-2. VF-20.
This coin has gray-brown surfaces. At this level and lower, sharpness of the original strike diminishes in importance, as star centers, hair, leaves, and so on show significant wear.

F-12, 15 (Fine)

Obverse. The hair details are fewer than on the preceding, but many are still present. Stars have flat centers. F-15 shows slightly more detail.

Reverse. The wreath leaves are worn flat, but their edges are distinct. F-15 shows slightly more detail.

Illustrated coin: 1811, B-2, C-2. F-15.
Smooth, even wear characterizes this example of the scarce 1811 half cent. Some light porosity or granularity is normal at this grade level.

VG-8, 10 (Very Good)

Obverse. The portrait is well worn, although the eye and ear can be seen, as can some hair detail. The border is well defined in most areas.

Reverse. The wreath, bow, and lettering are seen in outline form, and some leaves and letters may be indistinct in parts. The border is well defined in most areas.

Illustrated coin: 1811, B-1, C-1. VG-8.
Here is a "poster example" of this grade—smooth, with even wear, a nice planchet, and overall attractive appearance.

G-4, 6 (Good)

Obverse. The portrait is worn smooth and is seen only in outline form. Much of LIBERTY on the headband is readable, but the letters are weak. The stars are bold in outline. Much of the rim can be discerned.

Reverse. Extensive wear is seen overall. Lettering in UNITED STATES OF AMERICA ranges from weak but complete (although the ANA grading guidelines allow for only half to be readable; the ANA text illustrates the words in full) to having perhaps a third of the letters missing. HALF CENT is usually bold.

Illustrated coin: 1811, B-2, C-2. G-4.

AG-3 (About Good)

Obverse. Wear is more extensive than on the preceding. The portrait is visible only in outline. A few letters of LIBERTY are discernible in the headband. The stars are weak or worn away on their outer edges. The date is light.

Reverse. The wreath is visible in outline form. Most or even all of UNITED STATES OF AMERICA is worn away. HALF CENT is usually readable.

Illustrated coin: 1828. AG-3.

Proof Classic Head Half Cents, PF-60 to 70

Proofs were struck of various years in the 1820s and 1830s, with 1831 and 1836 being great rarities (these dates were also restruck at the Mint circa 1859 and later). Some prooflike circulation strikes (especially of the 1833 date) have been certified as Proofs. Except for the years 1831 and 1836, for which Proofs are unequivocal, careful study is advised when contemplating the purchase of a coin described as Proof. Blotchy and recolored Proofs are often seen, but hardly ever described as such. Probably fewer than 25 of the Proofs of this type are truly pristine—without one problem or another.

Illustrated coin: 1831, First Restrike, B-2. PF-66 RB.

Obverse and Reverse. Proofs that are extensively hairlined or have dull surfaces, this being characteristic of many issues (1831 and 1836 usually excepted), are graded PF-60 to 62 or 63. This includes artificially toned and recolored coins, a secret that isn't really secret among knowledgeable collectors and dealers, but is rarely described in print. To qualify as PF-65 or higher, hairlines should be microscopic, and there should be no trace of friction. Surfaces should be prooflike or, better, fully mirrored, without dullness.

1840–1857 BRAIDED HAIR

History. Half cents of this design were introduced in 1840, a year after the motif made its appearance on copper cents. As there was little commercial call for this denomination, only Proofs were struck from 1840 to 1848 and in 1852. The Act of February 21, 1857, abolished the half cent, after which pieces were rapidly withdrawn from circulation. By 1860 virtually all had disappeared from commerce.

Striking and Sharpness. Many if not most are well struck, and nearly all are on good planchet stock. Points to check for sharpness are the dentils on both sides, the star centers and hair detail on the obverse, and the leaf detail on the reverse.

Availability. As coins of this design did not circulate after the 1850s, and as circulation strikes were not made until 1849, such pieces never acquired extensive wear. Typical grades are from EF-40 upward. Coins in lesser grades are seen now and again, but are not in particular demand, as Extremely Fine and About Uncirculated coins are relatively inexpensive.

MS-60 to 70 (Mint State)

Illustrated coin: 1855. MS-64 RB.
Red and brown on the obverse, this example is
mostly brown on the reverse.

Note: All coins are shown enlarged, for clarity.

Obverse. In the lower Mint State grades, MS-60 and 61, some slight abrasion can be seen on the
portrait, most evidently on the cheek. Check the tip of the coronet as well. Luster in the field is
complete, or nearly so. At MS-63, luster should be complete, and no abrasions evident. At higher
levels, the luster is complete and deeper, and some original mint color may be seen. Mint frost
on this type is usually deep, sometimes satiny, but hardly ever prooflike. MS-64 coins may have
some slight discoloration or scattered contact marks. A well-graded MS-65 or higher coin has full,
rich luster; no contact marks visible except under magnification; and a nice blend of brown toning or nicely mixed (not stained or blotchy) mint color and natural brown toning. The late Walter Breen stated that he had never seen an 1853 (common date) half cent with extensive *original*
mint color, but these are plentiful with brown-toned surfaces.

Reverse. In the lower Mint State grades some abrasions are seen on the higher areas of the leaves.
Mint luster is complete in all Mint State grades, as the open areas are protected by the lettering
and wreath.

AU-50, 53, 55, 58 (About Uncirculated)

Obverse. Wear is evident on the cheek, the hair
above the forehead, and the tip of the coronet.
Friction is evident in the field. At AU-58, luster
may be present except in the center of the fields.
As the grades go down to AU-50, wear is more
evident on the portrait. Wear is seen on the
stars, but is not as easy to discern as it is elsewhere. At AU-50 there is either no luster or only
traces of luster close to the letters and devices.

Illustrated coin: 1851. AU-58.
This coin shows Full Details on both sides, and has eye-pleasing
light-brown surfaces.

Reverse. Wear is most evident on the highest
areas of the leaves and the ribbon bow. Luster
is present in the fields. As the grades go downward from AU-58 to 50, wear increases and luster decreases. At the AU-50 level there is either
no luster or traces of luster close to the letters
and devices.

EF-40, 45 (Extremely Fine)

Obverse. Wear is more extensive on the portrait, including the cheek, hair, and coronet. The star centers are worn down slightly. Traces of luster are minimal, if at all existent.

Reverse. The centers of the leaves are well worn, with detail visible only near the edges of the leaves and nearby, with the higher parts worn flat. Letters show significant wear. Luster, if present, is minimal.

Illustrated coin: 1854. EF-40.

VF-20, 30 (Very Fine)

Obverse. Wear is more extensive than on the foregoing. Some of the strands of hair are fused together. The center radials of the stars are worn nearly completely away.

Reverse. The leaves show more extensive wear, with details visible at the edges, and only minimally and not on all leaves. The lettering shows smooth, even wear.

Illustrated coin: 1855. VF-20.

The Braided Hair half cent is seldom collected in grades lower than VF-20.

Proof Braided Hair Half Cents, PF-60 to 70

For the issues of 1840 to 1848, 1849 Small Date, and 1852, only Proofs were made, without related examples for circulation. All were restruck at the Mint. Generally, the quality of these Proofs is very good, with excellent striking of details and nice planchet quality.

Obverse and Reverse. Superb gems at PF-65 and 66 show hairlines only under high magnification, and at PF-67 none are seen. The fields are deeply mirrorlike. There is no evidence of friction. At lower levels, hairlines increase, with a profusion at PF-60 to 62 (and also a general dullness of the fields). Typical color for an undipped coin ranges from light or iridescent brown to brown with some traces of mint color. Except for issues in the 1850s, Proofs are nearly always BN or, less often, RB. The rare Proofs of the 1840s are sometimes seen with light wear and can be classified according to the About Uncirculated and Extremely Fine comments above, except in place of "luster" read "Proof surface."

Illustrated coin: 1852, First Restrike. PF-64 RB. A high-quality coin with a generous amount of original mint color, this piece could just as easily be designated PF-64 RD, for some "RD" coins do not have this much color. Some light hairlines keep it from a higher grade. Excellent eye appeal.

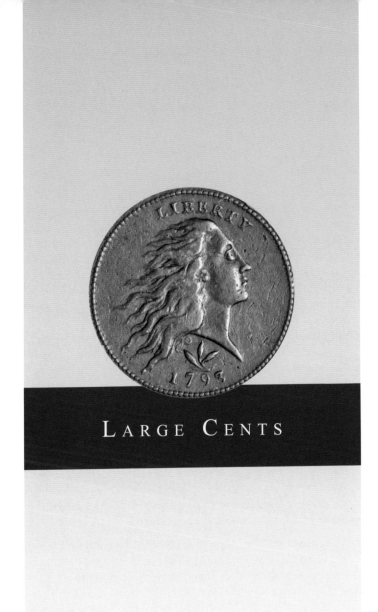

LARGE CENTS

LARGE CENTS, 1793–1857

Note that early copper coins of all kinds may exhibit "tooling" (engraving done outside the Mint in order to simulate worn-away or weakly struck details). These old coppers have also sometimes been burnished, to smooth out areas of porosity. Learn to recognize the signs of these alterations. They are considered to be damage, and significantly decrease the coin's value.

1793 CHAIN REVERSE

History. The first copper one-cent pieces for circulation were struck at the Mint from February 27 through March 12, 1793. These, of the Chain motif, were made to the extent of 36,103 pieces. Several varieties were struck, today attributed by Sheldon numbers. The first, or Sheldon-1, had AMERICA abbreviated as AMERI. A contemporary account noted that Miss Liberty appeared to be "in a fright," and that the chain motif on the reverse, 15 links intended to symbolize unity of the states in the Union, was an "ill omen" for a land of liberty. Accordingly, the design was used for only a short time. The rims on both sides are raised, without dentils or beads.

Ever since numismatics became a popular hobby in the United States, beginning in the 1850s, copper cents of 1793 of the various types have been highly admired and eagerly sought. The market demand for them seems to be everlasting.

Striking and Sharpness. The details of Miss Liberty's hair are often indistinct or missing, including on many higher-grade specimens. For all grades and varieties, the reverse is significantly sharper than the obverse. Hence, if split grading were popular today (as it once was), a Chain AMERI. cent might be correctly graded as VG-8 / F-12, or similar. An enlightened cataloger will carefully describe both sides of an offered coin. In the marketplace, grading interpretations are often quite liberal. The portrait of Miss Liberty is shallow and is often weak, especially on the S-1 variety (which is often missing the date). Each coin is apt to have its own "personality" within an assigned grade, certified or otherwise. Some expanded comments about this are given below.

Availability. All varieties are rare in the context of the demand for them, with probably fewer than 1,000 or so surviving today. Most are in lower grades, from Fair-2 to VG-8. Even Fair and About Good coins are highly collectible, for although the date may be worn away, the chain device identifies the type. Very Fine and Extremely Fine coins are few and far between, and About Uncirculated and Mint State coins are very rare.

MS-60 to 70 (Mint State)

Illustrated coin: 1793, Sheldon 4. MS-65 BN.
This variety has a distinctive obverse with a period after the date and LIBERTY.

Note: Abbreviations used in die-variety attributions, along with the reference works on which the attributions are based, are discussed on the first page of this chapter. All coins are shown enlarged, for clarity.

Obverse. In the lower Mint State grades, MS-60 and 61, some slight abrasions can be seen on the higher areas of the portrait. The large open field shows light contact marks and perhaps a few nicks. At MS-63 the luster should be complete, although some very light abrasions or contact marks may be seen on the portrait. At MS-64 or higher—a nearly impossible level for a Chain cent—there is no sign of abrasion anywhere. Mint color is not extensive on any known Mint State coin, but traces of red-orange are sometimes seen around the rim and devices on both sides.

Reverse. In the lower Mint State grades some abrasions are seen on the chain links. There is some abrasion in the field. At MS-63, luster should be unbroken. Some abrasion and minor contact marks may be evident. In still higher grades, luster is deep and there is no sign of abrasion.

AU-50, 53, 55, 58 (About Uncirculated)

Obverse. Light wear is seen on the highest areas of the portrait. Some luster is seen in the large open fields at the AU-58 level, less at 55, and little if any for 53 and 50. Scattered marks are normal and are most evident in the field. At higher levels, some vestiges of luster may be seen among the letters, numerals, and between the hair tips.

Reverse. Light wear is most evident on the chain, as this is the most prominent feature. The letters show wear, but not as extensive. Luster may be seen at the 58 and 55 levels, usually slightly more on the reverse than on the obverse. Generally, the reverse grades higher than the obverse, usually by a step, such as a 50 obverse and a 53 reverse (such a coin would be listed as the lower of the two, or AU-50).

Illustrated coin: 1793, S-1. AU-50.
Described by an auction cataloger: "Very well defined, some softness on the usually weak highest point of the hair, other fine details well delineated. Some very faint planchet granularity is seen, and a few short parallel fissures are noted around the central reverse. Some scattered nicks, old thin curved scratch from nose through chin and below, another pin scratch on the high forehead."

EF-40, 45 (Extremely Fine)

Obverse. The center of the portrait is well worn, with the hair visible only in thick strands, although extensive detail remains in the hair tips at the left. No luster is seen. Contact marks are normal in the large expanse of open field, but should be mentioned if they are distracting.

Reverse. The chain is bold and shows light wear. Other features show wear, as well—more extensive in *appearance,* as the relief is lower. The fields show some friction, but not as much as on the obverse.

Illustrated coin: 1793, S-2. EF-40.
A cut or void is seen in Miss Liberty's hair, as are some pinpricks and marks. Light scratches are seen at the top of the head. The reverse is especially bold. Surfaces are microscopically granular on both sides.

VF-20, 30 (Very Fine)

Obverse. More wear is seen on the portrait, with perhaps half or slightly more of the hair detail showing, mostly near the left edge of the hair. The ear usually is visible (but might not be, depending on the sharpness of strike). The letters in LIBERTY show wear. The rim remains bold (more so than on the reverse).

Reverse. The chain shows more wear than on the preceding, but is still bold. Other features show more wear and may be weak in areas. The rim may be weak in areas.

Illustrated coin: 1793, S-3. VF-20.
Nice detail is seen in the hair strands at the left. There are some marks near the neck and in the right field, not unusual for this grade. The reverse has a dig below the T in CENT.

F-12, 15 (Fine)

Obverse. The hair details are mostly worn away, with about one-third visible, that being on the left. The rim is distinct on most specimens. The bottoms of the date digits are weak or possibly worn away.

Reverse. The chain is bold, as is the lettering within the chain. Lettering around the border shows extensive wear, but is complete. The rim may be flat in areas.

Illustrated coin: 1793, S-1. F-15.
This coin has a planchet flaw and many tiny pin scratches, with a few heavier scratches above the portrait. Overall, this coin is better than F-15, but the grade compensates for the scratches. This points to the necessity for astute buyers to go beyond an alphanumeric grading number and study the coin itself. The same can be said for most early copper cents.

VG-8, 10 (Very Good)

Obverse. The portrait is well worn, although Miss Liberty's eye remains bold. Hair detail is gone at the center, but is evident at the left edge of the portrait. LIBERTY is always readable, but may be faded or partly missing on shallow strikes. The date is well worn, with the bottom of the numerals missing (published standards vary on this point, and it *used to be* the case that a full date was mandatory).

Reverse. The chain remains bold, and the center letters are all readable. Border letters may be weak or incomplete. The rim is smooth in most areas.

Illustrated coin: 1793, S-4. Certified as F-12, but more closely fitting, perhaps, VG-10 if one deducts for overall porosity. Sometimes, early copper cents cannot be neatly pigeonholed into grade categories.

G-4, 6 (Good)

Obverse. The portrait is worn smooth and is seen only in outline form, although the eye position can be discerned. LIBERTY may be weak. The date is weak, but the tops of the numerals can be discerned.

Reverse. The chain is fully visible in outline form. Central lettering is mostly or completely readable, but light. Peripheral lettering is mostly worn away.

Illustrated coin: 1793, S-4. G-4. The date can barely be discerned, but LIBERTY is sharp. The reverse is a "poster example" of the grade. Remarkably, for a coin so extensively worn, bumps and marks are absent. Few G-4 coins are this nice overall.

AG-3 (About Good)

Obverse. The portrait is visible as an outline. LIBERTY and the date are mostly or even completely worn away. Contact marks may be extensive.

Reverse. The chain is fully visible in outline form. Traces of the central letters—or, on better strikes, nearly all of the letters—can be seen. Around the border all letters are worn away.

Illustrated coin: 1793, S-3. AG-3. The date is completely worn away, but most of LIBERTY is readable. Two edge bumps on the left are unusual for this low grade. The reverse is quite bold, and some peripheral lettering can be seen.

1793 WREATH REVERSE

History. Between April 9 and July 17, 1793, the U.S. Mint struck and delivered 63,353 large copper cents. Certainly most of these, and perhaps all, were of the Wreath type, although records are silent on when design types were changed this year. The Wreath cent was named for the new reverse style—an elegant and dramatic change in design. Miss Liberty on the obverse is in very high relief, almost sculptured. On the reverse a wreath of leaves and sprays of berries enclose the denomination, while other inscriptions are around the border. Both sides have raised beads at the border, similar to the style used on 1793 half cents.

Striking and Sharpness. Usually fairly well struck, although high-grade pieces often exhibit some weakness on the highest hair tresses and on the leaf details. On lower-grade pieces these areas are worn, so the point is moot. Planchet quality varies widely, from smooth, glossy brown to dark and porous. The lettered-edge cents are often seen on defective planchets. Consult the Sheldon text and photographs to learn the idiosyncrasies of certain varieties. Some detailed auction listings reflect the truism that among early cents a grading number is only part of the story, as advanced collectors know well. The borders have raised beads, an artistic touch; on high-grade pieces these are usually very distinct, but they blend together on lower-grade coins and can sometimes be indistinct. The beads are not as prominent as those later used on the 1793 Liberty Cap cents.

Availability. At least several thousand examples exist of the different varieties of the type. Most are in lower grades, from AG-3 to VG-8, although Fine and Very Fine pieces are encountered with regularity. Choice Extremely Fine, About Uncirculated, and higher coins are highly sought numismatic prizes. Some Mint State coins have been billed as "specimen" or "presentation" coins, although this is supposition, as no records exist.

MS-60 to 70 (Mint State)

Illustrated coin: 1793, Sheldon 8. MS-64 BN.
This near-gem Wreath cent is well struck, with full separation on Liberty's curls. The planchet is of unusually high quality, lacking the usual streaks and pits common to early cents. The fields and devices are smooth and unblemished, and the color is a rich chocolate brown, with no specks or carbon spots. In addition to being in a high numerical grade, this coin has exceptional eye appeal.

Note: Abbreviations used in die-variety attributions, along with the reference works on which the attributions are based, are discussed on the first page of this chapter. All coins are shown enlarged, for clarity.

Obverse. On MS-60 and 61 coins there are some traces of abrasion on the higher areas of the portrait, most particularly the hair. As this area can be lightly struck, careful inspection is needed for evaluation, not as much in Mint State (as other features come into play), but in higher circulated grades. Luster in the field is incomplete at lower Mint State levels, but should be in generous quantity. At MS-63, luster should be complete, and no abrasion evident. At higher levels, the luster is deeper, and some original mint color may be seen. At MS-65 there might be some scattered contact marks and possibly bare traces of fingerprints or discoloration. Above MS-65, a coin should approach perfection. A Mint State 1793 Wreath cent is an object of rare beauty.

Reverse. In the lower Mint State grades some abrasion is seen on the higher areas of the leaves. Generally, luster is complete in all grades, as the open areas are protected by the lettering and wreath. In many ways, the grading guidelines for this type follow those of the 1793 half cent—also with sprays of berries (not seen elsewhere in the series).

AU-50, 53, 55, 58 (About Uncirculated)

Obverse. Friction is seen on the highest areas of the hair (which may also be lightly struck) and the cheek. Some scattered marks are normal in the field, ranging from more extensive at AU-50 to minimal at AU-58.

Reverse. Friction is seen on the higher wreath leaves and (not as easy to discern) on the letters. The fields, protected by the designs (including sprays of berries at the center), show friction, but not as noticeably as on the obverse. At AU-55 and 58, little if any friction is seen. Border beads, if well struck, are separate and boldly defined.

Illustrated coin: 1793 Wreath cent, S-8. AU-50.
Offered at auction with this description: "Glossy dark steel brown with appealing surface quality. Under a strong glass, the surfaces show extremely fine granularity . . . only really notable near the borders. A natural planchet flaw at the rim above O (OF) is a reminder of the tribulations the Mint endured in its first year of full operations. The marks that are present are utterly inoffensive, with just a dull scrape under 17 of the date and a minor old scratch under the last S of STATES. . . . The overall eye appeal, both in hand and under careful scrutiny, is very nice."

EF-40, 45 (Extremely Fine)

Obverse. More extensive wear is seen on the high parts of the hair, creating mostly a solid mass (without detail of strands) of varying width in the area immediately to the left of the face. The cheek shows light wear. Luster is minimal or nonexistent at EF-40, and may survive in traces in protected areas (such as between the letters) at EF-45.

Reverse. Wear is seen on the highest wreath and ribbon areas, and the letters. Luster is minimal, but likely more noticeable than on the obverse, as the fields are protected by the designs and lettering. Some of the beads blend together.

Illustrated coin: 1793, S-9. EF-40.
This coin shows some granularity and contact marks, with lighter brown color than usual.

VF-20, 30 (Very Fine)

Obverse. Wear on the hair is more extensive, and varies depending on the die variety and sharpness of strike. The ANA grading standards suggest that two-thirds of the hair is visible, which in practice can be said to be "more or less." More beads are blended together, the extent of which depends on the striking and variety. Certain parts of the rim are smooth, with beads scarcely visible at all. No luster is seen. The date, LIBERTY, and hair ends are bold.

Reverse. The leaf details are nearly completely worn away at VF-20, with slight detail at VF-30. The border beads are blended together, with many indistinct. Some berries in the sprays are light, but nearly all remain distinct. No luster is seen.

Illustrated coin: 1793, S-9. VF-25.
Note some tiny pin scratches, and overall planchet granularity. The sharpness is better than usually seen at this grade.

F-12, 15 (Fine)

Obverse. The hair details are mostly worn away, with about one-third visible, mainly at the edges. The ANA grading standards suggest that 50% are visible, seemingly applying to the total *area* of the hair. However, the visible part, at the left, also includes intermittent areas of the field. Beads are weak or worn away in areas. F-15 shows slightly more detail. By this grade, scattered light scratches, noticeable contact marks, and the like are the rule, not the exception. These are not mentioned at all on holders and are often overlooked elsewhere, except in some auction catalogs and price lists. Such marks are *implicit* for coins in lower grades, and light porosity or granularity is common as well.

Illustrated coin: 1793, S-9. F-12.
This is a sharp coin, but it shows some minor (non-distracting) pits near the base of the obverse. It has even color, superb visual appeal, and a mostly smooth surface.

Reverse. The wreath leaves are worn flat, but their edges are distinct. Border beads are weak or worn away in areas. F-15 shows slightly more detail.

VG-8, 10 (Very Good)

Obverse. The hair is well worn toward the face. Details at the left are mostly blended together in thick strands. The eye, nose, and lips often remain well defined. Border beads are completely gone, or just seen in traces, and part of the rim blends into the field. LIBERTY may be slightly weak. The 1793 date is fully visible, although there may be some lightness. Scattered marks are more common than on higher grades.

Illustrated coin: 1793, S-9. VG-8.
This is an attractive example for the grade, with just one tiny pit near the top of the 3 and some minor granularity.

Reverse. The wreath, bow, and lettering are seen in outline form, and some leaves and letters may be indistinct in parts. Most of the berries remain visible, but weak. Border beads are worn away, and the border blends into the field in most if not all of the periphery.

G-4, 6 (Good)

Obverse. The hair is worn smooth except for the thick tresses at the left. The eye, nose, and lips show some detail. LIBERTY is weak, with some letters missing. The date is discernible, although partially worn away. The sprig above the date is usually prominent. The border completely blends into the field.

Illustrated coin: 1793, S-9. G-4.
This coin's certified-grade holder noted that the surfaces are "corroded," a rather harsh term (oxidized or deeply oxidized might be gentler). At G-4, problems are expected. The date is weak, but most other features are discernible.

Reverse. Extensive overall wear. The wreath is seen in outline form, with some areas weak. Usually ONE CENT remains readable at the center. The border letters and fraction show extensive wear, with some letters very weak or even missing, although most should be discernible. Dark or porous coins may have more details on both sides in an effort to compensate for the roughness. Marks, edge bumps, and so on are normal.

AG-3 (About Good)

Obverse. Wear is more extensive than on the preceding. The eye, nose, and lips may still be discernible, and the sprig above the date can usually be seen. LIBERTY may be very weak or even missing. The date is gone, or just a trace will remain.

Reverse. Parts of the wreath are visible in outline form. ONE CENT might be readable, but this is not a requirement. Most border letters are gone. If a coin is dark or porous it may be graded AG-3 and may be sharper than just described, with the porosity accounting for the lower grade.

Illustrated coin: 1793, S-6. AG-3.
This piece is toned gray overall, and with porous surfaces. The date is gone, but other features on both sides are discernible, making for easy attribution as to die variety.

1793–1796 LIBERTY CAP

History. The Liberty Cap design was created in the summer of 1793 by artist and engraver Joseph Wright, who is also believed to have been the designer of the 1793 half cent (see listing). On the cent, Miss Liberty faces to the right, rather than to the left (as on the half cent). Liberty Cap cents of 1793 are classic rarities and are also the only issues with raised beaded borders. Other issues have dentils. Cents of 1794 and some of 1795 are on thick planchets with the edge lettered ONE HUNDRED FOR A DOLLAR, while those made later in 1795, and in 1796, are on thinner planchets and have a plain edge.

Striking and Sharpness. The depth of relief and striking characteristics vary widely, depending on the variety. Points to check are the details of the hair on Miss Liberty, the leaf details on the wreath, and the dentils on both sides. Generally, the earlier, thick-planchet issues are better strikes than are the thin-planchet coins. Plain-edge 1795 cents often have low or shallow rims. To determine the difference between lightness caused by shallow dies and lightness caused by wear, it is necessary to study the characteristics of the die variety involved (see in particular the reverses of 1793, S-13, and 1793, S-12/S-15).

Availability. Cents of this type are readily available, although those of 1793 are rare and in great demand, and certain die varieties of the other dates are rare and can command high prices. Typical grades range from About Good upward to Fine, Very Fine, and, less often, Extremely Fine. Attractive About Uncirculated and Mint State coins are elusive, and when found are usually dated 1795, the thin planchet variety.

MS-60 to 70 (Mint State)

Illustrated coin: 1794, Sheldon 30. MS-66 BN.
This light brown example is sharply struck and shows no trace of wear. The planchet has mildly grainy areas, but the overall texture is glossy. The blemish in the left obverse field is due to a chip in the die rather than damage to the coin. Despite a few minor spots on the reverse, this coin would be the centerpiece of an advanced collection.

Note: Abbreviations used in die-variety attributions, along with the reference works on which the attributions are based, are discussed on the first page of this chapter. All coins are shown enlarged, for clarity.

Obverse. On MS-60 and 61 coins there are some traces of abrasion on the higher areas of the portrait. Luster is incomplete, particularly in the field. At MS-63, luster should be complete, and no abrasion evident. At higher levels, the luster is deeper, and some original mint color may be seen on some examples. At the MS-65 level there may be some scattered contact marks and possibly some traces of fingerprints or discoloration, but these should be very minimal and not at all distracting. Generally, Liberty Cap cents of 1793 (in particular) and 1794 are harder to find with strong eye appeal than are those of 1795 and 1796. Mint State coins of 1795 often have satiny luster. Above MS-65, a coin should approach perfection, especially if dated 1795 or 1796. Certified Mint State cents can vary in their strictness of interpretation.

Reverse. In the lower Mint State grades some abrasion is seen on the higher areas of the leaves. Generally, luster is complete in all grades, as the open areas are protected by the lettering and wreath. Often on this type the reverse is shallower than the obverse and has a lower rim.

AU-50, 53, 55, 58 (About Uncirculated)

Obverse. Very light wear is evident on the highest parts of the hair above and to the left of the ear. Friction is seen on the cheek and the liberty cap. Coins at this level are usually on smooth planchets and have nice eye appeal. Color is very important. Dark and porous coins are relegated to lower grades, even if AU-level sharpness is present.

Reverse. Very light wear is evident on the higher parts of the leaves and the ribbon, and, to a lesser extent, on the lettering. The reverse may have original luster, toned brown, varying from minimal (at lower About Uncirculated grades) to extensive. Grading at the About Uncirculated level is mainly done by viewing the *obverse*, as many reverses are inherently shallow from lower-relief dies.

Illustrated coin: 1794, S-70. AU-55.
On this particular die variety the obverse rim dentils are particularly bold, helping to shield the field from wear. The motifs and inscriptions on both sides are cut deeply into the dies. Some porosity can be seen in the dentils above I (LIBERTY). Excellent eye appeal overall.

EF-40, 45 (Extremely Fine)

Obverse. The center of the coin shows wear or a small, flat area, for most dies. Other hair details are strong. Luster is minimal or nonexistent at EF-40, and may survive in traces in protected areas (such as between the letters) at EF-45.

Reverse. Wear is seen on the highest wreath and ribbon areas and the letters. Luster is minimal, but likely more noticeable than on the obverse, as the fields are protected by the designs and lettering. Sharpness varies depending on the die variety but is generally shallower than on the obverse, this being particularly true for many 1795 cents.

Illustrated coin: 1794, S-71. EF-40.
This coin has attractive light-brown surfaces. The flatness at the center of the obverse is partly from striking, not entirely from wear. Marks are evident, and on the reverse there is a rim bruise opposite the U in UNITED.

VF-20, 30 (Very Fine)

Obverse. Wear on the portrait has reduced the hair detail to indistinct or flat at the center, and on most varieties the individual strands at the left edge are blended together. One rule does not fit all. The ANA grading standards suggest that 75% of the hair shows, while PCGS suggests 30% to 70% on varieties struck from higher-relief dies, and less than 50% for others. Examples such as this reflect the artistic, rather than scientific, nature of grading.

Reverse. The leaf details are nearly completely worn away at VF-20, and with slight detail at VF-30. Some border letters may be weak, and ditto for the central letters (on later varieties of this type). The border dentils are blended together with many indistinct. No luster is seen. The sharpness of details depends on the die variety.

Illustrated coin: 1793, S-13. VF-20.
This is the rarest of the three major types of 1793—eagerly sought in all grades. Unlike later Liberty Cap cents, those of 1793 have raised beads instead of dentils at the border. This one has a dark planchet with some scattered marks, not unusual for the date and type.

F-12, 15 (Fine)

Obverse. The hair details are mostly worn away, with about one-third visible, mainly at the lower edges. Border dentils are weak or worn away in areas, depending on the height of the rim when the coin was struck. F-15 shows slightly more detail.

Reverse. The wreath leaves are worn flat, but their edges are distinct. Border dentils are weak or worn away in areas. F-15 shows slightly more detail. At this level and lower, planchet darkness and light porosity are common, as are scattered marks.

Illustrated coin: 1794, S-72. F-12.
Some lines and contact marks are expected for the grade.

VG-8, 10 (Very Good)

Obverse. The hair is more worn than on the preceding, with detail present only in the lower areas. Detail can differ, and widely, depending on the dies. Border dentils are worn away on some issues (not as much for 1793 and 1794 coins), and the border will blend into the field in areas in which the rim was low to begin with, or in areas struck slightly off center. LIBERTY and the date are bold. VG-10 is sometimes applied to especially nice Very Good coins.

Reverse. The wreath, bow, and lettering are seen in outline form, and some leaves and letters may be indistinct in parts. Border dentils are worn away, and the border blends into the field in most if not all of the periphery. In certain die varieties and die states, especially of 1797, some letters may be very weak, or missing.

Illustrated coin: 1794, S-49. VG-10.
This coin is sharp in some areas, and lightly struck at the upper-right border and on the corresponding part of the reverse, probably from the die faces not being parallel in the coining press. Note scattered light pitting and marks.

G-4, 6 (Good)

Obverse. The portrait is worn smooth and is seen only in outline form, although the eye and nose can be discerned. LIBERTY and the date are complete, although the date may be weak. Dentils are gone on varieties struck with low or shallow rims.

Reverse. Extensive wear is seen overall. From half to two-thirds of the letters in UNITED STATES OF AMERICA and the fraction numerals are worn away. Certain shallow-relief dies may have letters missing. G-6 is often assigned to finer examples in this category. Darkness, porosity, and marks characterize many coins.

Illustrated coin: 1796, S-84. G-4.
Note the dark and lightly porous planchet. ONE CENT not visible on the reverse due to the shallow die and striking (such situations can vary from one die to another). Otherwise, this coin is close to VG-8.

AG-3 (About Good)

Obverse. Wear is more extensive than on the preceding. The portrait is visible only in outline. LIBERTY will typically have some letters worn away. The date is weak, but discernible.

Reverse. Parts of the wreath are visible in outline form, and all but a few letters are gone. Grading of AG-3 is usually done by the reverse, as the obverse typically appears to be in a slightly higher grade.

Illustrated coin: 1794, S-68. AG-3.
This coin is fully G-4 on the obverse, but weak on the reverse, prompting a more conservative grade. It has no serious marks or edge bumps (somewhat unusual for an AG-3).

1796–1807 DRAPED BUST

History. The Draped Bust cent made its debut in 1796, following a coinage of Liberty Cap cents the same year. The motif, from a drawing by Gilbert Stuart, was first employed on certain silver dollars of 1795. Its use on half cents did not take place until 1800.

Striking and Sharpness. Most are struck on high-quality planchets, often imported from Boulton & Watt, of Birmingham, England. (This high planchet quality is less predictable for varieties of 1796, and almost never present for those of 1799 and 1800.) Sharpness of details varies among the die varieties. When weakness is found, likely as not it is on the hair behind the forehead, on the upper leaves, and among the dentils. However, lightness can occur in other areas as well. Many coins of this type are not perfectly centered, so dentils can be bold on one side of a die and light or even missing on the other; this can occur on obverse and reverse. Not much attention has been paid to this, and values are unaffected. Certain Draped Bust cents of 1796 have semi-prooflike surfaces and are from the Nichols Find. Those of 1799 often have rough or porous surfaces and are found in lower grades (the finest is the Henry Hines Collection About Uncirculated coin).

Availability. As a type, cents of this style are readily available, although the 1799, 9 Over 8, and 1799 are the keys to the series, and the 1804 is elusive. A different scenario evolves when considering engraving errors, repunched dates, and recut letters and numerals; many of these varieties are very difficult to locate. The eye appeal of these rarities is apt to be below par. Other years are generally available in high grades, Very Fine and above, well struck (except for some reverse leaves, in instances), on high-quality planchets, and with excellent eye appeal. The quality of lower grades varies, depending on the rigors of circulation. Dark and porous coins are plentiful among coins graded below VF. True Mint State coins tend to be in lower levels, MS-60 to 63, when found.

MS-60 to 70 (Mint State)

Illustrated coin: 1797, Reverse of 1797, Stems, Sheldon 123. MS-62 BN.
This handsome crimson-brown example is well struck, especially on the obverse. The tiny divot in the field in front of Liberty's throat is a planchet flaw, rather than damage. The coin has no significant blemishes on either side. (Note on the reverse what appears to be a scratch across the two Ns in ONE and CENT. This is actually a scratch on the plastic slab, not on the coin; if one were to examine the coin in person and tilt the slab, the scratch would appear to move in relation to the coin.)

Note: Abbreviations used in die-variety attributions, along with the reference works on which the attributions are based, are discussed on the first page of this chapter. All coins are shown enlarged, for clarity.

Obverse. In the lower Mint State grades, MS-60 and 61, some slight abrasion can be seen on the higher areas of the portrait, especially the cheek, and the hair behind the forehead. Luster in the field is incomplete, particularly in the center of the open areas, which on this type are very open, especially at the right. At MS-63, luster should be nearly complete, and no abrasions evident. In higher levels, the luster is complete and deeper, and some original mint color should be seen. MS-64 coins may have some slight discoloration or scattered contact marks. A well-graded MS-65 or higher coin will have full, rich luster; no marks visible except under magnification; and a nice blend of brown toning or nicely mixed (not stained or blotchy) mint color and natural brown toning.

Reverse. In the lower Mint State ranges some abrasions are seen on the higher areas of the leaves. Generally, luster is complete in all Mint State ranges, as the open areas are protected by the lettering and wreath. Sharpness of the leaves can vary by die variety, so check this aspect. Otherwise, the same comments apply as for the obverse.

AU-50, 53, 55, 58 (About Uncirculated)

Obverse. Friction is seen on the higher parts, particularly the hair of Miss Liberty and the cheek. Friction and scattered marks are in the field, ranging from more extensive at AU-50 to minimal at AU-58. Luster may be seen in protected areas, minimal at AU-50, more visible at AU-58. At AU-58 the field may retain some luster, as well. In many instances, the luster is smaller in area and lesser in "depth" than on the reverse of this type. Cents of this type can be very beautiful in About Uncirculated.

Illustrated coin: 1803, Small Date, Small Fraction, S-247. AU-50.
This is the popular "Mumps" variety, with a bulge below the chin. The coin has many tiny scattered marks, but is pleasing overall.

Reverse. Friction is seen on the higher wreath leaves and (not as easy to discern) on the letters. Again, the die variety should be checked. The fields, protected by the designs, show friction, but not as noticeably as on the obverse. At AU-55 and 58, little if any friction is seen. The reverse may have original luster, toned brown, minimal on lower About Uncirculated grades, often extensive at the AU-58 level. General rules for cents follow the half cents of the same type.

EF-40, 45 (Extremely Fine)

Obverse. Wear is seen on the portrait overall, with reduction or elimination of some separation of hair strands on the highest part. By the standards of the Early American Coppers society, if the "spit curl" in front of Liberty's ear is missing, the coin is not EF. The cheek shows more wear than on higher grades, and the drapery covering the bosom is lightly worn on the higher areas. Often weakness in the separation of the drapery lines can be attributed to weakness in striking. Luster is minimal or nonexistent at EF-40, and may survive in among the letters of LIBERTY at EF-45.

Illustrated coin: 1803, S-256. EF-45.
This is a high-level coin from the aspect of sharpness, with details perhaps befitting AU-50, but reduced slightly due to some planchet porosity. Nice eye appeal overall.

Reverse. Wear is seen on the highest wreath and ribbon areas, and on the letters. Luster is minimal, but likely more noticeable than on the obverse, as the fields are protected by the designs and lettering. The ANA grading standards state that at EF-45 nearly all of the "ribbing" (veins) in the leaves is visible, and that at EF-40 about 75% is sharp. In practice, striking plays a part as well, and some leaves may be weak even in higher grades.

VF-20, 30 (Very Fine)

Obverse. Wear on the portrait has reduced the hair detail further, especially to the left of the forehead. The rolling curls are solid or flat on their highest areas, as well as by the ribbon behind the hair. The border dentils are blended together, with many indistinct. No luster is seen.

Reverse. The leaf details are nearly completely worn away at VF-20, and with slight detail at VF-30. The ANA grading standards are a bit stricter: 30% remaining at VF-20 and 50% at VF-30. In the marketplace, fewer details can be seen on most certified coins at these levels.

The border dentils are blended together with many indistinct. No luster is seen.

Illustrated coin: 1803, S-260. VF-20.
The wreath is bold, but most leaves are worn flat on their high parts.

F-12, 15 (Fine)

Obverse. Many hair details are worn away, with perhaps one-half to one-third visible, mainly at the edges and behind the shoulder. Border dentils are weak or worn away in areas. F-15 shows slightly more detail. Porosity and scattered marks become increasingly common at this level and lower.

Reverse. The wreath leaves are worn flat, but their edges are distinct. Little if anything remains of leaf vein details. Border dentils are weak or worn away in areas. F-15 shows slightly more detail.

Illustrated coin: 1799, 9 Over 8, S-188. F-12.
Note the gray, toned surfaces, with very light porosity and some scattered marks. The date is full and clear (sometimes a challenge). Cents of 1799, 9 Over 8, and 1799 are the keys to the series and often are graded liberally.

VG-8, 10 (Very Good)

Obverse. The portrait is well worn, although the eye can be seen, as can hints of hair detail. Some hair at the left shows separation. Curls now appear as mostly solid blobs. Border dentils are worn away on most varieties, and the rim, although usually present, begins to blend into the field. LIBERTY and the date are bold in most areas, with some lightness toward the rim. VG-10 is sometimes applied to especially nice Very Good coins.

Reverse. The wreath, bow, and lettering are seen in outline form, and some leaves and letters may be indistinct in parts. The border may blend into the field on some of the periphery. The strength of the letters is dependent to an extent on the specific die variety.

Illustrated coin: 1803, Small Date, Small Fraction, S-245. VG-8.
This is a late die state with a massive "cud" break on the lower-right reverse rim.

G-4, 6 (Good)

Obverse. The portrait is worn smooth and is seen only in outline form, although the eye position can be discerned and some curls can be made out. LIBERTY is readable, but the tops of the letters may fade away. The date is clearly readable, but the lower part of the numerals may be very weak or worn away. The border will blend into the field more extensively than on the preceding, but significant areas will still be seen.

Reverse. Extensive wear is seen overall. From half to two-thirds of the letters in UNITED STATES OF AMERICA and the fraction numerals are worn away. On most varieties, ONE CENT is fairly strong. G-6 is often assigned to finer examples in this category.

Illustrated coin: 1799, S-189. G-4.
Note the dark planchet, as typical, and some light porosity.

AG-3 (About Good)

Obverse. Wear is more extensive than on the preceding. The portrait is visible only in outline. LIBERTY is weak, partially worn away, but usually discernible. The date is weak, and the bottoms of the digits may be worn away, but must be identifiable.

Reverse. Parts of the wreath are visible in outline form, and all but a few letters are gone. ONE CENT is usually mostly or completely discernible, depending on the variety.

Illustrated coin: 1799, 9 Over 8, S-188. AG-3.
The obverse if graded separately would qualify as G-4, but the reverse does not come up to that level.

1808–1814 CLASSIC HEAD

History. The Classic Head design, by John Reich, assistant engraver at the Mint, was introduced in 1808 and was continued through 1814. The same motif was used on half cents beginning in 1809 and on Classic Head $5 gold coins of 1834 to 1838. The War of 1812 with Britain ended the importation of high-quality planchets from England, with the result that copper quality was poor after this time.

Striking and Sharpness. Striking sharpness varies, but is often poor. The cents of 1809 are notorious for having obverses much weaker than their reverses. Points to look for include sharpness of the dentils (which are often mushy, and in *most* instances inconsistent), star centers (a key area), hair details, and leaf details. These cents are often dark and porous due to the copper stock used.

Availability. Examples are readily available in grades from well worn to Very Fine and Extremely Fine, although overall quality often leaves much to be desired. About Uncirculated and Mint State coins are elusive, and a true Mint State coin with Full Details and on a high-quality planchet is a first-class rarity. Grading numbers do not mean much, and connoisseurs might well prefer a high-quality EF-45 to a poorly struck MS-63. Overall eye appeal of obverse and reverse is often sub-par, a characteristic of this type. Cherrypicking is the order of the day, with a wide field open, for most buyers in competition are not aware of differences in quality.

MS-60 to 70 (Mint State)

Illustrated coin: 1814, Sheldon 295. MS-64 BN.
This example is sharply struck and generally well centered. Medium-brown and golden-brown in color, the surface has a trace of original Mint luster in protected areas. The only notable blemish is a tiny vertical nick in the obverse field in front of Liberty's throat, which on a coin of this caliber has no particular market effect. Even the finest of early coppers are apt to show some tiny normal marks.

Note: Abbreviations used in die-variety attributions, along with the reference works on which the attributions are based, are discussed on the first page of this chapter. All coins are shown enlarged, for clarity.

Obverse. In the lower Mint State grades, MS-60 and 61, some slight abrasions can be seen on the portrait, most evidently on the cheek, as the hair details are complex on this type. Luster in the field is complete or nearly complete; the field is not as open on this type as on the Draped Bust issues. At 63, luster should be complete, and no abrasion evident. In higher levels, the luster is complete and deeper, and some original mint color may be seen. MS-64 coins may have some slight discoloration or scattered contact marks. A well-graded MS-65 or higher coin will have full, rich luster; no marks visible except under magnification; and a nice blend of brown toning or nicely mixed (not stained or blotchy) mint color and natural brown toning. Incomplete striking of some details, especially the obverse stars, is the rule.

Reverse. In the lower Mint State grades, some abrasion is seen on the higher areas of the leaves. Mint luster is complete in all Mint State grades, as the open areas are protected by the lettering and wreath. Sharpness of the leaves can vary by die variety, so check this aspect. Otherwise, the same comments apply as for the obverse.

AU-50, 53, 55, 58 (About Uncirculated)

Obverse. Friction is seen on the higher parts, particularly the cheek. The hair will have friction and light wear, but will not be as obvious. Friction and scattered marks are in the field, ranging from more extensive at AU-50 to minimal at AU-58. Luster may be seen in protected areas, minimal at AU-50, but more visible at AU-58. At AU-58 the open field may retain some luster, as well.

Reverse. Friction is seen on the higher wreath leaves and on the letters. Fields, protected by the designs, show less friction. At the AU-55 and 58 levels little if any friction is seen. The reverse may have original luster, toned brown, minimal on lower About Uncirculated grades, often extensive at AU-58.

Illustrated coin: 1813, S-292. AU-50.
Note the dark planchet, typical due to the copper stock used this year. The light striking at the star centers is normal, and some lightness of strike is seen on the hair, especially above LIBERTY. The dentils on Classic Head cents are nearly always off center on one side or the other—here on the reverse.

EF-40, 45 (Extremely Fine)

Obverse. Wear is seen on the portrait overall, but most hair detail will still be present. The cheek shows light wear. Luster is minimal or nonexistent at EF-40, and may survive in among the letters of LIBERTY at EF-45.

Reverse. Wear is seen on the highest wreath and ribbon areas and the letters. Leaf veins are visible except in the highest areas. Luster is minimal, but likely more noticeable than on the obverse, as the fields are protected by the designs and lettering.

Illustrated coin: 1814, Plain 4, S-295. EF-45.
A very attractive coin, far above average in sharpness, but with some "old oxidation" seen around certain of the elements.

VF-20, 30 (Very Fine)

Obverse. Wear on the portrait has reduced the hair detail, especially on the area to the right of the cheek and neck, but much can still be seen.

Reverse. The wreath details, except for the edges of the leaves and certain of the tips (on leaves in lower relief), are worn away at VF-20, and with slightly more detail at VF-30.

Illustrated coin: 1810, 10 Over 09, S-281. VF-35.
This is an attractive example, conservatively graded. The VF-35 grade is not "official" but is widely used.

F-12, 15 (Fine)

Obverse. The hair details are fewer than on the preceding, but many are still present. The central hair curl is visible. Stars have flat centers. F-15 shows slightly more detail. The portrait on this type held up well to wear.

Reverse. The higher areas of wreath leaves are worn flat, but their edges are distinct. F-15 shows slightly more detail.

Illustrated coin: 1812. F-12.
Note the planchet—dark and lightly porous, as is often seen on cents of this type.

VG-8, 10 (Very Good)

Obverse. The portrait is well worn, although the eye and ear can be seen clearly. The hair is mostly blended, but some slight separation can be seen in areas. The border is raised in most or all areas.

Reverse. The wreath is more worn than on the preceding grade, but there will still be some detail on the leaves. On most coins, ONE CENT is bold. Border letters are light or weak but are fully readable. The border is well defined in most areas.

Illustrated coin: 1809, S-280. VG-8.

This is a dark and somewhat porous example of what is considered to be the key issue of the Classic Head type.

G-4, 6 (Good)

Obverse. The portrait is worn smooth and is seen only in outline form. Much or even all of LIBERTY on the headband is readable, but the letters are weak. The stars are weak, only in outline form, and several may scarcely be discerned.

Reverse. Extensive wear is seen overall. Lettering in UNITED STATES OF AMERICA is weak, but completely discernible. The wreath is in outline, but still fairly bold, and ONE CENT is usually strong.

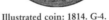

Illustrated coin: 1814. G-4.

AG-3 (About Good)

Obverse. Wear is more extensive than on the preceding. The portrait is visible only in outline. Most letters of LIBERTY are discernible, as this feature is in low relief. The stars are weak or worn away on their outer edges, and the date is light.

Reverse. The wreath is visible in outline form but remains fairly strong. Most or even all of UNITED STATES OF AMERICA is worn away. ONE CENT is usually easily readable.

Illustrated coin: 1808. AG-3.

1816–1839 MATRON HEAD

History. *Matron Head* generally describes cents of 1816 to 1839 (no cents were struck in 1815). Engraver Christian Gobrecht experimented with various portraits, described in the Red Book as well as specialized texts, through 1839. The *Silly Head* and *Booby Head* styles are particularly interesting. These were popular in their time and were made in large quantities. Cents of this type circulated until the late 1850s, by which time some of the earlier dates wore down to become nearly smooth.

Striking and Sharpness. Planchet quality is generally very good. Color tends to be lighter on coins of the 1830s than on earlier dates. Check the obverse stars (in particular), the highest hair details, and the leaves on the reverse. Dentils range from sharp to weak, and centering is often irregular. The reverse design is essentially the same as on the type of 1808 to 1814, and can be graded the same way. This motif stood up to circulation particularly well. Striking can vary; for idiosyncrasies, refer to auction catalogs and pictorial reference guides (Newcomb book does not treat this aspect).

Availability. As a type, cents of these years are easily available. The scarcest date by far is 1823 (and the related 1823, 3 Over 2 overdate). Cents of 1816 to 1820 (particularly 1818 and 1820) are readily available in Mint State, mostly from the famous Randall Hoard. Otherwise, Mint State coins are generally scarce, although those of the 1830s are more readily available than those of the teens and 1820s. Circulated examples exist in approximate relationship to their mintages. Planchet quality and striking sharpness vary in all grades, and careful selection is recommended. Enough coins with excellent eye appeal exist that forming a specialized collection can be a pleasure.

MS-60 to 70 (Mint State)

Illustrated coin: 1826. MS-63 BN.
This 1826 cent is lovely to look at—and would be still nicer to own. Early copper cents have a wide appeal.

Note: Abbreviations used in die-variety attributions, along with the reference works on which the attributions are based, are discussed on the first page of this chapter. All coins are shown enlarged, for clarity.

Obverse. In the lower Mint State grades, MS- 60 and 61, some slight abrasions can be seen on the portrait, most evidently on the cheek, which on this type is very prominent. Higher areas of the hair can be checked, particularly the top and back of Liberty's head, but do not confuse with lightness of strike. Luster in the field is complete or nearly complete. At MS-63, luster should be complete, and no abrasion is evident. In higher levels, the luster is complete and deeper, and some original mint color may be seen. MS-64 coins may have some minimal discoloration or scattered contact marks. A well-graded MS-65 or higher coin will have full, rich luster; no marks visible except under magnification; and a nice blend of brown toning or nicely mixed mint color and natural brown toning. Randall Hoard coins of the 1816 to 1820 years usually have much mint red and some black spotting.

Reverse. In the lower Mint State grades some abrasion is seen on the higher areas of the leaves. Mint luster is complete in all Mint State grades, as the open areas are protected by the lettering and wreath. Sharpness of the leaves can vary by die variety, so check this aspect. Otherwise, the same comments apply as for the obverse.

AU-50, 53, 55, 58 (About Uncirculated)

Obverse. Friction is seen on the higher parts, particularly the cheek. The hair has friction and light wear, usually most notable in the general area above BER (LIBERTY). Friction and scattered marks are in the field, ranging from extensive at AU-50 to minimal at AU-58. Luster may be seen in protected areas, minimal at the AU-50 level, more visible at AU-58. At AU-58 the field may retain some luster as well.

Reverse. Friction is seen on the higher wreath leaves and on the letters. Fields, protected by the designs, show friction. At the AU-55 and 58 levels little if any friction is seen. The reverse may have original luster, toned brown, minimal on lower About Uncirculated grades, often extensive at AU-58.

Illustrated coin: 1828. AU-55 BN.
This example has rich brown surfaces. Among early copper cents, selected About Uncirculated coins such as this one can have eye appeal matching that of lower-level Mint State pieces.

EF-40, 45 (Extremely Fine)

Obverse. Wear is seen on the portrait overall, but most hair detail is still present, except in higher areas. The cheek shows light wear. Luster is minimal or nonexistent at EF-40, and may survive in among the letters of LIBERTY at EF-45.

Reverse. Wear is seen on the highest wreath and ribbon areas, and on the letters. Leaf veins are visible except in the highest areas. Luster is minimal, but likely more noticeable than on the obverse, as the fields are protected by the designs and lettering.

Illustrated coin: 1829, N-6. EF-40.
Here is a well-centered coin. On this variety the obverse dentils are larger (reducing the area of the field somewhat) than those on the reverse.

VF-20, 30 (Very Fine)

Obverse. Wear on the portrait has reduced the hair detail, especially on the area to the right of the cheek and neck, but much can still be seen.

Reverse. The wreath details, except for the edges of the leaves and certain of the tips (on leaves in lower relief), are worn away at VF-20, and with slightly more detail at VF-30.

Illustrated coin: 1839, 9 Over 6, N-1. VF-20.
Some light granularity is most noticeable on the reverse.

F-12, 15 (Fine)

Obverse. The hair details are fewer than on the preceding, but still many are present. Wear is extensive above and below the LIBERTY coronet, with the area from the forehead to the coronet worn flat. Stars have flat centers. F-15 shows slightly more detail.

Reverse. The higher areas of wreath leaves are worn flat, but their edges are distinct. F-15 shows slightly more detail.

Illustrated coin: 1823, N-2. F-15.

VG-8, 10 (Very Good)

Obverse. The portrait is well worn, although the eye and ear can be seen clearly. The hair is mostly blended, but some slight separation can be seen in lower areas. The border is raised in most or all areas.

Reverse. The wreath is more worn than on the preceding, but still there is some detail on the leaves. On most coins, ONE CENT is bold. Border letters are light or weak but are fully readable. The border is well defined in most areas.

Illustrated coin: 1823, 3 Over 2, N-1. VG-8.
Note the tiny scratches on the cheek, and many tiny marks in the field. This coin has a pleasing light-brown color, and overall good eye appeal.

G-4, 6 (Good)

Obverse. The portrait is worn smooth and is seen only in outline form. Much or even all of LIBERTY on the headband is readable, but the letters are weak, and L may be missing. The stars are weak. The rim is usually discernible all around.

Reverse. Extensive wear is seen overall. Lettering in UNITED STATES OF AMERICA is weak, but completely discernible. The wreath is in outline, but still fairly bold, and ONE CENT is usually strong. The rim is usually faded into the field in many areas (depending on the die variety).

Illustrated coin: 1831, N-12. G-6.
Here is an advanced die state with a cud break at the lower right of the obverse, and with cracks connecting most of the stars. Note the double profile to the portrait, caused by die "chatter" during the coining process.

AG-3 (About Good)

Obverse. Wear is more extensive than on the preceding. The portrait is visible only in outline. Most letters of LIBERTY remain discernible in the headband, as this feature is in low relief. The stars are weak or worn away on their outer edges, and the date is light.

Reverse. The wreath is visible in outline form, but remains fairly strong. Most of UNITED STATES OF AMERICA is worn away. ONE CENT is usually readable, but light.

Illustrated coin: 1818. AG-3.

Proof Matron Head Large Cents, PF-60 to 70

Proofs were made for cents from 1817 onward. Often, what are called "Proofs" are only partially mirrorlike, and sometimes the striking is casual, e.g., with weakness on certain of the stars. Complicating the situation is the fact that all but one of the same die pairs were also used to make circulation strikes. Many misattributions were made generations ago, some of which have been perpetuated. Except among large-cent specialists, debate is effectively ended when a certification service seals a coin as a Proof (logic aside). True Proofs with deeply mirrored surfaces are in the small minority.

Illustrated coin: 1838, N-11. PF-64 BN.
Note some light striking of the stars, and excellent centering.

Obverse and Reverse. Proofs that are extensively hairlined or have dull surfaces, this being characteristic of many issues (exceptions, when found, are usually dated in the 1830s) are graded PF-60 to 62 or 63. Artificially toned and recolored coins may be graded lower. To qualify as PF-65 or higher, hairlines should be microscopic, and there should be no trace of friction. Surfaces should be prooflike or, better, fully mirrored and without dullness.

1839–1857 BRAIDED HAIR

History. In 1839 Christian Gobrecht's Braided Hair motif was introduced, loosely following the design he had created for the 1838 gold eagle. On issues of 1839 through part of 1843, Miss Liberty's portrait is tilted forward, with the left tip of her neck truncation over the 8 of the date. For most issues of 1843 and all later dates her head is larger and aligned in a more vertical position, and the tip of her neck is over the first digit of the date. The reverse lettering was made larger beginning in 1844. The net result is that cents after 1843 are less delicate in appearance than are those of earlier dates. These coins were made in large quantities, except for the last year, 1857. They remained in circulation in the United States until the late 1850s, not long enough to be worn down to very low levels. Exceptions are provided by cents that circulated in the eastern part of *Canada,* as they did throughout the 1860s.

Striking and Sharpness. Sharpness can vary. On the obverse, the star centers can be a problem, especially for dates in the 1850s, and, less often, there can be lightness on the front of the coronet and the hair. On the reverse the leaves can be light, but most are well struck. The dentils can be mushy and indistinct on either side, this being particularly true of dates in the early and mid-1850s. Flaky or laminated planchets can be a problem, again among coins of the 1850s, in which tiny pieces of metal fall away from the surface, leaving areas in the field that interrupt the luster on Mint State coins. As grading numbers do not reflect sharpness of strike, once again there is ample opportunity for cherrypicking.

Availability. All dates are readily available, with the 1857 somewhat less so (it was minted in January 1857 in low quantity; seemingly not all were released). The delicate-featured issues of 1839 to 1843 are becoming more difficult to find in Extremely Fine or finer conditions without surface problems. Cents dated in the 1850s are usually seen in Very Fine or higher grades. Certain die varieties attributed by Newcomb numbers can be scarce or rare. For issues in the 1850s the differences can be microscopic, thus limiting their numismatic appeal and making them unattributable unless in high grades. Hoards were found of some dates, particularly 1850 to 1856, making Mint State coins of these years more readily available than would otherwise be the case. Grades below VF-20 are not widely collected and, for many issues, are too worn to attribute by die variety. Lower grades are not analyzed here.

MS-60 to 70 (Mint State)

Illustrated coin: 1845. MS-64 RB.
This attractive coin has mixed Mint red and brown coloring.

Note: Abbreviations used in die-variety attributions, along with the reference works on which the attributions are based, are discussed on the first page of this chapter. All coins are shown enlarged, for clarity.

Obverse. In the lower Mint State grades, MS-60 and 61, some slight abrasions can be seen on the portrait, most evidently on the cheek. Check the tip of the coronet and the hair above the ear, as well. Luster in the field is complete or nearly so. At MS-63, luster should be complete, and no abrasion evident. If there is weakness on the hair it is due to light striking, not to wear; this also applies for the stars. In higher levels, the luster is complete and deeper, and some original mint color may be seen. Mint frost on this type is usually deep, sometimes satiny, but hardly ever prooflike. MS-64 coins may have some slight discoloration or scattered contact marks. A well-graded MS-65 or higher coin will have full, rich luster; no marks visible under magnification; and a nice blend of brown toning or nicely mixed (not stained or blotchy) mint color and natural brown toning. MS-64 RD or higher coins with *original* color range from scarce to very rare for dates prior to 1850, but those of the 1850s are seen regularly (except for 1857).

Reverse. In the lower Mint State grades some abrasion is seen on the higher areas of the leaves. Mint luster is complete in all Mint State ranges, as the open areas are protected by the lettering and wreath. The quality of the luster is the best way to grade both sides of this type.

AU-50, 53, 55, 58 (About Uncirculated)

Obverse. Wear is evident on the cheek, the hair above the ear, and the tip of the coronet. Friction is evident in the field. At AU-58, luster may be present except in the center of the fields. As the grade goes down to AU-50, wear becomes more evident on the cheek. Wear is seen on the stars, but is not as easy to discern as it is elsewhere and, in any event, many stars are weakly struck. At AU-50 there will be either no luster or only traces of luster close to the letters and devices.

Illustrated coin: 1849. AU-58.
Some friction is present, but the coin has nearly full luster and outstanding eye appeal. Note some lightness of strike on the stars, as usual (and not reflective of the grade).

Reverse. Wear is most evident on the highest areas of the leaves and the ribbon bow. Luster is present in the fields. As grade goes down from AU-58 to 50, wear increases and luster decreases. At AU-50 there will be either no luster or just traces close to the letters and devices.

EF-40, 45 (Extremely Fine)

Obverse. Wear is more extensive on the portrait, including the cheek, the hair above the ear, and the coronet. The star centers are worn down slightly (if they were sharply struck to begin with). Traces of luster are minimal, if at all existent.

Illustrated coin: 1856, Slanting 5 in date. EF-40.
Note the light wear on the higher areas; and lightly struck stars, as is typical. This coin has attractive light-brown surfaces.

Reverse. The centers of the leaves are well worn, with detail visible only near the edges of the leaves and nearby, with the higher parts worn flat. Letters show significant wear. Luster, if present, is minimal.

VF-20, 30 (Very Fine)

Obverse. Wear is more extensive than on the preceding. Some of the strands of hair are fused together at the top of the head, above the ear, and on the shoulder. The center radials of the stars are nearly completely worn away.

Reverse. The leaves show more extensive wear. Details are visible at the leaves' edges only minimally and not on all the leaves. The lettering shows smooth, even wear.

Illustrated coin: 1855, Upright 5's. VF-20.

F-12, 15 (Fine)

Obverse. About two-thirds of the hair detail is visible. Extensive wear is seen below the coronet. On the coronet the beginning of the word LIBERTY shows wear, with L sometimes only partially visible. The hair behind the neck is flat. The stars are flat.

Reverse. The leaves show more wear and are flat except for the lower areas. The ribbon has very little detail.

Illustrated coin: 1857, Large Date. F-12.

The Braided Hair large cent is seldom collected in grades lower than F-12.

Proof Braided Hair Large Cents, PF-60 to 70

Except for 1841, Proof Braided Hair cents before 1855 range from rare to very rare. Those from 1855 to 1857 are seen with some frequency. Most later Proofs are well struck and of nice quality, but there are exceptions. Most pieces from this era that have been attributed as Proofs really are such, but beware of deeply toned "Proofs" that are actually prooflike, or circulation strikes with polished fields, and recolored.

Illustrated coin: 1857, N-3. PF-63 BN.
Early Proofs from this period are scarce to extremely rare. This example is well struck (the reverse is slightly off-center), with a generally light-brown color except for a few darker areas on the reverse, not unusual for a coin with the BN designation.

Obverse and Reverse. Superb gems PF-65 and 66 show hairlines only under high magnification, and at PF-67 none are seen. The fields usually are deeply mirrorlike on issues after 1843, sometimes less so on earlier dates of this type. Striking should be sharp, including the stars (unlike the situation for many Proofs of the Matron Head type). There is no evidence of friction. In lower grades, hairlines are more numerous, with a profusion of them at the PF-60 to 62 levels, and there is also a general dullness of the fields. Typical color for an undipped coin ranges from light or iridescent brown to brown with some traces of mint color. Except for issues after 1854, Proofs are nearly always BN or, less often, RB. Prooflike pieces are sometimes offered as Proofs. Beware deeply toned "Proofs" and those that do not have full mirrorlike fields.

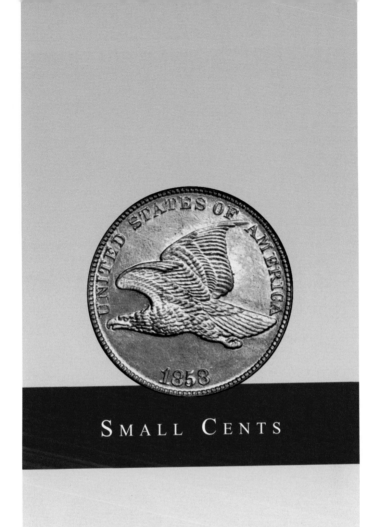

SMALL CENTS

SMALL CENTS, 1856 TO DATE

1856–1858 FLYING EAGLE

History. Large copper cents were becoming increasingly expensive to produce. During the 1850s the Mint experimented with smaller versions, finally deciding on the Flying Eagle cent of small diameter and 72 grains' weight. Many patterns were made of this design in 1856, and restrikes were extensive, with the result that many numismatists have adopted it into the regular series. Distribution of the new cents for circulation commenced on May 25, 1857. Problems resulted from striking the design properly, and the motif was discontinued in 1858. Examples remained in circulation until the early 1900s, by which time survivors were well worn.

Striking and Sharpness. The heavy wreath on the reverse was opposite in the dies (while in the press) from the head and tail of the eagle on the obverse, and, accordingly, many pieces were weakly struck in these areas. Today, this lightness of strike is most visible at each end of the eagle and on the wreath, particularly the higher areas, and on the vertical separation at the middle of the ribbon knot. Striking weakness is most obvious (especially for novice collectors) on the eagle's tail feathers. Many Flying Eagle cents are quite well struck, however.

Availability. As a type the Flying Eagle cent is easy to find, although some varieties, such as 1856 and 1858, 8 Over 7, range from scarce to rare. Most are seen in worn grades. In Mint State, many are in the marketplace, although dipping, cleaning, and recoloring (causing staining and spotting) have eliminated the majority from consideration by connoisseurs. Cherrypicking for quality is easy enough to do and will not take long.

MS-60 to 70 (Mint State)

Illustrated coin: 1857, Snow-2. MS-65.
This very popular variety coin was struck using the obverse hub type of the 1856 cent. It is very scarce at the gem grade level. Both sides exhibit crisp striking detail and smooth, satiny luster. Pinkish-rose in general, it has a splash of light red tinting on the obverse over the eagle's right wing.

Note: All coins are shown enlarged, for clarity.

Obverse. Contact marks, most obvious in the field, are evident at MS-60, diminishing at MS-61, 62, and higher. The eagle, the feathers of which usually hide marks, shows some evidence as well. At Gem MS-65 or finer there is no trace of friction or rubbing. A few tiny nicks or marks may be seen, but none are obvious. At MS-67 and higher levels the coin will approach perfection. A theoretically perfect MS-70 will have no marks at all evident, even under a strong magnifier. Although in practice this is not always consistent, at MS-66 and higher there should be no staining or other problems, and the coin should have good eye appeal overall.

Reverse. Check the higher parts of the wreath for slight abrasions at MS-60 to 62. Otherwise, the above guidelines apply.

AU-50, 53, 55, 58 (About Uncirculated)

Obverse. At AU-50, light wear is seen on the breast of the eagle, the top edge of the closest wing, and, less so, on the head. As both the head and tail tip can be lightly struck, these are not reliable indicators of grade. Luster is present in traces among the letters. At higher About Uncirculated levels the evidence of wear diminishes. An AU-58 coin will have nearly full luster, but friction is seen in the fields, as are some marks.

Illustrated coin: 1856. AU-50.
This is a well-struck example of this rate date. Some slightly mottled toning is on the obverse.

Reverse. At AU-50, light wear is seen on the ribbon bow and the highest areas of the leaves. Some luster is seen (more than on the obverse). Friction is evident, as are some marks, but these will not be as distracting as those on the obverse, as the heavy wreath and lettering are more protective of the reverse field. In higher grades, wear is less, and at AU-58 nearly full—or even completely full—luster is seen.

EF-40, 45 (Extremely Fine)

Obverse. Wear is more extensive, especially on the eagle's breast and the top of the closest wing. Wear will also show on the other wing in the area below OF. Marks may be more extensive in the field. The wear is slightly greater at EF-40 than at EF-45, although in the marketplace these two grades are not clearly differentiated.

Illustrated coin: 1856. EF-40.

Reverse. More wear shows on the higher areas of the wreath, but most detail will still be present. There may be tinges of luster in protected areas, more likely at EF-45 than at 40.

VF-20, 30 (Very Fine)

Obverse. Wear is appreciable, with the breast feathers gone over a larger area and with more wear on the wings. The tail shows significant wear, negating the aspect as to whether it was well struck originally. Marks are more extensive, although across all grades the durable copper-nickel metal resisted heavy marks and cuts; any such should be separately described. Staining and spotting, not related to grade, is common. Cherrypicking at this and lower grades will yield nice coins in any given category.

Illustrated coin: 1838. VF-20.

Reverse. The wreath is worn flat in the higher and medium-relief areas, although some detail is seen in the lower areas close to the field. ONE / CENT may be slightly weak, depending on the quality of original strike. Marks are fewer than on the obverse.

F-12, 15 (Fine)

Obverse. The eagle shows extensive wear, with about half of the feathers gone. Some detail is still seen, especially on the underside of the closest wing, above the breast.

Reverse. Wear is even more extensive, with the wreath nearing flatness, but still with some detail in the lower areas.

Illustrated coin: 1857. F-12.

VG-8, 10 (Very Good)

Obverse. On the obverse the eagle is clear in outline form, but only a small number of feathers can be discerned, mostly above the breast. Letters and the date show extensive wear but are complete and clear.

Reverse. The wreath is now mostly an outline, although some lower-relief features can be differentiated. ONE / CENT may be weak (depending on the strike).

Illustrated coin: 1858. VG-8.

G-4, 6 (Good)

Obverse. The eagle is nearly completely flat, with just a few feathers, if any, discernible. The rim is worn down, making the outer parts of the letters and the lower part of the date slightly weak, but all are readable.

Reverse. The wreath is basically in outline form, with hardly any detail. ONE / CENT is weak, usually with CENT weakest. The rim is worn down.

Illustrated coin: 1858. G-6.

AG-3 (About Good)

Obverse. Wear is extensive, but most of the eagle is visible in outline form. The letters are mostly worn away, with vestiges remaining here and there. The date is partially worn away at the bottom, but is distinct and readable.

Reverse. The wreath is so worn that it cannot be distinguished from the field in areas, usually toward the top. ONE / CENT is mostly gone, but much of CENT can be discerned (unless the coin was a weak strike to begin with).

Illustrated coin: 1856. AG-3.

Proof Flying Eagle Cents, **PF-60 to 70**

Proof Flying Eagle cents dated 1856 are plentiful, surviving from perhaps 2,000 to 2,500 or more restruck in 1859 and later. Proofs of 1857 are very rare. Proofs of 1858 are rare, but are significantly more readily available than for 1857. A first-class Proof should have a fully and deeply mirrored field on both sides, except for those of 1856, which are usually a combination of mirrorlike and grainy in character. Some prooflike Mint State coins have been called Proofs. Quality is a challenge, and problem-free examples are in the minority.

Illustrated coin: 1858, Large Letters. PF-66 Cameo.

Obverse and Reverse. Gem PF-65 coins have very few hairlines, and these are visible only under a strong magnifying glass. At the PF-67 level or higher there should be no evidence of hairlines or friction at all. PF-60 coins can be dull from repeated dipping and cleaning (remember, hairlines on any Proof were caused by cleaning with an abrasive agent; they had no hairlines when struck). At PF-63 the mirrorlike fields should be attractive, and hairlines should be minimal, best seen when the coin is held at an angle to the light. No rubbing is seen. PF-64 coins are even nicer.

1859–1909 INDIAN HEAD

History. After nearly a dozen varieties of patterns were made in 1858, in 1859 the Indian Head was adopted as the new motif for the cent. The reverse of the 1859 coin illustrates an olive (or laurel) wreath. In 1860 this was changed to a wreath of oak and other leaves with a shield at the apex, a design continued through the end of the series in 1909. From 1859 through spring 1864 cents were struck in copper-nickel, the alloy used earlier for Flying Eagle cents. In the latter year a new 48-grain bronze alloy was adopted.

Indian Head cents remained in circulation through the 1940s, but were rarely seen by the early 1950s. In the 1930s, when coin albums and folders became widely available for collectors, many key dates were picked out of circulation, the typical grades for the scarce issues of the 1870s being Good or so, and for the 1908-S and 1909-S, Very Fine or so.

Striking and Sharpness. The striking can vary widely. On the obverse the points to check include the details at the tips of the feathers and the diamonds on the ribbon. Popular convention notwithstanding, the diamonds *cannot* be used as a grading marker, and the feather tips can be used only if you have familiarity with how sharp the coin was struck to begin with. In general, the reverse is usually sharper, but check the leaf and shield details. On many bronze cents beginning in the 1870s the bottom of N (ONE) and tops of EN (CENT) are light, as they were in the dies (not factored when grading). Check the dentils on both sides. Generally, copper-nickel cents of the early 1860s are candidates for light striking as are later issues in the bronze format, of the 1890s onward.

Availability. In worn grades Indian Head cents are available in proportion to their mintages, in combination with survival rates being higher for the later issues. The low-mintage 1909-S was saved in larger quantities than the higher-mintage 1877, as an example. Mint State coins survive as a matter of chance, with those of 1878 and before being much scarcer than those of 1879 and later, and some of the 1900s being readily available. Collectors desiring single pieces often bought Proofs. Many if not most higher-grade Mint State coins have been dipped or recolored, unless they are a warm orange-red color with traces of natural brown. The search for quality among bronze cents is particularly challenging. Some tiny toning flecks are to be expected on many coins, and as long as they are microscopic they can often be ignored (except in grades on the far side of MS-65). A set of MS-65 coins in RB or RD can be formed quickly, but one with *original* color, sharp strike, and excellent eye appeal may take *several years*. Again, knowledge is king, and the better coins go to the informed buyer, often at little or no more cost than that of dipped or recolored coins.

MS-60 to 70 (Mint State)

Illustrated coin: 1894. MS-66+ RD.
This lovely gem is one of the highest-certified circulation-strike 1894 cents known. Absolutely unblemished, it retains every bit of its original, reddish-orange Mint color and frosty texture.

Note: All coins are shown enlarged, for clarity.

Obverse. Contact marks, most obvious in the field, are evident at MS-60, diminishing at MS-61, 62, and higher. This abrasion is most noticeable on copper-nickel cents, for it blends in with the background on bronze issues. The cheek of the Indian and the field show some evidence as well. Typical color is BN, occasionally RB at MS-63 and 64, unless dipped to be RD. At gem MS-65 or finer there is no trace of abrasion. A few tiny nicks or marks may be seen, but none are obvious. At MS-67 and finer the coin will approach perfection. Check "RD" coins for originality. A theoretically perfect MS-70 will have no marks at all, even under a strong magnifier. Although in practice this is not always consistent, at MS-66 and higher there should be no staining or other problems, and the coin should have good eye appeal overall.

Reverse. Check the high parts of the wreath for abrasion. Otherwise the above comments apply.

AU-50, 53, 55, 58 (About Uncirculated)

Obverse. At AU-50, wear is most noticeable on the hair above the ear, on the central portion of the ribbon, on the curl to the right of the ribbon, and near the feather tips, although the last is not a reliable indicator due to striking. Luster is present, but mostly in protected areas. At AU-53 and 55, wear is less. At AU-58 friction is evident, rather than actual wear. Luster, toned brown, is nearly complete at AU-58, but may be incomplete in the field.

Illustrated coin: 1873, Close 3, with doubled LIBERTY. AU-50.
Its glossy brown surfaces retain some luster. This is a coin with excellent eye appeal.

Reverse. At AU-50, light wear is seen on the ribbon and the higher-relief areas of the leaves, while the lower areas retain their detail. Some luster may be present in protected areas. At AU-53 and 55, wear is less and luster is more extensive. An AU-58 coin will have nearly full luster and show only light friction.

EF-40, 45 (Extremely Fine)

Obverse. Wear is more extensive, but all of LIBERTY is very clear. Wear is seen on the hair above and below the ear, on the central portion of the ribbon, and on the feather tips. Overall the coin is bold. Scattered marks are normal for this and lower grades, most often seen on the cheek and in the field.

Reverse. The higher-relief parts of the leaves and ribbon bow show light wear, but details are sharp in lower areas. Some tiny lines in the vertical stripes in the shield may be blended. Scattered marks may be present, but on all grades they are usually fewer on the reverse than on the obverse.

Illustrated coin: 1869. EF-45.
In the marketplace there is little observable difference between EF-40 and 45.

VF-20, 30 (Very Fine)

Obverse. Wear is more extensive. LIBERTY shows significant wear on BE but is sharp overall. Most hair detail is gone. The feather tips show greater wear (the extent of which will depend on the original strike). The ribbon and hair no longer show separation.

Reverse. Wear is more extensive than on the preceding, and many tiny vertical lines are fused together. Detail is still good on lower levels of the leaves.

Illustrated coin: 1877. VF-30.
Note the slight granularity to the surfaces.

F-12, 15 (Fine)

Obverse. By tradition the word LIBERTY should be fully readable, but weak on the higher letters of LIB. PCGS suggests this is true except if a coin was lightly struck. Full or incomplete, well struck or lightly struck, no matter what the coin, most buyers still want the word to be discernible. Other areas have correspondingly more wear than on the next-higher grade.

Illustrated coin: 1909-S. F-12.

Reverse. The higher areas of the leaves and the bow show wear. The shield shows greater wear than on the preceding. Overall, the reverse appears to be less worn than the obverse, this being generally true of all circulated grades.

VG-8, 10 (Very Good)

Obverse. A total of at least three letters in LIBERTY must be visible. This can be a combination of several partial letters. PCGS does not adhere to this rule and suggests that wear on the feathers is a better indicator. The rim may blend into the field in areas, depending on striking.

Reverse. Wear is even more extensive. Leaves on the left have hardly any detail, while those on the right may have limited detail. The rim is complete.

Illustrated coin: 1877. VG-8.
The weakness at the base of N (ONE) is due to the nature of the dies, not to wear.

G-4, 6 (Good)

Obverse. The coin is worn flat, with the portrait visible mostly in outline form, with only slight indication of feathers. Lettering and date are complete. Part of the rim is usually gone. At G-6, the rim is clearer.

Reverse. The wreath is nearly flat, although some hints of detail may be seen on the right side. All letters are readable, although the inscription is light at the center (on issues from the 1870s onward). The rim is discernible all around, but is light in areas. At G-6 the rim is clearly delineated.

Illustrated coin: 1877. G-4 or slightly better.
This is a "strong" Good, a candidate for G-6 (not an official ANA grade, but widely used), with excellent definition within that grade. The weakness at the base of N (ONE) is due to the nature of the dies, not to wear.

AG-3 (About Good)

Obverse. Most letters are worn away, as is the rim. The portrait is in outline form. The date is clearly readable, but may be weak or missing at the bottom.

Reverse. Extensive wear prevails, although the rim will usually be more discernible than on the obverse. Most lettering, or sometimes all, is readable.

Illustrated coin: Here is a problem-free AG-3 cent.
As is often the case, the reverse, if evaluated separately, could be graded G-4. Some light spotting is acceptable.

Proof Indian Head Cents, PF-60 to 70

Proof Indian Head cents were made of all dates 1859 to 1909. The 1864 bronze variety with a tiny L (for designer James B. Longacre) on the ribbon is a rarity, with only about two dozen known. Generally, Proofs are sharp strikes until the 1890s, when some can be weak. On bronze coins tiny carbon flecks are typical, but should be microscopic. If larger, avoid, and at PF-65 or higher, avoid as well. The majority of Proofs have been dipped, and many bronze pieces have been retoned. Most undipped coins are either rich brown (can be very attractive) or red and brown. The late John J. Pittman spent 50 years trying to find a Gem Proof 1907 Indian Head cent with brilliant *original* color! Cherrypicking is the order of the day. Extra value can be found in BN and RB, simply because investors won't buy them; instead, they are drawn to RD coins, most of which have been "improved," as noted.

Proofs are generally designated BN if the surfaces are mainly brown or iridescent, or have up to perhaps 30% original mint red-orange color (there is little consistency in this determination). RB is the designation if the surface is a mixture of red-orange and brown, best if blended together nicely, but often with patches of mint color among brown areas. RD designates a coin with original (in theory) mint-red orange, always blending to slight natural brown toning unless the coin has been dipped. Likely, *any* RD coin with even a few hairlines has been cleaned (or at least mishandled) at one time; in most such cases, the RD is not original. Certification services take no notice of this. For this reason, a connoisseur will prefer a gem BN coin with no hairlines to a PF-65 or 66 RD coin with some hairlines. The BN coin can always be dipped and cleaned (not advised).

Proof copper-nickel Indian Head cents of 1859 to 1864 need no letter to indicate color. As a general rule, these survive in higher grades and with greater eye appeal, as they stayed "brilliant" (the watchword for most collectors until recent decades) and did not need dipping. Moreover, when such pieces were cleaned and acquired hairlines, they tended to be fewer than on a bronze coin, due to the very hard nature of the alloy.

Obverse and Reverse. Gem PF-65 coins will have very few hairlines, and these are visible only under a strong magnifying glass. At any level and color, a Proof with hairlines likely (though not necessarily) has been cleaned. At PF-67 or higher there should be no evidence of hairlines or friction at all. Such a coin is fully original. PF-60 coins can be dull from repeated dipping and cleaning and are often toned iridescent colors. At PF-63 the mirrorlike fields should be attractive, and hairlines should be minimal. These are easiest to see when the coin is held at an angle to the light. No rubbing is seen. PF-64 coins are even nicer.

Illustrated coin: 1864. Gem PF-66.
Lightly toned and free of hairlines, this coin could possibly be graded even higher.

1909–1958 LINCOLN, WREATH REVERSE

History. Lincoln cents, designed by Victor David Brenner, were first released on August 2, 1909. The earliest issues had tiny V.D.B. initials on the reverse, soon discontinued. In 1943, during World War II, zinc-coated steel was used for planchets, as copper was needed for the war effort. The Philadelphia, Denver, and San Francisco mints all produced these coins, but not in all years. Produced by the billions, cents of this type are plentiful today, although certain varieties are scarce.

Striking and Sharpness. As a rule, cents of 1909 through 1914 are fairly well struck. From 1915 through the end of the 1920s, many are weak, with Denver Mint coins being particularly egregious. Issues of the 1930s onward are mostly well struck. With many different die pairs used over a long period of time, striking quality varies. On the obverse, check for details in Lincoln's hair and beard. Also check the lettering and the inner edge of the rim. *Tiny marks on the shoulder of Lincoln indicate a weak strike there*, a checkpoint not known to many; this area cannot be used to determine *wear* on high-grade coins. (During striking, there was not enough die pressure to fill this, the deepest point of the obverse die; therefore, stray marks on the raw planchet remain evident in this spot.) On the reverse check the wheat stalks, letters, and inner rim. A weak strike will usually manifest itself on the O of ONE (the area directly opposite Lincoln's shoulder). Coins struck from overused or "tired" dies can have grainy or even slightly wavy fields on either side; avoid these.

Availability. Cents of the first year, 1909, are easily found in Mint State, after which they become scarcer, although Philadelphia varieties were made in higher quantities and are more often seen. Beginning in the early 1930s, bank-wrapped rolls of Mint State cents were saved in large quantities (starting mainly in 1934, though the low-mintage 1931-S was also hoarded). Dates after this time all are plentiful, although some more so than others. Along the way there are a number of scarce and rare varieties. In the 1930s collectors retrieved many earlier coins from circulation, with typical grades for the key 1909-S V.D.B. and 1914-D being Fine or so. The search continued, and by the 1950s, most early-date coins were apt to be worn down to G-4. The demand for scarcer Lincoln cents and higher-grade issues is intense, resulting in a strong market. Many Mint State coins before the 1930s have been dipped and recolored, this being particularly true of pieces listed as RD. Others are stained and blotchy. See the Indian Head cents commentary for similar situations. To assemble a truly choice collection, well struck, of Lincoln cents of the 1910 to 1929 years takes a lot of patience. Otherwise, if quality is not a concern, a set can be put together quickly.

MS-60 to 70 (Mint State)

Illustrated coin: 1943. MS-68.
This zinc-coated steel cent is an ultra gem in quality.
Note: All coins are shown enlarged, for clarity.

Obverse and Reverse. At MS-65 and higher, the luster is rich on all areas, except perhaps the shoulder (which may be grainy and show original planchet surface). There is no rubbing, and no contact marks are visible except under magnification. Coins with full or nearly full mint orange-red color can be designated RD; those with full or nearly full brown-toned surfaces can be designated BN; and those with a substantial percentage of red-orange and of brown can be called RB. Ideally, MS-65 or finer coins should have good eye appeal, which in the RB category means nicely blended colors, not stained or blotched. Below MS-65, full RD coins become scarce, and at MS-60 to 62 are virtually non-existent, unless they have been dipped. Copper is a very active metal, and influences such as slight abrasions, contact marks, and so on that define the grade also affect the color. The ANA grading standards allow for "dull" and/or "spotted" coins at MS-60 and 61, as well as incomplete luster. In the marketplace, interpretations often vary widely. BN and RB coins at MS-60 and 61 are apt to be more attractive than (dipped) RD coins.

AU-50, 53, 55, 58 (About Uncirculated)

Obverse. Slight wear shows on Lincoln's cheekbone to the left of his nose, and also on his beard. At AU-55 or 58 there may be some hints of mint red-orange. Most coins in About Uncirculated are BN, but are often not designated by color.

Reverse. Slight wear is evident on the stalks of wheat to the left and right. Otherwise, the same standards apply as for the obverse.

Illustrated coin: 1909-S, VDB. AU-50 BN.
This is a sharp example of the most famous Lincoln cent issue.

EF-40, 45 (Extremely Fine)

Obverse. Light wear is seen on Lincoln's portrait, and hair detail is gone on the higher areas, especially above the ear.

Reverse. Light wear is seen overall, but the parallel lines in the wheat stalks are clearly separated.

Illustrated coin: 1909. EF-45.

VF-20, 30 (Very Fine)

Obverse. Lincoln's portrait is worn all over, with most hair detail gone at the center. Hair separation is seen at the back and the top of the head, but hairs are blended together. The jaw outline is clear. The center of the ear is defined and the bowtie is clear. The date and lettering is sharp.

Reverse. More wear is seen, but still the lines in the wheat stalks are separated. Lettering shows wear but is very clear.

Illustrated coin: 1909-S V.D.B. VF-20. Some gray discoloration is hardly noticeable near the rims.

F-12, 15 (Fine)

Obverse. More wear is seen overall. Hair definition is less. The center of the ear is partially visible. The jaw outline and bowtie are clear.

Reverse. Most lines in the wheat stalks are either weak or blended with others, but more than half of the separating lines are clear.

Illustrated coin: 1914-D. F-12.

VG-8, 10 (Very Good)

Obverse. The portrait is more worn, with only slight hair strands visible (thick strands blended). The ear opening is visible. The bowtie and jacket show fewer details.

Reverse. The lines in the wheat stalks are blended together in flat areas. Perhaps 40% to 50% of the separating lines can be seen. The rim may be weak in areas.

Illustrated coin: 1910-S. VG-8.

G-4, 6 (Good)

Obverse. The portrait is well worn. Some slight details are seen at the top of the head and the bottom of the coat. LIBERTY is weak. The rim may touch or blend with the tops of the letters forming IN GOD WE TRUST. The date and mintmark (if any) are very clear.

Reverse. The wheat stalks are flat, with just a few scattered details visible.

Illustrated coin: 1911. G-4.

AG-3 (About Good)

Obverse. Wear is extensive. The portrait is mostly in outline form, with only scattered details visible. LIBERTY is weak and perhaps with some letters missing. IN GOD WE TRUST blends in with the rim, and several letters are very weak or missing.

Reverse. The rim is worn down to blend with the outside of the wheat stalks in some areas, although some hints of the edge of the stalks can be seen. Lettering is weak, with up to several letters missing.

Illustrated coin: 1913-D. AG-3.
A coin such as this might have been found in circulation in the 1950s or early 1960s.

Matte Proof Lincoln/Wreath Cents, PF-60 to 70

Matte Proof Lincoln cents of a new style were made from 1909 to 1916. These have minutely matte or pebbled surfaces caused by special treatment of the dies. The rims are square and sharp. Such pieces cannot easily be told from certain circulation strikes with similar borders. Certified holders usually list these simply as "Proof," not "Matte Proof." Buy only coins that have been verified by an expert. Most are brown, or brown with tinges of red. Nearly all full "red" coins have been dipped or recolored.

Illustrated coin: 1912. Matte PF-64 RD.
This lovely coin has above-average eye appeal.

Mirror-finish Proofs were made from 1936 to 1942 and again from 1950 to 1958. Proofs of this era are mostly from dies polished overall (including the portrait), although some later issues have frosted ("cameo") portraits. Quality can be a problem for the 1936 to 1942 issues. Check for carbon spots and recoloring. Proofs of later dates are easy to find.

Generally, Proofs below 63 are unattractive and are not desired by most collectors.

Obverse and Reverse. At the Matte PF-65 level or higher there are no traces of abrasion or contact marks. Color will range from brown (BN)—the most common—to brown with significant tinges of mint red-orange (RB), or with much mint color (RD). Most RD coins have been dipped. Some tiny flecks are normal on coins certified as PF-65 but should be microscopic or absent above that. Coins in the PF-60 to 63 range are BN or sometimes RB—almost impossible to be RD unless dipped. Lower-grade Proofs usually have poor eye appeal.

Mirror Proof Lincoln/Wreath Cents, PF-60 to 70

Obverse and Reverse. PF-65 and higher coins are usually RB (colors should be nicely blended) or RD, the latter with bright red-orange fading slightly to hints of brown. Some tiny flecks are normal on coins certified as PF-65 but should be microscopic or absent above that. PF-60 and 61 coins can be dull, stained, or spotted but still have some original mint color. Coins with fingerprints must be given a low numerical grade. Lower-grade Proofs usually have poor eye appeal.

Illustrated coin: 1936. Mirror PF-65 RD.
A few flecks are seen here and there.

1959–2008 LINCOLN, MEMORIAL REVERSE

History. In 1959 the new Memorial reverse by Frank Gasparro was introduced. This was used from that time until 2009, when new reverse designs were struck for the bicentennial of Abraham Lincoln's birth. Coins have been struck at the Philadelphia, Denver, and San Francisco mints, with the latter in smaller numbers. Partway through 1982 the bronze alloy was discontinued in favor of copper-coated zinc.

Striking and Sharpness. Striking varies and can range from "sloppy" to needle sharp. On the obverse, check Lincoln's hair and beard (although the sharpness of this feature varied in the dies, and if you are *serious,* buy or borrow a copy of *A Guide Book of Lincoln Cents*). *Tiny marks on the shoulder of Lincoln indicate a weak strike there,* a checkpoint not known to many. On the reverse the sharpness can vary, including on the tiny statue of Lincoln and the shrubbery. On the reverse there can be light striking on the steps of the Memorial, and at IBU and M (E PLURIBUS UNUM). The quality of the fields can vary, as well. Some early copper-coated zinc cents, particularly of 1982 and 1983, can have planchet blisters or problems. The good news is that so many were made that for any given date and mintmark a little patience will reward you with a sharp coin.

Availability. Plentiful across the board for standard dates and mintmarks.

MS-60 to 70 (Mint State)

Illustrated coin: 1970-S. MS-65 RD.
Note this coin has a few flecks.

Note: All coins are shown enlarged, for clarity.

Obverse and Reverse. At MS-65 and higher, the luster is rich on all areas, except perhaps the shoulder (which may be grainy and show original planchet surface). There is no rubbing, and no contact marks are visible except under magnification. Coins with full or nearly full mint orange-red color can be designated RD; those with full or nearly full brown-toned surfaces can be designated BN; and those with a substantial percentage of red-orange and of brown can be called RB. Ideally, MS-65 or finer coins should have good eye appeal, which in the RB category means nicely blended colors, not stained or blotched. Below MS-65, full RD coins become scarce, and at MS-60 to 62 are virtually non-existent, unless they have been dipped. Copper is a very active metal, and influences such as slight abrasions, contact marks, and so on that define the grade also affect the color. The ANA grading standards allow for "dull" and/or "spotted" coins at MS-60 and 61, as well as incomplete luster. In the marketplace, interpretations often vary widely. BN and RB coins at MS-60 and 61 are apt to be more attractive than (dipped) RD coins.

AU-50, 53, 55, 58 (About Uncirculated)

Obverse. Same guidelines as for the preceding type except that tinges of original mint-red are sometimes seen on coins that have *not* been cleaned.

Reverse. Slight wear is seen on the Lincoln Memorial, particularly on the steps, the columns, and the horizontal architectural elements above.

Illustrated coin: 1996-D. AU-50.

EF-40, 45 (Extremely Fine)

Obverse. Light wear is seen on Lincoln's portrait, and hair detail is gone on the higher areas, especially above the ear.

Reverse. Most detail is gone from the steps of the Lincoln Memorial, and the columns and other higher-relief architectural elements show wear.

Illustrated coin: 1962-D. EF-40.

The Lincoln cent with Memorial reverse is seldom collected in grades lower than EF-40.

Proof Lincoln/Memorial Cents, PF-60 to 70

All Proof Lincoln Memorial cents are of the mirror type, usually with cameo or frosted contrast between the devices and the fields. High quality is common. Special Mint Set (SMS) coins were struck in lieu of Proofs from 1965 to 1967 and in some instances closely resemble Proofs.

Illustrated coin: 1979-S. PF-68 Cameo RD. A hint of toning is on Lincoln's jacket. Note the deep cameo contrast.

Obverse and Reverse. PF-65 and higher coins are usually RB (colors should be nicely blended) or RD, the latter with bright red-orange fading slightly to hints of brown. Some tiny flecks are normal on coins certified as PF-65 but should be microscopic or absent above that. PF-60 and 61 coins can be dull, stained, or spotted and still have some original mint color. Coins with fingerprints must be given a low numerical grade. Lower-grade Proofs usually have poor eye appeal. Generally, Proofs below PF-64 are not desired by most collectors.

2009 (BICENTENNIAL REVERSE), 2010 TO DATE (SHIELD REVERSE) LINCOLN

History. One-cent coins with new motifs were issued in 2009 in recognition of the bicentennial of the birth of Abraham Lincoln, as well as the 100th anniversary of the Lincoln cent. Four different reverse designs, one released every three months, represent four major aspects of President Lincoln's life: Birth and Early Childhood in Kentucky, Formative Years in Indiana, Professional Life in Illinois, and Presidency in Washington, D.C. The traditional obverse portrait of Lincoln, in use since 1909, was retained. Regular circulating coins were of the same copper-plated-zinc composition used since 1982. Special versions for collector sets used the original 1909 cent composition (95% copper, 5% tin and zinc).

For 2010 onward, the reverse design was change to a federal shield, "an image emblematic of President Lincoln's preservation of the United States of America as a single and united country."

Striking and Sharpness. Striking is generally sharp.

Availability. Each of the four Lincoln Bicentennial cents was minted for circulation in the hundreds of millions, and today's Shield cents are also minted in large quantities (billions annually). All are readily available in the numismatic marketplace, and they are being seen with greater and greater frequency in the normal channels of commerce.

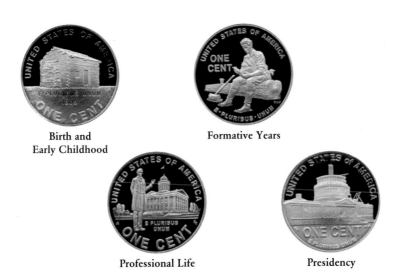

Birth and
Early Childhood

Formative Years

Professional Life

Presidency

MS-60 to 70 (Mint State)

Illustrated coin: 2009, Formative Years. MS-63.

Note: All coins are shown enlarged, for clarity.

Obverse and Reverse. At MS-65 and higher, luster is rich on all areas; there is no rubbing, and no contact marks are visible except under magnification. Coins with full or nearly full mint orange-red color can be designated RD; those with a substantial percentage of red-orange and of brown can be called RB; and those with full (or nearly full) brown-toned surfaces can be designated BN. Some 2009 cents, even from original rolls and bags, have surface marks that look like water spots.

The Lincoln cent with Bicentennial or Shield reverse is seldom collected in grades lower than MS-60.

Proof Lincoln/Bicentennial or Shield Cents, PF-60 to 70

All Proof Lincoln Bicentennial and Shield cents are mirror Proofs, usually with cameo or frosted contrast between the devices and the fields. High quality (PF-69 and 70) is common.

Illustrated coin: 2009-S, Shield. PF-69 RD Ultra Cameo.

Obverse and Reverse. PF-65 and higher coins are RB (with colors nicely blended) or RD, the latter with bright red-orange color sometimes fading to hints of brown. Some tiny flecks are normal on coins certified as PF-65 but should be microscopic or absent above that level. PF-60 and 61 coins can be dull, stained, or spotted and still have some original mint luster. Proof coins with fingerprints are impaired and must be given a lower numerical grade. Lower-grade Proofs usually have poor eye appeal. Generally, Proofs of these types below PF-65 are not desired by most collectors.

TWO-CENT PIECES

TWO-CENT PIECES, 1864–1873

History. The two-cent coin, struck in bronze, made its debut in 1864 under the authorization of the Mint Act of that year, which also provided that Indian Head cents be made of bronze. Coins were scarce in circulation at the time, due to hoarding. The outcome of the Civil War was uncertain, and "hard money" was desired by the public. Large quantities were struck in 1864, after which the mintage declined, due to once-hoarded Indian Head cents becoming available again and to the new nickel three-cent coins being introduced in 1865. Ever-decreasing quantities continued to be made through 1872, then only Proofs in 1873.

Striking and Sharpness. Points to check for sharpness on the obverse include WE in the motto, the leaves, and the horizontal shield lines. On the reverse check the wreath details and the border letters. Check the dentils on both sides. Most coins are quite well struck.

Availability. Most Mint State coins are dated 1864 or 1865, after which the availability declines sharply, especially for the issues of 1872. Among 1864 coins most seen are of the Large Motto variety. Small Motto coins are elusive. Coins with much or nearly all *original* mint red-orange color are rare for the later years, with most in the marketplace being recolored.

MS-60 to 70 (Mint State)

Illustrated coin: 1872. MS-65 RD.
This exceptional example is of a date that is rarely found at this grade level.

Note: All coins are shown enlarged, for clarity.

Obverse and Reverse. At MS-65 and higher, the luster is rich on all areas. There is no rubbing, and no contact marks are visible except under magnification. Coins with full or nearly full mint orange-red color can be designated RD (the color on this is often more orange than red), those with full or nearly full brown-toned surfaces can be designated BN, and those with a substantial percentage of red-orange and of brown can be called RB. Ideally, MS-65 or finer coins should have good eye appeal, which in the RB category means nicely blended colors, not stained or blotched, the latter problem mostly with dipped and irregularly retoned coins. Below MS-65, full RD coins become scarce, although MS-64 RD coins can be attractive. These usually have more flecks and tiny spots, while the color remains bright. At MS-60 to 62, RD coins are virtually non-existent, unless they have been dipped. The ANA standards allow for "dull" and/or "spotted" coins at MS-60 and 61 as well as incomplete luster. As a rule, MS-60 to 63 BN coins can be fairly attractive if not spotted or blotched, but those with hints of color usually lack eye appeal.

AU-50, 53, 55, 58 (About Uncirculated)

Obverse. WE shows light wear, this being the prime place to check. The arrowheads and leaves also show light wear. At AU-50, level wear is more noticeable. At AU-53 and 55, wear is less. At AU-58, friction is evident, rather than actual wear. Luster, toned brown, is nearly complete at AU-58, but may be incomplete in the field.

Reverse. At AU-50, light wear is seen on the ribbon and the higher-relief areas of the leaves and grains, while the lower areas retain their detail. Some luster may be present in protected areas. At AU-53 and 55, wear is lesser and luster is more extensive. An AU-58 coin will have nearly full luster and show only light friction.

Illustrated coin: 1871. AU-55.

EF-40, 45 (Extremely Fine)

Obverse. Wear is more extensive. WE shows wear extensively, but still is clear. The leaves lack detail on their highest points. Some scattered marks are normal at this and lower grades.

Reverse. The higher-relief parts of the leaves and ribbon bow show further wear, as do other areas.

Illustrated coin: 1864, Small Motto. EF-45.

VF-20, 30 (Very Fine)

Obverse. WE is clear, but not strong. Leaves show more wear, as do all other areas.

Reverse. Still more wear is seen, but the leaves still are separately defined. The wheat grains are very clear.

Illustrated coin: 1867. VF-20.

F-12, 15 (Fine)

Obverse. WE is the defining factor and is very weak, but readable, if only barely. Other areas show more wear. The edges of some leaves are gone, blending them into adjacent leaves.

Reverse. Wear is more extensive. Near the apex of the wreath the edges of some leaves are gone, blending them into adjacent leaves. The grains of wheat are clear, but some are slightly weak.

Illustrated coin: 1864, Small Motto. F-12.
WE is very weak. Some scratches on the shield should be separately described.

VG-8, 10 (Very Good)

Obverse. WE is gone, although the ANA grading standards and *Photograde* suggest "very weak." IN GOD and TRUST are readable, but some areas may be weak. The inner edges of most leaves are gone.

Reverse. The wear appears to be less extensive than on the obverse. All lettering is bold. A few grains of wheat may be well worn or even missing.

Illustrated coin: 1864, Large Motto. VG-8.

G-4, 6 (Good)

Obverse. Wear is more extensive, and the leaf bunches are in flat clumps. IN GOD and TRUST are very worn, with a letter or two not visible.

Reverse. All letters are clear. The wreath is mostly in outline on G-4. On G-6, perhaps half the grains are visible.

Illustrated coin: 1872. G-6.

AG-3 (About Good)

Obverse. The motto shows only a few letters. The leaves are flat. Only a few horizontal shield stripes can be seen.

Reverse. The wreath is in outline form. The letters are weak, with 20% to 40% worn away entirely.

Illustrated coin: 1865. AG-3.

Proof Two-Cent Pieces, PF-60 to 70

Proof two-cent pieces were struck each year from 1864 to 1873. The 1864 Small Motto Proof is a great rarity, with fewer than two dozen estimated to exist. Coins of 1873 were made only in Proof format, of the Close 3 and Open 3 styles. Proofs of most dates are easily enough acquired. Very few have *original* color, and a set of these (excluding 1864, Small Motto) in PF-65 RD or better, *with original color and with no hairlines,* would take a decade or more to assemble. Ignore the *original* aspect, and many are offered. Use connoisseurship, the same as needed for Proof Indian Head cents. Do not overlook the many nice brown and red-and-brown pieces on the market ("investment" advisors often suggest that only "red" copper is worth buying, leaving many great values among other coins!). Refer to the comments under Proof Indian Head cents.

Illustrated coin: 1873, Close 3. PF-67 RD.
This superb, fully red Gem is one of the finest known. The strike is razor sharp, and the only irregularity is a hint of pale lilac toning at the lower edge of the reverse. Its value for most readers is not the availability of such, but as a handsome benchmark against which to measure others.

Obverse and Reverse. Gem PF-65 two-cent pieces will have very few hairlines, and these visible only under a strong magnifying glass. At any level and color, a Proof with hairlines has likely been cleaned, a fact usually overlooked. At PF-67 or higher there should be no evidence of hairlines or friction at all. Such a coin is fully original. PF-60 coins can be dull from repeated dipping and cleaning and are often toned iridescent colors or have mottled surfaces. At PF-63, the mirrorlike fields should be attractive, and hairlines should be minimal, most easily seen when the coin is held at an angle to the light. No rubbing is seen. PF-64 coins are even nicer. As a general rule, Proofs of 1873 are of very high quality but, unless dipped or cleaned, are nearly always toned light brown.

THREE-CENT PIECES

THREE-CENT PIECES, 1851–1889

NICKEL THREE-CENT PIECES, 1865–1889

History. The nickel three-cent piece was launched in 1865, when silver coins were still being hoarded by the public (as they would be until 1876). At the time, the highest-denomination coin in circulation was the recently introduced two-cent piece. After 1875, when silver coins circulated once again, the three-cent denomination became redundant and mintages dropped. The last pieces were coined in 1889.

Striking and Sharpness. On the obverse check the hair and other portrait details. On the reverse the tiny vertical lines in the Roman numeral III can be weak. Check the dentils on both sides of the coin. Among circulation strikes, clashed dies are common, particularly for the earlier high-mintage years. Generally, coins of the 1860s and 1870s have weakness in one area or another, while many if not most dated in the 1880s are well struck.

Availability. Circulated examples of dates from 1865 to the mid-1870s are readily available. Mint State coins are easily found, particularly from the 1860s, but often have areas of weakness or lack aesthetic appeal. Mint State coins of the 1880s are readily found for most dates (except for 1883, 1884, 1885, and 1887), some of them probably sold as Proofs. Many Proofs of the era had slight to extensive mint luster.

MS-60 to 70 (Mint State)

Illustrated coin: 1870. MS-65.
This example is lightly toned.
Note: All coins are shown enlarged, for clarity.

Obverse and Reverse. Mint luster is complete in the obverse and reverse fields. Lower grades such as MS-60, 61, and 62 can show some evidence of abrasion. This is usually on the area of the hair to the right of the face (on the obverse), and on the highest parts of the wreath (on the reverse). Abrasion can appear as scattered contact marks elsewhere. At MS-63, these marks are few, and on MS-65 they are fewer yet. In grades above MS-65, marks can only be seen under magnification.

AU-50, 53, 55, 58 (About Uncirculated)

Obverse. Light wear is seen on the portrait, most notably on the upper cheek and on the hair to the right of the face. Mint luster is present in the fields, ranging from partial at AU-50 to nearly complete at AU-58. All details are sharp, unless lightly struck.

Reverse. Light wear is seen on the top and bottom horizontal edges of the III and the wreath. Luster is partial at AU-50, increasing to nearly full at AU-58. All details are sharp, unless lightly struck.

Illustrated coin: 1868. AU-50.

EF-40, 45 (Extremely Fine)

Obverse. More wear is seen on the cheek and the hair to the right of the face and neck. The hair to the right of the coronet beads shows light wear.

Reverse. The wreath still shows most detail on the leaves. Some wear is seen on the vertical lines within III (but striking can also cause weakness). Overall the reverse appears to be very bold.

Illustrated coin: 1881. EF-40.

VF-20, 30 (Very Fine)

Obverse. Most hair detail is gone, with a continuous flat area to the right of the face and neck, where the higher hair strands have blended together. The hair to the right of the coronet beads shows about half of the strands.

Reverse. Higher details of the leaves are worn away; the central ridges are seen on some. Wear on the vertical lines in III has caused some to merge, but most are separate.

Illustrated coin: 1873, Open 3. VF-20.

F-12, 15 (Fine)

Obverse. Wear is more extensive. The forehead blends into the hair above it. About 10% to 29% of the hair detail to the right of the coronet remains, and much detail is seen lower, at the right edge opposite the ear and neck. Dentils are distinct.

Reverse. The top (highest-relief) part of most leaves is flat. Many vertical lines in III are fused. Dentils are distinct.

Illustrated coin: 1874. F-12.

VG-8, 10 (Very Good)

Obverse. Less hair detail shows. Dentils all are clear.

Reverse. The leaves show more wear. The inner edges of some leaves are worn away, causing leaves to merge. Only about half, or slightly fewer, of the lines in III are discernible.

Illustrated coin: 1865. VG-10.

G-4, 6 (Good)

Obverse. Most hair details are gone, but some remain at the lower right. The rim is worn smooth in areas, and many dentils are missing. The lettering is weak, but readable.

Reverse. The leaves mostly are worn flat. Very few lines remain in III. The rim is worn smooth in areas, and many dentils are missing.

Illustrated coin: 1867. G-4.

AG-3 (About Good)

Obverse. The rim is worn away and into the tops of most of the letters. The date remains bold.

Reverse. The rim is worn away and into some of the leaves.

Illustrated coin: 1867. AG-3.

Proof Nickel Three-Cent Pieces, PF-60 to 70

Proofs were struck of all dates and can be found easily enough in the marketplace. The rarest is the first year of issue, 1865, of which only an estimated 500 or so were made. The vast majority of 1865s have a repunched date. Second rarest (not counting PF-only date of 1877) is the 1887 (perfect date, not the overdate) with a production of about 1,000 coins. Proofs of the years 1865 to 1876 can be difficult to find as true gems, while later Proofs are nearly all gems. Proofs from 1878 onward often have satiny or frosty fields, rather than mirrored surfaces, and resemble circulation strikes.

Illustrated coin: 1884. PF-67.
This superb gem, with delicate toning, is a connoisseur's delight.

Obverse and Reverse. PF-60, 61, and 62 coins show varying amounts of hairlines in the field, decreasing as the grade increases. Fields may be dull or cloudy on lower-level pieces. At PF-65, hairlines are visible only under magnification and are very light; the cheek of Miss Liberty does not show any friction or "album slide marks." Above PF-65, hairlines become fewer, and in ultra-high grades are nonexistent, this meaning that the coins have never been subject to wiping or abrasive cleaning. At PF-65 or better, expect excellent aesthetic appeal. Blotched, deeply toned, or recolored coins are sometimes seen at Proof levels from PF-60 through 65 or even 66 and should be avoided, but these are less often seen than on contemporary Proof nickel five-cent pieces.

SILVER THREE-CENT PIECES, 1851–1873

History. The influx of gold from California after 1848 made this metal "common" in comparison to its earlier status. Gold traditionally was priced at 15.5 to 16 times the value of silver by weight; with the influx, silver was undervalued. Beginning in 1850, American silver coins from the half dime to the dollar began disappearing from circulation. To provide a small coin for commerce, the Mint introduced the silver three-cent piece or *trime*, made of just 75% (instead of the usual 90%) silver. Intrinsically these were worth less than face value, and thus there was no incentive to hoard or melt them. Three different designs were made, of which the 1851–1853 type is the first. Such coins were popular in their time and circulated widely. These are distinguished by having no outline or frame around the obverse star. After the Act of February 21, 1853, reduced the authorized amount of silver in other denominations from the half dime to the half dollar (but not the dollar), those other coins circulated once again. The 14 mm–diameter trime, thought by many to be too tiny to handle easily, fell from favor, and mintages decreased.

In 1854 the trime design was changed considerably, creating the Type II, which was made through 1858. The alloy was modified to the regular standard for other issues—90% silver and 10% copper—and the overall weight was lightened from 12.375 grains to 11.52 grains. A raised border was added to the obverse star plus two line frames around it. On the reverse an olive branch was placed above the III denomination and a bundle of arrows below it. The new motif proved to be very difficult to strike up properly.

In 1859 the design of the trime was modified again, creating the Type III. Demand for the denomination continued to be small, and after 1862 very few were made for circulation, as silver coins were hoarded by the war-weary public and began to trade at a premium. Under the Coinage Act of 1873 the trime was discontinued. In that year only Proofs were made.

Striking and Sharpness. On the obverse of the Type I the tiny shield at the center of the star is often lacking certain details. On the reverse check the details and strength of the III denomination. On both sides check the rims. Needle-sharp coins are in the minority. As sharpness of strike has been nearly completely overlooked in the marketplace, cherrypicking will pay dividends.

Trimes of Type II are usually miserably struck, with some or all of these characteristics: obverse lettering weak in places; frames around the star of inconsistent strength or missing in certain areas; shield weak in places; reverse stars irregular and poorly formed; olive branch and arrows weak in areas; weak or irregular rims. Now and then a sharp 1855 is found—ironic, as this has the lowest mintage of the type.

Most Type III trimes are sharply struck. Points to look for include full outlines around the star, full shield on the star, and full leaf details and sharp stars.

Availability. Circulated examples of the Type I trimes are plentiful. Mint State coins are often seen, although the solitary branch-mint issue of the series, the 1851-O, is scarce in Mint State and high circulated grades. Most Mint State coins are lustrous and attractive, especially at MS-63 and above. Circulated Type II coins are scarce in all grades. Mint State coins are scarce, particularly so at MS-64 and higher. With a needle-sharp strike, gems are *rarities*. This is far and away the scarcest of the three trime design types. Among Type III trimes, circulated coins of the years 1859 to 1862 are easy to find. All later dates range from scarce to rare in circulation-strike format. Choice and Gem Mint State coins 1865 and later are very rare.

MS-60 to 70 (Mint State)

Illustrated coin: 1851-O. MS-66.
This is an exceptional example of the only branch-mint coin in the trime series.

Note: All coins are shown enlarged, for clarity.

Obverse and Reverse. At MS-60, some abrasion and very minor contact marks are evident, most noticeably on the obverse star and the C ornament on the reverse. At MS-63, abrasion is hard to detect except under magnification. An MS-65 coin will have no abrasion. Luster should be full and rich (not grainy). Grades above MS-65 are defined by having fewer marks as perfection is approached. Most high-grade Mint State coins are of the Type III design.

AU-50, 53, 55, 58 (About Uncirculated)

Obverse. Light wear is most obvious on the star arms and shield on Type I, and on the points of the frames on Type II and Type III. At AU-50, luster is evident, but only on part of the field. At AU-58 luster is nearly complete.

Reverse. Light wear is seen on the C ornament and III. On Type II and III, light wear is seen on the leaves and arrows.

Illustrated coin: 1868, Type III. AU-50.
Overall this is a decent strike, but with some reverse stars flat at their centers.

EF-40, 45 (Extremely Fine)

Obverse. More wear is seen, most noticeable on the ridges of the star arms, this in addition to more wear on the frames (Type II and Type III). Luster is absent, or seen only in traces.

Reverse. More wear is seen on the C ornament and III. On Type II and Type III more wear is seen on the leaves and arrows.

Illustrated coin: 1863, Type III. EF-45.
This is sharply struck, as are most Type III trimes.

VF-20, 30 (Very Fine)

Obverse. Further wear reduced the relief of the star. On Type II and Type III the frames show further wear and begin to blend together. The center shield shows wear, and its border is indistinct in areas, but its horizontal and vertical stripes are fully delineated (unless the coin was weakly struck).

Reverse. Still more wear is seen on the C ornament and III. On Type II and Type III the high-relief areas of the leaves and the feathers of the arrow are partially worn away. Stars are flat at their centers (on sharply struck coins in addition to, as expected, on weak strikes).

Illustrated coin: 1869, Type III. VF-20.

F-12, 15 (Fine)

Obverse. The star is worn so as to have lost most of its relief. On Type II and Type III the frames are mostly blended together. The center shield shows wear, and its border is flat (or else showing only slight separation of its two outlines), but its horizontal and vertical stripes still are delineated (unless the coin was weakly struck).

Reverse. Still more wear is seen on the C ornament and III. On Type II and Type III the high-relief areas of the leaves, and the feathers of the arrow, have slight if any detail. Stars are flat. The designs within the C ornament are missing much detail.

Illustrated coin: 1851, Type I. F-12.

VG-8, 10 (Very Good)

Obverse. The border is incomplete in places, but all lettering is bold. The horizontal and vertical stripes within the shield begin to blend together, but most remain well delineated.

Reverse. Still more wear is seen on all areas. The designs within the C ornament have more detail gone.

Illustrated coin: 1852, Type I. VG-10.

G-4, 6 (Good)

Obverse. The border is worn into the tops of the letters and the bottom of the date. The shield is blended into the star, and only traces of the shield outline remain. In this grade most coins seen are Type I.

Reverse. The border is worn into the outer parts of the stars. Additional wear is seen in all other areas.

Illustrated coin: 1853, Type I. G-4.

AG-3 (About Good)

Obverse. The star is flat. Strong elements of the shield are seen, but the tiny lines are mostly or completely blended together. Lettering and date are weak and partially missing, but the date must be identifiable. In this grade most coins seen are Type I.

Reverse. The border is worn into the stars, with outer elements of the stars now gone. Additional wear is seen in all other areas. The designs within the C ornament are only in outline form.

Illustrated coin: 1851, Type I. AG-3.

Proof Silver Three-Cent Pieces, PF-60 to 70

A few Proofs were made in the early 1850s and are great rarities today. After 1857, production increased to an estimated 210 or so in 1858, through 500 to 700 or so as a yearly average in the 1860s to 1873. Most are needle sharp and have mirrored surfaces, although some of the late 1860s and early 1870s can have slightly grainy or satiny lustrous surfaces. Striking quality varies. Lint marks and surface problems are not unusual. Careful examination is recommended.

Illustrated coin: 1873. PF-61.
Many hairlines are mostly masked by attractive toning, yielding a highly collectible coin at this lower Proof grade level.

Obverse and Reverse. Proofs that are extensively cleaned and have many hairlines, or that are dull and grainy, are lower level, such as PF-60 to 62. These are difficult to verify as Proofs. For a trime with medium hairlines and good reflectivity, an assigned grade of PF-64 is indicated, and with relatively few hairlines, gem PF-65. PF-66 should have hairlines so delicate that magnification is needed to see them. Above that, a Proof should be free of such lines.

NICKEL FIVE-CENT
PIECES

NICKEL FIVE-CENT PIECES, 1866 TO DATE

1866–1883 SHIELD

History. Nickel five-cent pieces were introduced in 1866, a time when silver coins (except the trime) did not circulate in the East or Midwest. The denomination proved popular and is still in wide use today. Nickels of the Shield type were made continuously from 1866 to 1883. All 1866 nickels have rays between the stars on the reverse, as do a minority of 1867 issues, after which this feature was dropped. In 1877 and 1878 only Proofs were made, with no circulation strikes. The design by Chief Engraver James B. Longacre is somewhat similar to the obverse of the two-cent piece. Shield nickels were still seen in circulation in the 1930s, by which time most had been worn nearly smooth.

Striking and Sharpness. Sharpness can be a problem for dates in the 1860s through 1876, much less so for later years. On the obverse the horizontal shield stripes, vertical stripes, and leaves should be checked. The horizontal stripes in particular can be blended together. On the reverse the star centers can be weak. Check all other areas as well. Die cracks are seen on *most* circulation-strike Shield nickels, and do not affect value.

Availability. Circulated coins generally are available in proportion to their mintage quantities (exceptions being the 1873 Open 3 and Close 3 varieties, which tend to be elusive in all grades despite their relatively high mintage). Mint State coins are similarly available, except that 1880 is a rarity. Those dated 1882 and 1883 are plentiful.

MS-60 to 70 (Mint State)

Illustrated coin: 1872. MS-66.
This is a gem with rich luster, light golden toning, and great eye appeal.

Note: All coins are enlarged, for clarity.

Obverse and Reverse. At MS-60 some abrasion and very minor contact marks are evident, most noticeably on high points of the shield on the obverse and the field on the reverse. Sometimes light striking on the shield and stars can be mistaken for light wear, and marks on the numeral 5 on the reverse can be from the original planchet surface not struck up fully. At MS-63 abrasions are hard to detect except under magnification. An MS-65 coin will have no abrasion. Luster should be full and rich (not grainy). Grades above MS-65 are defined by having no marks that can be seen by the naked eye. Higher-grade coins display deeper luster or virtually perfect proof-like surfaces, depending on the dies used.

AU-50, 53, 55, 58 (About Uncirculated)

Obverse. Light wear is on the outside edges of the leaves, the frame of the shield, and the horizontal stripes (although the stripes can also be weakly struck). Mint luster is present in the fields, ranging from partial at AU-50 to nearly complete at AU-58. All details are sharp, unless lightly struck.

Reverse. Light wear is seen on the numeral 5, and friction is seen in the field, identifiable as a change of color (loss of luster). Luster is partial at AU-50, increasing to nearly full at AU-58. All details are sharp, unless lightly struck.

Illustrated coin: 1881. AU-50.
This is a rare, low-mintage date.

EF-40, 45 (Extremely Fine)

Obverse. Nearly all shield border and leaf detail is visible. Light wear is seen on the shield stripes (but the horizontal stripes can be weakly struck).

Reverse. More wear is seen on the numeral 5. The radial lines in the stars (if sharply struck to begin with) show slight wear. The field shows more wear.

Illustrated coin: 1881. EF-40.

VF-20, 30 (Very Fine)

Obverse. The frame details and leaves show more wear, with much leaf detail gone. The shield stripes show more wear, and some of the vertical lines will begin to blend together.

Reverse. More wear is seen overall, but some radial detail can still be seen on the stars.

Illustrated coin: 1868. VF-20.

F-12, 15 (Fine)

Obverse. Most leaves are flat and have little detail, but will remain outlined. The shield frame is mostly flat. Most horizontal lines are blended together, regardless of original strike. Many vertical lines in the stripes are blended together. IN GOD WE TRUST is slightly weak.

Reverse. All areas are in outline form except for slight traces of the star radials. Lettering is bold.

Illustrated coin: 1867, Without Rays. F-12.

VG-8, 10 (Very Good)

Obverse. Many leaves are flat and blended with adjacent leaves. The frame is blended and has no details. Only a few horizontal lines may show. Vertical lines in the stripes are mostly blended. IN GOD WE TRUST is weak.

Reverse. All elements are visible only in outline form. The rim is complete.

Illustrated coin: 1866. VG-8.

G-4, 6 (Good)

Obverse. The shield and elements are seen in outline form except the vertical stripe separations. IN GOD WE TRUST is weak, and a few letters may be missing.

Reverse. The rim is mostly if not completely worn away and into the tops of the letters.

Illustrated coin: 1866. G-4.
Overall this coin is slightly better than G-4, but the 5 in the date is weak, making G-4 an appropriate attribution.

AG-3 (About Good)

Obverse. The rim is worn down and blended with the wreath. Only traces of IN GOD WE TRUST can be seen. The date is fully readable.

Reverse. The rim is worn down and blended with the letters, some of which may be missing.

Illustrated coin: 1868. AG-3.

Proof Shield Nickels, PF-60 to 70

Proof Shield nickels were struck of all dates 1866 to 1883, including two varieties of 1867 (With Rays, a great rarity, and the usually seen Without Rays). Fields range from deeply mirrorlike to somewhat grainy in character to mirror-surface, depending on a given year. Many of 1878, a date struck only in Proof format, have *lustrous* surfaces or prooflike surfaces combined with some luster, resembling a circulation strike. While most Proofs are sharp, some have weakness on the shield on the obverse and/or the star centers on the reverse. Lint marks or tiny recessed marks from scattered debris on the die faces are sometimes encountered, especially on issues of the 1870s, but not factored into the grade in commercial certification unless excessive.

Illustrated coin: 1877. PF-67 Cam.
The 1877 Proof Shield nickel is very popular because of its Proof-only status. This fully struck, superb gem coin, with good contrast between the field and the devices, is a very attractive example. There is no noticeable toning, nor are there any hints of grade-limiting or other blemishes.

Obverse and Reverse. PF-60, 61, and 62 coins show varying amounts of hairlines in the reverse field in particular, decreasing as the grade increases. Fields may be dull or cloudy on lower-level pieces. At PF-65, hairlines are visible only under magnification and are very light and usually only on the reverse. Above PF-65, hairlines become fewer, and in ultra-high grades are nonexistent, this meaning that the coins have never been subject to wiping or abrasive cleaning. At PF-65 or better, expect excellent aesthetic appeal.

1883–1913 Liberty Head

History. Liberty Head nickels were made in large quantities for most dates. These were popular in their time, and remained in circulation through the 1940s, by which time most were worn down to grades such as AG-3 and G-4. Stray coins could still be found in the early 1950s. Serious numismatic interest in circulated examples began in the 1930s with the popularity of Whitman, Raymond, and other coin folders and albums. Many of the scarcer dates were plucked from circulation at that time.

Striking and Sharpness. Many coins have areas of light striking. On the obverse, this is often seen at the star centers, particularly near the top border. The hair above the forehead can be light as well, and always is thus on 1912-S (the obverse die on this San Francisco issue is slightly bulged). On the reverse, E PLURIBUS UNUM can vary in sharpness of strike. Weakness is often seen at the wreath bow and on the ear of corn to the left (the kernels in the ear can range from indistinct to bold). Even Proofs can be weakly struck in areas. Mint luster can range from minutely pebbly or grainy, but still attractive, to a deep, rich frost. Some later Philadelphia coins show stress marks in the field, particularly the obverse, from the use of "tired" dies. Such can be determined only by observation, as "slabbed" grades for Mint State coins do not treat the quality of the luster or surfaces. Liberty Head nickels in higher grades can be a cherrypicker's delight, as commercial grading services take no note of sharpness of strike or aesthetic appeal.

Availability. All issues from 1883 to 1912 are readily collectible, although the 1885 (in particular), 1886, and 1912-S are considered to be key dates. Most readily available are well-worn coins in AG-3 and G-4 grades taken from circulation in the 1930s and later. As a class, Very Fine, Extremely Fine, and About Uncirculated pieces are very scarce in relation to the demand for them. Mint State coins are generally scarce in the 1880s, except for 1883 without CENTS coins, which are plentiful in all grades. Mint State pieces are less scarce in the 1890s and are easily found for most 20th-century years, save for 1909, 1912-D, and 1912-S, all of which are elusive.

MS-60 to 70 (Mint State)

Illustrated coin: 1900. MS-64.
Often an MS-64 coin offers exceptional value for the price paid. This one is lightly toned and lustrous.

Note: All coins are enlarged, for clarity.

Obverse and Reverse. Mint luster is complete in the obverse and reverse fields. Lower grades such as MS-60, 61, and 62 can show some evidence of abrasion, usually on the portrait on the obverse and highest parts of the wreath on the reverse, and scattered contact marks elsewhere. At MS-63 these marks are few, and at MS-65 they are fewer yet. In grades above MS-65, marks can only be seen under magnification.

AU-50, 53, 55, 58 (About Uncirculated)

Obverse. Light wear is seen on the portrait and on the hair under LIB. Mint luster is present in the fields, ranging from partial at AU-50 to nearly complete at AU-58. All details are sharp, unless lightly struck.

Reverse. Light wear is seen on the V, the other letters, and the wreath. Luster is partial at AU-50, increasing to nearly full at AU-58. All details are sharp, unless lightly struck.

Illustrated coin: 1887. AU-50.
E PLURIBUS UNUM shows some light striking.

EF-40, 45 (Extremely Fine)

Obverse. Nearly all hair detail is visible, save for some lightness above the forehead. Stars show radial lines (except for those that may have been lightly struck). Overall bold appearance.

Reverse. The wreath still shows most detail on the leaves. Dentils are bold inside the rim.

Illustrated coin: 1883, Without CENTS. EF-40.
This coin shows some light striking at the bottom of the wreath, especially to the left of the ribbon bow. This is a plentiful variety that was hoarded in its time, as the public thought they would be recalled, due to the missing CENTS, and would become rare.

VF-20, 30 (Very Fine)

Obverse. Letters in LIBERTY are all well defined. Hair detail is seen on the back of the head and some between the ear and the coronet. Dentils are bold. Some stars show radial lines.

Reverse. Detail is seen in the wreath leaves. Lettering and dentils are bold, although E PLURIBUS UNUM may range from medium-light to bold (depending on the strike).

Illustrated coin: 1912-S. VF-20.
The hair detail on this date and mint is usually not as well defined as on Philadelphia issues.

F-12, 15 (Fine)

Obverse. All of the letters in LIBERTY are readable, although the I may be weak. The detail beginning at the front of hair is visible. Dentils are well defined.

Reverse. Detail of the leaves begins to fade in the wreath. Dentils are well defined all around the border. E PLURIBUS UNUM has medium definition, and is complete.

Illustrated coin: 1912-S. F-12.

VG-8, 10 (Very Good)

Obverse. Three or more letters in LIBERTY can be discerned. This can be a combination of two full letters and two or more partial letters. Some hair detail shows at the back of the head. The rim is well outlined and shows traces of most or even all dentils.

Reverse. The wreath and lettering are bold, but in outline form. E PLURIBUS UNUM is readable, but may be weak. The rim is complete all around, with traces of most dentils present.

Illustrated coin: 1885. VG-8.
This is the key Philadelphia Mint issue in the series.

G-4, 6 (Good)

Obverse. The rim is complete all around. Some dentils show on the inside of the rim. The date, Liberty head, and stars are in outline form. No letters of LIBERTY are visible in the coronet.

Reverse. V and the wreath are visible in outline form. Most letters are complete, but may be faint. E PLURIBUS UNUM is very weak (this feature can vary, and on some G-4 coins it is better defined). The rim is complete in most areas, but may blend with the field in some parts.

Illustrated coin: 1885. G-4.
This coin probably was taken from circulation in the late 1930s or the 1940s.

AG-3 (About Good)

Obverse. The head is outlined, with only the ear hole as a detail. The date is well worn; the bottom of the digits can be weak or incomplete. The stars are solid, without detail; some may be incomplete. The rim is indistinct or incomplete in some areas.

Reverse. Details are nearly all worn away, showing greater effects of wear than does the obverse. V is in outline form. The wreath is in outline form, and may be indistinct in areas. Lettering ranges from faint to missing, but with some letters readable. The rim is usually worn down into the letters.

Illustrated coin: 1886. AG-3.
This coin may have been taken from circulation in the 1940s.

Proof Liberty Head Nickels, PF-60 to 70

Proof Liberty Head nickels were struck of all dates 1883 to 1912, plus both varieties of 1883 (with and without CENTS). The fields range from deeply mirrorlike to somewhat grainy character to mirror-surface, depending on a given year. While most Proofs are sharp, some have weakness at the star centers and/or the kernels on the ear of corn to the left of the ribbon bow. These weaknesses are overlooked by the certification services. Generally, later issues are more deeply mirrored than are earlier ones. Some years in the 1880s and 1890s can show graininess, a combination of mint luster and mirror quality. Lint marks or tiny recessed marks from scattered debris on the die faces are sometimes encountered, but not factored into third-party–certified grades unless excessive.

Illustrated coin: 1911. PF-66.
This Proof shows medium-toned surfaces.

Obverse and Reverse. PF-60, 61, and 62 coins show varying amounts of hairlines in the field, decreasing as the grade increases. Fields may be dull or cloudy on lower-level pieces. At PF-65, hairlines are visible only under magnification and are very light; the cheek of Miss Liberty does not show any abrasion or "album slide marks." Above PF-65, hairlines become fewer, and in ultra-high grades are nonexistent, this meaning that the coins have never been subject to wiping or abrasive cleaning. At PF-65 or better, expect excellent aesthetic appeal. Blotched, deeply toned, or recolored coins can be found at most Proof levels from PF-60 through 65 or even 66, and should be avoided. Watch for artificially toned lower-grade Proofs colored to mask the true nature of the fields.

1913–1938 Buffalo (Indian Head)

History. The Indian Head nickel five-cent piece with a bison on the reverse, nearly always called the "Buffalo" nickel now, made its debut in 1913. Its designer was James Earle Fraser, a sculptor well known in the private sector. The obverse features an authentic portrait of a Native American, modeled as a composite from life with three subjects posing. Unlike any preceding coin made for circulation, the Buffalo nickel had little in the way of open, smooth field surfaces. Instead, most areas on the obverse and reverse were filled with design elements or, especially on the reverse, an irregular background as on a bas-relief plaque.

Upon reflection soon after the first coins were released, it was thought that the inscription FIVE CENTS, on a high area of the motif, would wear too quickly. Accordingly, the ground under the bison, which had been arranged in the form of a mound on Type I, was lowered to become flat, creating the next style (Type II).

Buffalo nickels attracted widespread numismatic interest beginning in the 1930s. Collectors picked scarce early varieties out of circulation until the 1960s, after which time they were hardly ever seen.

Striking and Sharpness. Most Buffalo nickels are poorly struck in one or more areas, and for many Denver and San Francisco issues of the 1920s the striking is miserable. However, enough sharp strikes exist among common dates of the 1930s that one can be found with some patience. Certification services do not reflect the quality of strike on their labels, so examination is up to you. The matter of striking sharpness on Buffalo nickels is an exceedingly important aspect for the connoisseur (who might prefer, for example, a sharply struck 1925-D in AU-58 over a fully lustrous Mint State example with much shallower detail). Points to check on the obverse include the center of the coin, especially the area immediately above the tie on the braid. On the reverse the fur on the head of the bison, and the fur "line" above the bison's shoulder on its back, should be checked. On both sides, overall striking of letters and other details can be examined.

Availability. Among circulated varieties of standard dates and mintmarks, availability is in proportion to their mintages. Among early issues the 1913-S, Type II, is the scarcest. The date wore away more quickly on the Type I coins than on the modified design used from later 1913 through the end of the series. In the 1920s the 1926-S is the hardest to find. Buffalo nickels became widely popular to collect beginning about 1935, when cardboard panels and pages became popular. By that time, issues dated in the teens were apt to be worn down to Fine or VF, those of the 1920s Very Fine to EF, and those of recent times About Uncirculated or lower Mint State grades. Collectors sought Buffalo nickels from circulation until the 1960s, after which most were gone. By that time the dates in the teens were apt to have their dates completely worn away, or be AG-3 or G-4. Among Mint State nickels, the issues of 1913 were saved in quantity as novelties, although 1913-S, Type II, is slightly scarce. Philadelphia Mint issues are readily available through the 1920s, while Choice and Gem mintmarked issues from 1914 to 1927 can range from scarce to rare. From 1931 to 1938, all dates and mintmarks were saved in roll quantities, and all are plentiful today. Many Buffalo nickels in Mint State are very rare if with Full Details, this being especially true for mintmarked issues after 1913, into the early 1930s.

MS-60 to 70 (Mint State)

Illustrated coin: 1937-D, 3-Legged. MS-65.
A gem example with exceptional eye appeal, this coin has smooth, satiny surfaces free of toning or notable detractions. An uncommonly sharp strike is also notable on this ever-popular die error, especially on the reverse.

Note: All coins are enlarged, for clarity.

Obverse and Reverse. Mint luster is complete in the obverse and reverse fields, except in areas not fully struck up, in which graininess or marks from the *original planchet surface* can be seen. Lower grades such as MS-60, 61, and 62 can show some evidence of abrasion, usually on the center of the obverse above the braid, and on the reverse at the highest parts of the bison. These two checkpoints are often areas of light striking, so abrasion must be differentiated from original planchet marks. At MS-63 evidences of abrasion are few, and at MS-65 they are fewer yet. In grades above MS-65, a Buffalo nickel should be mark-free. Sharpness of strike is not noted on certification holders, but a connoisseur would probably rather own a Full Details coin in MS-65 than an MS-66 or higher that is a flat strike.

AU-50, 53, 55, 58 (About Uncirculated)

Obverse. Light wear is seen on the highest area of the cheek, to the left of the nose, this being the most obvious checkpoint. Light wear is also seen on the highest-relief areas of the hair. Luster is less extensive, and wear more extensive, at AU-50 than at higher grades. An AU-58 coin will have only slight wear and will retain the majority of luster.

Illustrated coin: 1918-D, 8 Over 7. AU-58.
This lovely example has sharply defined details, though it is slightly light at the centers. This is an exceptional grade for this very rare overdate variety.

Reverse. Light wear is seen on the shoulder and hip, these being the key checkpoints. Light wear is also seen on the flank of the bison and on the horn and top of the head. Luster is less extensive, and wear more extensive, at AU-50 than at higher grades. An AU-58 coin will have only slight wear and will retain the majority of luster.

EF-40, 45 (Extremely Fine)

Obverse. More wear is seen on the cheek (in particular) and the rest of the face. The center of the coin above the braid is mostly smooth. Other details are sharp.

Reverse. More wear is evident. The tip of the horn is well defined on better strikes. The shoulder, flank, and hip show more wear. The tip of the tail may be discernible, but is mostly worn away.

Illustrated coin: 1937-D. EF-40.

VF-20, 30 (Very Fine)

Obverse. The hair above the braid is mostly flat, but with some details visible. The braid is discernible. The feathers lack most details. On Type I coins the date is light.

Reverse. Wear is more extensive, with most fur detail on the high area of the shoulder gone, the tip of the tail gone, and the horn flat. Ideally the tip of the horn should show, but in the marketplace many certified coins do not show this. On some coins this is due to a shallow strike.

Illustrated coin: 1937-D. VF-20.

F-12, 15 (Fine)

Obverse. Only slight detail remains in the hair above the braid. Some of the braid twists are blended together. LIB-ERTY is weak, and on some coins the upper part of the letters is faint. The rim still is separate. On all coins, the date shows extensive wear. On Type I coins it is weak.

Reverse. The horn is half to two-thirds visible. Fur details are gone except on the neck at the highest part of the back.

Illustrated coin: 1918-D, 8 Over 7. F-12.

VG-8, 10 (Very Good)

Obverse. Hair details above the braid are further worn, as is the hair at the top of the head. Most braid twists are blended together. The rim is worn down to the tops of the letters in LIBERTY. The date is light on all coins and very weak on those of Type I.

Reverse. The base of the horn is slightly visible. Fur details are worn more, but details can still be seen on the neck and top of the back. The hip and flank beneath are worn flat.

Illustrated coin: 1918-D, 8 Over 7. VG-8.

G-4, 6 (Good)

Obverse. Scarcely any hair details are seen at the center, and the braid is flat. The rim and tops of the letters in LIBERTY are blended. The date is weak but readable, with at least the last two numerals showing on earlier issues.

Reverse. The rim is worn to blend into the tops of some or all letters in UNITED STATES OF AMERICA (except for Type I). E PLURIBUS UNUM and FIVE CENTS are full, and the mintmark, if any, is clear. The front part of the bison's head blends into the rim.

Illustrated coin: 1918-D, 8 Over 7. G-4.

AG-3 (About Good)

Obverse. The head is mostly flat, but the facial features remain clear. LIBERTY is weak and partly missing. The date may be incomplete but must be identifiable.

Reverse. Further wear is seen. On Type I coins, UNITED STATES OF AMERICA is full and readable. On the Type II the rim is worn further into the letters. The reverse of the Type I nickels is bolder as the overall grade is defined by the date, which wore away more quickly than on the Type II.

Illustrated coin: 1913-S, Type II. AG-3.
This coin is barely identifiable as to date but with its mintmark clear.

Matte Proof Buffalo Nickels, PF-60 to 70

Proof Buffalo nickels are of two main styles. Matte Proofs were made from 1913 to 1916 and are rare. These have minutely granular or matte surfaces, are sharply struck with Full Details of the design on both sides, and have edges (as viewed edge-on) that are mirrored, a distinctive figure. These are easily confused with circulation strikes except for the features noted. Certified holders usually list these simply as "Proof," not "Matte Proof." Some early Proofs of 1936 have satiny rather than mirrorlike fields. Later Proofs of 1936 and all of 1937 have a mirror surface in the fields. The motifs of the 1936 and 1937 mirror Proofs are lightly polished in the die (not frosty or matte).

Illustrated coin: 1914. Matte PF-67.

Obverse and Reverse. Most Matte Proofs are in higher grades. Those with abrasion or contact marks can be graded PF-60 to 62; these are not widely desired. PF-64 can have some abrasion. Tiny flecks are not common, but are sometimes seen. At the Matte PF-65 level or higher there will no traces of abrasion or flecks. Differences between higher-grade Proofs are highly subjective, and one certified at PF-65 can be similar to another at PF-67, and vice-versa.

Mirror Proof Buffalo Nickels, PF-60 to 70

Obverse and Reverse. Most mirror Proofs are in higher grades. PF-60 to 62 coins can have abrasion or minor handling marks, but are usually assigned such grades because of staining or blotches resulting from poor cleaning. PF-63 and 64 can have minor abrasion and staining. Tiny flecks are not common, but are sometimes seen, as are dark stripe lines from the glued seams in the cellophane envelopes used by the Mint. PF-65 and higher coins should be free of stains, flecks, and abrasion of any kind. Differences between higher-grade Proofs are highly subjective, and one certified PF-65 can be similar to another at PF-67, and vice-versa.

Illustrated coin: 1916. PF-67.
This fully-struck Matte Proof example has a satiny sheen and no detracting blemishes. The obverse has a delicate, champagne-gold toning, while the reverse is an attractive silver-blue with pale rose highlights.

1938–2003 JEFFERSON

History. The Jefferson nickel, designed by Felix O. Schlag in a public competition, made its debut in 1938, and has been a numismatic favorite since. The obverse features a portrait of Jefferson after Jean Antoine Houdon, and the reverse depicts a front view of Jefferson's home, Monticello. In 2004 special designs observing the Westward Journey (Lewis and Clark expedition) were introduced, later followed by a new obverse portrait.

From partway through 1942 to 1945 a copper-silver-manganese alloy replaced the traditional 75% copper and 25% nickel composition. These silver-content coins bear a distinctive P, D, or S mintmark above the dome of Monticello.

Striking and Sharpness. On the obverse, check for weakness on the portrait, especially in the lower jaw area. On the reverse, most circulation strikes have weak details on the six steps of Monticello, especially under the third pillar from the left, as this section on the reverse was opposite in the dies (in the press) from the high parts of the Jefferson portrait, and metal could not effectively flow in both directions at once. Planchet weight allowance was another cause, the dies being spaced slightly too far apart. Jefferson nickels are sometimes classified as "Full Steps" (FS) if five or six steps are clear, or, more exactly, as 5FS and 6FS, giving a count. Even if the steps are mostly or fully defined, check other areas so that overall a coin has Full Details. Interestingly, coins of the 1950s and 1960s are among the most weakly struck. The silver-content coins of the 1940s are usually well struck, and in Mint State are exceptionally beautiful. Some coins of the 1950s to 1970s discolored easily, perhaps due to some impurities in the alloy.

Availability. All basic dates and mintmarks were saved in roll quantities. Scarce issues in Mint State include 1939-D and 1942-D. The low-mintage 1950-D was a popular speculation, and most of the mintage went into numismatic hands, making *worn* coins rare. Many different dates and mints are rare if with 5FS or 6FS. Consult *A Guide Book of Buffalo and Jefferson Nickels* for details in this regard.

MS-60 to 70 (Mint State)

Illustrated coin: 1939. MS-67.
A brilliant and attractive example, this coin displays a hint of toning.

Note: All coins are enlarged, for clarity.

Obverse and Reverse. Mint luster is complete in the obverse and reverse fields, except in areas not fully struck up, in which graininess or marks from the *original planchet surface* can be seen. This may include the jaw, the back of Jefferson's head, and the higher-relief central features of Monticello. Lower grades such as MS-60, 61, and 62 can show some evidence of abrasion, usually on the same areas that display weak striking. At MS-63, evidences of abrasion are few, and at MS-65 they are fewer yet. In grades above MS-65, a Jefferson nickel should be mark-free.

Note: For modern issues of 2003 to date, check the higher parts of the obverse and reverse for abrasion and contact marks. Otherwise the same rules apply.

AU-50, 53, 55, 58 (About Uncirculated)

Obverse. The cheekbone and the higher points of the hair show light wear, more at AU-50 than at AU-58. Some mint luster will remain on some AU-55 and most AU-58 coins.

Reverse. The central part of Monticello shows light wear, but is difficult to evaluate as this area often shows weakness of strike. Some mint luster will remain on some AU-55 and most AU-58 coins.

Illustrated coin: 1942-P. AU-50.

EF-40, 45 (Extremely Fine)

Obverse. More wear is evident on the cheekbone. The higher parts of the hair are without detail.

Reverse. Monticello shows wear overall. The bottom edge of the triangular area above the columns at the center are worn away.

Illustrated coin: 1938-S. EF-40.

VF-20, 30 (Very Fine)

Obverse. Most hair detail is lost, except for the back of the head and lower area. The cheekbone is flat and mostly blended into the hair at the right.

Reverse. Many shallow-relief architectural features are worn away. The windows remain clear and the four columns are distinct.

Illustrated coin: 1938-S. VF-20.

The Jefferson nickel is seldom collected in grades lower than VF-20.

Proof Jefferson Nickels, PF-60 to 70

Proofs were struck from 1938 to 1942, 1950 to 1964, and 1968 to date. All have mirror fields. Striking is usually with Full Details, although there are scattered exceptions. Most survivors are in high grade, PF-64 and upward. Most since the 1970s have frosted or cameo contrast on the higher features. Special Mint Set (SMS) coins were struck in lieu of Proofs from 1965 to 1967; these in some instances closely resemble Proofs.

Illustrated coin: 1939, Reverse of 1938. PF-68. This example has a uniformly mirrored finish. Its smooth, unblemished surfaces have a silver-rose, powder-blue, and pale gold iridescence. The higher parts of the portrait are lightly struck.

Obverse and Reverse. Most Proof Jefferson nickels are in higher grades. Those with abrasion or contact marks can be graded PF-60 to 62 or even 63; these are not widely desired by collectors. PF-64 can have some abrasion. Tiny flecks are sometimes seen on coins of 1938 to 1942, as are discolorations (even to the extent of black streaks); these flaws are from cellophane holders. You should avoid such coins. Undipped Proofs of the early era often have a slight bluish or yellowish tint. At PF-65 or higher there are no traces of abrasion or flecks. Evaluation of differences between higher-grade Jefferson Proofs is highly subjective; one certified at PF-65 might be similar to another at PF-67, and vice-versa.

2004 TO DATE WESTWARD JOURNEY/JEFFERSON MODIFIED

History. Westward Journey nickels commemorated the bicentennial of the Louisiana Purchase and the journey of Meriwether Lewis and William Clark to explore that vast territory.

Striking and Sharpness. Striking is generally sharp.

Availability. Westward Journey nickels were minted in large quantities for circulation (hundreds of millions of coins for each design). They are readily available in the numismatic marketplace, and are seen with normal frequency in everyday channels of commerce. Mint State coins generally range from MS-64 to 70, with many MS-65 and higher; they are easily obtainable and affordable.

Peace Medal
Reverse (2004)

Keelboat
Reverse (2004)

Obverse (2005)

American Bison
Reverse (2005)

Ocean in View
Reverse (2005)

Obverse
(2006 to Date)

Reverse
(2006 to Date)

MS-60 to 70 (Mint State)

Illustrated coin: 2004-D, Peace Medal. MS-66.

Note: All coins are enlarged, for clarity.

Obverse and Reverse. Mint luster is complete in the obverse and reverse fields. The highest parts of the design may have evidence of abrasion and/or contact marks in lower MS grades. In grades above MS-65, the coin should be mark-free.

The Westward Journey/Jefferson Modified nickel is seldom collected in grades lower than MS-60.

Proof Westward Journey/Jefferson Modified Nickels, PF-60 to 70

Nearly all Westward Journey and Jefferson Modified nickel Proofs are as issued, in PF-69 or 70.

Obverse and Reverse. All Proof Westward Journey and Jefferson Modified nickels have mirror fields. Striking is typically with full details, although there are scattered exceptions. At PF-69 and 70 there are no traces of abrasion, contact marks, or other flaws.

Illustrated coin: PF-70.

HALF DIMES

HALF DIMES, 1792–1873

1792 HALF DISMES

History. While the Philadelphia Mint was still in the planning stage (the cornerstone would be laid on July 31, 1792), dies were cut for the first federal coinage of that year. The engraver was probably Robert Birch. Denominated HALF DISME, for half dime, these pieces were struck in a private facility in mid-July. It is believed that 1,500 were made, of which most were placed into circulation. The obverse has the head of Miss Liberty, while the reverse features an eagle. This design was not continued later.

Striking and Sharpness. Usually fairly well struck, but with some lightness on Miss Liberty's hair above her ear, and on the eagle's breast. Some have adjustment marks from filing the planchet prior to striking.

Availability. Today, most of the estimated 200 to 300 surviving coins show extensive wear. Some About Uncirculated and Mint State coins exist and attract wide attention when offered for sale. Several are Choice or Gem, perhaps from the four examples Mint Director David Rittenhouse is said to have reserved for himself.

MS-60 to 70 (Mint State)

Illustrated coin: 1792. MS-64.

Note: All coins are shown enlarged, for clarity.

Obverse. No wear is visible. Luster ranges from nearly full at MS-60 to frosty at MS-65 or higher. Toning often masks the surface, so careful inspection is required.

Reverse. No wear is visible. The field around the eagle is lustrous, ranging from not completely full at MS-60 to deep and frosty at MS-65 and higher.

AU-50, 53, 55, 58 (About Uncirculated)

Obverse. Light wear is seen on the cheek and on the hair (not as easily observable, as certain areas of the hair may be lightly struck). Luster ranges from light and mostly in protected areas at AU-50, to extensive at AU-58. Friction is evident in the field, less so in the higher ranges.

Reverse. Light wear is seen on the eagle, but is less noticeable on the letters. Luster ranges from light and mostly in protected areas at AU-50, to extensive at AU-58. Friction is evident in the field, less in the higher ranges.

Illustrated coin: 1792. AU-58.

This is a problem-free example with nice definition, save for some normal lightness of strike at the centers.

EF-40, 45 (Extremely Fine)

Obverse. The hair shows medium wear to the right of the face and on the bust end. The fields have no luster. Some luster may be seen among the hair strands and letters.

Reverse. The eagle shows medium wear on its breast and the right wing, less so on the left wing. HALF DISME shows wear. The fields have no luster. Some luster may be seen among the design elements and letters.

Illustrated coin: 1792. EF-40.

VF-20, 30 (Very Fine)

Obverse. More wear is seen on the hair, including to the right of the forehead and face, where only a few strands may be seen. The hair tips at the right are well detailed. The bust end is flat on its high area. Letters all show light wear.

Reverse. The eagle displays significant wear, with its central part flat and most of the detail missing from the right wing. Letters all show light wear.

Illustrated coin: 1792. VF-35.
Note the medium wear on both sides. The coin has a scratch on the obverse from P (in PAR) to near the center of the head. Scattered marks of a minor nature are evident; these are not unexpected at this grade.

F-12, 15 (Fine)

Obverse. The portrait, above the neck, is essentially flat, but details of the eye, the nose, and, to a lesser extent, the lips can be seen. The bust end and neck truncation are flat. Some hair detail can be seen to the right of the neck and behind the head, with individual strands blended into heavy groups. Both obverse and reverse at this grade and lower are apt to show marks, minor digs, and other evidence of handling.

Illustrated coin: 1792. F-12.

Reverse. Wear is more advanced than on a Very Fine coin, with significant reduction of the height of the lettering, and with some letters weak in areas, especially if the rim nearby is flat.

VG-8, 10 (Very Good)

Obverse. The head has less detail than a Fine coin and is essentially flat except at the neck. Some hair, in thick strands, can be seen. The letters show extensive wear, but are readable.

Reverse. The eagle is mostly flat, and the letters are well worn, some of them incomplete at the borders. Detail overall is weaker than on the obverse.

Illustrated coin: 1792. VG-8.

G-4, 6 (Good)

Obverse. There is hardly any detail on the portrait, except that the eye can be seen, as well as some thick hair tips. The date is clear. Around the border the edges of the letters are worn away, and some are weak overall.

Reverse. The eagle is only in outline form. The letters are very worn, with some missing.

Illustrated coin: 1792. G-4.

AG-3 (About Good)

Obverse. Extreme wear has reduced the portrait to an even shallower state. Around the border some letters are worn away completely, some partially. The 1792 date can be seen but is weak and may be partly missing.

Reverse. Traces of the eagle will remain and there are scattered letters and fragments of letters. Most of the coin is worn flat.

Illustrated coin: 1792. AG-3.
The scratches on the obverse should be noted.

1794–1795 FLOWING HAIR

History. Half dimes dated 1794 and 1795, of the Flowing Hair type, were all struck in the calendar year 1795, although dies were ready by the end of 1794. The same motif was also used on half dollars and silver dollars of the same years, but not on other denominations.

Striking and Sharpness. Many have problems of one sort or another, including adjustment marks from the planchet being filed, and/or light striking in some areas. On the obverse, check the hair and stars, and on the reverse the breast of the eagle. It may not be possible to find a *needle-sharp* example, but with some extensive searching a fairly decent strike can be obtained. Sharp striking and excellent eye appeal will add dramatically to the value.

Availability. Examples appear on the market with frequency, typically in lower circulated grades. Probably 250 to 500 could be classified as Mint State, most being of the 1795 date. Some searching is needed to locate choice specimens within whatever grade level you desire. As a rule, half dimes are more readily available than are half dollars and dollars of the same design, and when found are usually more attractive and have fewer problems.

MS-60 to 70 (Mint State)

Illustrated coin: 1794, LM-2. MS-62.
Through the olive-charcoal patina, one can see that this satiny example is free of distracting abrasions.

Note: Abbreviations used in die-variety attributions, along with the reference works on which the attributions are based, are discussed on the first page of this chapter. All coins are shown enlarged, for clarity.

Obverse. At MS-60 some abrasion and contact marks are evident, most noticeably on the cheek and in the fields. Luster is present, but may be dull or lifeless, and interrupted in patches. At MS-63, contact marks are very few, and abrasion is hard to detect except under magnification. An MS-65 coin has no abrasion, and contact marks are so minute as to require magnification. Luster should be full and rich. Coins graded above MS-65 are more theoretical than actual for this type—but they do exist, and are defined by having fewer marks as perfection is approached.

Reverse. Comments apply as for the obverse, except that abrasion and contact marks are most noticeable on the eagle at the center. The field area is small and is protected by lettering and the wreath, and in any given grade shows fewer marks than on the obverse.

AU-50, 53, 55, 58 (About Uncirculated)

Obverse. Light wear is seen on the hair area immediately to the left of the face and neck, on the cheek, and on the top of the neck truncation, more so at AU-50 than at 53 or 55. An AU-58 coin will have minimal traces of wear. An AU-50 will have luster in protected areas among the stars and letters, with little in the open fields or on the portrait. At AU-58, most luster is present in the fields, but is worn away on the highest parts of the motifs.

Illustrated coin: 1795, LM-10. AU-50.
Note the toned surfaces. Lightness at the bottom of the obverse and on the eagle's breast and right wing is more from strike than wear. Scattered tiny marks and thin scratches are evident, but there are no severe dents or adjustment marks.

Reverse. Light wear is seen on the eagle's body and right wing. At AU-50, detail is lost in most feathers in this area. However, striking can play a part, and some coins are weak to begin with. Light wear is seen on the wreath and lettering. Luster is the best key to actual wear. This will range from perhaps 20% remaining in protected areas at AU-50 to nearly full mint bloom at AU-58.

EF-40, 45 (Extremely Fine)

Obverse. More wear is evident on the portrait, especially on the hair to the left of the face and neck; the cheek; and the tip of the neck truncation. Excellent detail remains in low-relief areas of the hair. The stars show wear, as do the date and letters. Luster, if present at all, is minimal and in protected areas.

Reverse. The eagle, this being the focal point to check, shows more wear. Observe in combination with a knowledge of the die variety, to determine the sharpness of the coin when it was first struck. Some were flat at the center at the time they were made. Additional wear is on the wreath and letters, but many details are present. Some luster may be seen in protected areas, and if present is slightly more abundant than on the obverse.

Illustrated coin: 1795, LM-8. EF-40.
Extensive adjustment marks on Miss Liberty's hair, forehead, nose, and eye prompt a grade slightly lower than might otherwise be the case. Note the light strike on the eagle. Some edge damage (noted on the coin's certified-grade label) is hidden by the holder.

VF-20, 30 (Very Fine)

Obverse. The hair is well worn at the VF-20 level, less so at VF-30. The strands are blended so as to be heavy. The cheek shows only slight relief, and the tip of the neck truncation is flat. The stars have more wear, making them appear larger (an optical illusion).

Reverse. The body of the eagle shows few if any feathers, while the wings have about half of the feathers visible, depending on the strike. The leaves lack detail and are in outline form. Scattered, non-disfiguring marks are normal for this and lower grades. Any major defects should be noted separately.

Illustrated coin: 1795, LM-3. VF-20.
Here is a pleasing example with smooth, even wear. At this level any lightness of strike is moot, as overall wear is present.

F-12, 15 (Fine)

Obverse. Wear is more extensive than on a Very Fine coin, reducing the definition of the thick strands of hair. The cheek has less detail, and the stars appear larger. The rim is distinct and many dentils remain visible.

Reverse. Wear is more extensive. Now, feather details are reduced, mostly remaining on the right wing. The wreath and lettering are more worn, and the rim is usually weak in areas, although some dentils can be seen.

Illustrated coin: 1795, LM-8. F-12.
This is an "as you like it" coin—ostensibly a nice example of the grade, problem free at quick glance, but with a slight planchet bend and some hairlines.

VG-8, 10 (Very Good)

Obverse. The portrait is mostly seen in outline form, with most hair strands gone, although the tips at the lower left are clear. The ear is discernible, as is the eye. The stars appear larger still, again an illusion. The rim is weak in areas. LIBERTY and the date are readable and usually full, although some letters may be weak at their tops.

Reverse. The eagle is mostly an outline, although some traces of feathers may be seen in the tail and the lower part of the inside of the right wing. The rim is worn, as are the letters, with some weak, but the motto is readable.

Illustrated coin: 1795, LM-8. VG-8.
This is a well-circulated example with no problems worthy of mention.

G-4, 6 (Good)

Obverse. Wear is more extensive, and some stars may be missing or only partially visible. The head is an outline, although a few elements of thick hair strands may be seen. The eye is visible only in outline form. The rim is well worn or even missing. LIBERTY is worn, and parts of some letters may be missing, but elements of all are readable. The date is readable, but worn.

Reverse. The eagle is flat and discernible in outline form. The wreath is well worn. Some of the letters may be partly missing. At this level some "averaging" can be done. If the letters are stronger than usual in one area, but some are missing in another area, the coin can still qualify as G-4.

Illustrated coin: 1795, LM-8. G-4.
This coin has slightly stronger detail on the reverse than on the obverse. Scattered marks are normal for the grade.

AG-3 (About Good)

Obverse. Wear is so extensive that the coin is barely identifiable. The head is in outline form, LIBERTY is mostly gone, and the date, while readable, may be partially missing.

Reverse. The reverse is well worn with parts of the wreath and lettering missing.

Illustrated coin: 1795, LM-10. AG-3.
This is a late state of the dies with a rim cut at upper right obverse. The coin has been through the mill, but is suitable as a filler for the type.

1796–1797 DRAPED BUST, SMALL EAGLE

History. Although the Draped Bust obverse was used on various copper and silver coins circa 1795 to 1808, it was employed in combination with the *Small Eagle* reverse only on silver coins of 1795 to 1798, and in the half dime series, only in 1796 and 1797.

Striking and Sharpness. Most coins are weak in at least one area, although there are some marvelous exceptions. Points to check for sharpness include the hair of Miss Liberty, the centers of the stars, the bust line, and, on the reverse, the center of the eagle. Also check for planchet adjustment marks, but these are infrequent. Dentils around the border are usually decent on this type, but may vary in strength from one part of the border to another. Sharp striking (hardly ever seen on this half dime type) and excellent eye appeal will add to the value dramatically.

Availability. Although this type is fairly scarce in all grades, probably no more than a few dozen MS-63 or higher coins have been traced. As is true of other early silver types, beware of deeply toned or vividly iridescent-toned pieces whose true surface characters are flawed, but which are offered as Mint State; in truth some of these are barely better than Extremely Fine. Many coins have nice eye appeal, and it will pay to find one of these, no matter what the grade.

MS-60 to 70 (Mint State)

Illustrated coin: 1797, LM-1, V-2. MS-62.
The bold cracks visible on the obverse of this bright, brilliant-white example were caused by the state of the obverse die, which was in an advanced stage of breakup when the coin was struck. The strike, although a bit soft at the center of the reverse, is quite bold by the standards of this early half-dime series. The surface on both sides has a nice, satiny texture.

Note: Abbreviations used in die-variety attributions, along with the reference works on which the attributions are based, are discussed on the first page of this chapter. All coins are shown enlarged, for clarity.

Obverse. At MS-60 some abrasion and contact marks are evident, most noticeably on the cheek, on the drapery, and in the right field. Luster is present, but may be dull or lifeless, and interrupted in patches. At MS-63, contact marks are very few, and abrasion is hard to detect except under magnification, although this type is sometimes graded liberally due to its rarity. An MS-65 coin has no abrasion, and contact marks are so minute as to require magnification. Luster should be full and rich. Coins graded above MS-65 are more theoretical than actual for this type—but they do exist, and are defined by having fewer marks as perfection is approached.

Reverse. Comments apply as for the obverse, except that abrasion and marks are most noticeable on the eagle at the center, a situation complicated by the fact that this area was often flatly struck. Grading is best done by the obverse, then verified by the reverse. The field area is small and is protected by lettering and the wreath, and in any given grade shows fewer marks than on the obverse.

AU-50, 53, 55, 58 (About Uncirculated)

Obverse. Light wear is seen on the hair area above the ear and extending to left of the forehead, on the ribbon, and on the bosom—more so at AU-50 than at 53 or 55. An AU-58 coin has minimal traces of wear. An AU-50 coin has luster in protected areas among the stars and letters, with little in the open fields or on the portrait. At AU-58, most luster is present in the fields, but is worn away on the highest parts of the motifs.

Reverse. Light wear is seen on the eagle's body (keep in mind this area might be lightly struck) and edges of the wings. Light wear is seen on the wreath and lettering. Luster is the best key to actual wear. This ranges from perhaps 20% remaining in protected areas at AU-50 to nearly full mint bloom at AU-58.

Illustrated coin: 1797, 16 stars. LM-3, 16 obverse stars. AU-50.
This coin has typical strike on both sides, with lightness on the higher areas. The eagle's wing feathers are well defined, but the head is missing. Attractive iridescent toning is visible.

EF-40, 45 (Extremely Fine)

Obverse. More wear is evident on the upper hair area and the ribbon and on the drapery and bosom. Excellent detail will remain in low relief areas of the hair. The stars show wear as will the date and letters. Luster, if present at all, is minimal and in protected areas.

Reverse. The eagle shows more wear, this being the focal point to check. On most examples, many feathers remain on the interior areas of the wings. Check the eagle in combination with a knowledge of the die variety to determine the sharpness of the coin when it was first struck. Additional wear is evident on the wreath and letters, but many details are present. Some luster may be seen in protected areas and, if present, is slightly more abundant than on the obverse.

Illustrated coin: 1796. LM-1. EF-45.
This is the "LIKERTY" variety, its fanciful name derived from the top and bottom lines of the B being defective. The strike is above average, indeed outstanding, at the center and elsewhere. Note the scrape in the right obverse field. The coin has peripheral "halo" toning, perhaps from being housed in a National (Raymond) holder for many years.

VF-20, 30 (Very Fine)

Obverse. The higher-relief areas of hair are well worn at VF-20, less so at VF-30. The drapery and bosom show extensive wear. The stars have more wear, making them appear larger (an optical illusion seen on most worn silver coins of this era).

Reverse. The body of the eagle shows few if any feathers, while the wings have about half of the feathers visible, depending on the strike. The leaves lack most detail and are in outline form. Scattered, non-disfiguring marks are normal for this and lower grades; any major distractions should be noted separately.

Illustrated coin: 1796. LM-1. VF-30.
This coin is nice overall, with good detail for the grade. At this grade lightness of strike is not very important, as wear prevails.

F-12, 15 (Fine)

Obverse. Wear is more extensive than on a Very Fine coin. Wear is particularly noticeable on the hair, face, and bosom, and the stars appear larger. About half the hair detail remains, most noticeably behind the neck and shoulder. The rim may be partially worn away and may blend into the field.

Reverse. Wear is more extensive. Feather details are diminished, with fewer than half remaining on the wings. The wreath and lettering are worn further, and the rim is usually weak in areas, although some dentils can be seen.

Illustrated coin: 1797. LM-1, 15 obverse stars. F-15.

This is a lovely coin with excellent eye appeal; certainly a high-end or conservatively graded example.

VG-8, 10 (Very Good)

Obverse. The portrait is mostly seen in outline form, with most hair strands gone, although there is some definition at the back of the hair and behind the shoulder. The ear is discernible, as is the eye. The stars appear larger still, again an illusion. The rim is weak in areas. LIBERTY and the date are readable and usually full, although some letters may be weak at their tops.

Reverse. The eagle is mostly an outline, with parts blending into the field (on lighter strikes). The rim is worn, as are the letters, with some weak, but the motto is readable.

Illustrated coin: 1797, 15 stars. LM-1, 15 obverse stars. VG-8.

Scattered marks, particularly on the obverse, are more plentiful than regularly seen at this level.

G-4, 6 (Good)

Obverse. Wear is more extensive, and some stars may be partly missing. The head is an outline. The eye is visible only in outline form. The rim is well worn or even missing in areas. LIBERTY is worn, and parts of some letters may be missing, but elements of all should be readable. The date is readable, but worn.

Reverse. The eagle is flat and discernible in outline form, and may be blending into the field. The wreath is well worn. Some of the letters may be partly missing. At this level some "averaging" can be done. If the letters are stronger than usual in one area, but some are missing in another area, the coin can still qualify as G-4.

Illustrated coin: 1796. G-4.

AG-3 (About Good)

Obverse. Wear is so extensive that the coin is barely identifiable. The head is in outline form. LIBERTY is mostly gone, as are some of the stars. The date, while readable, may be partially worn away.

Reverse. The reverse is well worn, with parts of the wreath and lettering missing.

Illustrated coin: 1796, LM-1. AG-3.

Note the significant scratches on the obverse. While problems are expected at this low grade, prominent defects should be mentioned.

1800–1805 DRAPED BUST, HERALDIC EAGLE

History. The combination of Draped Bust obverse / Heraldic Eagle reverse was used in the silver half dime series from 1800 to 1805—an ephemeral existence. The obverse style, now standardized with 13 stars, is the same as used in 1796 and 1797. During this span the rare 1802 was produced, and none were minted with the date 1804. The majority of pieces surviving today are dated 1800, and *nearly all* of the About Uncirculated or finer coins are of this date.

Striking and Sharpness. Most are lightly struck in one area or another. The obverse stars usually show some weakness. On many coins the central details of Miss Liberty are not sharp. On the reverse the upper right of the shield and the adjacent part of the eagle's wing are often soft, and several or even most stars may be lightly defined (sharp stars show sharply peaked centers); high parts of the clouds are often weak. The area on the reverse opposite the bosom of Miss Liberty may be flat or weak, due to the metal having to flow in both directions when the coins were struck. (The area curving obliquely up and to the right of the eagle's head—exactly mirroring the curvature of the bust on the obverse—is especially prone to weakness of strike.) Dentils are likely to be weak or missing in areas. Expect to compromise on the striking issue. As if this were not enough, many have Mint-caused planchet adjustment marks. In summary, *a sharply struck coin is a goal, not necessarily a reality.* Sharp striking and excellent eye appeal will add to the coin's value dramatically, this being particularly true for all issues from 1801 to 1805. When top-grade Mint State coins are found they are usually dated 1800.

Availability. This is a challenging type to find "nice," and cherrypicking is recommended. This is particularly true of the dates after 1800. Grading is often optimistic, and many toned pieces are recolored. Some are porous or have other problems. Take your time.

MS-60 to 70 (Mint State)

Illustrated coin: 1800, LM-1, V-1. MS-63.
Both sides of this example are suitably well struck, with surfaces free of outwardly distracting abrasions. The obverse has a rich antique-copper patina, with hints of pale gold and rose. The reverse is lighter in color, with cobalt-blue and champagne-pink highlights around a pinkish-silver center.

Note: Abbreviations used in die-variety attributions, along with the reference works on which the attributions are based, are discussed on the first page of this chapter. All coins are shown enlarged, for clarity.

Obverse. At MS-60 some abrasion and contact marks are evident, most noticeably on the cheek, on the drapery, and in the right field. Luster is present, but may be dull or lifeless, and interrupted in patches. At MS-63, contact marks are very few, and abrasion is hard to detect except under magnification, although this type is sometimes graded liberally due to its rarity. An MS-65 coin will have no abrasion, and contact marks are so minute as to require magnification. Luster should be full and rich. Coins graded above MS-65 are more theoretical than actual for this type—but they do exist, and are defined by having fewer marks as perfection is approached.

Reverse. Comments apply as for the obverse, except that abrasion and contact marks are most noticeable on the eagle's neck, the tips of the wing, and the tail. The field area is complex—with stars above the eagle, the arrows and olive branch, and other features, there is not much open space. Accordingly, marks will not be as noticeable as on the obverse.

AU-50, 53, 55, 58 (About Uncirculated)

Obverse. Light wear is seen on the hair area above the ear and extending to left of the forehead, on the ribbon, and on the bosom, more so at AU-50 than at AU-53 or 55. An AU-58 coin will have minimal traces of wear. An AU-50 coin will have luster in protected areas among the stars and letters, with little in the open fields or on the portrait. At AU-58, most luster is present in the fields, but is worn away on the highest parts of the motifs.

Reverse. Comments as for Mint State coins, except that the eagle's neck, the tips and top of the wings, the clouds, and the tail show noticeable wear, as do other features. Luster ranges from perhaps 20% remaining in protected areas at AU-50 to nearly full mint bloom at AU-58. Often the reverse of this type retains much more luster than the obverse.

Illustrated coin: 1800, LM-3. AU-58.
Note the lightness of strike at the center obverse and stars, and on the reverse the upper left of the shield. This coin has light iridescent toning.

EF-40, 45 (Extremely Fine)

Obverse. More wear is evident on the upper hair area and the ribbon, and on the drapery and bosom. Excellent detail remains in low-relief areas of the hair. The stars show wear, as do the date and letters. Luster, if present at all, is minimal and only in protected areas.

Reverse. Wear is greater than on an About Uncirculated coin, overall. The neck lacks feather detail on its highest points. Feathers lose some detail near the edges of the wings, and some areas of the horizontal lines in the shield may be blended together. Some traces of luster may be seen, more so at EF-45 than at EF-40.

Illustrated coin: 1805, LM-1. EF-40.
Note lightness of strike on the bust at the right, and, on the reverse, on the eagle at the right. Half dimes of this date are very rare in Extremely Fine and higher grades.

VF-20, 30 (Very Fine)

Obverse. The higher-relief areas of hair are well worn at VF-20, less so at VF-30. The drapery and bosom show extensive wear. The stars have more wear, making them appear larger (an optical illusion seen on most worn silver coins of this era).

Reverse. Wear is greater, including on the shield and wing feathers. Star centers are flat. Other areas have lost detail as well.

Illustrated coin: 1805, LM-1. VF-30.
This is a very acceptable example of this scarce date. It has light striking in the same areas as the EF-40 coin above.

F-12, 15 (Fine)

Obverse. Wear is more extensive than on a Very Fine coin, particularly noticeable on the hair, face, and bosom, and the stars appear larger. About half the hair detail remains, most noticeably behind the neck and shoulder. The rim may be partially worn away and may blend into the field.

Reverse. Wear is even more extensive, with the shield and wing feathers being points to observe. The incuse E PLURIBUS UNUM may have a few letters worn away. The clouds all seem to be connected. The stars are weak. Parts of the border and lettering may be weak.

Illustrated coin: 1800, LM-1. F-12.
This coin has smooth, even wear—a nice example of the grade.

VG-8, 10 (Very Good)

Obverse. The portrait is mostly seen in outline form, with most hair strands gone, although there is some definition at the back of the hair and behind the shoulder. The ear is discernible, as is the eye. The stars appear larger still, again an illusion. The rim is weak in areas. LIBERTY and the date are readable and usually full, although some letters may be weak at their tops.

Reverse. Half or so of the letters in the motto are worn away. Most feathers are worn away, although separation of some of the lower feathers may be seen. Some stars are faint. The border blends into the field in areas, and some letters are weak.

Illustrated coin: 1800, LM-3. VG-8.

G-4, 6 (Good)

Obverse. Some stars may be partly missing. The head is an outline. The eye is visible only in outline form. The rim is well worn or even missing in areas. LIBERTY is worn, and parts of some letters may be missing, but elements of all should be readable. The date is readable, but worn.

Reverse. The upper part of the eagle is flat, and feathers are noticeable only at the lower edge of the wings and do not have detail. The upper part of the shield is flat. Only a few letters of the motto can be seen. The rim is worn extensively, and a few letters may be missing.

Illustrated coin: 1805. G-4.

AG-3 (About Good)

Obverse. Wear is so extensive that the coin is barely identifiable. The head is in outline form. LIBERTY is mostly gone; same for the stars. The date, while readable, may be partially worn away.

Reverse. Extensive wear is seen overall, with the rim worn away and some areas worn smooth. The eagle can be discerned in outline form, but not necessarily completely. A few stray motto letters may remain.

Illustrated coin: 1803, LM-2. AG-3.
This coin is extensively worn, but defect free.

1829–1837 CAPPED BUST

History. Half dimes of this design were first struck in the wee hours of the morning of July 4, 1829, to have a supply on hand for insertion in the cornerstone of the new (second) Philadelphia Mint building and, presumably, to have some inexpensive coins on hand for distribution as souvenirs. Engraver John Reich's Capped Bust motif was not new and had been used on half dollars as early as 1807. It was logical to employ it on the new half dime, a coin of which none had been made since 1805. The new half dimes proved popular and remained in circulation for many years.

Striking and Sharpness. Striking varies, and most show lightness in one area or another. On the obverse, check the hair details to the left of the eye and the star centers. On the reverse, check the eagle's feathers and neck. The motto, which can be a problem on certain other coins of this design (notably half dollars), is usually bold on the half dimes. Dentils range from well defined to somewhat indistinct, and, in general, are sharper on the obverse than on the reverse.

Availability. Finding an example in any desired grade will not be a challenge. Finding one with Full Details will take more time. Connoisseurship is required at the Mint State level, due to overgraded and recolored coins.

MS-60 to 70 (Mint State)

Illustrated coin: 1831, LM-4, V-4. MS-67.
This example is nearly pristine. Rich with original Mint luster, the softly frosted surfaces thin to hints of reflectivity in the fields. The strike, however, is strong from rim to center, delineating the intricate design elements clearly. Brilliant, save for a faint champagne-colored iridescence, the coin has no distracting abrasions.

Note: Abbreviations used in die-variety attributions, along with the reference works on which the attributions are based, are discussed on the first page of this chapter. All coins are shown enlarged, for clarity.

Obverse. At MS-60 some abrasion and contact marks are evident, most noticeably on the cheek, on the hair below the left part of LIBERTY, and on the area near the drapery clasp. Luster is present, but may be dull or lifeless, and interrupted in patches. At MS-63, contact marks are very few, and abrasion is hard to detect except under magnification. An MS-65 coin has no abrasion, and has contact marks so minute as to require magnification. Luster should be full and rich, usually more so on half dimes than larger coins of the Capped Bust type. Grades above MS-65 are seen now and again, and are defined by having fewer marks as perfection is approached.

Reverse. Comments apply as for the obverse, except that abrasion and contact marks are most noticeable on the eagle's neck, the top of the wings, the claws, and the flat band that surrounds the incuse motto. The field is mainly protected by design elements and does not show abrasion as much as does the obverse.

AU-50, 53, 55, 58 (About Uncirculated)

Obverse. Light wear is seen on the cap, the hair below LIBERTY, the hair near the clasp, and the drapery at the bosom. At AU-58, the luster is extensive except in the open area of the field, especially to the right. At AU-50 and 53, luster remains only in protected areas.

Reverse. Wear is visible on the eagle's neck, the top of the wings, the claws, and the flat band above the eagle. An AU-58 coin will have nearly full luster. At AU-50 and 53, there will still be significant luster, more than on the obverse.

Illustrated coin: 1835, LM-9.1. AU-53.
Vivid iridescent toning is evident, perhaps as acquired from longtime storage in a cardboard album. The light areas on the obverse coincidentally showcase the points of wear to be observed at this level. Some lightness of strike is seen at the centers and at the eagle's neck.

EF-40, 45 (Extremely Fine)

Obverse. Wear is most noticeable on the higher areas of the hair. The cap shows more wear, as does the cheek. Stars, usually protected by the rim on the half dime, still show their centers (unless lightly struck). Luster, if present, is in protected areas among the star points and close to the portrait.

Reverse. The wings show wear on the higher areas of the feathers, and some details are lost. Feathers in the neck are light. The eagle's claws and the leaves show wear. Luster may be present in protected areas, even if there is little or none on the obverse.

Illustrated coin: 1835, LM-10. EF-45.
This is an attractive example, with much luster remaining.

VF-20, 30 (Very Fine)

Obverse. Wear has caused most of the hair to be combined into thick tresses without delicate features. The curl on the neck is flat. Most stars, unless they were weakly struck, retain their interior lines.

Reverse. Wear is most evident on the eagle's neck, to the left of the shield, and on the leaves and claws. Most feathers in the wing remain distinct.

Illustrated coin: 1830, LM-5. VF-30.
The obverse die, which had been used in other die marriages, probably failed soon after the present pairing, as evidenced by the prominent cud break on the rim.

F-12, 15 (Fine)

Obverse. Wear is more extensive, with much of the hair blended together. The drapery is indistinct at its upper edge. Stars have lost some detail at the centers, but still have relief (are not flat).

Reverse. Wear is more extensive, now with only about half of the feathers remaining on the wings. Some of the horizontal lines in the shield may be worn away.

Illustrated coin: 1837. F-12.

VG-8, 10 (Very Good)

Obverse. The hair is less distinct, with the area surrounding the face blended into the facial features. LIBERTY is complete, but weak in areas. The stars are nearly flat, although some interior detail can be seen on certain strikings.

Reverse. Feathers are fewer and mostly appear on the right wing. Other details are weaker. All lettering remains easily visible.

Illustrated coin: 1829. VG-8.

G-4, 6 (Good)

Obverse. The portrait is mostly in outline, with few interior details discernible. LIBERTY may still be readable or may be partially worn away, depending on the variety. Stars are flat at their centers.

Reverse. The eagle mostly is in outline form, although some feathers can be seen in the right wing. All letters around the border are clear. E PLURIBUS UNUM may be weak, sometimes with a few letters worn away.

Illustrated coin: 1837. G-6.

AG-3 (About Good)

Obverse. The portrait is an outline, although traces of LIBERTY can still be seen. The rim is worn down, and some stars are weak. The date remains clear.

Reverse. The reverse shows more wear overall than the obverse, with the rim indistinct in areas and many letters worn away.

Illustrated coin: 1835. AG-3.

Proof Capped Bust Half Dimes, PF-60 to 70

Proofs were struck in small quantities, generally as part of silver Proof sets, although perhaps some were made to mark the Mint cornerstone event (see introduction); facts are scarce. True Proofs have fully mirrored fields. Scrutinize deeply toned pieces (deep toning often masks the true nature of a coin, e.g., if it is not a true Proof, or if it has been cleaned or repaired). Some pieces attributed as "Proofs" are not Proofs. This advice applies across the entire Capped Bust silver series.

Illustrated coin: 1829, LM-2, V-3. PF-64. Both sides of this Proof example are fully defined, even at the denticles. The fields have a glittering reflectivity, while the devices have a satin texture, providing for a cameo-like appearance overall. There are no detracting blemishes, and only a hint of light olive-russet toning.

Obverse and Reverse. Proofs that are extensively cleaned and have many hairlines, or that are dull and grainy, are lower level, such as PF-60 to 62. These are not of great interest to specialists unless they are of rare die varieties (such as 1829, LM-1 to 3, described in the image caption). With medium hairlines, an assigned grade of PF-64 may be in order, and with relatively few hairlines, gem PF-65. PF-66 should have hairlines so delicate that magnification is needed to see them. Above that, a Proof should be free of such lines. Grading is highly subjective with early Proofs, and eye appeal also is a factor.

1837–1838 LIBERTY SEATED, NO STARS

History. The Liberty Seated design without obverse stars was used in the half dime and dime series only at the Philadelphia Mint in 1837 and the New Orleans Mint in 1838 (1838-O). The design, by Christian Gobrecht, follows the obverse inaugurated on the 1836 silver dollar. Miss Liberty has no drapery at her elbow. These coins are very attractive, and the starless obverse gives them a cameo-like appearance.

Striking and Sharpness. Check the highest parts of the Liberty Seated figure (especially the head and horizontal shield stripes) and, on the reverse, the leaves. Check the dentils on both sides.

Availability. The Philadelphia coins are easily available in all grades. The 1838-O is a rarity in true Mint State, often is overgraded, and typically has low eye appeal.

MS-60 to 70 (Mint State)

Illustrated coin: 1837. MS-62.
This is an attractive example with a hint of toning.

Note: All coins are shown enlarged, for clarity.

Obverse. At MS-60 some abrasion and contact marks are evident, most noticeably on the bosom, thighs, and knees. Luster is present, but may be dull or lifeless, and interrupted in patches in the large open field. At MS-63, contact marks are very few, and abrasion is hard to detect except under magnification. An MS-65 coin has no abrasion, and contact marks are so minute as to require magnification. Luster should be full and rich. Half dimes of this type can be very beautiful at this level. Grades above MS-65 are seen with regularity, more often than the related No Stars dimes.

Reverse. Comments apply as for the obverse, except that abrasion and contact marks are most noticeable on the highest parts of the leaves and the ribbon. The field is mainly protected by design elements and does not show abrasion as much as does the open-field obverse on a given coin.

AU-50, 53, 55, 58 (About Uncirculated)

Obverse. Light wear is seen on the thighs and knees, bosom, and head. At AU-58, the luster is extensive, but incomplete. Friction is seen in the large open field. At AU-50 and 53, luster is less.

Reverse. Wear is noticeable on the leaves and ribbon. An AU-58 coin has nearly full luster—more so than on the obverse, as the design elements protect the small field areas. At AU-50 and 53, there still is significant luster, more than on the obverse.

Illustrated coin: 1837. AU-58.

EF-40, 45 (Extremely Fine)

Obverse. Further wear is seen on all areas, especially the thighs and knees, bosom, and head. Little or no luster is seen.

Reverse. Further wear is seen on all areas, most noticeably at the leaves to each side of the wreath apex, and on the ribbon bow knot. Leaves retain details except on the higher areas.

Illustrated coin: 1838-O. EF-40.

VF-20, 30 (Very Fine)

Obverse. Further wear is seen. Most details of the gown are worn away, except in the lower-relief areas. Hair detail are mostly gone.

Reverse. Wear is more extensive. The highest leaves are flat.

Illustrated coin: 1837. VF-25.

F-12, 15 (Fine)

Obverse. The seated figure is well worn, with little detail remaining. LIBERTY on the shield is fully readable.

Reverse. Most detail of the leaves are gone. The rim is worn, but most if not all dentils are visible.

Illustrated coin: 1837. F-12.

VG-8, 10 (Very Good)

Obverse. The seated figure is mostly flat, without detail. The shield is discernible. In LIBERTY, at least three letters are readable at VG-8, with a few more at VG-10.

Reverse. Further wear has combined the details of most leaves. The rim is complete, but weak in areas.

Illustrated coin: 1837. VG-8.

G-4, 6 (Good)

Obverse. The seated figure is worn smooth. At G-4 there are no letters in LIBERTY remaining. At G-6, traces of one or two can be seen.

Reverse. Wear is more extensive. The leaves are all combined and in outline form. The rim is well worn and missing in some areas, causing the outer parts of the peripheral letters to be worn away in some instances.

Illustrated coin: 1837. G-4.

AG-3 (About Good)

Obverse. The seated figure is mostly visible in outline form, with no detail. The rim is worn away. The date remains clear.

Reverse. Many if not most letters are worn away, as are parts of the wreath.

Illustrated coin: 1837. AG-3.

Proof Liberty Seated / No Stars Half Dimes, PF-60 to 70

It is likely that at least several dozen Proofs were made of the 1837 half dime, although perhaps more were made of the related dime. Today, attractive examples exist and are rare. Nearly all designated as Proofs are, indeed, Proofs. If you aspire to acquire one, select an example with deep mirror surfaces.

Obverse and Reverse. Proofs that are extensively cleaned and have many hairlines, or that are dull and grainy, are lower level, such as PF-60 to 62. These command little attention. Both the half dime and dime Proofs of this year were often cleaned, resulting in coins which have lost much of their mirror surface. With medium hairlines and good reflectivity, an assigned grade of PF-64 is indicated, and with relatively few hairlines, gem PF-65. In various grades hairlines are most easily seen in the obverse field. PF-66 should have hairlines so delicate that magnification is needed to see them. Above that, a Proof should be free of such lines.

Illustrated coin: 1837. PF-67.
Note the brown tone. Fully mirrored fields are seen when the coin is held at an angle to the light.

1838–1859 LIBERTY SEATED, WITH STARS

History. The Liberty Seated motif is essentially the same as before, but with 13 obverse stars added in 1838, and in 1839 a restyling (drapery added to the elbow) by Robert Ball Hughes. The reverse features an open wreath enclosing HALF DIME, with UNITED STATES OF AMERICA around the border.

Striking and Sharpness. Varies widely. Most from 1838 to 1852 are sharper than later ones, but there are exceptions. (Coins with "mushy" details are especially common among the high-mintage dates of the mid- to late 1850s.) On the obverse, check the star centers, the head and center of Miss Liberty, and the dentils. On the reverse, check the wreath leaves and dentils.

Availability. Easily available as a type, but with many scarce varieties. Such issues as 1849-O and 1846 are extreme rarities at the true Mint State level. Quality varies widely, and many Mint State coins are artificially toned. Cherrypicking is advised.

MS-60 to 70 (Mint State)

Illustrated coin: 1851. MS-65.

Note: All coins are shown enlarged, for clarity.

Obverse. At MS-60 some abrasion and contact marks are evident, most noticeably on the bosom and knees. Luster is present, but may be dull or lifeless. At MS-63, contact marks are very few, and abrasion is hard to detect except under magnification. An MS-65 coin will have no abrasion, and contact marks are so minute as to require magnification. Luster should be full and rich.

Reverse. Comments apply as for the obverse, except that in lower Mint State grades abrasion and contact marks are most noticeable on the highest parts of the leaves and the ribbon. At MS-65 or higher there are no marks visible to the unaided eye. The field is mainly protected by design elements and does not show abrasion as much as does the obverse on a given coin.

AU-50, 53, 55, 58 (About Uncirculated)

Obverse. Light wear is seen on the knees, bosom, and head. At AU-58, the luster is extensive, but incomplete. At AU-50 and 53, luster is less.

Reverse. Wear is evident on the leaves (especially at the top of the wreath) and ribbon. An AU-58 coin has nearly full luster, more so than on the obverse, as the design elements protect the small field areas. At AU-50 and 53, there still is significant luster.

Illustrated coin: 1849-O. AU-50.

EF-40, 45 (Extremely Fine)

Obverse. Further wear is seen on all areas, especially the knees, bosom, and head. Little or no luster is seen.

Reverse. Further wear is seen on all areas, most noticeably at the leaves to each side of the wreath apex, and on the ribbon. Leaves retain details except on the higher areas.

Illustrated coin: 1856-O. EF-40.

VF-20, 30 (Very Fine)

Obverse. Further wear is seen. Most details of the gown are worn away, except in the lower-relief areas. Hair detail is mostly gone.

Reverse. Wear is more extensive. The highest leaves are flat.

Illustrated coin: 1857. VF-30.

F-12, 15 (Fine)

Obverse. The seated figure is well worn, with little detail remaining. LIBERTY on the shield is readable, but weak in areas.

Reverse. Most detail of the leaves is gone. The rim is worn, but most if not all dentils are visible.

Illustrated coin: 1846. F-12.

VG-8, 10 (Very Good)

Obverse. The seated figure is mostly flat, without detail. The shield is discernible. IN LIBERTY at least three letters are readable but very weak at VG-8; a few more appear at VG-10.

Reverse. Further wear combines the details of most leaves. The rim is complete, but weak in areas. The reverse appears to be in a slightly higher grade than the obverse.

Illustrated coin: 1843. VG-8.

G-4, 6 (Good)

Obverse. The seated figure is worn smooth. At G-4 there are no letters in LIBERTY remaining. At G-6, traces of one or two can barely be seen.

Reverse. The leaves are all combined and in outline form. The rim is well worn and missing in some areas, causing the outer parts of the peripheral letters to be worn away in some instances.

Illustrated coin: 1846. G-4.

AG-3 (About Good)

Obverse. The seated figure is mostly visible in outline form, with no detail. Much of the rim is worn away. The date remains clear.

Reverse. Many if not most letters are worn away at least in part. The wreath and interior letters are discernible.

Illustrated coin: 1854. AG-3.

Proof Liberty Seated / Stars Half Dimes, PF-60 to 70

Proofs were first widely sold to collectors in 1858, in which year an estimated 210 silver sets were distributed. It is believed that 800 Proofs were struck of 1859, of which slightly more than 400 found buyers. Proofs were made of earlier dates, but in much smaller numbers. Excellent strike and deeply mirrored fields characterized nearly all. The quality of Proofs on the market varies widely, mainly due to cleaning and dipping. Patience and care are needed to find a choice example.

Illustrated coin: 1849. PF-64.
This glittering example has sharp, frosty devices and fully mirrored fields. Essentially brilliant at the centers, the surface develops a pale champagne toning toward the rims.

Obverse and Reverse. Proofs that are extensively cleaned and have many hairlines, or that are dull and grainy, are lower level, such as PF-60 to 62. These are not widely desired, save for the rare (in any grade) date of 1846. With medium hairlines and good reflectivity, an assigned grade of PF-64 is justified, and with relatively few hairlines, gem PF-65. In various grades hairlines are most easily seen in the obverse field. PF-66 should have hairlines so delicate that magnification is needed to see them. Above that, a Proof should be free of such lines.

1860–1873 LEGEND OBVERSE

History. In 1860 the UNITED STATES OF AMERICA inscription was moved to the obverse of the half dime, in place of the stars. The reverse displayed a "cereal wreath" (as it was called in Mint records) enclosing HALF DIME.

Striking and Sharpness. Points to check include the head of Miss Liberty on the obverse, the wreath details on the reverse (particularly at the inside upper left, above H of HALF) and the dentils on both sides. Generally, Mint State coins have excellent luster, although some struck from relapped dies tend to be prooflike and with many striae. The word LIBERTY is not an infallible guide to grading at lower levels, as on some dies the shield was in lower relief, and the letters wore away less quickly. This guideline should be used in combination with other features.

Availability. Easily available as a type, although some dates and varieties are rare. San Francisco coins, first made in 1863, are rare in Mint State for the first several years.

MS-60 to 70 (Mint State)

Illustrated coin: 1872-S, Mintmark Below Bow. MS-66.
Both sides of this beautiful gem display full Mint luster, with no toning. The coin is very sharply struck, with no marks or abrasions.

Note: All coins are shown enlarged, for clarity.

Obverse. At MS-60 some abrasion and contact marks are evident, most noticeably on the bosom and knees. Luster is present, but may be dull or lifeless. At MS-63, contact marks are very few, and abrasion is hard to detect except under magnification. An MS-65 coin has no abrasion, and contact marks are so minute as to require magnification. Luster should be full and rich, except for Philadelphia (but not San Francisco) half dimes of the early and mid-1860s. Most Mint State coins of 1861 to 1865, Philadelphia issues, will have extensive die striae (from the dies being incompletely finished). Some low-mintage Philadelphia issues may be prooflike (and some may even be mislabeled as Proofs). Clashmarks are common in this era.

Reverse. Comments apply as for the obverse, except that in lower Mint State grades abrasion and contact marks are most noticeable on the highest parts of the leaves and the ribbon, less so on HALF DIME. At MS-65 or higher there are no marks visible to the unaided eye. The field, mainly protected by design elements, does not show abrasion as much as does the obverse on a given coin.

AU-50, 53, 55, 58 (About Uncirculated)

Obverse. Light wear is seen on the knees, bosom, and head. At AU-58 the luster is extensive, but incomplete. At AU-50 and 53, luster is less evident.

Reverse. Wear is observable on the leaves and ribbon. An AU-58 coin will have nearly full luster, more so than on the obverse, as the design elements protect the small field areas. At AU-50 and 53 there will still be significant luster.

Illustrated coin: 1863. AU-55.
Ample traces of luster remain on the light silver surfaces of this example.

EF-40, 45 (Extremely Fine)

Obverse. Further wear is seen on all areas, especially the knees, bosom, and head. Little or no luster is seen.

Reverse. Further wear is seen on all areas, most noticeably at the high areas of the wreath and on the ribbon. Leaves retain excellent details except on the higher areas.

Illustrated coin: 1866. EF-40.

VF-20, 30 (Very Fine)

Obverse. Further wear is seen. Most details of the gown are worn away, except in the lower-relief areas above and to the right of the shield. Hair detail is gone on the higher points.

Reverse. Wear is more extensive. The highest leaves are flat, particularly the larger leaves at the top of the wreath.

Illustrated coin: 1865. VF-35.

F-12, 15 (Fine)

Obverse. The seated figure is well worn, but with some detail above and to the right of the shield. LIBERTY is readable but weak in areas.

Reverse. Much detail of the leaves in the higher areas is gone. The rim remains bold.

Illustrated coin: 1861. F-12.

VG-8, 10 (Very Good)

Obverse. The seated figure is more worn, but some detail can be seen above and to the right of the shield. The shield is discernible. In LIBERTY, at least the equivalent of two or three letters (can be a combination of partial letters) is readable—very weak—at VG-8. A few more letters are readable at VG-10.

Reverse. Further wear has combined the details of many leaves. The rim is bold. On most coins the reverse appears to be in a slightly higher grade than the obverse.

Illustrated coin: 1872. VG-8.

G-4, 6 (Good)

Obverse. The seated figure is worn smooth. At G-4 there are no letters in LIBERTY remaining. At G-6, traces of one or two can barely be seen.

Reverse. The leaves are all combined and in outline form. The rim is clear. On most coins the reverse appears to be in a slightly higher grade than the obverse.

Illustrated coin: 1872. G-4

AG-3 (About Good)

Obverse. The seated figure is mostly visible in outline form, with no detail. Much of the rim is worn away. The date remains clear.

Reverse. The wreath and interior letters are partially worn away. The rim can usually be seen, but is weak.

Illustrated coin: 1867. AG-3

Proof Legend Obverse Half Dimes, PF-60 to 70

Proof coins were made in fair quantities each year and are readily available today. Generally, they are well made, with deeply mirrored fields, although some of the late 1860s and early 1870s can have weak areas. Average quality in the marketplace is higher than for larger Liberty Seated denominations.

Obverse and Reverse. Proofs that are extensively cleaned and have many hairlines, or that are dull and grainy, are lower level, such as PF-60 to 62. These are not widely desired. With medium hairlines and good reflectivity, an assigned grade of PF-64 is appropriate, and with relatively few hairlines, Gem PF-65. In various grades hairlines are most easily seen in the obverse field. PF-66 should have hairlines so delicate that magnification is needed to see them. Above that, a Proof should be free of such lines.

Illustrated coin: 1864. PF-65 UC.
The sharp contrast between the fields and devices on this example is easy to see, thanks to the brilliant-white surfaces. Fully struck throughout, the coin is free of distracting blemishes.

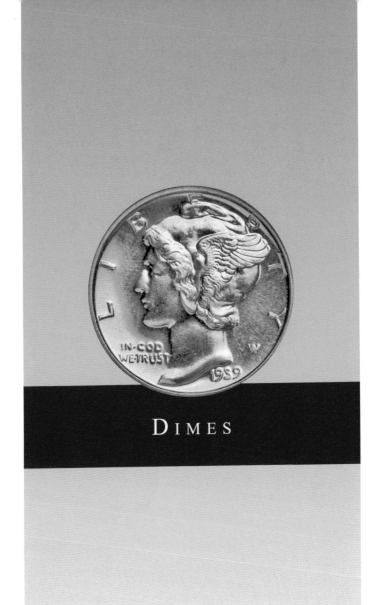

DIMES

DIMES, 1796 TO DATE

1796–1797 DRAPED BUST, SMALL EAGLE

History. Dimes or ten-cent pieces were first minted in 1796, with no known fanfare or publicity at the time. They were struck with the Draped Bust obverse, as employed on cents and other silver coins, in combination with the Small Eagle reverse. Some dimes of 1796 exhibit prooflike surfaces, suggesting that they may have been "presentation pieces," but no documentation exists.

Striking and Sharpness. Most dimes of this type have weakness or problems in one area or another, usually more so on those dated 1797. Points to check for sharpness include the hair of Miss Liberty, the drapery lines on the bust, the centers of the stars, and, on the reverse, the breast and wing feathers of the eagle. Also check for adjustment marks. In summary, *a sharply struck coin is a goal, not necessarily a reality.* Sharp striking and excellent eye appeal dramatically add to the value.

Availability. This type is the rarest and most expensive in the dime series. Within any desired grade, examples should be selected with great care, as many have problems of one sort or another. Mint State coins are especially rare. When seen they are usually dated 1796. Dimes of 1797 are much rarer in all grades and nearly impossible to find in Choice Mint State.

MS-60 to 70 (Mint State)

Illustrated coin: 1796, John Reich 4. MS-61.
This coin is significantly above average in strike, but shows numerous contact marks in the right obverse field. The luster is especially rich on the reverse.

Note: Abbreviations used in die-variety attributions, along with the reference works on which the attributions are based, are discussed on the first page of this chapter. All coins are shown enlarged, for clarity.

Obverse. At MS-60, some abrasion and contact marks are evident, most noticeably on the cheek, the drapery, and the right field. Luster is present, but may be dull or lifeless, and interrupted in patches. At MS-63, contact marks are very few, and abrasion is hard to detect except under magnification, although this type is sometimes graded liberally due to its rarity. An MS-65 coin has no abrasion, and contact marks are so minute as to require magnification. Luster should be full and rich. Coins graded above MS-65 are more theoretical than actual for this type—but they do exist, and are defined by having fewer marks as perfection is approached.

Reverse. Comments apply as for the obverse, except that abrasion and marks are most noticeable on the eagle at the center, a situation complicated by the fact that this area was sometimes lightly struck. The field area is small and is protected by lettering and the wreath, and in any given grade shows fewer marks than on the obverse.

AU-50, 53, 55, 58 (About Uncirculated)

Obverse. Light wear is seen on the hair area above the ear and extending to left of the forehead, on the ribbon, and on the bosom, more so at AU-50 than at 53 or 55. An AU-58 coin has minimal traces of wear. An AU-50 coin has luster in protected areas among the stars and letters, with little in the open fields or on the portrait. At AU-58, most luster is present in the fields, but is worn away on the highest parts of the motifs. Generally, grading guidelines for this dime type follow those of the related half dimes.

Illustrated coin: 1796, JR-4. AU-55.
This coin is attractive overall. Some scattered marks are evident, and it possibly was cleaned long ago and retoned.

Reverse. Light wear is seen on the eagle's body (keep in mind that the higher parts of this area might be lightly struck) and the edges of the wings. Light wear is seen on the wreath and lettering. Luster is the best key to actual wear. This ranges from perhaps 20% remaining in protected areas (at AU-50) to nearly full mint bloom (at AU-58).

EF-40, 45 (Extremely Fine)

Obverse. More wear is evident on the upper hair area and the ribbon, and on the drapery and bosom. Excellent detail remains in low-relief areas of the hair. The stars show wear as do the date and letters. Luster, if present at all, is minimal and in protected areas.

Reverse. The eagle shows more wear, this being the focal point to check. Many feathers remain on the interior areas of the wings. Additional wear is on the wreath and letters, but many details are present. Some luster may be seen in protected areas, and if present is slightly more abundant than on the obverse.

Illustrated coin: 1797, JR-1. EF-45.
This is the only 1797 obverse die with 16 stars. Note some adjustment marks in and behind the hair.

VF-20, 30 (Very Fine)

Obverse. The higher-relief areas of hair are well worn at VF-20, less so at VF-30. The drapery and bosom show extensive wear. The stars have more wear, making them appear larger (an optical illusion seen on most worn silver coins of this era).

Reverse. The body of the eagle shows few if any feathers, while the wings have about half of the feathers visible, depending on the strike. At VF-30 more than half of the feathers may show. The leaves lack most detail and are in outline form. Scattered, non-disfiguring marks are normal for this and lower grades. Any major defects should be noted separately.

Illustrated coin: 1796, JR-1. VF-30.
Note the thin scratch from star 5 to the back of the head, and a tiny planchet flaw in front of the forehead. This is a late state of the obverse die, with a large cud break at lower left.

F-12, 15 (Fine)

Obverse. Wear is more extensive than on a Very Fine coin, particularly noticeable on the hair, face, and bosom, and the stars appear larger. About half the hair detail remains, most noticeably behind the neck and shoulder. The rim may be partially worn away and blend into the field.

Reverse. Wear is more extensive. Now, feather details are diminished, with fewer than half remaining on the wings. The wreath and lettering are worn further, and the rim is usually weak in areas, although some dentils can be seen.

Illustrated coin: 1797. F-15.

VG-8, 10 (Very Good)

Obverse. The portrait is mostly seen in outline form, with most hair strands gone, although there is some definition at the back of the hair and behind the shoulder. The ear is discernible, as is the eye. The stars appear larger still, again an illusion. The rim is weak in areas. LIBERTY and the date are readable and usually full, although some letters may be weak at their tops.

Reverse. The eagle is mostly an outline with parts blending into the field (on lighter strikes). The rim is worn, as are the letters, with some weak, but the motto is readable.

Illustrated coin: 1797. VG-10.

G-4, 6 (Good)

Obverse. Wear is more extensive, and some stars may be partly missing. The head is an outline. The eye is visible only in outline form. The rim is well worn or even missing in areas. LIBERTY is worn, and parts of some letters may be missing, but elements of all should be readable. The date is readable, but worn.

Reverse. The eagle is flat and discernible in outline form, and may be blending into the field. The wreath is well worn. Some of the letters may be partly missing. At this level some "averaging" can be done. If the letters are stronger than usual in one area, but some are missing in another area, the coin can still qualify as G-4.

Illustrated coin: 1796, JR-1. G-6. This is a late die state, with a cud break at lower-left obverse. The reverse, if graded alone, would be higher than G-6.

AG-3 (About Good)

Obverse. Wear is so extensive that the coin is barely identifiable. The head is in outline form. LIBERTY is mostly gone, same for the stars. The date, while readable, may be partially worn away.

Reverse. The reverse is well worn with parts of the wreath and lettering missing.

Illustrated coin: 1796, JR-1. AG-3. This is a late die state, with a cud break at lower-left obverse.

1798–1807 DRAPED BUST, HERALDIC EAGLE

History. Dimes of this style were minted each year from 1798 to 1807 (with the exception of 1799 and 1805). The designs follow those of other silver coins of the era.

Striking and Sharpness. Nearly all have one area or another of light striking. On the obverse, check the hair details and drapery lines, and the star centers. On the reverse, the upper right of the shield and the adjacent part of the eagle's wing are often soft, and several or even most stars may be lightly defined (sharp stars show sharply peaked centers); high parts of the clouds are often weak. Dentils are likely to be weak or missing in areas on either side. Expect to compromise on the strike. In summary, *a sharply struck coin is a goal, not necessarily a reality.* Certain reverse dies of this type were also used to coin quarter eagles. Sharp striking and excellent eye appeal dramatically add to a Draped Bust dime's value, this being particularly true for 1805 and 1807, which are usually weakly struck, especially 1807, the dates most often seen in Mint State.

Availability. Although certain die varieties are rare, the basic years are available, with 1805 and 1807 being the most often seen. As a class, Mint State coins are rare. Again, when seen they are usually dated 1805 or 1807, and have areas of striking weakness. Coins of 1801 through 1804 are scarce in Very Fine and higher grades, very scarce in About Uncirculated and better.

MS-60 to 70 (Mint State)

Illustrated coin: 1805, John Reich 2, 4 berries in branch. MS-66. Some planchet adjustment marks at the left obverse are not particularly noticeable at a casual glance. The reverse shows some strike weakness on the stars above and to the left of the eagle's beak and on the horizontal stripes on the shield, particularly to the right. For an 1805 dime this is an above-average strike.

Note: Abbreviations used in die-variety attributions, along with the reference works on which the attributions are based, are discussed on the first page of this chapter. All coins are shown enlarged, for clarity.

Obverse. At MS-60 some abrasion and contact marks are evident, most noticeably on the cheek, the drapery at the shoulder, and the right field. Luster is present, but may be dull or lifeless, and interrupted in patches. At MS-63, contact marks are very few, and abrasion is hard to detect except under magnification. An MS-65 coin has no abrasion, and contact marks are so minute as to require magnification. Luster should be full and rich. Coins graded above MS-65 are more theoretical than actual for this type—but they do exist, and are defined by having fewer marks as perfection is approached.

Reverse. Comments apply as for the obverse, except that abrasion and marks are most noticeable on the eagle's neck, the tips of the wing, and the tail. The field area is complex, without much open space, given the stars above the eagle, the arrows and olive branch, and other features. Accordingly, marks are not as noticeable as on the obverse.

AU-50, 53, 55, 58 (About Uncirculated)

Obverse. Light wear is seen on the hair area above the ear and extending to left of the forehead, on the ribbon, and on the drapery at the shoulder, more so at AU-50 than at 53 or 55. An AU-58 coin has minimal traces of wear. An AU-50 coin has luster in protected areas among the stars and letters, with little in the open fields or on the portrait. At AU-58, most luster is present in the fields, but is worn away on the highest parts of the motifs.

Illustrated coin: 1802, JR-2. AU-50.
Note some marks below the Y in LIBERTY.

Reverse. Comments as preceding, except that the eagle's neck, the tips and top of the wings, the clouds, and the tail now show noticeable wear, as do other features. As always, a familiarity with a given die variety will help differentiate striking weakness from actual wear. Luster ranges from perhaps 20% remaining in protected areas (at AU-50) to nearly full mint bloom (at AU-58). Often the reverse of this type will retain much more luster than the obverse.

EF-40, 45 (Extremely Fine)

Obverse. More wear is evident on the upper hair area and the ribbon and on the drapery and bosom. Excellent detail remains in low-relief areas of the hair. The stars show wear, as do the date and letters. Luster, if present at all, is minimal and in protected areas.

Illustrated coin: 1800, JR-2. EF-40.
Note two small digs on the bosom and scattered other marks.

Reverse. The neck lacks feather detail on its highest points. Feathers have lost some detail near the edges of the wings, and some areas of the horizontal lines in the shield may be blended together, particularly at the right (an area that is also susceptible to weak striking). Some traces of luster may be seen, more so at EF-45 than at EF-40.

VF-20, 30 (Very Fine)

Obverse. The higher-relief areas of hair are well worn at VF-20, less so at VF-30. The drapery and bosom show extensive wear. The stars have more wear, making them appear larger (an optical illusion seen on most worn silver coins of this era).

Illustrated coin: 1801, JR-1. VF-20.
Here is a problem-free example with normal wear for this grade.

Reverse. Wear is greater, including on the shield and wing feathers. Star centers are flat. Other areas have lost detail, as well. E PLURIBUS UNUM is complete (this incuse feature tended to wear away slowly).

F-12, 15 (Fine)

Obverse. Wear is more extensive than on a Very Fine coin, particularly noticeable on the hair, face, and bosom, and the stars appear larger. About half the hair detail remains, most noticeably behind the neck and shoulder. The rim may be partially worn away and blend into the field.

Reverse. Wear is even more extensive, with the shield and wing feathers being points to observe. About half of the feathers are visible (depending on striking). E PLURIBUS UNUM may have a few letters worn away. The clouds all seem to be connected. The stars are weak. Parts of the border and lettering may be weak.

Illustrated coin: 1807, JR-1. F-12.
This is one of the more readily available die varieties of the type; nearly always weakly struck, but at F-12 this is not as important as it would be in higher grades.

VG-8, 10 (Very Good)

Obverse. The portrait is mostly seen in outline form, with most hair strands gone, although there is some definition at the back of the hair and behind the shoulder. The ear may be discernible. The eye is evident. The stars appear larger still, again an illusion. The rim is weak in areas. LIBERTY and the date are readable and usually full, although some letters may be weak at their tops.

Reverse. Half or so of the letters in the motto are worn away. Most feathers are worn away, although separation of some may be seen. Some stars are faint. The border blends into the field in areas, and some letters are weak. Sharpness can vary widely depending on the die variety. At this level, grading by the obverse first, then checking the reverse, is recommended.

Illustrated coin: 1802, JR-4. VG-10.
This coin has a dig on the obverse near star 2, a few other marks (not unusual for the grade), and attractive iridescent toning.

G-4, 6 (Good)

Obverse. Some stars may be partly missing. The head is an outline. The eye is visible only in outline form. The rim is well worn or even missing in areas. LIBERTY is worn, and parts of some letters may be missing, but elements of all should be readable. The date is readable, but worn.

Reverse. The upper part of the eagle is flat, and feathers are noticeable at the lower edge of the wing. Some scattered feather detail may or may not be seen. The upper part of the shield is flat or nearly so, depending on the variety. Only a few letters of the motto can be seen, although this depends on the variety. The rim is worn extensively, and a few letters may be missing.

Illustrated coin: 1798, JR-4, Medium 8. G-6.
This is a late state of the obverse die, with cracks in the right field. Due to the original relief of the dies of this particular specimen, the reverse is better defined than the obverse and is a candidate for VG. On some other dimes the opposite can be true.

AG-3 (About Good)

Obverse. Wear is very extensive, and some stars and letters are extremely weak or missing entirely. The date is readable.

Reverse. Extensive wear is seen overall, with the rim worn away and some areas worn smooth. The eagle can be discerned in outline form, but not necessarily completely. A few stray motto letters may remain. Sometimes the obverse can be exceedingly worn (but the date must be readable) and the reverse with more detail, or vice-versa.

Illustrated coin: 1805, JR-2, 4 berries in branch. AG-3.
This coin has extensive wear overall, but is remarkably free of marks and problems for this low grade.

1809–1828 CAPPED BUST, WIDE BORDER

History. Dimes of this design were struck intermittently from 1809 to 1828. The design by John Reich closely follows that inaugurated with the Capped Bust half dollars of 1809 (themselves a modification of the earlier Capped Bust design).

Striking and Sharpness. Many if not most have areas of light striking. On the obverse, check the star centers, the hair details, and the drapery at the bosom. On the reverse, check the eagle, especially the area in and around the upper right of the shield. Dentils are sometimes weak, but are usually better defined on the reverse than on the obverse. The height of the rims on both sides can vary, and coins with a low rim or rims tend to show wear more quickly.

Availability. There are no extremely rare dates in this series, so all are available to collectors. Most are scarce in Mint State, with some being rare. Those exhibiting a strong strike, with Full Details, command a premium, especially the earlier dates.

MS-60 to 70 (Mint State)

Illustrated coin: 1814, John Reich 1, Small Date. MS-65.
This coin is sharply struck at the centers, and lightly struck on some stars, border areas, and dentils. It has deep, rich mint luster.

Note: Abbreviations used in die-variety attributions, along with the reference works on which the attributions are based, are discussed on the first page of this chapter. All coins are shown enlarged, for clarity.

Obverse. At MS-60 some abrasion and contact marks are evident, most noticeably on the cheek and on the area near the drapery clasp. Luster is present, but may be dull or lifeless, and interrupted in patches. At MS-63, contact marks are very few, and abrasion is hard to detect except under magnification. An MS-65 coin has no abrasion, and contact marks are so minute as to require magnification. Luster should be full and rich. Grades above MS-65 are seen now and again, and are defined by having fewer marks as perfection is approached.

Reverse. Comments apply as for the obverse, except that abrasion and contact marks are most noticeable on the eagle's neck, the top of the wings, the claws, and the flat band that surrounds the incuse motto. The field is mainly protected by design elements and does not show abrasion as much as does the obverse.

AU-50, 53, 55, 58 (About Uncirculated)

Obverse. Light wear is seen on the cap, the hair below LIBERTY, the hair near the clasp, and the drapery at the bosom. At AU-58, the luster is extensive except in the open area of the field, especially to the right. At AU-50 and 53, luster remains only in protected areas. As is true of all high grades, sharpness of strike can affect the perception of wear.

Illustrated coin: 1823, 3 Over 2, JR-1, Small E's in legend. AU-50.
This coin shows some tiny adjustment marks (scarcely visible). It is lightly struck at the center, and grading was mostly done by observing the luster.

Reverse. Wear is evident on the eagle's neck, the top of the wings, and the claws. An AU-58 has nearly full luster. At AU-50 and 53, there still is significant luster, more than on the obverse.

EF-40, 45 (Extremely Fine)

Obverse. Wear is more extensive, most noticeable on the higher areas of the hair. The cap shows more wear, as does the cheek. Stars still show their centers (unless lightly struck, and *many* are). Luster, if present, is in protected areas among the star points and close to the portrait.

Reverse. The wings show wear on the higher areas of the feathers (particularly on the right wing), and some details are lost. Feathers in the neck are light. The eagle's claws show wear. Luster may be present in protected areas, even if there is little or none on the obverse.

Illustrated coin: 1827, JR-7. EF-45.
This coin is lightly struck on some stars, but fairly well struck at the center. It may be useful to compare the detail with that on the lightly struck coin used to illustrate the About Uncirculated level, a reminder that multiple factors need to be considered when grading early coins. Overall, a nice example of the grade.

VF-20, 30 (Very Fine)

Obverse. Wear is more extensive, and most of the hair is combined into thick tresses without delicate features. The curl on the neck is flat. Unless they were weakly struck to begin with, most stars retain their interior lines.

Reverse. Wear is most evident on the eagle's neck, to the left of the shield, and on the leaves and claws. Most feathers in the wing remain distinct.

Illustrated coin: 1811, 11 Over 09, JR-1. VF-20.
The reverse has multiple die cracks (but not as many as on later states of this die). It is a wonder how the reverse die held together.

F-12, 15 (Fine)

Obverse. Wear is more extensive, with much of the hair blended together. The drapery is indistinct along part of its upper edge. Stars have lost detail at the center and some may be flat. The height of obverse rim is important in the amount of wear the coin has received.

Reverse. Wear is more extensive, now with only about a third to half of the feathers remaining on the wings, more on the wing to the left. Some of the horizontal lines in the shield may be worn away.

Illustrated coin: 1821, JR-2. F-12.
Some pin scratches are evident. This is a rare die variety; slightly more than a dozen are known. The die failed at stars 1 to 3, soon ending its life. Traces of a resultant bulge can be seen.

VG-8, 10 (Very Good)

Obverse. The hair is less distinct, with the area surrounding the face blended into the facial features. LIBERTY is complete, but weak in areas. Stars are nearly flat.

Reverse. Feathers are fewer and mostly visible on the eagle's left wing. Other details are weaker. All lettering remains easily readable, although some letters may be faint.

Illustrated coin: 1827, JR-1. VG-8.
Here is a mint error double struck while in the press, with some of the first-strike features still visible.

G-4, 6 (Good)

Obverse. The portrait is mostly in outline, with few interior details discernible. LIBERTY may still be readable or may be partially worn away, depending on the variety (this varies due to the strike characteristics of some die marriages). Stars are flat at their centers.

Reverse. The eagle is mostly in outline form, although some feathers can be seen in the right wing. All letters around the border are clear on a sharp strike; some letters are light or missing on a coin with low rims. E PLURIBUS UNUM may be weak, often with some letters worn away.

Illustrated coin: 1820. G-4.
This is an attractive, problem-free coin at this grade.

AG-3 (About Good)

Obverse. The portrait is an outline, although traces of LIBERTY can still be seen. The rim is worn down, and some stars are weak. The date remains clear although weak toward the rim.

Reverse. The reverse shows more wear overall than the obverse, with the rim indistinct in areas and many if not most letters worn away.

Illustrated coin: 1821, JR-1. AG-3.
This is a well-worn but still attractive example.

Proof Capped Bust / Wide Border Dimes, PF-60 to 70

Proof Capped Bust dimes of 1809 to 1828 were struck in small numbers, likely mostly as part of presentation sets. As is the case with any and all early Proofs, you should insist on a coin with deeply and fully (not partially) mirrored surfaces, well struck, and with good contrast. Carefully examine deeply toned pieces (deep toning can mask the true nature of a coin, e.g., if it is not a true Proof, or if it has been cleaned or repaired). More than just a few pieces attributed as "Proofs" are not Proofs at all.

Illustrated coin: 1825, JR-2. PF-66.
Some lightness of strike left of the neck on the obverse and at the upper right of the shield on the reverse.

Obverse and Reverse. Proofs of this type can have areas of light striking, such as at the star centers. Proofs that are extensively cleaned and have many hairlines, or that are dull and grainy, are lower level, such as PF-60 to 62. These are not of great interest to specialists unless they are of rare die varieties. A PF-64 has fewer hairlines, but they are obvious, perhaps slightly distracting. A Gem PF-65 should have fewer still and full mirrored surfaces (no trace of cloudiness or dullness). PF-66 should have hairlines so delicate that magnification is needed to see them. Above that, a Proof should be free of such lines. Grading is highly subjective with early Proofs, and eye appeal also is a major factor.

1828–1837 CAPPED BUST, MODIFIED DESIGN

History. Capped Bust dimes of this slightly modified design have smaller dentils in the border and differ slightly in other features from the preceding type. Made in fairly large quantities, these circulated widely in their era.

Striking and Sharpness. Most dimes of this type are fairly well struck, with fewer irregularities of strike than the 1809–1828 type. On the obverse, check the hair and the brooch, and don't overlook the stars (but these are usually sharp). On the reverse, check the details of the eagle. The dentils are usually sharp.

Availability. All dates are readily available, but certain die varieties range from rare to extremely rare. In Mint State the dates of the early 1830s to 1835 are the most readily available. Most have nice eye appeal.

MS-60 to 70 (Mint State)

Illustrated coin: 1835, John Reich 1. MS-65.
This coin is a "just right" gem, sharply struck and with light toning.

Note: Abbreviations used in die-variety attributions, along with the reference works on which the attributions are based, are discussed on the first page of this chapter. All coins are shown enlarged, for clarity.

Obverse. The rims are more uniform than for the 1809–1828 type, striking is usually very sharp, and any abrasion occurs evenly on both sides. At MS-60, some abrasion and contact marks are evident, most noticeably on the cheek and on the area near the drapery clasp. Luster is present, but may be dull or lifeless, and interrupted in patches. At MS-63, contact marks are very few, and abrasion is hard to detect except under magnification. An MS-65 coin has no abrasion, and contact marks are so minute as to require magnification. Luster should be full and rich. Grades above MS-65 are seen now and again and are defined by having fewer marks as perfection is approached.

Reverse. Abrasion and contact marks are most noticeable on the eagle's neck, the top of the wings, the claws, and the flat band that surrounds the incuse motto.

AU-50, 53, 55, 58 (About Uncirculated)

Obverse. The rims are more uniform than for the 1809–1828 type, striking is usually very sharp, and any abrasion occurs evenly on both sides. Light wear is seen on the cap, the hair below LIBERTY, the hair near the clasp, and the drapery at the bosom. At AU-58, the luster is extensive except in the open area of the field, especially to the right. At AU-50 and 53, luster remains only in protected areas. As is true of all high grades, sharpness of strike can affect the perception of wear.

Illustrated coin: 1832, JR-2. AU-50.

Reverse. Wear is evident on the eagle's neck, the top of the wings, and the claws. At AU-58, luster is nearly full. At AU-50 and 53, there still is significant luster.

EF-40, 45 (Extremely Fine)

Obverse. The rims are more uniform than for the 1809–1828 type, striking is usually very sharp, and the wear occurs evenly on both sides. Wear is most noticeable on the higher areas of the hair. The cap shows wear, as does the cheek. Stars still show their centers. Luster, if present, is in protected areas among the star points and close to the portrait.

Reverse. The wings show wear on the higher areas of the feathers (particularly on the right wing), and some details are lost. Feathers in the neck are light. The eagle's claws show wear. Luster may be present in protected areas.

Illustrated coin: 1835, JR-1. EF-40.
This coin shows some digs at the neck. Iridescent toning frames the borders.

VF-20, 30 (Very Fine)

Obverse. The rims are more uniform than for the 1809–1828 type, striking is usually very sharp, and wear occurs evenly on both sides. Most of the hair is combined into thick tresses without delicate features. The curl on the neck is flat. Most stars retain their interior lines.

Reverse. Wear is most evident on the eagle's neck, to the left of the shield, and on the leaves and claws. Most feathers in the wing remain distinct.

Illustrated coin: 1832, JR-1. VF-30.

F-12, 15 (Fine)

Obverse. The rims are more uniform than for the 1809–1828 type, striking is usually very sharp, and wear occurs evenly on both sides. (For both types the striking is not as important at this and lower grades.) Much of the hair is blended together. The drapery is indistinct along part of its upper edge. Stars have lost detail at the center and some may be flat.

Reverse. Only about a third to half of the feathers remain on the wings (more on the left wing). Some of the horizontal lines in the shield may be worn away.

Illustrated coin: 1835, JR-9. F-12.

VG-8, 10 (Very Good)

Obverse. The hair is less distinct, with the area surrounding the face blended into the facial features. LIBERTY is complete, but weak in areas. Stars are nearly flat.

Reverse. Feathers are fewer and mostly visible on the eagle's left wing. Other details are weaker. All lettering remains easily readable, although some letters may be faint.

Illustrated coin: 1829, JR-10, Curl Base 2 in Date. VG-8.

G-4, 6 (Good)

Obverse. The portrait is mostly in outline, with few interior details discernible. LIBERTY may still be readable or may be partially worn away. Stars are flat at their centers.

Reverse. The eagle is mostly in outline form, although some feathers can be seen in the right wing. Some letters may be light or missing. E PLURIBUS UNUM may be weak, often with some letters worn away.

Illustrated coin: 1829, JR-10, Curl Base 2 in Date. G-4.
Note the scratch across the obverse. This is a well-worn example of this rare variety.

AG-3 (About Good)

Obverse. The portrait is an outline, although traces of LIBERTY can still be seen. The rim is worn down, and some stars are weak. The date remains clear although weak toward the rim.

Reverse. The reverse shows more wear overall than the obverse, with the rim indistinct in areas and many if not most letters worn away.

Illustrated coin: 1834. AG-3.

Proof Capped Bust / Modified Dimes, PF-60 to 70

Proofs were made of each year from 1828 to 1837 and are rare. Beware of "Proofs" that have deeply toned surfaces or fields that show patches of mint frost. Buy slowly and carefully.

Obverse and Reverse. Generally, Proof dimes of this type are of better quality than the 1809–1828 type and have Full Details in almost all areas. Proofs that are extensively cleaned and have many hairlines, or that are dull and grainy, are lower level, such as PF-60 to 62. While every Capped Bust Proof deserves attention, those of lower levels are not of great interest to specialists unless they are of rare die varieties. With medium hairlines, an assigned grade of PF-64 may be in order, and with relatively few hairlines, Gem PF-65. PF-66 should have hairlines so delicate that magnification is needed to see them. Above that, a Proof should be free of such lines.

Illustrated coin: 1835, JR-4. PF-65.
This coin displays a needle-sharp strike with deeply mirrored fields.

1837–1838 LIBERTY SEATED, NO STARS

History. This design with no stars on the obverse was inspired by Christian Gobrecht's silver dollar of 1836. The reverse is of a different design, with a wreath and inscription. The type was made only at the Philadelphia Mint in 1837 and the New Orleans Mint in 1838 (1838-O).

Striking and Sharpness. Check the highest parts of the Liberty Seated figure (especially the head and horizontal shield stripes) and, on the reverse, the leaves. Check the dentils on both sides. Grading and points of weakness on the dime are the same as for the related No Stars half dime.

Availability. The 1837 is readily available in all grades including MS-65 and higher, but is rarer than the half dime of the same type, especially at the Gem level and with good eye appeal. The 1838-O is usually seen with wear and is a rarity if truly MS-63 or above. Beware coins with deep or vivid iridescent toning that often masks friction or evidence of wear. Coins with uniformly grainy etching on both sides have been processed and should be avoided.

MS-60 to 70 (Mint State)

Illustrated coin: 1837. MS-65.
This coin is brilliant, with areas of toning.
Note: All coins are shown enlarged, for clarity.

Obverse. At MS-60, some abrasion and contact marks are evident, most noticeably on the bosom and thighs and knees. Luster is present, but may be dull or lifeless, and interrupted in patches in the large open field. At MS-63, contact marks are very few, and abrasion is hard to detect except under magnification. An MS-65 coin has no abrasion, and contact marks are so minute as to require magnification. Luster should be full and rich. Half dimes of this type can be very beautiful at this level. Grades above MS-65 are seen with regularity, more so than for the related No Stars dimes.

Reverse. Comments apply as for the obverse, except that abrasion and contact marks are most noticeable on the highest parts of the leaves and the ribbon. The field is mainly protected by design elements and does not show abrasion as much as does the open-field obverse on a given coin.

AU-50, 53, 55, 58 (About Uncirculated)

Obverse. Light wear is seen on the thighs and knees, bosom, and head. At AU-58, the luster is extensive, but incomplete. Friction is seen in the large open field. At AU-50 and 53, luster is less.

Reverse. Wear is evident on the leaves and ribbon. An AU-58 coin has nearly full luster, more so than on the obverse, as the design elements protect the small field areas. At AU-50 and 53, there still is significant luster, more than on the obverse.

Illustrated coin: 1838-O. AU-55.
Lustrous and lightly toned, this is an exceptional example of this scarce New Orleans dime.

EF-40, 45 (Extremely Fine)

Obverse. Further wear is seen on all areas, especially the thighs and knees, bosom, and head. Little or no luster is seen.

Reverse. Further wear is seen on all areas, most noticeably at the leaves to each side of the wreath apex and on the ribbon bow knot. Leaves retain details except on the higher areas.

Illustrated coin: 1837. EF-40.

VF-20, 30 (Very Fine)

Obverse. Further wear is seen. Most details of the gown are worn away, except in the lower-relief areas. Hair detail is mostly gone.

Reverse. Wear is more extensive. The highest leaves are flat.

Illustrated coin: 1837. VF-30.

F-12, 15 (Fine)

Obverse. The seated figure is well worn, with little detail remaining. LIBERTY on the shield is fully readable.

Reverse. Most detail of the leaves is gone. The rim is worn, but most if not all dentils are visible.

Illustrated coin: 1838-O. F-15.
The word LIBERTY is full but is weak at ER.

VG-8, 10 (Very Good)

Obverse. The seated figure is mostly flat, without detail. The shield is discernible. In LIBERTY at least three letters are readable at VG-8; a few more at VG-10.

Reverse. Further wear has combined the details of most leaves. The rim is complete, but weak in areas.

Illustrated coin: 1838-O. VG-8.

G-4, 6 (Good)

Obverse. The seated figure is worn smooth. At G-4 there are no letters in LIBERTY remaining. At G-6, traces of one or two can be seen.

Reverse. Wear is more extensive. The leaves are all combined and in outline form. The rim is well worn and missing in some areas, causing the outer parts of the peripheral letters to be worn away in some instances.

Illustrated coin: 1837. G-4.

AG-3 (About Good)

Obverse. The seated figure is mostly visible in outline form, with no detail. The rim is worn away. The date remains clear.

Reverse. Many if not most letters are worn away, as are parts of the wreath.

Illustrated coin: 1838. AG-3.

Proof Liberty Seated / No Stars Dimes, PF-60 to 70

Proofs of 1837 (but not 1838-O) were struck in an unknown small quantity, but seemingly more than the related 1837 half dime. Examples have deep-mirror surfaces and are mostly quite attractive. Carefully examine deeply toned pieces to ensure the toning does not hide flaws.

Illustrated coin: 1837. PF-65.

Obverse and Reverse. Proofs that are extensively cleaned and have many hairlines, or that are dull and grainy, are lower level, such as PF-60 to 62. These command less attention than more visually appealing pieces. Both the half dime and dime Proofs of this year were often cleaned, resulting in coins that have lost much of their mirror surface. With medium hairlines and good reflectivity, an assigned grade of PF-64 is indicated, and with relatively few hairlines, Gem PF-65. In various grades hairlines are most easily seen in the obverse field. PF-66 should have hairlines so delicate that magnification is needed to see them. Above that, a Proof should be free of such lines.

1838–1860 LIBERTY SEATED, WITH STARS

History. Liberty Seated coins of this type were first made without drapery at the elbow. These early issues have the shield tilted sharply to the left. Drapery was soon added, and the shield reoriented, this being the style of the 1840s onward. Made in large quantities, these dimes were widely used in their time.

Striking and Sharpness. On the obverse, check the head of Miss Liberty and the star centers. On the reverse, check the leaves. Check the dentils on both sides. Avoid coins from "tired" or overused dies, as evidenced by grainy rather than lustrous fields (on higher-grade coins).

Availability. These dimes are plentiful as a type, although certain dates and varieties are rare. Most Mint State coins on the market are dated in the 1850s and are often found in Choice and Gem grades.

MS-60 to 70 (Mint State)

Illustrated coin: 1853, With Arrows. MS-66.
The coin shown here is a gorgeous example of the popular Variety 3 type coin.

Note: All coins are shown enlarged, for clarity.

Obverse. At MS-60 some abrasion and contact marks are evident, most noticeably on the bosom and thighs and knees. Luster is present, but may be dull or lifeless. At MS-63, contact marks are very few, and abrasion is hard to detect except under magnification. An MS-65 coin has no abrasions, and contact marks are so minute as to require magnification. Luster should be full and rich.

Reverse. Comments apply as for the obverse, except that abrasion and contact marks are most noticeable on the highest parts of the leaves and the ribbon. The field is mainly protected by design elements and does not show abrasion as much as does the open-field obverse on a given coin.

AU-50, 53, 55, 58 (About Uncirculated)

Obverse. Light wear is seen on the thighs and knees, bosom, and head. At AU-58, the luster is extensive, but incomplete. At AU-50 and 53, luster is less.

Reverse. Wear is evident on the leaves (especially at the top of the wreath) and ribbon. An AU-58 coin has nearly full luster, more so than on the obverse, as the design elements protect the small field areas. At AU-50 and 53 there still is significant luster.

Illustrated coin: 1846. AU-50.
Medium toning is evident on this coin, which is an exceptional representative of this key date.

EF-40, 45 (Extremely Fine)

Obverse. Further wear is seen on all areas, especially the thighs and knees, bosom, and head. Little or no luster is seen.

Reverse. Further wear is seen on all areas, most noticeably at the leaves to each side of the wreath apex and on the ribbon bow knot. Leaves retain details except on the higher areas.

Illustrated coin: 1843-O. EF-40.

VF-20, 30 (Very Fine)

Obverse. Further wear is seen. Most details of the gown are worn away, except in the lower-relief areas. Hair detail is mostly gone.

Reverse. Wear is more extensive. The highest leaves are flat.

Illustrated coin: 1845-O. VF-20.

F-12, 15 (Fine)

Obverse. The seated figure is well worn, with little detail remaining. LIBERTY on the shield is readable but weak in areas. On the 1838–1840 subtype Without Drapery, LIBERTY is in higher relief and will wear more quickly; ER may be missing, but other details are at the Fine level.

Reverse. Most detail of the leaves is gone. The rim is worn, but most if not all dentils are visible.

Illustrated coin: 1838. F-12.

VG-8, 10 (Very Good)

Obverse. The seated figure is mostly flat, without detail. The shield is discernible. In LIBERTY at least three letters are readable but very weak at VG-8, with a few more visible at VG-10. On the 1838–1840 subtype Without Drapery, LIBERTY is in higher relief, and at Very Good only one or two letters may be readable.

Reverse. Further wear has combined the details of most leaves. The rim is complete, but weak in areas. The reverse appears to be in a slightly higher grade than the obverse.

Illustrated coin: 1844. VG-8 or slightly finer.

G-4, 6 (Good)

Obverse. The seated figure is worn smooth. At G-4 there are no letters in LIBERTY remaining. At G-6, traces of one or two can barely be seen (except on the early No Drapery coins).

Reverse. Wear is more extensive. The leaves are all combined and in outline form. The rim is well worn and missing in some areas, causing the outer parts of the peripheral letters to be worn away in some instances.

Illustrated coin: 1839-O. G-4.

AG-3 (About Good)

Obverse. The seated figure is mostly visible in outline form, with no detail. Much of the rim is worn away. The date remains clear.

Reverse. Many if not most letters are worn away, at least in part. The wreath and interior letters are discernible.

Illustrated coin: 1853, Arrows at Date. AG-3.

Proof Liberty Seated / Stars Dimes, PF-60 to 70

Proofs were made of most years and are mostly available from 1854 onward, with 1858 and especially 1859 being those often seen. Most are well struck.

Obverse and Reverse. Proofs that are extensively cleaned and have many hairlines, or that are dull and grainy, are lower level, such as PF-60 to 62. Generally, these are not widely desired, save for the scarce (in any grade) dates of 1844 and 1846. With medium hairlines and good reflectivity, an assigned grade of PF-64 is appropriate, and with relatively few hairlines, Gem PF-65. In various grades hairlines are most easily seen in the obverse field. PF-66 should have hairlines so delicate that magnification is needed to see them. Above that, a Proof should be free of such lines.

Illustrated coin: 1859. PF-64.
This coin displays medium to deep toning.

1860–1891 LIBERTY SEATED, LEGEND OBVERSE

History. Dimes of this type continue the Liberty Seated obverse, now with UNITED STATES OF AMERICA in place of the stars, in combination with a new reverse, designated in Mint correspondence as a "cereal wreath," enclosing ONE DIME in two lines.

Striking and Sharpness. Coins of this type are usually fairly well struck for the earlier years, somewhat erratic in the 1870s, and better from the 1880s to 1891. Many Civil War issues have parallel die striae, this being true of virtually all silver and gold issues of that period. Some issues are found prooflike, this being especially true of dates from 1879 to 1881. Points to check include the head of Miss Liberty on the obverse, the wreath details on the reverse, and the dentils on both sides. Issues of the Carson City Mint in the early 1870s, particularly 1873-CC With Arrows, are often seen with porous surfaces, a post-striking effect.

Note: The word LIBERTY on the shield is not an infallible key to attributing lower grades. On some dies such as those of the early 1870s the shield was in low relief on the coins and wore away slowly, with the result that part or all of the word can be readable in grades below F-12.

Availability. While certain issues of the 1860s through 1881 range from scarce to very rare, those from 1882 to 1891 are for the most part very common, even in choice and gem Mint State.

MS-60 to 70 (Mint State)

Illustrated coin: 1876. MS-66.
This brilliant example has "album toning" around the border, from storage in an old-time holder. This does not detract from its nice eye appeal.

Note: All coins are shown enlarged, for clarity.

Obverse. At MS-60, some abrasion and contact marks are evident, most noticeably on the bosom and thighs and knees. Luster is present, but may be dull or lifeless. At MS-63, contact marks are very few, and abrasion is hard to detect except under magnification. An MS-65 coin has no abrasion, and contact marks are so minute as to require magnification. Luster should be full and rich, except for Philadelphia (but not San Francisco) dimes of the early and mid-1860s. Most Mint State coins of the 1861 to 1865 years, Philadelphia issues, have extensive die striae (from not completely finishing the die). Some low-mintage Philadelphia issues may be prooflike. Clashmarks are common in this era. This is true of contemporary half dimes as well.

Reverse. Comments apply as for the obverse, except that in lower Mint State grades abrasion and contact marks are most noticeable on the highest parts of the leaves and the ribbon, less so on ONE DIME. At MS-65 or higher there are no marks visible to the unaided eye. The field is mainly protected by design elements and does not show abrasion as much as does the obverse on a given coin.

AU-50, 53, 55, 58 (About Uncirculated)

Obverse. Light wear is seen on the thighs and knees, bosom, and head. At AU-58, the luster is extensive, but incomplete. At AU-50 and 53, luster is less.

Reverse. Wear is evident on the leaves and ribbon. An AU-58 coin has nearly full luster, more so than on the obverse, as the design elements protect the small field areas. At AU-50 and 53, there still is significant luster.

Illustrated coin: 1886-S. AU-58.

EF-40, 45 (Extremely Fine)

Obverse. Further wear is seen on all areas, especially the thighs and knees, bosom, and head. Little or no luster is seen.

Reverse. Further wear is seen on all areas, most noticeably at on the high areas of the wreath and on the ribbon. Leaves retain excellent details except on the higher areas.

Illustrated coin: 1864. EF-40.

VF-20, 30 (Very Fine)

Obverse. Further wear is seen. Most details of the gown are worn away, except in the lower-relief areas above and to the right of the shield. Hair detail is mostly or completely gone.

Reverse. Wear is more extensive. The highest leaves are flat.

Illustrated coin: 1873-CC, With Arrows at Date. VF-20.

F-12, 15 (Fine)

Obverse. The seated figure is well worn, but with some detail above and to the right of the shield. LIBERTY is readable but weak in areas.

Reverse. Much detail of the leaves in the higher areas is gone. The rim remains bold.

Illustrated coin: 1871-CC. F-12.
This is a well-worn example of this rare variety. LIBERTY is sharper than seen on the average F-12 coin.

VG-8, 10 (Very Good)

Obverse. The seated figure is more worn, but some detail can be seen above and to the right of the shield. The shield is discernible. In LIBERTY at least the equivalent of two or three letters (can be a combination of partial letters) must be readable but can be very weak at VG-8, with a few more at VG-10. However, LIBERTY is not an infallible way to grade this type, as some varieties have the word in low relief on the die, so it wore away slowly.

Reverse. Further wear has made the wreath flat; now only in outline form with only a few traces of details. The rim is complete.

Illustrated coin: 1873-CC, With Arrows. VG-8. LIBERTY is sharper than usually seen on a Very Good coin, but overall wear indeed suggests this grade.

G-4, 6 (Good)

Obverse. The seated figure is worn smooth. At G-4 there are no letters in LIBERTY remaining on most (but not all) coins. At G-6, traces of one or two letters can barely be seen.

Reverse. The leaves are all combined and in outline form. The rim is clear. On most coins the reverse appears to be in a slightly higher grade than the obverse.

Illustrated coin: 1874-CC. G-4. Note full LIBERTY, but the *other* features are worn away to the G-4 level—an interesting exception to the normal G-4 coin.

AG-3 (About Good)

Obverse. The seated figure is mostly visible in outline form, with only a hint of detail. Much of the rim is worn away. The date remains clear.

Reverse. The wreath and interior letters are partially worn away. The rim is weak.

Illustrated coin: 1891-O. AG-3.

Proof Liberty Seated / Legend Dimes, PF-60 to 70

Proof Liberty Seated dimes of this type were made continuously from 1860 to 1891. They exist today in proportion to their mintages. Some of the 1860s and early 1870s can be carelessly struck, with areas of lightness and sometimes with lint marks. Those of the mid-1870s onward are usually sharply struck and without problems.

Illustrated coin: 1886. PF-67 Cameo.

Obverse and Reverse. Proofs that are extensively cleaned and have many hairlines, or that are dull and grainy, are lower level, such as PF-60 to 62. These are not widely desired, save for the rare (in any grade) dates of 1863 through 1867. With medium hairlines and good reflectivity, an assigned grade of PF-64 is appropriate, and with relatively few hairlines, Gem PF-65. In various grades hairlines are most easily seen in the obverse field. PF-66 should have hairlines so delicate that magnification is needed to see them. Above that, a Proof should be free of such lines.

1892–1916 BARBER

History. Designed by chief engraver Charles E. Barber, the dimes are part of a suite of silver coins including the quarter and half dollar. Each features a large Liberty Head modeled after French coinage. The reverse of the dime continues the "cereal wreath" of the late Liberty Seated era. Examples remained in circulation into the early 1950s, but were not often seen by that time.

Striking and Sharpness. Check the details of the hair on the obverse. The reverse is usually sharp. If weakness is seen, it is usually in the wreath details. The dentils are usually sharp on the obverse and reverse.

Availability. With the exception of the rare 1894-S, of which fewer than a dozen are known, all dates and mintmarks are collectible. Probably 90% or more of the survivors are in lower grades such as AG-3 and G-4. (The same is true of the quarters and half dollars of this design.) The word LIBERTY in the headband, a key to grading, tended to wear away quickly. Relatively few are in grades from Fine upward. Mint State coins are somewhat scarce, this being especially true of the mintmarked issues. Choice and Gem coins are usually of Philadelphia Mint varieties or, if of branch mints, dated after 1905.

MS-60 to 70 (Mint State)

Illustrated coin: 1897-O. MS-65.
This is a lustrous coin, with scattered areas of toning.

Note: All coins are shown enlarged, for clarity.

Obverse. At MS-60, some abrasion and contact marks are evident, most noticeably on the cheek and the obverse field to the right. Luster is present, but may be dull or lifeless. Many Barber coins have been cleaned, especially of the earlier dates. At MS-63, contact marks are very few; abrasion still is evident, but less than at lower levels. An MS-65 coin may have minor abrasion on the cheek, but contact marks are so minute as to require magnification. Luster should be full and rich.

Reverse. Comments apply as for the obverse, except that in lower Mint State grades abrasion and contact marks are most noticeable on the highest parts of the leaves and the ribbon, less so on ONE DIME. At MS-65 or higher, there are no marks visible to the unaided eye. The field is mainly protected by design elements and does not show abrasion as much as does the obverse on a given coin.

AU-50, 53, 55, 58 (About Uncirculated)

Obverse. Light wear is seen on the head, especially on the forward hair under LIBERTY. At AU-58, the luster is extensive, but incomplete, especially on the higher parts and in the right field. At AU-50 and 53, luster is less.

Reverse. Wear is seen on the leaves and ribbon. An AU-58 coin will have nearly full luster, more so than on the obverse, as the design elements protect the small field areas. At AU-50 and 53, there still is significant luster.

Illustrated coin: 1907-S. AU-50.

EF-40, 45 (Extremely Fine)

Obverse. Further wear is seen on the head. The hair above the forehead lacks most detail. LIBERTY shows wear but still is strong.

Reverse. Further wear is seen on all areas, most noticeably at the wreath and ribbon. Leaves retain excellent details except on the higher areas.

Illustrated coin: 1895-O. EF-40.

VF-20, 30 (Very Fine)

Obverse. The head shows more wear, now with nearly all detail gone in the hair above the forehead. LIBERTY shows wear, but is complete. The leaves on the head all show wear, as does the upper part of the cap.

Reverse. Wear is more extensive. The details in the highest leaves are weak or missing, but in lower levels the leaf details remain strong.

Illustrated coin: 1914-S. VF-30.

F-12, 15 (Fine)

Obverse. The head shows extensive wear. LIBERTY, the key place to check, is weak, especially at ER, but is fully readable. The ANA grading standards and *Photograde* adhere to this. PCGS suggests that lightly struck coins "may have letters partially missing." Traditionally, collectors insist on full LIBERTY.

Reverse. Much detail of the leaves in the higher areas is gone. The rim remains bold.

Illustrated coin: 1901-S. F-12.
LIBERTY is readable, but letters ER are light.

VG-8, 10 (Very Good)

Obverse. A net of three letters in LIBERTY must be readable. Traditionally LI is clear, and after that there is a partial letter or two.

Reverse. Further wear has made the wreath flat; now only in outline form with only a few traces of details. The rim is complete.

Illustrated coin: 1895-O. VG-8.

G-4, 6 (Good)

Obverse. The head is in outline form, with the center flat. Most of the rim is there. All letters and the date are full.

Reverse. The leaves are all combined and in outline form. The rim is weak in areas.

Illustrated coin: 1892. G-4.

AG-3 (About Good)

Obverse. The lettering is readable, but the parts near the border may be worn away. The date is clear.

Reverse. The wreath and interior letters are partially worn away. The rim is weak.

Illustrated coin: 1908-S. AG-3.

Proof Barber Dimes, PF-60 to 70

Proof Barber dimes survive in proportion to their mintages. Choice and Gem specimens are more easily found among dimes than among quarters and half dollars of this type. All were originally sold in silver-coin sets. The Proofs of 1892 to 1901 usually have cameo contrast between the designs and the mirror fields. Later Proofs vary in contrast.

Illustrated coin: 1911. PF-67 DC.

Proof dimes of 1911 are rare (only 543 minted), but one with a Deep Cameo finish, as displayed by this coin, is *extremely* rare. The coin is fully struck on both sides, and has not a blemish nor a trace of toning.

Obverse and Reverse. Proofs that are extensively cleaned and have many hairlines, or that are dull and grainy, are lower level, such as PF-60 to 62. These are not widely desired, save for the rare (in any grade) year of 1895, and even so most collectors would rather have a lustrous MS-60 than a dull PF-60. With medium hairlines and good reflectivity, an assigned grade of PF-64 is indicated. Tiny horizontal lines on Miss Liberty's cheek, known as *slide marks,* from National and other album slides scuffing the relief of the cheek, are endemic among Barber silver coins. With noticeable marks of this type, the highest grade assignable is PF-64. With relatively few hairlines, a rating of PF-65 can be given. PF-66 should have hairlines so delicate that magnification is needed to see them. Above that, a Proof should be free of any hairlines or other problems.

1916–1945 WINGED LIBERTY HEAD OR "MERCURY"

History. Designed by sculptor Adolph A. Weinman, who also created the 1916 half dollar, the new dime that replaced the Barber design was officially known as the Winged Liberty Head type, but numismatists nearly universally call it the Mercury dime. The reverse depicts a fasces (symbolic of unity) and an olive branch. Production was continuous from 1916 to 1945, except for 1922, 1932, and 1933, usually but not always at the Philadelphia, Denver, and San Francisco mints. Coins remained in circulation until the late 1960s, when all silver issues disappeared, as their meltdown value became greater than their face value.

Striking and Sharpness. Many Mercury dimes exhibit areas of light striking, most notably in the center horizontal band across the fasces, less so in the lower horizontal band. The bands are composed of two parallel lines with a separation or "split" between. The term FB, or Full Bands, denotes coins with both parallel lines in the center band distinctly separated. *In addition,* some dimes may display weak striking in other areas (not noted by certification services or others), including at areas of the obverse hair, rim, and date. Dimes of 1921 in particular can have FB but poorly struck dates.

Availability. Certain coins, such as 1916-D; 1921-P; 1921-D; 1942, 2 Over 1; and 1942-D, 2 Over 1, are elusive in any grade. Others are generally available in lower circulated grades, although some are scarce. In Mint State many of the issues before 1931 range from scarce to rare. If with FB and also sharply struck in other areas, some are rare. Mint State coins are usually very lustrous. In the marketplace certain scarce early issues such as 1916-D, 1921, and 1921-D are often graded slightly more liberally than are later varieties.

MS-60 to 70 (Mint State)

Illustrated coin: 1919-S. MS-65.
This lustrous example is lightly toned.

Note: All coins are shown enlarged, for clarity.

Obverse. At MS-60, some abrasion and contact marks are evident on the highest part of the portrait, including the hair immediately to the right of the face and the upper left part of the wing. At MS-63, abrasion is slight at best, less so for 64. Album slide marks on the cheek, if present, should not be at any grade above MS-64. An MS-65 coin should display no abrasion or contact marks except under magnification, and MS-66 and higher coins should have none at all. Luster should be full and rich.

Reverse. Comments apply as for the obverse, except that the highest parts of the fasces, these being the horizontal bands, are the places to check. The field is mainly protected by design elements and does not show contact marks readily.

AU-50, 53, 55, 58 (About Uncirculated)

Obverse. Light wear is seen on the cheek, the hair immediately to the right of the face, the left edge of the wing, and the upper right of the wing. At AU-58, the luster is extensive, but incomplete, especially on the higher parts and in the field. At AU-50 and 53, luster is less.

Reverse. Light wear is seen on the higher parts of the fasces. An AU-58 coin has nearly full luster, more so than on the obverse, as the design elements protect the field areas. At AU-50 and 53, there still is significant luster. Generally, the reverse appears to be in a slightly higher grade than the obverse.

Illustrated coin: 1942, 2 Over 1. AU-55.

EF-40, 45 (Extremely Fine)

Obverse. Further wear is seen on the head. Many of the hair details are blended together, as are some feather details at the left side of the wing.

Reverse. The horizontal bands on the fasces may be fused together. The diagonal bands remain in slight relief against the vertical lines (sticks).

Illustrated coin: 1921. EF-40.

VF-20, 30 (Very Fine)

Obverse. The head shows more wear, now with the forehead and cheek mostly blending into the hair. More feather details are gone.

Reverse. Wear is more extensive, but the diagonal and horizontal bands on the fasces still are separated from the thin vertical sticks.

Illustrated coin: 1942, 2 Over 1. VF-20.

F-12, 15 (Fine)

Obverse. The head shows more wear, the hair has only slight detail, and most of the feathers are gone. In the marketplace a coin in F-12 grade usually has slightly less detail than stated by the ANA grading standards or *Photograde*, from modern interpretations.

Reverse. Many of the tiny vertical sticks in the fasces are blended together. The bands can be barely discerned and may be worn away at the highest-relief parts.

Illustrated coin: 1916-D. F-12.

VG-8, 10 (Very Good)

Obverse. Wear is more extensive on the portrait, and only a few feathers are seen on the wing. The outlines between the hair and cap and of the wing are distinct. Lettering is clear, but light in areas.

Reverse. The rim is complete, or it may be slightly worn away in areas. Only a few traces of the vertical sticks remain in the fasces. Current interpretations in the marketplace are given here and are less strict than those listed by the ANA grading standards and *Photograde*. Often, earlier issues are graded more liberally than are later dates.

Illustrated coin: 1916-D. VG-8.

G-4, 6 (Good)

Obverse. Wear is more extensive, with not all of the outline between the hair and the wing visible. The rim is worn into the edges of the letters and often into the bottom of the last numeral in the date.

Reverse. The rim is worn away, as are the outer parts of the letters. The fasces is flat or may show a hint of a vertical stick or two. The leaves are thick from wear. The mintmark, if any, is easily seen.

Illustrated coin: 1916-D. G-4.

AG-3 (About Good)

Obverse. The rim is worn further into the letters. The head is mostly outline all over, except for a few indicates of edges. Folds remain at the top of the cap. The date is clearly visible.

Reverse. The rim is worn further into the letters. The mintmark, if any, is clear but may be worn away slightly at the bottom. The apparent wear is slightly greater on the reverse than on the obverse.

Illustrated coin: 1916-D. AG-3.

Proof Mercury Dimes, PF-60 to 70

Proofs were minted from 1936 to 1942 and are available in proportion to their mintages. The dies were completely polished, including the portrait.

Obverse and Reverse. Proofs that are extensively cleaned and have many hairlines, or that are dull and grainy, are lower level, such as PF-60 to 62. These are not widely desired, and represent coins that have been mistreated. With medium hairlines and good reflectivity, assigned grades of PF-63 or 64 are appropriate. Tiny horizontal lines on Miss Liberty's cheek, known as *slide marks,* from National and other album slides scuffing the relief of the cheek, are common; such coins should not be graded higher than PF-64, but sometimes are. With relatively few hairlines and no noticeable slide marks, a rating of PF-65 can be given. PF-66 should have hairlines so delicate that magnification is needed to see them. Above that, a Proof should be free of any hairlines or other problems.

Illustrated coin: 1939. PF-67.

1946 TO DATE ROOSEVELT

History. After the death of President Franklin D. Roosevelt in 1945 the Treasury rushed to create a ten-cent piece in his honor. This denomination was selected as he was stricken with polio and had been active in the March of Dimes fundraising effort. The obverse of the coin features his portrait, while the reverse illustrates a torch flanked by a branch of olive and a branch of oak.

Striking and Sharpness. Little attention has been paid to the sharpness of these coins. The obverse portrait is such that lightness of strike on the higher points is difficult to detect. On the reverse, check the leaves and the elements of the torch. Some with complete separation on the lower two bands have been called Full Torch (FT), but interest seems to be minimal at this time.

Availability. All are common, although some are more common than others. Mint State coins in higher grades are usually very lustrous.

MS-60 to 70 (Mint State)

Illustrated coin: 1964. MS-66.

Note: All coins are shown enlarged, for clarity.

Obverse. At MS-60, some abrasion and contact marks are evident on the cheek, the hair above the ear, and the neck. At MS-63, abrasion is slight at best, less so for MS-64. An MS-65 coin should display no abrasion or contact marks except under magnification, and MS-66 and higher coins should have none at all. Luster should be full and rich.

Reverse. Comments apply as for the obverse, except that the highest parts of the torch, flame, and leaves are the places to check. On both sides the fields are protected by design elements and do not show contact marks readily.

AU-50, 53, 55, 58 (About Uncirculated)

Obverse. Light wear is seen on the cheek and higher-relief part of the hair. At AU-58, the luster is extensive, but incomplete, especially on the higher parts and in the field. At AU-50 and 53, luster is less.

Reverse. Light wear is seen on the higher parts of the torch and leaves. An AU-58 coin has nearly full luster. At AU-50 and 53, there still is significant luster.

Illustrated coin: 1955. AU-50.

EF-40, 45 (Extremely Fine)

Obverse. Further wear is seen on the head. Some details are gone in the hair to the right of the forehead.

Reverse. Further wear is seen on the torch, but the vertical lines are visible, some just barely. The higher-relief details in the leaves, never strong to begin with, are worn away.

Illustrated coin: 1950-S. EF-40.

The Roosevelt dime is seldom collected in grades lower than EF-40.

Proof Roosevelt Dimes, PF-60 to 70

Proofs have been made of the 1950 to 1964 years, and again from 1968 to date. Those of the 1970s onward usually have frosted or cameo contrast. Special Mint Set (SMS) coins were struck in lieu of Proofs from 1965 to 1967 and in some instances closely resemble Proofs. The majority of Proofs made in recent decades are at high levels, MS-66 to 68 or higher.

Illustrated coin: 1959. PF-68.

Obverse and Reverse. Proofs that are extensively cleaned and have many hairlines, or that are dull and grainy, are lower level, such as PF-60 to 62. These are not widely desired, and represent coins that have been mistreated. Fortunately, only a few Proof Roosevelt dimes are in this category. With medium hairlines and good reflectivity, assigned grades of PF-63 or 64 are appropriate. PF-65 may have hairlines so delicate that magnification is needed to see them. Above that, a Proof should be free of any hairlines or other problems.

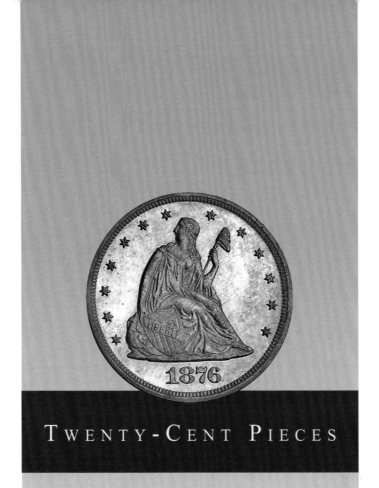

TWENTY-CENT PIECES

TWENTY-CENT PIECES, 1875–1878

History. Twenty-cent pieces were introduced in 1875 as a convenient way to make change in the West (at the time silver coins did not circulate in the East or Midwest). The Liberty Seated design on the obverse and their size caused them to be confused with quarter dollars. Mintage quantities dropped precipitately in 1876, and in 1877 and 1878 only Proofs were struck. Despite the brief time of their production, these coins were still seen in circulation through the early 20th century, by which time they were often casually used as quarters.

Striking and Sharpness. Areas of weakness are common. On the obverse, check the head of Miss Liberty and the stars. The word LIBERTY is *raised* on this coin, a curious departure from other Liberty Seated coins of the era, on which it is recessed or incuse (the Gobrecht silver dollars of 1836 and 1839 being exceptions). On the reverse, check the eagle's feathers, especially the top of the wing on the left, but other areas can be weak as well. Cherrypicking will pay rich dividends. Some 1875-S coins are highly prooflike.

Availability. Most often seen is the large-mintage 1875-S, although the 1875 and 1875-CC are encountered with frequency. The 1876 is quite scarce and when seen is usually in high grades and well struck. The 1876-CC is a rarity, and only about two dozen are known, nearly all of which are Mint State. The eye appeal of Mint State coins can vary widely. The number of letters in LIBERTY on certain coins from Very Good through Very Fine can vary widely in the marketplace.

MS-60 to 70 (Mint State)

Illustrated coin: 1875-S, S Over S. MS-61.
Light toning is evident on the lustrous surfaces of this coin.

Note: All coins are shown enlarged, for clarity.

Obverse. At MS-60, some abrasion and contact marks are evident, most noticeably on the bosom and thighs and knees. Luster is present, but may be dull or lifeless. At MS-63, contact marks are very few, and abrasion is hard to detect except under magnification. An MS-65 coin has no abrasion, and contact marks are sufficiently minute as to require magnification. Check the knees of Liberty and the right field. Luster should be full and rich.

Reverse. Comments apply as for the obverse, except that in lower Mint State grades abrasion and contact marks are most noticeable on the eagle's breast and the top of the wing to the left. At MS-65 or higher, there are no marks visible to the unaided eye. The field is mainly protected by design elements and does not show abrasion as much as does the obverse on a given coin.

AU-50, 53, 55, 58 (About Uncirculated)

Obverse. Light wear is seen on the thighs and knees, bosom, and head. At AU-58, the luster is extensive but incomplete, especially in the right field. At AU-50 and 53, luster is less.

Reverse. Wear is evident on the eagle's breast (the prime focal point) and the top of the wings. An AU-58 coin will have nearly full luster, more so than on the obverse, as the design elements protect the small field areas. At AU-50 and 53, there still are traces of luster.

Illustrated coin: 1875-CC. AU-50.

EF-40, 45 (Extremely Fine)

Obverse. Further wear is seen on all areas, especially the thighs and knees, bosom, and head. Little or no luster is seen on most coins. From this grade downward, sharpness of strike of the stars and the head does not matter to connoisseurs.

Reverse. Further wear is evident on the eagle's breast and wings. Some feathers may be blended together.

Illustrated coin: 1875. EF-40.

VF-20, 30 (Very Fine)

Obverse. Further wear is seen. Most details of the gown are worn away, except in the lower-relief areas above and to the right of the shield. Hair detail is mostly or completely gone. As to whether LIBERTY should be completely readable seems to be a matter of debate. On many coins in the marketplace the word is weak or missing on one to several letters. ANA grading standards and PCGS require full LIBERTY.

Reverse. Wear is more extensive, with more feathers blended together, especially in the right wing. The area below the shield shows more wear.

Illustrated coin: 1875-S. VF-20.

F-12, 15 (Fine)

Obverse. The seated figure is well worn, but with some detail above and to the right of the shield. LIBERTY has no more than two and a half letters missing (per ANA grading standards) or can have three letters missing (per PCGS). In the marketplace, some have four or five letters missing.

Reverse. Wear is extensive, with about half of the feathers flat or blended with others.

Illustrated coin: 1875-S. F-15.
Three letters of LIBERTY remain.

VG-8, 10 (Very Good)

Obverse. The seated figure is more worn, but some detail can be seen above and to the right of the shield. The shield is discernible. In LIBERTY at least a letter or two should be visible per ANA grading standards and PCGS. In the marketplace, many have no letters.

Reverse. Further wear has flattened about half of the feathers. Those remaining are on the inside of the wings. The rim is full and shows many if not most dentils.

Illustrated coin: 1875-CC. VG-8.

G-4, 6 (Good)

Obverse. The seated figure is worn nearly smooth, but with some slight detail above and to the right of the shield. At G-4, there are no letters in LIBERTY remaining. On some at the G-6 level, there may be a trace of letters.

Reverse. Most feathers in the eagle are gone. The border lettering is weak. The rim is visible partially or completely (depending on the strike).

Illustrated coin: 1875-S. G-4.
Note some scratches on this coin.

AG-3 (About Good)

Obverse. The seated figure is mostly visible in outline form, with only a hint of detail. Much of the rim is worn away. The date remains clear.

Reverse. The border letters are partially worn away. The eagle is mostly in outline form, but with a few details discernible. The rim is weak or missing.

Illustrated coin: 1875. AG-3.

Proof Twenty-Cent Pieces, PF-60 to 70

Proof coins were made of all years 1875 to 1878. Most often seen are those of 1875 and 1876. The 1877 and 1878 are Proof-only issues with no related circulation strikes. For some unexplained reason, high-quality Proofs of the last two years are very hard to find. Most have been cleaned or even lightly polished. Many Proofs in the marketplace have been convincingly retoned to mask problems. Proofs are usually well struck, but more than just a few are somewhat flat on the hair details of Miss Liberty.

Illustrated coin: 1876. PF-64.

Obverse and Reverse. Proofs that are extensively cleaned and have many hairlines, or that are dull and grainy, are lower level, such as PF-60 to 62. These are not widely desired. With medium hairlines and good reflectivity, an assigned grade of PF-64 is indicated, and with relatively few hairlines, Gem PF-65. In various grades hairlines are most easily seen in the obverse field. PF-66 should have hairlines so delicate that magnification is needed to see them. Above that, a Proof should be free of such lines.

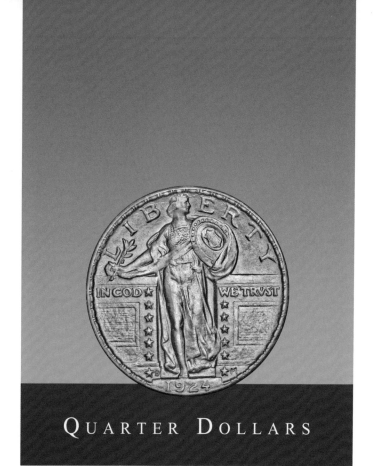

QUARTER DOLLARS

QUARTER DOLLARS, 1796 TO DATE

1796 Draped Bust, Small Eagle

History. The first U.S. quarter dollar was struck in 1796. The design followed that used on other silver coins. As circumstances would have it, only 6,146 were coined, after which there was a hiatus until 1804, by which time a new reverse was used. The 1796 was thus isolated as a one-year type.

Striking and Sharpness. On the obverse, check the hair details and the star centers. Most are well struck. On the reverse, most are well struck except for the head of the eagle, which can be shallow or flat, especially on the B-2 variety (there are two known die varieties for this year, B-1 being the rarer). Rarely is a Full Details coin encountered— a great unappreciated opportunity. The dentils are unusually bold on quarters of this type and serve to frame the motifs. Check for mint-caused planchet adjustment marks. Sharp striking (as on B-2) will add to the value. Most Mint State 1796 quarters have excellent eye appeal.

Availability. Examples are available in all grades from well worn to superb Mint State. Nearly all of the latter are highly prooflike, but there are some exceptions. The numismatic world awaits most of the prooflike gems seen by dealer Abe Kosoff in the early 1940s, but mostly untraced since.

MS-60 to 70 (Mint State)

Illustrated coin: 1796, Browning 2. MS-65.
This is well struck except on the eagle's breast and, especially, the eagle's head.

Note: Abbreviations used in die-variety attributions, along with the reference works on which the attributions are based, are discussed on the first page of this chapter. All coins are shown enlarged, for clarity.

Obverse. At MS-60, some abrasion and contact marks are evident, most noticeably on the cheek, the drapery, and the right field. Luster is present, but may be dull or lifeless, and interrupted in patches. On prooflike coins the contact marks are more prominent. At MS-63, contact marks are very few, and abrasion is hard to detect except under magnification, although this type is sometimes graded liberally due to its rarity. An MS-65 coin has no abrasion, and contact marks are so minute as to require magnification. Luster should be full and rich. Grades above MS-65 are defined by having fewer marks as perfection is approached.

Reverse. Comments apply as for the obverse, except that abrasion and contact marks are most noticeable on the eagle at the center, a situation complicated by the fact that this area is typically flatly struck (except on the B-2 variety). Grading is best done by the obverse, then verified by the reverse. The field area is small and is protected by lettering and the wreath and in any given grade shows fewer marks than on the obverse.

AU-50, 53, 55, 58 (About Uncirculated)

Obverse. Light wear is seen on the hair area above the ear and extending to left of the forehead, on the ribbon, on the drapery at the shoulder, and on the high points of the bust line, more so at AU-50 than at 53 or 55. An AU-58 coin has minimal traces of wear. An AU-50 coin has luster in protected areas among the stars and letters, with little in the open fields or on the portrait. At AU-58, most luster remains in the fields, but is worn away on the highest parts of the motifs.

Reverse. Light wear is seen on the eagle's body (keep in mind this area is nearly always lightly struck) and the edges of the wings. Light wear is seen on the wreath and lettering. Luster is the best key to actual wear. This ranges from perhaps 20% remaining in protected areas (at AU-50) to nearly full mint bloom (at AU-58).

Illustrated coin: 1796, B-2. AU-53.
This coin has rich iridescent toning. A few minor marks are not worthy of special notice.

EF-40, 45 (Extremely Fine)

Obverse. More wear is evident on the upper hair area and the ribbon, and on the drapery and bosom. Excellent detail remains in low-relief areas of the hair. The stars show wear as do the date and letters. Luster, if present at all, is minimal and in protected areas.

Reverse. The eagle shows more wear, this being the focal point to check. Most feathers remain on the interior areas of the wings. Additional wear is on the wreath and letters, but many details are present. Some luster may be seen in protected areas and if present is slightly more abundant than on the obverse.

Illustrated coin: 1796, B-2. EF-40.
Here is an attractive, problem-free coin.

VF-20, 30 (Very Fine)

Obverse. The higher-relief areas of hair are well worn at VF-20, less so at VF-30, although much detail remains on the areas below the ear. The drapery and bosom show extensive wear. The stars have more wear, making them appear larger (an optical illusion seen on most worn silver coins of this era).

Reverse. The body of the eagle shows few if any feathers, while the wings have about half of the feathers visible, mostly on the right wing, depending on the strike. The leaves lack most detail and are in outline form. Scattered, non-disfiguring marks are normal for this and lower grades. Any major defects should be noted separately.

Illustrated coin: 1796, B-2. VF-20.
A few faint scratches are not unusual for coins in this grade.

F-12, 15 (Fine)

Obverse. Wear is more extensive than on a Very Fine coin, particularly noticeable on the hair, face, and bosom. The stars appear larger. About half the hair detail remains, most noticeably behind the neck and shoulder. The dentils remain strong (while on most other silver denominations of this design they become weak at this grade level).

Reverse. Wear is more extensive. Now feather details are diminished, with fewer than half remaining on the wings. The wreath and lettering are worn further, and the rim is slightly weak in areas, although most dentils can be seen.

Illustrated coin: 1796, B-2. F-15.

VG-8, 10 (Very Good)

Obverse. The portrait is mostly seen in outline form, with most hair strands gone, although there is some definition at the back of the hair and behind the shoulder. The ear is discernible, as is the eye. The stars appear larger still, again an illusion. The rim is weak in areas. Most dentils are seen, some of them even bold. LIBERTY and the date are readable and usually full, although some letters may be weak at their tops (the high rim and dentils protect the design more on the quarter dollar than on other silver coins of this type).

Illustrated coin: 1796, B-2. VG-8.
Some granularity is not unusual for the grade.

Reverse. The eagle is mostly an outline, with parts blending into the field (on lighter strikes), although some slight feather detail can be seen on the right wing. The rim is worn, as are the letters, with some weak, but the motto is readable. Most dentils remain clear.

G-4, 6 (Good)

Obverse. Wear is more extensive. The head is an outline. The rim still is present, as are most of the dentils, most well defined. LIBERTY is worn, but complete. The date is bold.

Reverse. The eagle is flat and discernible in outline form, blending into the field in areas. The wreath is well worn. Some of the letters may be partly missing. Some rim areas and dentils are discernible. At this level some "averaging" can be done. If the letters are stronger than usual in one area, but some are missing in another area, the coin can still qualify as G-4.

Illustrated coin: 1796, B-2. G-4.
Overall this is a nice coin showing extensive wear. It has some pin scratches above the eagle.

AG-3 (About Good)

Obverse. Wear is so extensive that the coin is barely identifiable. The head is in outline form, LIBERTY is mostly gone, same for the stars, and the date, while readable, may be partially worn away.

Reverse. The reverse is well worn, with parts of the wreath and lettering missing.

Illustrated coin: 1796. AG-3.

1804–1807 DRAPED BUST, HERALDIC EAGLE

History. The production of silver coins during a given year was dependent upon requests made by depositors of silver, as such pieces were not made for the Mint's own account. After 1796 no quarters were struck until 1804, still using the Draped Bust obverse, but with the new Heraldic Eagle reverse. The latter was similar to that used on other silver (and gold) denominations of the time.

Striking and Sharpness. Virtually all are lightly struck in one area or another. Hope for sharpness, but expect weakness! On the obverse, check the hair details and the star centers. On the reverse, check the shield, stars, feathers, and other design elements. The dentils and rims on both sides often have problems. Quarters of the last year, 1807, are usually the lightest struck. Also check for adjustment marks. Sharp striking (seldom seen) and excellent eye appeal add to a coin's value. This is a series often misgraded due to lack of understanding of its strike anomalies.

Availability. All dates are collectible, with 1804 being scarcer than the others and a rarity in Mint State. Some die varieties are rare. High-grade coins with Full Details are very rare for all varieties.

MS-60 to 70 (Mint State)

Illustrated coin: 1806, Browning 9. MS-66.
This coin is lightly struck on the right obverse stars and at the center of the reverse. Some planchet adjustment marks are mostly hidden. Some tiny carbon streaks are on the obverse (seemingly typical for B-9). This is among the finest known for this variety.

Note: Abbreviations used in die-variety attributions, along with the reference works on which the attributions are based, are discussed on the first page of this chapter. All coins are shown enlarged, for clarity.

Obverse. At MS-60, some abrasion and contact marks are evident, most noticeably on the cheek, the drapery, and the right field. Luster is present, but may be dull or lifeless, and interrupted in patches. At MS-63, contact marks are very few, and abrasion is hard to detect except under magnification. An MS-65 coin will have no abrasion, and contact marks are so minute as to require magnification. Luster should be full and rich. Coins graded above MS-65 are more theoretical than actual for this type—but they do exist, and are defined by having fewer marks as perfection is approached. As noted in the introduction, expect weakness in some areas.

Reverse. Comments apply as for the obverse, except that abrasion and contact marks are most noticeable on the eagle's neck, the tips of the wing, and the tail. The field area is complex, without much open space, given the stars above the eagle, the arrows and olive branch, and other features. Accordingly, marks are not as noticeable as on the obverse.

AU-50, 53, 55, 58 (About Uncirculated)

Obverse. Light wear is seen on the hair area above the ear and extending to left of the forehead, on the ribbon, and on the drapery at the shoulder, more so at AU-50 than at 53 or 55. An AU-58 coin has minimal traces of wear. An AU-50 coin has luster in protected areas among the stars and letters, with little in the open fields or on the portrait. At AU-58, most luster is present in the fields, but is worn away on the highest parts of the motifs.

Illustrated coin: 1804, B-1. AU-58.
Lightly struck on the obverse stars. The reverse has some light areas but is sharp overall. A few planchet adjustment marks are visible. Abundant luster and good eye appeal rank this as an exceptional example of this date, the most difficult of the type to find in high grades.

Reverse. Comments as preceding, except that the eagle's neck, the tips and top of the wings, the clouds, and the tail now show noticeable wear, as do other features. Luster ranges from perhaps 20% remaining in protected areas (at AU-50) to nearly full mint bloom (at AU-58). Often the reverse retains much more luster than the obverse, more so on quarter dollars than on other denominations of this design.

EF-40, 45 (Extremely Fine)

Obverse. More wear is evident on the upper hair area and the ribbon, and on the drapery at the shoulder and the bosom. Excellent detail remains in low-relief areas of the hair. The stars show wear, as do the date and letters (note: on most coins of this type the stars are softly struck). Luster, if present at all, is minimal and in protected areas.

Reverse. Wear is greater than on an About Uncirculated coin, overall. The neck lacks feather detail on its highest points. Feathers have lost some detail near the edges of the wings, and some areas of the horizontal lines in the shield may be blended together. Some traces of luster may be seen, more so at EF-45 than at EF-40.

Illustrated coin: 1804, B-1. EF-45.

VF-20, 30 (Very Fine)

Obverse. The higher-relief areas of hair are well worn at VF-20, less so at VF-30. The drapery and bosom show extensive wear. The stars have more wear, making them appear larger (an optical illusion seen on most worn silver coins of this era).

Reverse. Wear is greater, including on the shield and wing feathers, although more than half of the feathers are defined. Star centers are flat. Other areas have lost detail as well. Some letters in the motto may be missing, depending on the strike.

Illustrated coin: 1807, B-2. VF-25.
Note some scattered marks and granularity. This date is notoriously weakly struck, but at Very Fine this is not as noticeable as in higher grades.

F-12, 15 (Fine)

Obverse. Wear is more extensive than on a Very Fine coin, particularly noticeable on the hair, face, and bosom. The stars appear larger. About half the hair detail remains with the tresses fused so as to appear thick, most noticeably behind the neck and shoulder. The rim may be partially worn away and blend into the field.

Reverse. Wear is even more extensive, with the shield and wing feathers being points to observe. About half of the feathers can be seen. The incuse E PLURIBUS UNUM may have a few letters worn away. The clouds all seem to be connected. The stars are weak. Parts of the border and lettering may be weak. As with most quarters of this type, peculiarities of striking can account for some weakness.

Illustrated coin: 1805, B-1. F-12.
Note some scratches on the shield.

VG-8, 10 (Very Good)

Obverse. The portrait is mostly seen in outline form, with most hair strands gone, although there is slight definition at the back of the hair and behind the shoulder. The ear is discernible, as is the eye. The stars appear larger still, again an illusion. The rim is weak in areas. LIBERTY and the date are readable and usually full, although some letters may be weak at their tops.

Reverse. Wear is more extensive. Half or so of the letters in the motto are worn away. Most feathers are worn away, although separation of some of the lower feathers may be seen. Some stars are faint. The border blends into the field in areas (depending on striking), and some letters are weak.

Illustrated coin: 1805, B-4. VG-8.

G-4, 6 (Good)

Obverse. Wear is more extensive, and some stars may be partly missing. The head is an outline. The eye is visible only in outline form. The rim is well worn or even missing in areas. LIBERTY is worn, and parts of some letters may be missing, but elements of all should be readable. The date is readable, but worn.

Reverse. Wear is more extensive. The upper part of the eagle is flat, and feathers are noticeable only at some (but not necessarily all) of the lower edge of the wings, and do not have detail. The shield lacks most of its detail. Only a few letters of the motto can be seen (depending on striking). The rim is worn extensively, and a few letters may be missing.

Illustrated coin: 1805, B-1. G-4.
Note the small edge cut near the first star.

AG-3 (About Good)

Obverse. Wear is so extensive that the coin is barely identifiable. The head is in outline form, LIBERTY is mostly gone. Same for the stars. The date, while readable, may be partially worn away.

Reverse. Extensive wear is seen overall, with the rim worn away and some areas worn smooth. The eagle can be discerned in outline form, but not necessarily completely. A few stray motto letters may remain. Sometimes the obverse appears to be more worn than the reverse, or vice-versa.

Illustrated coin: 1807, B-1. AG-3.
This coin is slightly finer than AG-3 overall, but is reduced in grade due to a circular scratch at the center of the reverse.

1815–1828 CAPPED BUST, LARGE DIAMETER

History. John Reich's Capped Bust motif introduced on the half dollar of 1807 was not used on the quarter until 1815. This motif was continued until 1828, although none were coined with the dates 1816, 1817, or 1826.

Striking and Sharpness. Striking sharpness varies. On the obverse, check the hair of Miss Liberty, the broach clasp (a particular point of observation), and the star centers. On this type the stars are often well defined (in contrast with half dollars of the same design). On the reverse, check the neck of the eagle and its wings, and the letters. Dentils on both sides should be examined. When weakness occurs it is usually in the center.

Availability. Most quarters of this type range from slightly scarce to rare, with the 1823, 3 Over 2, and the 1827 being famous rarities. Typical coins range from well worn to Fine and Very Fine. About Uncirculated and Mint State coins are elusive (and are usually dated before the 1820s), and gems are particularly rare.

MS-60 to 70 (Mint State)

Illustrated coin: 1818, 8 Over 5, Browning 1. MS-65.

Note some lightness of strike on the lower curls on the obverse and the eagle's neck on the reverse. This is an attractive example of a popular overdate.

Note: Abbreviations used in die-variety attributions, along with the reference works on which the attributions are based, are discussed on the first page of this chapter. All coins are shown enlarged, for clarity.

Obverse. At MS-60, some abrasion and contact marks are evident, most noticeably on the cheek, the hair below LIBERTY, and the area near the drapery clasp. Luster is present, but may be dull or lifeless, and interrupted in patches. At MS-63, contact marks are very few, and abrasion is hard to detect except under magnification. An MS-65 coin has no abrasion, and contact marks are so minute as to require magnification. Luster should be full and rich. Grades above MS-65 are seen now and again and are defined by having fewer marks as perfection is approached.

Reverse. Comments apply as for the obverse, except that abrasion and contact marks are most noticeable on the eagle's neck, the top of the wings, the claws, and the flat band that surrounds the incuse motto. The field is mainly protected by design elements and does not show abrasion as much as does the obverse on a given coin.

AU-50, 53, 55, 58 (About Uncirculated)

Obverse. Light wear is seen on the cap, the hair below LIBERTY, the curl on the neck, the hair near the clasp, and the drapery. At AU-58, the luster is extensive except in the open area of the field, especially to the right. At AU-50 and 53, luster remains only in protected areas.

Reverse. Wear is evident on the eagle's neck, the top of the wings, the claws, and the flat band above the eagle. An AU-58 coin has nearly full luster. At AU-50 and 53, there still is significant luster, more than on the obverse. Generally, light wear is most obvious on the obverse.

Illustrated coin: 1815. AU-50.
This About Uncirculated example has gray and light lilac toning.

EF-40, 45 (Extremely Fine)

Obverse. Wear is more extensive, most noticeably on the higher areas of the hair. The cap shows more wear, as does the cheek. Most or all stars have some radial lines visible (unless lightly struck, as *many* are). Luster, if present, is in protected areas among the star points and close to the portrait.

Reverse. The wings show wear on the higher areas of the feathers, and some details are lost. Feathers in the neck are light on some (but not on especially sharp strikes). The eagle's claws and the leaves show wear. Luster may be present in protected areas, even if there is little or none on the obverse.

Illustrated coin: 1818, B-2. EF-40.
This coin was lightly cleaned long ago and has nicely retoned, although most graders would probably simply call it EF-40. It is attractive for the grade.

VF-20, 30 (Very Fine)

Obverse. Wear is more extensive, and most of the hair is combined into thick tresses without delicate features. The curl on the neck is flat. Details of the drapery are well defined at the lower edge. Unless they were weakly struck, the stars are mostly flat although a few may retain radial lines.

Reverse. Wear is most evident on the eagle's neck, to the left of the shield, and on the leaves and claws. Most feathers in the wing remain distinct, but some show light wear. Overall, the reverse on most quarters at this level shows less wear than the obverse.

Illustrated coin: 1825, 5 Over 4, B-2. VF-20.
Overall this is a pleasing coin. A few tiny scratches are masked by the toning; as with any accurate description, these should be noted.

F-12, 15 (Fine)

Obverse. Wear is more extensive, with much of the hair blended together. The drapery is indistinct at its upper edge. The stars are flat.

Reverse. Wear is more extensive, now with only about half of the feathers remaining on the wings. The claws on the right are fused at their upper parts.

Illustrated coin: 1821, B-5. F-12 or slightly finer.
Note that some light scratches are mostly covered by toning.

VG-8, 10 (Very Good)

Obverse. The hair is less distinct, with the area above the face blended into the facial features. LIBERTY is complete, but can be weak in areas. At the left the drapery and bosom are blended together in a flat area. The rim is worn away in areas, and blends into the field.

Reverse. Feathers are fewer and mostly on the eagle's wing to the left. Other details are weaker. E PLURIBUS UNUM is weak, perhaps with some letters missing. All border lettering remains easily readable.

Illustrated coin: 1815, B-1.
This is a well-worn, problem-free example from the inaugural year of this type.

G-4, 6 (Good)

Obverse. The portrait is mostly in outline, with few interior details discernible. LIBERTY may still be readable or may be partially worn away, depending on the variety. Most or all of the border is worn away, and the outer parts of the stars are weak.

Reverse. The eagle mostly is in outline form, although some feathers can be seen in the wing to the left. All letters around the border are clear. E PLURIBUS UNUM is mostly or completely worn away.

Illustrated coin: 1822, 25 Over 50 C error reverse, B-2. G-4.

AG-3 (About Good)

Obverse. The portrait is an outline. Most of LIB-ERTY can still be seen. Stars are weak or missing toward what used to be the rim. The date remains clear, but may be weak at the bottom.

Reverse. The reverse shows more wear than at G-4, but parts of the rim may remain clear. On many coins the reverse, if graded separately, could be called G-4.

Illustrated coin: 1822, 25 Over 50 C error reverse, B-2. AG-3. This is a low-grade but very desirable example; the date is very clear and the die cutting error on the reverse is well defined.

Proof Capped Bust / Large Quarters, PF-60 to 70

Proofs were struck for inclusion in sets and for numismatists. All authentic Proofs are rarities. Some deeply toned coins, and coins with patches of mint luster, have been described as Proofs but are mostly impostors, some of which have been certified or have "papers" signed by Walter Breen. Be careful!

Obverse and Reverse. Proofs that are extensively cleaned and have many hairlines, or that are dull and grainy, are lower level, such as PF-60 to 62. While any early Proof garners collector interest, lower levels are not of great interest to specialists unless they are of rare die varieties. With medium hairlines, an assigned grade of PF-64 may be in order, and with relatively few, Gem PF-65. PF-66 should have hairlines so delicate that magnification is needed to see them. Above that, a Proof should be free of such lines. Grading is highly subjective with early Proofs, and eye appeal also is a factor.

Illustrated coin: 1825, 5 Over 3, B-2. PF-63.

1831–1838 CAPPED BUST, SMALL DIAMETER

History. Quarter dollars of this type are similar in overall appearance to the preceding, but with important differences. The diameter is reduced, the motto E PLURIBUS UNUM is no longer on the reverse, and the dentils are smaller and are restyled.

Striking and Sharpness. Nearly all coins of this type are very well struck. There are exceptions, which connoisseurs would be smart to avoid. Check all areas for sharpness. Some quarters of 1833 and 1834 are from rusted or otherwise imperfect dies and can be less attractive than coins from undamaged dies.

Availability. Examples are readily available of all dates, including many of the first year of issue. Mint frost ranges from satiny (usual) to deeply frosty.

MS-60 to 70 (Mint State)

Illustrated coin: 1831, Browning 2. MS-66.
This coin is well struck in most areas, with minor exceptions (such as stars 12 and 13); it has excellent eye appeal.

Note: Abbreviations used in die-variety attributions, along with the reference works on which the attributions are based, are discussed on the first page of this chapter. All coins are shown enlarged, for clarity.

Obverse. Grading is similar to the 1815–1828 type, except the rims are more uniform, striking is usually very sharp, and the wear occurs evenly on both sides. At MS-60, some abrasion and contact marks are evident, most noticeably on the cheek, the hair below LIBERTY, and the area near the drapery clasp. Luster is present, but may be dull or lifeless, and interrupted in patches. At MS-63, contact marks are very few, and abrasion is hard to detect except under magnification. An MS-65 coin has no abrasion, and contact marks are so minute as to require magnification. Luster should be full and rich. Grades above MS-65 are seen now and again, and are defined by having fewer marks as perfection is approached.

Reverse. Comments apply as for the obverse, except that abrasion and contact marks are most noticeable on the eagle's neck, the top of the wings, the claws, and the flat band that surrounds the incuse motto.

AU-50, 53, 55, 58 (About Uncirculated)

Obverse. Grading guidelines are the same as for the 1815–1828 type, except the rims are more uniform, striking is usually very sharp, and the wear occurs evenly on both sides. Light wear is seen on the cap, the hair below LIBERTY, the curl on the neck, the hair near the clasp, and the drapery. At AU-58, the luster is extensive except in the open area of the field, especially to the right. At AU-50 and 53, luster remains only in protected areas.

Illustrated coin: 1836, B-3. AU-50.

Reverse. Wear is evident on the eagle's neck, the top of the wings, the claws, and the flat band above the eagle. An AU-58 coin has nearly full luster. At AU-50 and 53, there still is significant luster, more than on the obverse.

EF-40, 45 (Extremely Fine)

Obverse. Grading guidelines are the same as for the 1815–1828 type, except the rims are more uniform, striking is usually very sharp, and the wear occurs evenly on both sides. Wear is most noticeable on the higher areas of the hair. The cap shows more wear, as does the cheek. Most or all stars have some radial lines visible. Luster, if present, is in protected areas among the star points and close to the portrait.

Illustrated coin: 1835. EF-40.

Reverse. The wings show wear on the higher areas of the feathers, and some details are lost. Feathers in the neck are light on some coins. The eagle's claws and the leaves show wear. Luster may be present in protected areas.

VF-20, 30 (Very Fine)

Obverse. Grading guidelines are the same as for the 1815–1828 type, except the rims are more uniform, striking is usually very sharp, and the wear occurs evenly on both sides. Most of the hair is combined into thick tresses without delicate features. The curl on the neck is flat. Details of the drapery are well defined at the lower edge. The stars are mostly flat, although a few may retain radial lines.

Illustrated coin: 1831, B-4. VF-30.

Reverse. Wear is most evident on the eagle's neck, to the left of the shield, and on the leaves and claws. Most feathers in the wing remain distinct, but some show light wear.

F-12, 15 (Fine)

Obverse. Grading guidelines are the same as for the 1815–1828 type, except the rims are more uniform, striking is usually very sharp, and the wear occurs evenly on both sides. For both types, the striking is not as important at this and lower grade levels. Much of the hair is blended together. The drapery is indistinct at its upper edge. The stars are flat.

Reverse. Wear is more extensive, now with only about half of the feathers remaining on the wings. The claws on the right are fused at their upper parts.

Illustrated coin: 1835, B-3. F-15.

VG-8, 10 (Very Good)

Obverse. The hair is less distinct, with the area above the face blended into the facial features. LIBERTY is complete, but can be weak in areas. At the left the drapery and bosom are blended together in a flat area. The rim is worn away in areas, and blends into the field.

Reverse. Feathers are fewer and mostly on the eagle's left wing. Other details are weaker. All border lettering remains easily readable.

Illustrated coin: 1832, B-1. VG-10.

G-4, 6 (Good)

Obverse. The portrait is mostly in outline, with few interior details discernible. LIBERTY may still be readable or may be partially worn away, depending on the variety. Most or all of the border is worn away, and the outer parts of the stars are weak.

Reverse. The eagle mostly is in outline form, although some feathers can be seen in the left wing. All letters around the border are clear.

Illustrated coin: 1834. G-6.

AG-3 (About Good)

Obverse. The portrait is an outline. Most of LIBERTY can still be seen. Stars are weak or missing toward what used to be the rim. The date remains clear, but may be weak at the bottom.

Reverse. The reverse shows more wear than at G-4, but parts of the rim may remain clear.

Illustrated coin: 1835. AG-3.
Note the planchet laminations on the reverse.

Proof Capped Bust / Small Quarters, PF-60 to 70

Proofs were struck of all dates for inclusion in sets and for sale or trade to numismatists. Most coins offered as Proofs are indeed of this format. Avoid any that show patches of mint frost or that are darkly toned.

Illustrated coin: 1835, B-7. PF-63.
Some scattered marks in the obverse field are mostly masked by toning.

Obverse and Reverse. Proofs that are extensively cleaned and have many hairlines, or that are dull and grainy, are lower level, such as PF-60 to 62. While any early Proof coin will attract attention, lower-level specimens are not of great interest to specialists unless they are of rare die varieties. With medium hairlines, an assigned grade of PF-64 may be in order and with relatively few, Gem PF-65. PF-66 should have hairlines so delicate that magnification is needed to see them. Above that, a Proof should be free of such lines. Grading is highly subjective with early Proofs, and eye appeal also is a factor.

1838–1891 LIBERTY SEATED

History. Liberty Seated quarters were introduced in 1838. Early issues lack drapery at the elbow and have small lettering on the reverse, giving them a particularly attractive appearance. Drapery was added in 1840 and continued afterward. Mintages varied. These coins were popular in their era and remained in circulation through the early 20th century.

Striking and Sharpness. On the obverse, check the head of Miss Liberty and the star centers. If these are sharp, then check the central part of the seated figure. On the reverse, check the eagle, particularly the area to the lower left of the shield. Check the dentils on both sides. Generally, the earliest issues are well struck, as are those of the 1880s onward. The word LIBERTY is not an infallible guide to grading at lower levels, as on some dies the shield was in lower relief, and the letters wore away less quickly. This guideline should be used in combination with other features.

Availability. Coins of this type are available in proportion to their mintages. Mint State coins can range from rare to exceedingly rare, as they were mostly ignored by numismatists until the series ended. Quality can vary widely, especially among branch-mint coins.

MS-60 to 70 (Mint State)

Illustrated coin: 1853, With Arrows. MS-66.
This coin is an ultra gem.

Note: All coins are shown enlarged, for clarity.

Obverse. At MS-60, some abrasion and contact marks are evident, most noticeably on the bosom and thighs and knees. Luster is present, but may be dull or lifeless. At MS-63, contact marks are very few, and abrasion is hard to detect except under magnification. An MS-65 coin has no abrasion, and contact marks are sufficiently minute as to require magnification. Check the knees of Liberty and the right field. Luster should be full and rich. Most Mint State coins of the 1861 to 1865 years, Philadelphia issues, have extensive die striae (from not completely finishing the die).

Reverse. Comments apply as for the obverse, except that in lower Mint State grades abrasion and contact marks are most noticeable on the eagle's neck, the claws, and the top of the wings (harder to see there, however). At MS-65 or higher there are no marks visible to the unaided eye. The field is mainly protected by design elements and does not show abrasion as much as does the obverse on a given coin.

AU-50, 53, 55, 58 (About Uncirculated)

Obverse. Light wear is seen on the thighs and knees, bosom, and head. At AU-58, the luster is extensive, but incomplete, especially in the right field. At AU-50 and 53, luster is less.

Reverse. Wear is evident on the eagle's neck, claws, and top of the wings. An AU-58 coin has nearly full luster, more so than on the obverse, as the design elements protect the small field areas. At AU-50 and 53, there still are traces of luster.

Illustrated coin: 1840. AU-53.
The example shown has light gray and golden toning.

EF-40, 45 (Extremely Fine)

Obverse. Further wear is seen on all areas, especially the thighs and knees, bosom, and head. Little or no luster is seen on most coins. From this grade downward, sharpness of strike of the stars and the head does not matter to connoisseurs.

Reverse. Further wear is evident on the eagle's neck, claws, and wings. Some feathers in the right wing may be blended together.

Illustrated coin: 1851-O. EF-40.

VF-20, 30 (Very Fine)

Obverse. Further wear is seen. Most details of the gown are worn away, except in the lower-relief areas above and to the right of the shield. Hair detail is mostly or completely gone.

Reverse. Wear is more extensive, with more feathers blended together, especially in the right wing. The area below the shield shows more wear.

Illustrated coin: 1870-CC. VF-20.

F-12, 15 (Fine)

Obverse. The seated figure is well worn, but with some detail above and to the right of the shield. LIBERTY is readable but weak in areas.

Reverse. Wear is extensive, with about half of the feathers flat or blended with others.

Illustrated coin: 1864-S. F-12.

VG-8, 10 (Very Good)

Obverse. The seated figure is more worn, but some detail can be seen above and to the right of the shield. The shield is discernible. In LIBERTY at least the equivalent of two or three letters (can be a combination of partial letters) must be readable but can be very weak at VG-8, with a few more visible at VG-10. However, LIBERTY is not an infallible guide to grade this type, as some varieties had the word in low relief on the die, so it wore away slowly.

Illustrated coin: 1849-O. VG-8.

Reverse. Further wear has flattened all but a few feathers, and the horizontal lines of the shield are indistinct. The leaves are only in outline form. The rim is visible all around, as are the ends of most dentils.

G-4, 6 (Good)

Obverse. The seated figure is worn smooth. At G-4 there are no letters in LIBERTY remaining on most (but not all) coins; some coins, especially of the early 1870s, are exceptions. At G-6, traces of one or two can barely be seen.

Reverse. The designs are only in outline form, although some vertical shield stripes can be seen on some. The rim is worn down, and tops of the border letters are weak or worn away, although the inscription can still be read.

Illustrated coin: 1872-CC. G-4.
Assigned this grade by a third-party certification service, the reverse of this coin is slightly more worn than usual for G-4—probably the result of a bit of optimism in view of the rarity of this issue.

AG-3 (About Good)

Obverse. The seated figure is mostly visible in outline form, with only a hint of detail. Much of the rim is worn away. The date remains clear.

Reverse. The border letters are partially worn away. The eagle is mostly in outline form, but with a few details discernible. The rim is weak or missing.

Illustrated coin: 1856-O. AG-3.

Proof Liberty Quarter Dollars, PF-60 to 70

Proofs of the earlier years are very rare. Beginning with 1856, they were made in larger numbers, and from 1859 onward the yearly production was in the multiple hundreds. Examples of the later era are readily available today. Some (1858 is an example) have lint marks, and others can have light striking (particularly in the 1870s and 1880s). Avoid "problem" coins and those with deep or artificial (and often colorful) toning.

Illustrated coin: 1843. PF-53.
This circulated Proof has some of the original mirror surface remaining in protected areas.

Obverse and Reverse. Proofs that are extensively cleaned and have many hairlines, or that are dull and grainy, are lower level, such as PF-60 to 62. These are not widely desired by connoisseurs. With medium hairlines and good reflectivity, an assigned grade of PF-64 is appropriate and with relatively few hairlines, Gem PF-65. In various grades hairlines are most easily seen in the obverse field. PF-66 should have hairlines so delicate that magnification is needed to see them. Above that, a Proof should be free of such lines.

1892–1916 BARBER

History. Designed by Charles E. Barber, the "Barber" or Liberty Head quarters have the same motif used on dimes and half dollars of the era. The reverse depicts a heraldic eagle. Production was continuous from 1892 to 1916.

Striking and Sharpness. On the obverse, check the hair details and other features. On the reverse, the eagle's leg at the lower right and the arrows can be weak, aspects hardly ever mentioned. Also check the upper right of the shield and the nearby wing. Cherry-picking is advised. The design of the Barber dime, quarter, and half dollar is such that once pieces entered circulation and acquired wear, the word LIBERTY on the headband tended to disappear quickly. There was little interest in saving Barber coins from circulation until the 1930s, with interest accelerating in the 1940s. By that time most were in grades of AG-3 or G-4, occasionally VG-8, and hardly ever finer. Today, among circulation-strike Barber quarters, probably 90% or more in existence are G-4 or below, a curious situation repeated in the dime and half dollar series.

Availability. Most seen in the marketplace are well worn. Coins that are Fine or better are much scarcer. Mint State coins are available of all dates and mints, but some are very elusive. The 1896-S, 1901-S, and 1913-S are the key dates in all grades.

MS-60 to 70 (Mint State)

Illustrated coin: 1913. MS-62.
This is an attractive, lightly toned example of a later-date Barber quarter.

Note: All coins are shown enlarged, for clarity.

Obverse. At MS-60, some abrasion and contact marks are evident, most noticeably on the cheek and the obverse field to the right. Luster is present, but may be dull or lifeless. Many Barber coins have been cleaned, especially of the earlier dates. At MS-63, contact marks are very few. Abrasion still is evident, but less than at lower levels. Indeed, the cheek of Miss Liberty virtually showcases abrasion. An MS-65 coin may have minor abrasion, but contact marks are so minute as to require magnification. Luster should be full and rich.

Reverse. Comments apply as for the obverse, except that in lower Mint State grades abrasion and contact marks are most noticeable on the head and tail of the eagle and on the tips of the wings. At MS-65 or higher, there are no marks visible to the unaided eye. The field is mainly protected by design elements, and often appears to grade a point or two higher than the obverse.

AU-50, 53, 55, 58 (About Uncirculated)

Obverse. Light wear is seen on the head, especially on the forward hair under LIBERTY. At AU-58, the luster is extensive but incomplete, especially on the higher parts and in the right field. At AU-50 and 53, luster is less.

Reverse. Wear is evident on the head and tail of the eagle and on the tips of the wings. At AU-50 and 53, there still is significant luster. An AU-58 coin (as determined by the obverse) can have the reverse appear to be full Mint State.

Illustrated coin: 1915-S. AU-50.
Note the typical light striking on the eagle's talons and arrows at lower right. This coin has some lightness at the upper right of the shield.

EF-40, 45 (Extremely Fine)

Obverse. Further wear is seen on the head. The hair above the forehead lacks most detail. LIBERTY shows wear, but still is strong.

Reverse. Further wear is seen on the head and tail of the eagle and on the tips of the wings, most evident at the left and right extremes of the wings. At this level and below, sharpness of strike on the reverse is not important.

Illustrated coin: 1916. EF-40.

VF-20, 30 (Very Fine)

Obverse. The head shows more wear, now with nearly all detail gone in the hair above the forehead. LIBERTY shows wear, but is complete. The leaves on the head all show wear, as does the upper part of the cap.

Reverse. Wear is more extensive, particularly noticeable on the outer parts of the wings, the head, the shield, and the tail.

Illustrated coin: 1913-S. VF-30.

F-12, 15 (Fine)

Obverse. The head shows extensive wear. LIBERTY, the key place to check, is weak, especially at ER, but is fully readable. The ANA grading standards and *Photograde* adhere to this. PCGS suggests that lightly struck coins "may have letters partially missing." Traditionally, collectors insist on full LIBERTY.

Reverse. More wear is seen on the reverse in the places as above. E PLURIBUS UNUM is light, with one to several letters worn away.

Illustrated coin: 1907. F-12.

VG-8, 10 (Very Good)

Obverse. A net of three letters in LIBERTY must be readable. Traditionally, LI is clear, and after that there is a partial letter or two.

Reverse. Further wear has smoothed more than half of the feathers in the wing. The shield is indistinct except for a few traces of interior lines. The motto is partially worn away. The rim is full, and many if not most dentils can be seen.

Illustrated coin: 1901-S. VG-8.

G-4, 6 (Good)

Obverse. The head is in outline form, with the center flat. Most of the rim is there. All letters and the date are full.

Reverse. The eagle shows only a few feathers, and only a few scattered letters remain in the motto. The rim may be worn flat in some or all of the area, but the peripheral lettering is clear.

Illustrated coin: 1913-S. G-4.

AG-3 (About Good)

Obverse. The stars and motto are worn, and the border may be indistinct. Distinctness varies at this level. The date is clear. Grading is usually determined by the reverse.

Reverse. The rim is gone and the letters are partially worn away. The eagle is mostly flat, perhaps with a few hints of feathers.

Illustrated coin: 1901-S. AG-3.
This is a pleasing example of the grade, with bold date and mintmark and no problems.

Proof Barber Quarters, PF-60 to 70

Proofs exist in proportion to their mintages. Choicer examples tend to be of later dates. Most are sharply struck, although more than just a few are weak on the eagle's leg at the lower right and on certain parts of the arrows. The Proofs of 1892 to 1901 usually have cameo contrast between the designs and the mirror fields.

Obverse and Reverse. Proofs that are extensively cleaned and have many hairlines, or that are dull and grainy, are lower level, such as PF-60 to 62. These are not widely desired by collectors. With medium hairlines and good reflectivity, an assigned grade of PF-64 is appropriate. Tiny horizontal lines on Miss Liberty's cheek, known as slide marks, from National and other album slides scuffing the relief of the cheek, are endemic on all Barber silver coins. With noticeable marks of this type, the highest grade assignable is PF-64. With relatively few hairlines, a rating of PF-65 can be given. PF-66 should have hairlines so delicate that magnification is needed to see them. Above that, a Proof should be free of any hairlines or other problems.

Illustrated coin: 1894. PF-63.
Light gray and lilac toning combine to create a beautiful coin.

1916–1917 STANDING LIBERTY • TYPE I

History. Designed by sculptor Hermon A. MacNeil, the Standing Liberty quarter was widely acclaimed from its first appearance. All of 1916 and many of 1917 are of the Type I design, with the right breast of Miss Liberty exposed on the obverse and with no stars below the eagle on the reverse. Type II (see next section) has modified designs.

Striking and Sharpness. Many if not most 1916 quarters are somewhat lightly struck on the head and body of Miss Liberty. The 1917 Type I quarters are usually quite well struck. When light striking is found, it is usually on the higher-relief parts of the head, the right knee (not as obvious), and the rivets on the left side of the shield. For some reason, the 1917 Philadelphia Mint coins are usually sharper than the other varieties of this type. A misleading term, Full Head (FH), is widely used to describe quarters that have only *partial* head details. See further comments regarding Type II coins, wherein the problem is more serious.

Availability. The 1916 quarter is the key to the series. Examples tend to be liberally graded in the real-life marketplace, especially in Extremely Fine and About Uncirculated, this in contrast to more careful grading for the less valuable 1917 issues. Circulated coins of 1916 and 1917 often have the date worn partly away, due to the high position of this feature in the design. On Mint State coins the luster is usually rich and attractive.

MS-60 to 70 (Mint State)

Illustrated coin: 1917. MS-67.
This gorgeous coin has sharply struck details and full luster.

Note: All coins are shown enlarged, for clarity.

Obverse. At MS-60 some abrasion and contact marks are evident on the higher areas, which are also the areas most likely to be weakly struck. This includes the rivets on the shield to the left and the central escutcheon on the shield, the head, and the right leg of Miss Liberty. The luster may not be complete in those areas on weakly struck coins, even those certified above MS-65—the *original planchet surface* may be revealed as it was not smoothed out by striking. Accordingly, grading is best done by evaluating abrasion and mint luster as it is observed. Luster may be dull or lifeless at MS-60 to 62 but should have deep frost at MS-63 or better, particularly in the lower-relief areas. At MS-65 or better, it should be full and rich.

Reverse. Striking is usually quite good. Check the eagle's breast and the surface of the right wing. Luster may be dull or lifeless at MS-60 to 62 but should have deep frost at MS-63 or better, particularly in the lower-relief areas. At MS-65 or better, it should be full and rich.

AU-50, 53, 55, 58 (About Uncirculated)

Obverse. Light wear is seen on the figure of Miss Liberty, especially noticeable around her midriff and right knee. The shield shows wear, as does the highest part of the sash where it crosses Miss Liberty's waist. At AU-58 the luster is extensive, but incomplete on the higher areas, although it should be nearly full in the panels of the parapet to the left and right, and in the upper field. At AU-50 and 53, luster is less.

Illustrated coin: 1916. AU-55.
The original luster is still present in some areas of this lightly struck coin.

Reverse. Wear is most evident on the eagle's breast, the edges of both wings, and the interior area of the right wing. Luster is nearly complete at AU-58, but at AU-50, half or more is gone.

EF-40, 45 (Extremely Fine)

Obverse. Wear is more extensive, with the higher parts of Miss Liberty now without detail and the front of the right leg flat. The shield is worn. The date shows wear at the top. Little or no luster is seen, except perhaps among the letters.

Reverse. The eagle shows more wear, with the surface of the right wing being mostly flat. Little or no luster is evident.

Illustrated coin: 1917. EF-40.

VF-20, 30 (Very Fine)

Obverse. Wear is more extensive. The higher-relief areas of Miss Liberty are flat, and the sash crossing her waist is mostly blended into it (some sharply struck pieces being exceptions). The left side of the shield is mostly flat, although its outline can be seen. The top of the date shows more wear.

Reverse. The eagle shows further wear, with the body blending into the wing above it. Much feather detail is gone from the wing to the left. Most detail is gone from the right wing.

Illustrated coin: 1916. VF-30.

F-12, 15 (Fine)

Obverse. Miss Liberty is worn nearly flat. Most detail in her gown is gone, except to the left of her leg and below her knee to the right. The stars on the parapet are well worn, with some indistinct. The top of the date is weak. Quarters of the rare 1916 date are slightly weaker than those of 1917 in this and lower grades.

Reverse. The eagle shows further wear.

Illustrated coin: 1916. F-12.

VG-8, 10 (Very Good)

Obverse. The obverse is worn further, with fewer details in the skirt, and part of the shield border to the left blended into the standing figure. The date is partially worn away at the top.

Reverse. The eagle is worn further, with only about a third of the feathers now discernible, these mostly on the wing to the left.

Illustrated coin: 1917. VG-8.

G-4, 6 (Good)

Obverse. The wear is more extensive. Most coins have the stars missing, the standing figure flat, and much of the date worn away, although still clearly identifiable.

Reverse. The eagle is mostly in outline form, with only a few feather details visible. The rim is worn into the letters. E PLURIBUS UNUM is very faint.

Illustrated coin: 1916. G-6.

AG-3 (About Good)

Obverse. The obverse is worn nearly smooth, and the date is mostly gone. On some coins, just one or two digits are seen. Fortunately, those digits are usually on the right, such as a trace of just a 6, which will identify the coin as a 1916.

Reverse. The eagle is flat, and the border is worn down further. E PLURIBUS UNUM is extremely faint or even missing in areas; it remains readable on quarters of later dates.

Illustrated coin: 1917. AG-3.

1917–1930 STANDING LIBERTY • TYPE II

History. Type II quarter of this design was introduced in 1917 and continued to the end of the series. It features Miss Liberty encased in a jacket of armor, and a slightly redesigned reverse. This redesign came at the suggestion of the designer, Hermon A. MacNeil. Mintage was continuous through 1930, except for 1922.

Striking and Sharpness. Most coins of this design have areas of light striking. On the obverse these are most notable on the head of Miss Liberty and on the shield, the latter often with the two lower-left rivets weak or missing and with the center emblem on the shield weak. The center of the standing figure can be weak as well, as can the upper-left area at and near the date. After 1924 the date was slightly recessed, eliminating that problem. On the reverse, check the eagle's breast. A misleading term, Full Head (FH), is widely used to describe quarters that have only *partial* head details. Such coins often the have two lower-left shield rivets miserably struck or not visible at all! Save your money and pay "Full Head" prices only for coins with completely Full Details. If the certification services ever label coins as Full Details and mean it, some varieties in this series may not exist in this degree of excellence. Most third-party grading services define these criteria for "Full Head" designation (in order of importance): a full, unbroken hairline from Liberty's brow down to the jawline; all three leaves on the head showing; and a visible earhole.

Availability. The 1918-S, 8 Over 7, is recognized as the key issue, and the 1919-D, 1921, 1923-S, and 1927-S as quite scarce. Mint State coins are readily available for most issues, but Full Details coins can be *extreme* rarities. Circulated coins dated from 1917 through 1924 often have the date worn partly away, due to the high position of this feature in the design. On Mint State coins the luster is usually rich and attractive.

MS-60 to 70 (Mint State)

Illustrated coin: 1917-D. MS-64.
Brilliant, lustrous, and attractive, this is a very nice coin overall.

Note: All coins are shown enlarged, for clarity.

Obverse. At MS-60, some abrasion and contact marks are evident on the higher areas, which are also the areas most likely to be weakly struck. This includes the lower left two rivets and the ornament at the center of the shield, the head, and the right leg of Miss Liberty. The luster may not be complete in those areas on weakly struck coins, even those certified above MS-65—the *original planchet surface* may be revealed as it was not smoothed out by striking. Accordingly, grading is best done by evaluating abrasion as it is observed, plus evaluation of the mint luster. This may be dull or lifeless at MS-60 to 62, but should have deep frost at MS-63 or better, particularly in the lower-relief areas. At MS-65 or better, it should be full and rich.

Reverse. Striking is usually better, permitting observation of luster in all areas. Check the eagle's breast and the surface of the right wing. Luster may be dull or lifeless at MS-60 to 62, but should have deep frost at MS-63 or better, particularly in the lower-relief areas. At MS-65 or better, it should be full and rich.

AU-50, 53, 55, 58 (About Uncirculated)

Obverse. Light wear is seen on the figure of Miss Liberty, especially noticeable around her midriff and right leg. The shield shows wear, as does the highest part of the sash where it crosses Miss Liberty's waist. At AU-58, the luster is extensive but incomplete on the higher areas, although it should be nearly full in the panels of the parapet to the left and right, and in the upper field. At AU-50 and 53, luster is less.

Reverse. Wear is most evident on the eagle's breast, the edges of both wings, and the interior area of the right wing. Luster is nearly complete at AU-58, but at AU-50, half or more is gone.

Illustrated coin: 1921. AU-53.
Mint luster is seen in protected areas of the coin. Light striking at the center should not be mistaken for wear.

EF-40, 45 (Extremely Fine)

Obverse. Wear is more extensive, with the higher parts of Miss Liberty now without detail and the front of the right leg flat. The shield is worn. On coins dated from 1917 to 1924 the date shows wear at the top (on those of 1925 to 1930, with the date recessed, the numbers are bold). Little or no luster is seen, except perhaps among the letters.

Reverse. The eagle shows more wear, with the surface of the right wing being mostly flat. Little or no luster is evident.

Illustrated coin: 1927-S. EF-40.

VF-20, 30 (Very Fine)

Obverse. Wear is more extensive. The higher-relief areas of Miss Liberty are flat, and the sash crossing her waist is mostly blended into it (some sharply struck pieces being exceptions). The left side of the shield is mostly flat, although its outline can be seen. On quarters dated 1917 to 1924 the top of the date shows more wear.

Reverse. The eagle shows further wear, with the body blending into the wing above it. Much feather detail is gone from the wing to the left (on quarters dated 1925 to 1930; less so for those dated 1917 to 1924). Most detail is gone from the right wing.

Illustrated coin: 1927-S. VF-20.

F-12, 15 (Fine)

Obverse. Miss Liberty is worn nearly flat. Most detail in her gown is gone, except to the left of her leg and below her knee to the right. The stars on the parapet are well worn, with some indistinct. On quarters of 1917 to 1924 the top of the date is weak. On those dated 1925 to 1930 the date remains strong.

Reverse. The eagle shows further wear, this being greater on 1925 to 1930 issues than on the earlier dates.

Illustrated coin: 1928-D. F-15.

VG-8, 10 (Very Good)

Obverse. The obverse is worn further, with fewer details in the skirt, and part of the shield border to the left blended into the standing figure. Quarters from 1917 to 1924 have less detail, and the date is partially worn away at the top. Those from 1925 to 1930 retain more detail, and the date is full.

Reverse. The eagle is worn further, with only about a third of the feathers now discernible, these mostly on the wing to the left.

Illustrated coin: 1927. VG-10.

G-4, 6 (Good)

Obverse. The wear is more extensive. Most 1917 to 1924 coins have the stars missing, the standing figure flat, and much of the date worn away, although still clearly identifiable. Quarters of 1925 to 1930 show more detail and the date is clear.

Reverse. The eagle is mostly in outline form, with only a few feather details visible. The rim is worn into the letters. On quarters of 1917 to 1924, E PLURIBUS UNUM is very faint; it is clear on quarters of later dates.

Illustrated coin: 1927. G-6.

AG-3 (About Good)

Obverse. On quarters of 1917 to 1924 the obverse is worn nearly smooth, and the date is mostly gone. On some coins just one or two digits are seen. Fortunately, those digits are usually on the right, permitting attribution. On quarters of 1925 to 1930 the wear is more extensive than for G-4, but most features are discernible and the date is clear.

Reverse. The eagle is flat, and the border is worn down further. On quarters of 1916 to 1924, E PLURIBUS UNUM is extremely faint or even missing in areas; it remains readable on quarters of later dates.

Illustrated coin: 1927. AG-3.

1932–1998 WASHINGTON

History. Washington quarters were intended to be commemorative coins, but ideas changed and they were produced as regular issues. Designed by John Flanagan, the obverse is from a bust by Jean Antoine Houdon. The reverse features a modernistic eagle. Mintage has been continuous except for the dates 1933 and 1975. In 1975 and 1976 a special Bicentennial design was used (with all coins dual-dated 1776–1976).

Striking and Sharpness. The relief of both sides of the Washington quarter issues from 1932 to 1988 is shallow. Accordingly, any lightness of strike is not easily seen. Nearly all are well struck. On all quarters of 1932 and some of 1934 the motto IN GOD WE TRUST is light, as per the design. It was strengthened in 1934.

Availability. The 1932-D and S are key issues but not rarities. All others are readily available in high grades, but some are scarcer than others.

MS-60 to 70 (Mint State)

Illustrated coin: 1932-S. MS-64.
This is a brilliant and lustrous example with excellent eye appeal.

Note: All coins are shown enlarged, for clarity.

Obverse. At MS-60, some abrasion and contact marks are evident on the hair above the ear and at the top of the head below E (LIBERTY). At MS-63, abrasion is slight at best, less so for MS-64. An MS-65 coin should display no abrasion or contact marks except under magnification, and MS-66 and higher coins should have none at all. Luster should be full and rich.

Reverse. Comments apply as for the obverse, except that the eagle's breast and legs are the places to check. On both sides the fields are protected by design elements and do not show contact marks readily.

AU-50, 53, 55, 58 (About Uncirculated)

Obverse. Light wear is seen on the cheek, the high areas of the hair, and the neck. At AU-58, the luster is extensive but incomplete, especially on the higher parts and in the field. At AU-50 and 53, luster is less.

Reverse. Light wear is seen on the breast, legs, and upper edges of the wings of the eagle. An AU-58 coin has nearly full luster. At AU-50 and 53, there still is significant luster.

Illustrated coin: 1932-D. AU-53.
Some of the original luster remains on the obverse of this example, while most of the luster remains on the reverse.

EF-40, 45 (Extremely Fine)

Obverse. Further wear is seen on the head. Higher-relief details are gone in the hair. The higher-relief parts of the neck show wear, most noticeably just above the date.

Reverse. Further wear is seen on the eagle. Most breast feathers, not strong to begin with, are worn away.

Illustrated coin: 1940. EF-40.

VF-20, 30 (Very Fine)

Obverse. Most hair detail is worn away, except above the curls. The delineation between the temple and the edge of the hair is faint. The curl by the ear is worn flat. Tips of the letters in LIBERTY and the date digits touch the rim in some instances.

Reverse. More details of the eagle are worn away, and the outlines of the feathers in the wing, while nearly all present, are faint. Tips of the letters touch the rim in some instances on this and lower grades, but this can vary from coin to coin depending on the strength of the rim.

Illustrated coin: 1937. VF-20.

F-12, 15 (Fine)

Obverse. Most of the hair is worn flat, with no distinction between the face and the beginning of the hair. There is some detail remaining just above and below the curls.

Reverse. More feathers are worn away. The end of the branch at the left is worn so as to blend into the wing. The edge of the rim is barely visible and in some areas is worn away. (In this and the Very Good grade, opinions concerning the rim vary in the ANA grading standards and in *Photograde;* PCGS is silent on the matter.)

Illustrated coin: 1934, Doubled-die obverse. F-12.

VG-8, 10 (Very Good)

Obverse. Further wear is seen on the head, with most of the upper part of the curls now blending into the hair above.

Reverse. The rim is worn into the tops of the letters. There is no detail on the leaves. About half of the feathers are outlined, but only faintly.

Illustrated coin: 1935-D. VG-8.

G-4, 6 (Good)

Obverse. Further wear is seen in all areas. On 1932 and some 1934 coins the IN GOD WE TRUST motto is so worn that some letters are missing.

Reverse. The rim is worn further into the letters. Fewer details are seen on the eagle's wing. On both sides the coin appears to be "worn flat," with little in relief.

Illustrated coin: 1932-D. G-4.

AG-3 (About Good)

Obverse. Wear is more extensive, with about half of the letters gone.

Reverse. Wear is more extensive, with about half of the letters gone. Slight detail remains in the eagle's wings. The mintmark, if any, is very clear.

Illustrated coin: 1942. AG-3.

Proof Washington Quarters, PF-60 to 70

Dates available are 1936 to 1942 and 1950 to 1964 (from the Philadelphia Mint) and 1968 to 1998 (from San Francisco). Certain later Proofs are available in clad metal as well as silver strikings. Special Mint Set (SMS) coins were struck in lieu of Proofs from 1965 to 1967; these in some instances closely resemble Proofs. The majority of Proofs made in recent decades are in high levels, PF-66 to 68 or higher.

Illustrated coin: 1938. PF-66.

Obverse and Reverse. Proofs that are extensively cleaned and have many hairlines, or that are dull and grainy, are lower level, such as PF-60 to 62. These are not widely desired, and represent coins that have been mistreated. Most low-level Proofs are of the 1936 to 1942 dates. With medium hairlines and good reflectivity, assigned grades of PF-63 or 64 are appropriate. PF-66 should have hairlines so delicate that magnification is needed to see them. Above that, a Proof should be free of any hairlines or other problems.

1999–2021, STATEHOOD, D.C./ TERRITORIAL, AND NATIONAL PARKS

History. In 1999 the Statehood quarters were introduced at the rate of five new reverse designs each year, in combination with a restyled obverse, through 2008. These became very popular and are still widely collected with great enthusiasm. In 2009 a new program of quarter dollars for Washington, D.C., and the five U.S. territories was issued. A similar program for national parks and historic sites started in 2010 and will run through 2021. Circulation strikes are made at the Philadelphia and Denver mints, and special silver-content and Proof issues are struck at San Francisco. Each coin combines a modified obverse depicting George Washington, without date. The reverses are distinctive and bear the date of issue, the date of statehood (for the state quarters), and other design elements. Each state or district/territory selected its own designs.

Striking and Sharpness. Statehood, D.C./Territorial, and National Parks quarters can have light striking on the highest area of the obverse. On the reverse there can be weak areas depending on the particular design, seemingly more often seen on Denver Mint coins. Many in the Statehood quarter series have been struck through grease, obliterating portions of both the obverse (usually) and reverse designs.

Availability. All are readily available in high grades. Typical Mint State coins are MS-63 and 64 with light abrasion. MS-65 and higher coins are in the minority, but enough exist that finding them is no problem. Around MS-68 many issues are scarce, and higher grades are scarcer yet.

MS-60 to 70 (Mint State)

Illustrated coin: 2006-P, South Dakota. MS-68.

Note: All coins are shown enlarged, for clarity.

Obverse. At MS-60, some abrasion and contact marks are evident on the highest-relief parts of the hair and the cheek. At MS-63, abrasion is slight at best, less so at MS-64. An MS-65 coin should display no abrasion or contact marks except under magnification, and MS-66 and higher coins should have none at all. Luster should be full.

Reverse. Check the highest-relief areas of the design (these differ from coin to coin). Otherwise, comments are as for the obverse.

AU-50, 53, 55, 58 (About Uncirculated)

Obverse. Light wear is seen on the cheek, the high areas of the hair, and the neck. At AU-58, the luster is extensive, but incomplete, especially on the higher parts and in the field. At AU-50 and 53, luster is less. About Uncirculated coins usually lack eye appeal.

Reverse. Light wear is seen on the higher-relief areas. Otherwise, comments are as for the obverse.

Illustrated coin: 2006-P, Colorado. AU-50.

Statehood, D.C./Territorial, and National Parks quarter dollars are seldom collected in grades lower than AU-50.

Proof Statehood, D.C./Territorial, and National Parks Quarters, PF-60 to 70

Statehood, D.C./Territorial, and National Parks quarter dollar Proofs are made in San Francisco. For certain later issues of Washington quarters as well as Statehood, D.C./Territorial, and National Parks issues, Proofs are available in clad metal as well as silver strikings. On some Proofs over-polishing of dies has eliminated some details, as on part of the WC (for William Cousins) initials on certain 1999 Delaware pieces.

Illustrated coin: 2000-S, New Hampshire. PF-70.

Obverse and Reverse. These coins are so recent, and as only a few have been cleaned, most approach perfection and can be designated PF-68 to 70, the latter only if no contact marks or other problems can be seen under magnification. A cleaned coin with extensive hairlines would not be collectible for most numismatists and would be classified at a lower level such as PF-60 to 63. Those with lighter hairlines qualify for PF-64 or 65.

HALF DOLLARS

HALF DOLLARS, 1794 TO DATE

1794–1795 FLOWING HAIR

History. Half dollars of this type inaugurated the denomination. The Flowing Hair motif was also used on half dimes and silver dollars of the same years.

Striking and Sharpness. Many have problems of one sort or another, including adjustment marks from filing the planchet, and mushy dentils. On the obverse, check the hair details and the stars. On the reverse, check the breast of the eagle in particular, but other areas as well. As with other silver coins of this design, it may not be possible to find a *needle-sharp* example, but with some extensive searching a fairly decent strike can be obtained. Sharp striking and excellent eye appeal will add to the value dramatically. However, very few 1794 and 1795 halves are uniformly sharp on both sides.

Availability. Probably 3,500 to 6,000 exist. Most are dated 1795, the 1794 being considered a rare date. Typical grades are Good to Fine. Extremely Fine and About Uncirculated grades are elusive in regard to the total population. Probably 100 or so could be classified as Mint State, nearly all being of the 1795 date. Unlike half dollars of the 1796–1797 type, none of these are known to have been made with prooflike surfaces. "Gradeflation" has increased the number in recent years. Given strong demand from type-coin collectors, Flowing Hair half dollars and dollars are far more likely than later issues to end up in certified holders, regardless of evidence of cleaning.

MS-60 to 70 (Mint State)

Illustrated coin: 1795, Overton-110a. MS-63.
This is a well-struck example with superb eye appeal.

Note: Abbreviations used in die-variety attributions, along with the reference works on which the attributions are based, are discussed on the first page of this chapter. All coins are shown enlarged, for clarity.

Obverse. At MS-60, some abrasion and contact marks are evident, most noticeably on the cheek and in the fields. This denomination, heavier than the half dime of the same design, was more susceptible to contact and other outside influences. A typical half dollar certified at MS-60 or 61 today might well have been designated as About Uncirculated a generation ago. Luster is present, but may be dull or lifeless, and interrupted in patches, perhaps as much from old cleaning as from contact the coin may have received. At MS-63, contact marks are very few, and abrasion is present, but not as noticeable. An MS-65 coin has no abrasion, and contact marks are very few. Luster should be full and rich. Higher grades are seldom seen in this type, but are defined in theory by having fewer marks as perfection is approached.

Reverse. Comments apply as for the obverse, except that abrasion and contact marks are most noticeable on the eagle at the center. This area is often lightly struck, so in all grades do not mistake weak striking for actual wear. Knowledge of specific die varieties is helpful in this regard. The field area is small and is protected by lettering and the wreath, and in any given grade shows fewer marks than on the obverse.

AU-50, 53, 55, 58 (About Uncirculated)

Obverse. Light wear is seen on the hair area immediately to the left of the face and above the forehead, on the cheek, and, to a lesser extent, on the top of the neck truncation, more so at AU-50 than at 53 or 55. An AU-58 coin has minimal traces of wear. An AU-50 coin has luster in protected areas among the stars and letters, with little in the open fields or on the portrait. At AU-58, much luster is present in the fields but is worn away on the highest parts of the motifs.

Illustrated coin: 1795. AU-55.
Significant luster remains in protected areas on this attractive early half dollar.

Reverse. Light wear is seen on the eagle's body and the upper part of both wings. On well-struck pieces the details of the wing features are excellent. At AU-50, detail is lost in some feathers in this area. However, striking can play a part, as some coins were weakly struck to begin with. Light wear is seen on the wreath and lettering, but is harder to discern. Luster is the best key to actual wear. This will range from perhaps 20% remaining in protected areas (at AU-50) to nearly full mint bloom (at AU-58), although among certified coins the amounts of luster can vary widely. See comments about gradeflation under "Availability."

EF-40, 45 (Extremely Fine)

Obverse. More wear is evident on the portrait, especially on the hair to the left of and above the forehead, and in the back below LI (LIBERTY). The tip of the neck truncation shows flatness, and the cheek is worn. Excellent detail remains in low-relief areas of the hair. The stars show wear, as do the date and letters. Luster, if present at all, is minimal and in protected areas.

Illustrated coin: 1794, Overton-101. EF-40.
Note some lightness of the stars at the right and at the reverse center, as struck. The scrape on the reverse below the ribbon knot was mentioned by the cataloger in an auction offering.

Reverse. The eagle shows more wear on the body and on the tops of the wings. Interior wing detail is good on most coins (depending on the variety and the striking), and the tail feathers can be discerned. Additional wear is on the wreath and letters, but many details are present. Some luster may be seen in protected areas and if present is slightly more abundant than on the obverse.

VF-20, 30 (Very Fine)

Obverse. The hair is well worn at VF-20, less so at VF-30, and is most noticeable in the upper part of the head, the area above the level of the eye, and extending to the back. The strands are blended as to be heavy. The cheek shows only slight relief, and the tip of the neck truncation is flat. The stars have more wear, making them appear larger (an optical illusion). Scattered marks are common on half dollars at this level and below, and should be mentioned if particularly serious.

Illustrated coin: 1795, Overton-109. VF-20.
On this variety in this grade, the dentils are especially prominent on each side. Such aspects vary from coin to coin.

Reverse. The body of the eagle shows few if any feathers, while the wings have perhaps a quarter or a third of the feathers visible depending on the strike, with sharper strikes having up to half visible (as PCGS suggests). *Photograde* and the ANA grading standards suggest half of the feathers on all, which may be the case on coins that were well struck to begin with. The leaves lack detail and are in outline form. Scattered, non-disfiguring marks are normal for this and lower grades. Any major defects should be noted separately.

F-12, 15 (Fine)

Obverse. Wear is more extensive than on the preceding, with less hair visible. The ear position can be seen, as can the eye. The cheek is nearly flat, and the stars appear larger. The rim is distinct and most dentils remain visible.

Reverse. Wear is more extensive. Now, feather details are fewer, mostly remaining on the wing to the left. The wreath and lettering are more worn, and the rim is usually weak in areas, although most dentils can be seen.

Illustrated coin: 1795, Overton-107. F-12.

VG-8, 10 (Very Good)

Obverse. The portrait is mostly seen in outline form, with most hair strands gone save for an area centered behind the neck. The hair tips at the lower left are clear. The eye location is barely discernible. The stars appear larger still and often quite bold, again an illusion. The rim is weak in areas. LIBERTY and the date are readable and usually full, although some letters may be weak at their tops.

Illustrated coin: 1795, Overton-109. VG-8.

Note a spot, a tiny edge bruise, and some adjustment marks. A cataloger mentioned that "the top of the obverse is slightly soft due to axial misalignment"— a technical note. On any half dollar of this era, knowledge of the varieties and peculiarities of striking is useful.

Reverse. The eagle is mostly an outline, although traces of the separation between the body and the right wing can sometimes be seen. The rim is worn, as are the letters, with some weak, but the motto is readable. On many coins the rim remains fairly prominent.

G-4, 6 (Good)

Obverse. Wear is more extensive, and some stars may be missing or only partially visible. The head is an outline, although a few elements of thick hair strands may be seen. The rim is well worn or even missing. LIBERTY is worn, and parts of some letters may be missing, but elements of all should be readable. The date is readable, but worn.

Illustrated coin: 1794, Overton-106. G-6.

Reverse. The eagle is flat and discernible in outline form. The wreath is well worn. Some of the letters may be partly missing. At this level some "averaging" can be done. If the letters are stronger than usual in one area, but some are missing in another area, the coin can still qualify as G-4. Often on this type in lower grades the reverse is more detailed than the obverse.

AG-3 (About Good)

Obverse. Wear is very extensive. The head is in outline form (perhaps partly blended into the field). LIBERTY is mostly gone. The date, while readable, may be partially worn away. Some stars are missing.

Reverse. The reverse is well worn, with parts of the wreath and lettering very weak or even missing. The details that remain and those that do not is often dependent on the particular die variety.

Illustrated coin: 1795, Overton-116. AG-3.

1796–1797 Draped Bust, Small Eagle

History. This is the Holy Grail among silver coin types, the most acclaimed (although the 1839 Gobrecht dollar edges it in rarity, but most are restrikes). The design is similar to that used on the half dime, dime, quarter, and silver dollar of the era. While the other denominations are scarce, only 3,918 half dollars of both dates were struck.

Striking and Sharpness. On the obverse, check the hair details and the stars. On the reverse, the breast of the eagle is the first place to look, but examine other areas as well. Also check the dentils on both sides. Look especially for coins that do not have significant adjustment marks. Coins of this denomination are on average better struck than are half dimes, dimes, quarters (which have reverse problems), and dollars.

Availability. Examples are rare in any grade. Mint State coins are particularly rare, and when seen are nearly always dated 1796. Some of these have partially prooflike surfaces. Any half dollar of this type has strong market demand.

MS-60 to 70 (Mint State)

Illustrated coin: 1797, Overton-101a. MS-66.

This superb gem, with prooflike surfaces, is a classic, pedigreed to the Norweb (1988) and Baldenhofer (1955) collections. It was bought by Baldenhofer as a Proof.

Note: Abbreviations used in die-variety attributions, along with the reference works on which the attributions are based, are discussed on the first page of this chapter. All coins are shown enlarged, for clarity.

Obverse. At MS-60, some abrasion and contact marks are evident, most noticeably on the cheek, the drapery at the shoulder, and the right field. Also check the hair to the left of the forehead. Luster is present, but may be dull or lifeless, and interrupted in patches. At MS-63, contact marks are few, and abrasion is hard to detect, although this type is sometimes graded liberally due to its rarity. An MS-65 coin has no abrasion, and contact marks are so minute as to require magnification. Luster should be full and rich. Coins graded above MS-65 are more theoretical than actual for this type, although some notable pieces have crossed the auction block. These are defined by having fewer marks as perfection is approached.

Reverse. Comments apply as for the obverse, except that abrasion and contact marks are most noticeable on the eagle at the center, a situation that should be evaluated by considering the original striking (which can be quite sharp, but with many exceptions). The field area is small and is protected by lettering and the wreath, and in any given grade shows fewer marks than on the obverse.

AU-50, 53, 55, 58 (About Uncirculated)

Obverse. Light wear is seen on the hair area above the ear and extending to the left of the forehead, on the ribbon, and on the drapery at the shoulder, more so at AU-50 than at 53 or 55. An AU-58 coin has minimal traces of wear. An AU-50 coin has luster in protected areas among the stars and letters, with little in the open fields or on the portrait. At AU-58, most luster is present in the fields, but is worn away on the highest parts of the motifs.

Illustrated coin: 1797, Overton-101a. AU-50.

Reverse. Light wear is seen on the eagle's body and the edges of the wings. Light wear is seen on the wreath and lettering. Luster is the best key to actual wear. This ranges from perhaps 20% remaining in protected areas (at AU-50) to nearly full mint bloom (at AU-58).

EF-40, 45 (Extremely Fine)

Obverse. More wear is evident on the upper hair area, particularly to the left of the forehead and also below LI (LIBERTY), in the ribbon, and on the drapery and bosom. Excellent detail remains in low-relief areas of the hair. The stars show wear as do the date and letters. Luster, if present at all, is minimal and in protected areas.

Reverse. The eagle shows more wear, this being the focal point to check. Many feathers remain on

Illustrated coin: 1796, Overton-101, 15 stars. EF-40.

the interior areas of the wings. Additional wear is on the wreath and letters, but many details are present. Some luster may be seen in protected areas and if present is slightly more abundant than on the obverse.

VF-20, 30 (Very Fine)

Obverse. The higher-relief areas of hair are well worn at VF-20, less so at VF-30. The drapery and bosom show extensive wear. The stars have more wear.

Reverse. The body of the eagle shows few if any feathers, while the wings have about half or more of the feathers visible, depending on the strike. The leaves lack most detail and are outlined. Scattered, non-disfiguring marks are normal for this and lower grades; major defects should be noted separately.

Illustrated coin: 1796, Overton-103, 16 stars. VF-20.

F-12, 15 (Fine)

Obverse. Wear is more extensive than on a Very Fine coin, particularly noticeable on the hair, face, and bosom. The stars appear larger (an optical illusion). About half the hair detail remains, most noticeably behind the neck and shoulder. The rim may be partially worn away and blend into the field, but on many coins it remains intact.

Reverse. Wear is more extensive. Now, feather details are diminished, with fewer than half remaining on the wings. The wreath and lettering are worn further, and the rim is usually weak in areas, but most dentils can be seen.

Illustrated coin: 1797, Overton-101a. F-15.

VG-8, 10 (Very Good)

Obverse. The portrait is mostly seen in outline form, with most hair strands gone, although there is some definition at the back of the hair and behind the shoulder. The ear is barely discernible and the eye is fairly distinct. The stars appear larger still, again an illusion. The rim is weak in areas, but shows most dentils. LIBERTY and the date are readable and usually full, although some letters may be weak at their tops.

Reverse. The eagle is mostly an outline, with parts blending into the field (on lighter strikes). The rim is worn, as are the letters, with some weak, but the motto is readable.

Illustrated coin: 1796, Overton-102, 16 stars. VG-10.

G-4, 6 (Good)

Obverse. Wear is more extensive, and some stars may be partly missing. The head is an outline. The eye is visible only in outline form. The rim is well worn or even missing in areas, but many dentils remain. LIBERTY is worn. The letters and date are weak but fully readable.

Reverse. The eagle is flat and discernible in outline form, and may be blending into the field. The wreath is well worn. Some of the letters may be partly missing. At

Illustrated coin: 1797. G-4.

this level some "averaging" can be done. If the letters are stronger than usual in one area, but some are missing in another area, the coin can still qualify as G-4.

AG-3 (About Good)

Obverse. Wear is so extensive that the coin is barely identifiable. The head is in outline form. LIBERTY is mostly gone; same for the stars. The date, while readable, may be partially worn away.

Reverse. The reverse is well worn, with parts of the wreath and lettering missing. On most coins the reverse shows more wear than the obverse.

Illustrated coin: 1793. AG-3.

1801–1807 DRAPED BUST, HERALDIC EAGLE

History. This design is similar to that seen on other silver coins of the era. Earlier years are scarce, beginning with the elusive 1801 and including the 1802, after which they are more readily available. These half dollars were very popular in their time, with the result that most show extensive wear.

Striking and Sharpness. Most have light striking in one area or another; on the obverse, check the hair details and, in particular, the star centers. On the reverse, check the stars above the eagle, the clouds, the details of the shield, and the eagle's wings. Check the dentils on both sides. Adjustment marks are sometimes seen, but not as often as on earlier types of this denomination. As a rule of thumb, the earlier years are better struck, and many of 1806 and nearly all of 1807 are poorly struck. Sharp striking and excellent eye appeal add to the value dramatically, this being particularly true for 1805 to 1807, which are often weak (particularly 1807). When top-grade Mint State coins are found they are usually dated 1805 to 1807.

Availability. All dates are readily collectible, although some die varieties are scarce. Mint State coins are mostly dated 1806 and 1807, but all are scarce. Finding sharply struck high-grade coins is almost impossible, a goal more than a reality.

MS-60 to 70 (Mint State)

Illustrated coin: 1803, Overton-101, Large 3. MS-63. This is an extraordinary strike with superb eye appeal. A connoisseur might prefer this coin to an MS-65 example with flat striking.

Note: Abbreviations used in die-variety attributions, along with the reference works on which the attributions are based, are discussed on the first page of this chapter. All coins are shown enlarged, for clarity.

Obverse. At MS-60, some abrasion and contact marks are evident, most noticeably on the cheek, the drapery at the shoulder, and the right field. Luster is present, but may be dull or lifeless, and interrupted in patches. At MS-63, contact marks are very few, and abrasion is hard to detect except under magnification. An MS-65 coin has no abrasion, and contact marks are so minute as to require magnification. Luster should be full and rich. Coins grading above MS-65 are more theoretical than actual for this type—but they do exist, and are defined by having fewer marks as perfection is approached. Later years usually have areas of flat striking.

Reverse. Comments apply as for the obverse, except that abrasion and contact marks are most noticeable on the eagle's neck, the tips of the wing, and the tail. The field area is complex, without much open space, given the stars above the eagle, the arrows and olive branch, and other features. Accordingly, marks are not as noticeable as on the obverse.

AU-50, 53, 55, 58 (About Uncirculated)

Obverse. Light wear is seen on the hair area above the ear and extending to left of the forehead, on the ribbon, and on the bosom, more so at AU-50 than at 53 or 55. An AU-58 coin has minimal traces of wear. An AU-50 coin has luster in protected areas among the stars and letters, with little in the open fields or on the portrait. At AU-58, most luster is present in the fields, but is worn away on the highest parts of the motifs.

Illustrated coin: 1806. Overton-109. AU-50. This example has gray and lilac toning.

Reverse. Comments as preceding, except that the eagle's neck, the tips and top of the wings, the clouds, and the tail now show noticeable wear, as do other features. Luster ranges from perhaps 20% remaining in protected areas (at AU-50) to nearly full mint bloom (at AU-58). Often the reverse of this type retains much more luster than the obverse.

EF-40, 45 (Extremely Fine)

Obverse. More wear is evident on the upper hair area and the ribbon, and on the drapery and bosom. Excellent detail remains in low-relief areas of the hair. The stars show wear, as do the date and letters. Luster, if present at all, is minimal and in protected areas.

Reverse. Wear is greater than on an About Uncirculated coin, overall. The neck lacks feather detail on its highest points. Feathers have lost some detail near the edges of the wings, and some areas of the horizontal lines in the shield may be blended together. Some traces of luster may be seen, more so at EF-45 than at EF-40.

Illustrated coin: 1807, Overton-105. EF-40.
Light striking at the obverse center is normal for this die variety.

VF-20, 30 (Very Fine)

Obverse. The higher-relief areas of hair are well worn at VF-20, less so at VF-30. The drapery on the shoulder and the bosom show extensive wear. The stars have more wear, making them appear larger (an optical illusion seen on most worn silver coins of this era).

Reverse. Wear is greater, including on the shield and wing feathers. Half to two-thirds of the feathers are visible. Star centers are flat. Other areas have lost detail as well.

Illustrated coin: 1806, 6 Over Inverted 9, Overton-111a. VF-30.
Note the cud break on the reverse rim over the E in UNITED.

F-12, 15 (Fine)

Obverse. Wear is more extensive than on a Very Fine coin, particularly noticeable on the hair, face, and bosom. The stars appear larger. About half the hair detail remains, most noticeably behind the neck and shoulder, but the fine hair is now combined into thicker tresses. The rim may be partially worn away and blend into the field.

Reverse. Wear is even more extensive, with the shield and wing feathers being points to observe. The incuse E PLURIBUS UNUM may have half or more of the letters worn away (depending on striking). The clouds all appear connected. The stars are weak. Parts of the border and lettering may be weak.

Illustrated coin: 1805, Overton-109. F-15.

VG-8, 10 (Very Good)

Obverse. The portrait is mostly seen in outline form, with most hair strands gone, although there is some definition at the back of the hair and behind the shoulder. The ear is discernible as is the eye. The stars appear larger still, again an illusion. The rim is weak in areas. LIBERTY and the date are readable and usually full, although some letters may be weak at their tops.

Reverse. Wear is more extensive. Half or more of the letters in the motto are worn away. Most feathers are worn away, although separation of some of the lower feathers may be seen. Some stars are faint (depending on the strike). The border blends into the field in areas and some letters are weak.

Illustrated coin: 1805, 5 Over 4, Overton-103. VG-8.
This is a scarce variety. Note the many tiny marks; still, this coin is attractive for the grade.

G-4, 6 (Good)

Obverse. Wear is more extensive, and some stars may be partly missing. The head is mostly an outline, although some hair strand outlines may be visible on some strikings. The rim is well worn or even missing in areas. LIBERTY is worn, and parts of some letters may be missing, but elements should be readable. The date is readable, but worn.

Reverse. Wear is more extensive. The upper part of the eagle is flat. Feathers are noticeable only at the lower edge of the wings, and do not have detail. The upper part of the shield is flat or mostly so (depending on the strike). Only a few letters of the motto can be seen. The rim is worn extensively, and a few letters may be missing.

Illustrated coin: 1805, Overton-111. G-4.

AG-3 (About Good)

Obverse. Wear is so extensive that the coin is barely identifiable. The head is in outline form. LIBERTY is mostly gone; same for the stars. The date, while readable, may be partially worn away.

Reverse. Extensive wear is seen overall, with the rim worn away and some areas worn smooth. The eagle can be discerned in outline form, but not necessarily completely. A few stray motto letters may remain.

Illustrated coin: 1801. AG-3.

1807–1836 Capped Bust, Lettered Edge

History. Created at the Mint by assistant engraver John Reich, the Capped Bust design in several variations was widely used on much of the coinage of the era. The half dollar is best known today. Minted continuously from 1807 to 1836, except 1816, these were the largest silver coins of the realm at the time (as silver dollars had not been struck since 1804).

Striking and Sharpness. On the obverse, check the hair and broach details. Stars are often flatly struck on half dollars, much more so than on other Capped Bust silver denominations. On the reverse, check the motto band and the eagle's head, and the wing to the left, as well as other areas (neck feathers, often lightly struck on other denominations of Capped Bust silver, are usually fairly sharp on half dollars). The E PLURIBUS UNUM band is often weak in the area left of its center; this does not normally occur on other Capped Bust silver denominations. Inspect the dentils on both sides. Generally, later dates are better struck than are earlier ones. It is not unusual to find an 1807 with flatness on many features, although it may be fully lustrous Mint State. In contrast, a typical 1834 is apt to be well struck. Many half dollars have semi-prooflike surfaces, or patches of mirrorlike character interspersed with luster. Others can have nearly full prooflike surfaces, with patches of luster being in the minority (and often in the left obverse field); some of these have been mischaracterized as "Proofs." Some issues from the early 1830s have little digs or "bite marks" on the portrait, possibly from some sort of a gadget used to eject them from the press. Unlike the Capped Bust half dime, dime, and quarter dollar, the half dollar is particularly subject to very wide variations in striking quality. Because of this, familiarity with the Overton text and commentaries as published in the *John Reich Journal,* and observation of illustrations in catalogs, on the Internet, and in person are very valuable adjuncts to grading. In this series, experts often differ widely in opinions on strike and sharpness.

Availability. Examples of most dates and overdates are easily found in just about any grade desired, from Fine and Very Fine to Mint State. (As the largest silver coin struck between 1803 and 1836, these half dollars spent much of their time in bags, transferred from bank to bank, rather than wearing down in circulation.) The later years are the most readily available and are also seen in higher average grades. Many die varieties range from scarce to rare. As so many coins are in the marketplace, these are widely collected by Overton numbers, with great competition when a rarity crosses the auction block.

MS-60 to 70 (Mint State)

Illustrated coin: 1827. MS-60.
An exceptional coin at the low Mint State level, this could find a home in a connoisseur's collection.

Note: Abbreviations used in die-variety attributions, along with the reference works on which the attributions are based, are discussed on the first page of this chapter. All coins are shown enlarged, for clarity.

Obverse. At MS-60, some abrasion and contact marks are evident, most noticeably on the cheek, the hair below the left part of LIBERTY, the cap, and the front part of the bosom and drapery. These areas also coincide with the highest parts of the coin and are thus susceptible to lightness of strike. Complicating matters is that when an area is lightly struck, and the planchet is not forced into the deepest parts of the die, the *original planchet surface* (which may exhibit scuffing and nicks) is visible. A lightly struck coin can have virtually perfect luster in the fields, deep and rich, and yet appear to be "worn" on the higher parts, due to the lightness of strike. This is a very sophisticated concept and is hard to quantify. In practice, the original planchet surface will usually be considered as wear on the finished coin, which of course is not true. Such grades as high About Uncirculated and low Mint State levels are often assigned to pieces that, if well struck, would be MS-64 and MS-65. As a matter of practicality, but not of logic, you will need to do the same. If a coin has original planchet abrasions, but otherwise is a Gem, those abrasions must be taken into consideration. Apart from this, on well-struck coins in lower Mint State grades, luster is present, but may be dull or lifeless, and interrupted in patches. At MS-63, on a well-struck coin, contact marks are very few, and abrasion is hard to detect except under magnification. A well-struck MS-65 coin has no abrasion, and contact marks are so minute as to require magnification. Luster should be full and rich. Grades above MS-65 are seen now and again and are defined by having fewer marks as perfection is approached.

Reverse. Comments apply as for the obverse, except that nearly all coins with weak striking on the obverse (so as to reveal original planchet surface) do not show such original surface on the reverse, except perhaps on the motto ribbon. Accordingly, market grading is usually by the obverse only, even if the reverse seems to be in much better preservation. On well-struck coins, abrasion and contact marks are most noticeable on the eagle's head, the top of the wings, the claws, and the flat band that surrounds the incuse motto. The field is mainly protected by design elements and does not show abrasion as much as does the obverse on a given coin.

AU-50, 53, 55, 58 (About Uncirculated)

Obverse. Light wear is seen on the cheek, the hair below the left part of LIBERTY, the cap, and the front part of the bosom and drapery. Some of this apparent "wear" may be related to the original planchet surface (as noted under Mint State, above), but at the About Uncirculated level the distinction is less important. On a well-struck coin, at AU-58 the luster is extensive except in the open area of the field, especially to the right. At AU-50 and 53, luster remains only in protected areas.

Reverse. Wear is evident on the eagle's head, the top of the wings, the claws, and the flat band above the eagle. An AU-58 coin has nearly full luster. At AU-50 and 53, there still is significant luster, more than on the obverse.

Illustrated coin: 1820. AU-55.
An attractive coin by any measure, this has light toning and ample areas of original luster.

EF-40, 45 (Extremely Fine)

Obverse. Wear is more extensive, most noticeably on the higher areas of the hair. The cap shows more wear, as does the cheek. Luster, if present, is in protected areas among the star points and close to the portrait.

Reverse. The wings show wear on the higher areas of the feathers, and some details are lost. The top of the head and the beak are flat. The eagle's claws and the leaves show wear. Luster may be present in protected areas, even if there is little or none on the obverse.

Illustrated coin: 1810, Overton-110. EF-45.
This coin probably was lightly cleaned years ago so as to give a light silver color, which added some hairlines, but now it has halo toning around the borders that adds attractiveness.

VF-20, 30 (Very Fine)

Obverse. Wear is more extensive, and most of the hair is combined into thick tresses without delicate features. The curl on the neck is flat. The cap shows significant wear at its top, and the left part of the drapery and bosom is nearly flat. Stars are flat at their centers (even if sharply struck to begin with).

Reverse. Wear is most evident on the eagle's head, the tops of the wings, and the leaves and claws. Nearly all feathers in the wing remain distinct.

Illustrated coin: 1815, 5 Over 2, Overton-101. VF-30.
The areas of wear appear exaggerated due to the light toning, a feature often observed on half dollars of this date but not as often among other years.

F-12, 15 (Fine)

Obverse. Wear is more extensive, with much of the hair blended together. The drapery is indistinct on most of its upper edge. The stars are flat at their centers. LIBERTY remains bold.

Reverse. Wear is more extensive, now with only about half of the feathers remaining on the wings, more on the right wing. The head shows the eye, nostril, and beak but no details. The claws show more wear. Other features are worn as well, but not as noticeable as the key points mentioned.

Illustrated coin: 1827, Overton-122. F-12.

VG-8, 10 (Very Good)

Obverse. The hair is less distinct, with the forehead blended into the hair above. LIBERTY is complete, but may be slightly weak in areas. The stars are flat. The rim is distinct, with most if not all dentils visible.

Reverse. Feathers are fewer and mostly on the right wing, although sharp strikes can show detail in both wings. Other details are weaker. All lettering remains easily readable.

Illustrated coin: 1831, Overton-120. VG-8.
This coin was cleaned and partially retoned. It is sharply struck on the reverse.

G-4, 6 (Good)

Obverse. The portrait is mostly in outline, with few interior details discernible. LIBERTY may still be readable or may be partially worn away, depending on the variety. The rim is weak, but distinct in most areas.

Reverse. The eagle is mostly in outline form, although some feathers can be seen in the right wing. All letters around the border are clear. E PLURIBUS UNUM may be weak. Overall, a typical coin has the reverse in a slightly higher grade than the obverse.

Illustrated coin: 1808. G-4.

AG-3 (About Good)

Obverse. The portrait is an outline, although some of LIBERTY can still be seen. The rim is worn down, and some stars are blended into it. The date remains clear, but is weak at the bottom (on most but not all).

Reverse. At this level the reverse shows more wear overall than the obverse, with the rim indistinct in areas and many letters worn away. This is an interesting turnabout from the situation of most G-4 coins.

Illustrated coin: 1824. AG-3.

Proof Capped Bust / Lettered Half Dollars, PF-60 to 70

Proofs were made in limited numbers for presentation purposes and for distribution to numismatists. True Proofs have deeply mirrored surfaces. Impostors are often seen, with deeply toned surfaces or with patches of mint luster. This situation is more prevalent with half dollars than with any other Capped Bust denomination. Proceed slowly, and be careful. There are some crushed-lettered-edge ("CLE") Proofs of the 1833 to 1835 era that are especially beautiful and are more deeply mirrorlike than original issues. Some of these are restrikes (not necessarily an important consideration, but worth mentioning), believed to have been made at the Mint beginning in the spring of 1859.

Illustrated coin: 1836, Overton-108. PF-64 Cameo.
This coin has some minor marks, but exceptional eye appeal.

Obverse and Reverse. Proofs of this type have confused experts for a long time (as have large copper cents of the same era). Proofs that were extensively cleaned and therefore have many hairlines, or that are dull and grainy, are lower level, such as PF-60 to 62. While any early Proof half dollar will generate interest among collectors, lower levels are not of great interest to specialists unless they are of rare die varieties. With medium hairlines, an assigned grade of PF-64 may be in order and with relatively few, Gem PF-65. PF-66 should have hairlines so delicate that magnification is needed to see them. Above that, a Proof should be free of such lines. Grading is highly subjective with early Proofs, with eye appeal being a major factor.

1836–1839 CAPPED BUST, REEDED EDGE

History. The obverse of this type features John Reich's Capped Bust, now restyled slightly, and of smaller diameter, made with a reeded edge. The reverse is of two variations, the 1836–1837 type with 50 CENTS and the 1838–1839 with HALF DOL. New Orleans Mint varieties include 1838-O (a rarity) and 1839-O.

Striking and Sharpness. Check the stars on the obverse, the key point for observation. On the reverse, check the border letters and the details of the eagle. The 1839-O nearly always shows die cracks, often extensive (these have no effect on desirability or market value).

Availability. The 1836 is rare. The 1838-O is a famous rarity (ranked among the top 25 in *100 Greatest U.S. Coins,* by Jeff Garrett and Ron Guth), and the 1839-O is scarce. The others are easily available in nearly any grade desired, with 1837 being the most common.

MS-60 to 70 (Mint State)

Illustrated coin: 1837. MS-62.
This example displays light gray toning with a sprinkling of gold over fully lustrous surfaces.

Note: All coins are shown enlarged, for clarity.

Obverse and Reverse. Grading guidelines are the same as for the 1807–1836 type, except on this type the rims are more uniform. On the 1836–1837 dates the reverse rim is generally lower than the obverse, causing the reverse to wear slightly more quickly. On the 1838–1839 type (with slightly different lettering) the wear occurs evenly on both sides, and light striking showing areas of the original planchet on the obverse does not occur here.

AU-50, 53, 55, 58 (About Uncirculated)

Obverse and Reverse. Grading guidelines are the same as for the 1807–1836 type, except on this type the rims are more uniform. On the 1836–1837 dates the reverse rim is generally lower than the obverse, causing the reverse to awear slightly more quickly. On the 1838–1839 type (with slightly different lettering) the wear occurs evenly on both sides.

Illustrated coin: 1836. AU-53.

EF-40, 45 (Extremely Fine)

Obverse and Reverse. Grading guidelines are the same as for the 1807–1836 type, except on this type the rims are more uniform. On the 1836–1837 dates the reverse rim is generally lower than the obverse, causing the reverse to wear slightly more quickly. On the 1838–1839 type (with slightly different lettering) the wear occurs evenly on both sides.

Illustrated coin: 1836. EF-40.

VF-20, 30 (Very Fine)

Obverse and Reverse. Grading guidelines are the same as for the 1807–1836 type, except on this type the rims are more uniform. On the 1836–1837 dates the reverse rim is generally lower than the obverse, causing the reverse to wear slightly more quickly. On the 1838–1839 type (with slightly different lettering) the wear occurs evenly on both sides.

Illustrated coin: 1836. VF-20.

F-12, 15 (Fine)

Obverse and Reverse. Grading guidelines are the same as for the 1807–1836 type, except on this type the rims are more uniform. On the 1836–1837 dates the reverse rim is generally lower than the obverse, causing the reverse to wear slightly more quickly. On the 1838–1839 type (with slightly different lettering) the wear occurs evenly on both sides.

Illustrated coin: 1839-O. F-15.

VG-8, 10 (Very Good)

Obverse and Reverse. Grading guidelines are the same as for the 1807–1836 type, except on this type the rims are more uniform. On the 1836–1837 dates the reverse rim is generally lower than the obverse, causing the reverse to wear slightly more quickly. On the 1838–1839 type (with slightly different lettering) the wear occurs evenly on both sides.

Illustrated coin: 1836. VG-10.

G-4, 6 (Good)

Obverse and Reverse. Grading guidelines are the same as for the 1807–1836 type, except on this type the rims are more uniform. On the 1836–1837 dates the reverse rim is generally lower than the obverse, causing the reverse to wear slightly more quickly. On the 1838–1839 type (with slightly different lettering) the wear occurs evenly on both sides.

Illustrated coin: 1838. G-4.

AG-3 (About Good)

Obverse and Reverse. Grading guidelines are the same as for the 1807–1836 type, except on this type the rims are more uniform. On the 1836–1837 dates the reverse rim is generally lower than the obverse, causing the reverse to wear slightly more quickly. On the 1838–1839 type (with slightly different lettering) the wear occurs evenly on both sides.

Illustrated coin: 1836. AG-3.

Proof Capped Bust / Reeded Half Dollars, PF-60 to 70

Proofs are occasionally encountered of the year 1836 and are quite rare. Authentic Proofs of 1837 exist but for all practical purposes are unobtainable. Most 1838-O (a rarity) and a few 1839-O have been called branch-mint Proofs.

Obverse and Reverse. Proofs in grades of PF-60 to 62 show extensive hairlines and cloudiness. At PF-63, hairlines are obvious, but the mirrored fields are attractive. PF-64 and 65 coins have fewer hairlines, but they still are obvious when the coin is slowly turned while held at an angle to the light. PF-66 coins require a magnifier to discern hairlines, and higher grades should have no hairlines.

Illustrated coin: 1836. PF-64 Cameo.
Note the lightly toned surfaces on both sides.

1839–1891 Liberty Seated

History. Liberty Seated half dollars were made continuously from 1839 to 1891, with several different types along the way. The basic obverse and reverse motifs remained the same. These were very popular in their time, and large quantities were made until 1879, at which time silver coins were a glut in commerce, and mintages were reduced.

Striking and Sharpness. On the obverse, first check the head of Miss Liberty and the star centers. On Arrows at Date coins, especially 1855, LIBERTY tends to wear more quickly compared to other varieties. On the reverse, check the eagle at the lower left. Afterward, check all other features. Generally, the higher-mintage issues are the least well struck, and many New Orleans Mint coins can be lightly struck as well, particularly those in the 1850s. Mint State luster is usually lovely. Resurfaced dies are often prooflike, some, especially the 1877-S, with the drapery polished away.

Above and beyond issues of strike, the Small Letters varieties of 1839 to 1842 have narrower, lower rims that afforded less protection to the central devices of the reverse. In contrast, the No Motto, Large Letters varieties have wider, higher rims that tended to better protect the central devices.

Many pre–Civil War dates, particularly of the 1840s, show evidence of extensive die polishing in the fields (especially evident in the open expanses of the obverse).

Availability. These are popular with many collectors, including members of the Liberty Seated Collectors Club. Examples of the higher-mintage dates are readily available, with earlier years being much scarcer than later ones. Most often seen among Mint State coins are issues from the mid-1870s onward. Circulated coins from well worn through About Uncirculated can be found of most dates and mintmarks, and are avidly sought.

MS-60 to 70 (Mint State)

Illustrated coin: 1856-O. MS-63. This lightly toned coin has nice eye appeal.

Note: All coins are shown enlarged, for clarity.

Obverse. At MS-60, some abrasion and contact marks are evident, most noticeably on the bosom and thighs and knees. Luster is present, but may be dull or lifeless. At MS-63, contact marks are very few, and abrasion is hard to detect except under magnification. An MS-65 coin has no abrasion, and contact marks are sufficiently minute as to require magnification. Check the knees of Liberty and the right field. Luster should be full and rich. Most Mint State coins of the 1861 to 1865 years, Philadelphia issues, have extensive die striae (from dies not being completely finished); note that these are *raised* (whereas cleaning hairlines are incuse).

Reverse. Comments as preceding, except that in lower Mint State grades abrasion and contact marks are most noticeable on the eagle's head, neck, and claws, and the top of the wings (harder to see there, however). At MS-65 or higher there are no marks visible to the unaided eye. The field is mainly protected by design elements and does not show abrasion as much as does the obverse on a given coin.

AU-50, 53, 55, 58 (About Uncirculated)

Obverse. Light wear is seen on the thighs and knees, bosom, and head. At AU-58, the luster is extensive, but incomplete, especially in the right field. At AU-50 and 53, luster is less.

Reverse. Wear is evident on the eagle's neck, the claws, and the top of the wings. An AU-58 coin has nearly full luster, more so than on the obverse, as the design elements protect the small field areas. At AU-50 and 53, there still are traces of luster.

Illustrated coin: 1841-O. AU-55.
Gray toning is evident on this coin. The reverse is lightly struck, a characteristic that should not be mistaken for wear.

EF-40, 45 (Extremely Fine)

Obverse. Further wear is seen on all areas, especially the thighs and knees, bosom, and head. Little or no luster is seen on most coins. From this grade downward, sharpness of strike of stars and the head does not matter to connoisseurs.

Reverse. Further wear is evident on the eagle's neck, claws, and wings.

Illustrated coin: 1839, No Drapery From Elbow. EF-40.

VF-20, 30 (Very Fine)

Obverse. Further wear is seen. Most details of the gown are worn away, except in the lower-relief areas above and to the right of the shield. Hair detail is mostly or completely gone.

Reverse. Wear is more extensive, with some of the feathers blended together.

Illustrated coin: 1839, No Drapery From Elbow. VF-20.

F-12, 15 (Fine)

Obverse. The seated figure is well worn, but with some detail above and to the right of the shield. LIBERTY is readable but weak in areas, perhaps with a letter missing (a slightly looser interpretation than the demand for full LIBERTY a generation ago).

Reverse. Wear is extensive, with about a third to half of the feathers flat or blended with others.

Illustrated coin: 1842-O, Small Date. F-12.

VG-8, 10 (Very Good)

Obverse. The seated figure is more worn, but some detail can be seen above and to the right of the shield. The shield is discernible, but the upper-right section may be flat and blended into the seated figure. In LIBERTY at least the equivalent of two or three letters (can be a combination of partial letters) must be readable, possibly very weak at VG-8, with a few more visible at VG-10. In the marketplace and among certified coins, parts of

Illustrated coin: 1873-CC, Arrows at Date. VG-8.

two letters seem to be allowed. Per PCGS, "localized weakness may obscure some letters." *However,* LIBERTY is not an infallible way to grade this type, as some varieties have the word in low relief on the die, so it wore away slowly.

Reverse. Further wear has flattened all but a few feathers, and many if not most horizontal lines of the shield are indistinct. The leaves are only in outline form. The rim is visible all around, as are the ends of most dentils.

G-4, 6 (Good)

Obverse. The seated figure is worn nearly smooth. At G-4 there are no letters in LIBERTY remaining on most (but not all) coins; some coins, especially of the early 1870s, are exceptions. At G-6, traces of one or two can barely be seen and more details can be seen in the figure.

Reverse. The eagle shows only a few details of the shield and feathers. The rim is worn down, and the tops of the border letters are weak or worn away, although the inscription can still be read.

Illustrated coin: 1873, Open 3. G-6.

AG-3 (About Good)

Obverse. The seated figure is visible in outline form. Much or all of the rim is worn away. The date remains clear.

Reverse. The border letters are partially worn away. The eagle is mostly in outline form, but with a few details discernible. The rim is weak or missing.

Illustrated coin: 1873, Open 3. AG-3.

Proof Liberty Seated Half Dollars, PF-60 to 70

Proofs were made in most years, with production beginning in a particularly significant way in 1858, when an estimated 210 silver sets were sold. Today, Proofs are readily available from 1858 through 1891. Quality is often lacking, with lint marks seen on some issues of the late 1850s and early 1860s. Light striking is occasionally seen on the star centers and the head of Miss Liberty; connoisseurs avoid these, but most buyers will not be aware. Slide marks (usually seen on the right knee) from coin albums can be a problem, more so on Liberty Seated halves than on lower denominations of this design.

Illustrated coin: 1889. PF-65.
This lovely gem has cameo contrast against mirrored fields.

Obverse and Reverse. Proofs that are extensively cleaned and have many hairlines, or that are dull and grainy, are lower level, such as PF-60 to 62. These are not widely desired, save for the low mintage (in circulation-strike format) years from 1879 to 1891. With medium hairlines and good reflectivity, an assigned grade of PF-64 is appropriate, and with relatively few hairlines, Gem PF-65. In various grades hairlines are most easily seen in the obverse field. PF-66 should have hairlines so delicate that magnification is needed to see them. Above that, a Proof should be free of such lines.

1892–1915 BARBER

History. Designed by Charles E. Barber, the "Barber" or Liberty Head half dollars have the same motifs used on Barber quarters. Production was continuous from 1892 to 1915, stopping one year short of the end of the Barber dime and quarter.

Striking and Sharpness. On the obverse, check the hair details and other features. On the reverse, the eagle's leg at the lower right and the arrows are often weak, and there can be weakness at the upper right of the shield and the nearby wing area. Barber coins tended to wear quickly in circulation. Only a tiny percentage of survivors grade Fine or better.

Availability. Most examples seen in the marketplace are well worn. There are no rarities, although some are scarcer than others. Coins that are Fine or better are much scarcer—in particular the San Francisco Mint issues of 1901, 1904, and 1907. Mint State coins are available of all dates and mints, but some are very elusive.

MS-60 to 70 (Mint State)

Illustrated coin: 1909. MS-62.
On this example, mottled light-brown toning appears over lustrous surfaces.

Note: All coins are shown enlarged, for clarity.

Obverse. At MS-60, some abrasion and contact marks are evident, most noticeably on the cheek and the obverse field to the right. Luster is present, but may be dull or lifeless. Many Barber coins have been cleaned, especially of the earlier dates. At MS-63, contact marks are very few; abrasion still is evident but less than at lower levels. Indeed, the cheek of Miss Liberty virtually showcases abrasion. This is even more evident on a half dollar than on lower denominations. An MS-65 coin may have minor abrasion, but contact marks are so minute as to require magnification. Luster should be full and rich.

Reverse. Comments apply as for the obverse, except that in lower Mint State grades abrasion and contact marks are most noticeable on the head and tail of the eagle and on the tips of the wings. At MS-65 or higher there are no marks visible to the unaided eye. The field is mainly protected by design elements, so the reverse often appears to grade a point or two higher than the obverse.

AU-50, 53, 55, 58 (About Uncirculated)

Obverse. Light wear is seen on the head, especially on the forward hair under LIBERTY. At AU-58, the luster is extensive but incomplete, especially on the higher parts and in the right field. At AU-50 and 53, luster is less.

Reverse. Wear is seen on the head and tail of the eagle and on the tips of the wings. At AU-50 and 53, there still is significant luster. An AU-58 coin (as determined by the obverse) can have the reverse appear to be full Mint State.

Illustrated coin: 1915-D. AU-53.
Areas of original Mint luster can be seen on this coin, more so on the reverse than on the obverse.

EF-40, 45 (Extremely Fine)

Obverse. Further wear is seen on the head. The hair above the forehead lacks most detail. LIBERTY shows wear but still is strong.

Reverse. Further wear is seen on the head and tail of the eagle and on the tips of the wings, most evident at the left and right extremes of the wings At this level and below, sharpness of strike on the reverse is not important.

Illustrated coin: 1908-S. EF-45.

VF-20, 30 (Very Fine)

Obverse. The head shows more wear, now with nearly all detail gone in the hair above the forehead. LIBERTY shows wear, but is complete. The leaves on the head all show wear, as does the upper part of the cap.

Reverse. Wear is more extensive, particularly noticeable on the outer parts of the wings, the head, the shield, and the tail.

Illustrated coin: 1897-S. VF-30.
This coin is seemingly lightly cleaned.

F-12, 15 (Fine)

Obverse. The head shows extensive wear. LIBERTY, the key place to check, is weak, especially at ER, but is fully readable. The ANA grading standards and *Photograde* adhere to this. PCGS suggests that lightly struck coins "may have letters partially missing." Traditionally, collectors insist on full LIBERTY.

Reverse. More wear is seen on the reverse, in the places as above. E PLURIBUS UNUM is light, with one to several letters worn away.

Illustrated coin: 1909-O. F-12.

VG-8, 10 (Very Good)

Obverse. A net of three letters in LIBERTY must be readable. Traditionally LI is clear, and after that there is a partial letter or two.

Reverse. Further wear has smoothed more than half of the feathers in the wing. The shield is indistinct except for a few traces of interior lines. The motto is partially worn away. The rim is full, and many if not most dentils can be seen.

Illustrated coin: 1915-S. VG-8.

G-4, 6 (Good)

Obverse. The head is in outline form, with the center flat. Most of the rim is there and all letters and the date are full.

Reverse. The eagle shows only a few feathers, and only a few scattered letters remain in the motto. The rim may be worn flat in some or all of the area, but the peripheral lettering is clear.

Illustrated coin: 1892-O. G-4.
On this coin the obverse is perhaps G-6 and the reverse AG-3. The grade might be averaged as G-4.

AG-3 (About Good)

Obverse. The stars and motto are worn, and the border may be indistinct. Distinctness varies at this level. The date is clear. Grading is usually determined by the reverse.

Reverse. The rim is gone and the letters are partially worn away. The eagle is mostly flat, perhaps with a few hints of feathers. Usually, the obverse appears to be in a slightly higher grade than the reverse.

Illustrated coin: 1896-S. AG-3.

Proof Barber Half Dollars, PF-60 to 70

Proofs exist in proportion to their mintages. Choicer examples tend to be of later dates, similar to other Barber coins. Most are sharply struck, although many are weak on the eagle's leg at the lower right and on certain parts of the arrows and/or the upper right of the shield and the nearby wing. The Proofs of 1892 to 1901 usually have cameo contrast between the designs and the mirror fields. Those of 1914 and 1915 are often with extensive hairlines or other problems.

Illustrated coin: 1914. PF-61.
This is an attractive coin at the relatively low PF-61 grade.

Obverse and Reverse. Proofs that are extensively cleaned and have many hairlines, or that are dull and grainy, are lower level, such as PF-60 to 62; these are not widely desired. With medium hairlines and good reflectivity, an assigned grade of PF-64 is appropriate. Tiny horizontal lines on Miss Liberty's cheek, known as slide marks, from National and other album slides scuffing the relief of the cheek, are endemic on all Barber silver coins. With noticeable marks of this type, the highest grade assignable is PF-64. With relatively few hairlines, a rating of PF-65 can be given. PF-66 should have hairlines so delicate that magnification is needed to see them. Above that, a Proof should be free of any hairlines or other problems.

1916–1947 LIBERTY WALKING

History. Designed by Adolph A. Weinman, the sculptor who also created the Mercury or Winged Liberty Head dime, the Liberty Walking half dollar is considered to be one of the most beautiful of all American coins. Mintage was intermittent, and none were struck in 1922, 1924 to 1926, and 1930 to 1932. Later years of this type were common in circulation until the rise of silver bullion value in the late 1960s.

Striking and Sharpness. A secret, an advantage and opportunity waiting to happen, is that most circulation-strike half dollars of this type are lightly struck. In this respect they are similar to Standing Liberty quarters of the same era. On the obverse, the key points to check are Miss Liberty's left hand, the higher parts and lines in the skirt, and her head; after that, check all other areas. *Very few* coins are sharply struck in these areas, and for some issues sharp strikes might not exist at all! On the reverse, check the breast of the eagle. No one has ever assembled a complete set with Full Details. If certification services ever recognized and tagged Full Details coins, or even those with 90% details, prices would explode for issues that are very rare if well struck! In the meantime, the opportunity to cherrypick beckons; seek the sharpest strike you can locate.

Availability. All dates and mintmarks are readily collectible, although some, such as 1917-S (obverse mintmark), 1919-D, the three issues of 1921, and 1938-D, are scarce. Earlier years are often seen with extensive wear. Mint State coins are most often seen of the three issues of 1916, the 1917, and from 1933 to 1947. Issues in the 1940s were saved in quantities and are common. As noted, coins with Full Details can range from scarce to extremely rare for certain dates.

MS-60 to 70 (Mint State)

Illustrated coin: 1917. MS-65.
The pictured coin is a lustrous gem example of this early Liberty Walking half dollar date.

Note: All coins are shown enlarged, for clarity.

Obverse. At MS-60, some abrasion and contact marks are evident on the higher areas, which are also the areas most likely to be weakly struck. This includes Miss Liberty's left arm, her hand, and the areas of the skirt covering her left leg. The luster may not be complete in those areas on weakly struck coins (even those certified above MS-65)—the *original planchet surface* may be revealed, as it was not smoothed out by striking. Accordingly, grading is best done by evaluating abrasion as it is observed *in the right field*, plus evaluating the mint luster. Luster may be dull or lifeless at MS-60 to 62, but should have deep frost at MS-63 or better, particularly in the lower-relief areas. At MS-65 or better, it should be full and rich. Sometimes, to compensate for flat striking, certified coins with virtually flawless luster in the fields, evocative of an MS-65 or 66 grade, are called MS-63 or a lower grade. Such coins would seem to offer a lot of value for the money, if the variety is one that is not found with Full Details (1923-S is one of many examples).

Reverse. Striking is usually better, permitting observation of luster in all areas except the eagle's body, which may be lightly struck. Luster may be dull or lifeless at MS-60 to 62, but should have deep frost at MS-63 or better, particularly in the lower-relief areas. At MS-65 or better, it should be full and rich.

AU-50, 53, 55, 58 (About Uncirculated)

Obverse. Light wear is seen on the higher-relief areas of Miss Liberty, the vertical area from her head down to the date. At AU-58, the luster in the field is extensive, but is interrupted by friction and light wear. At AU-50 and 53, luster is less.

Reverse. Wear is most evident on the eagle's breast immediately under the neck feathers, the left leg, and the top of the left wing. Luster is nearly complete at AU-58, but at AU-50 half or more is gone.

Illustrated coin: 1921-S. AU-50.

EF-40, 45 (Extremely Fine)

Obverse. Wear is more extensive, with the higher parts of Miss Liberty now without detail, and with no skirt lines visible directly over her left leg. Little or no luster is seen.

Reverse. The eagle shows more wear overall, with the highest parts of the body and left leg worn flat.

Illustrated coin: 1919-S. EF-40.

VF-20, 30 (Very Fine)

Obverse. Wear is more extensive, and Miss Liberty is worn mostly flat in the line from her head to her left foot. Her skirt is worn, but most lines are seen, except over the leg and to the left and right. The lower part of her cape (to the left of her waist) is worn.

Reverse. The eagle is worn smooth from the head to the left leg, and the right leg is flat at the top. Most feathers in the wings are delineated, but weak.

Illustrated coin: 1921-S. VF-20.

F-12, 15 (Fine)

Obverse. Wear is more extensive, now with only a few light lines visible in the skirt. The rays of the sun are weak below the cape, and may be worn away at their tips.

Reverse. Wear is more extensive, with most details now gone on the eagle's right leg. Delineation of the feathers is less, and most in the upper area and right edge of the left wing are blended together.

Illustrated coin: 1918-S. F-12.

VG-8, 10 (Very Good)

Obverse. Wear is slightly more extensive, but the rim still is defined all around. The tops of the date numerals are worn and blend slightly into the ground above.

Reverse. Wear is more extensive. On the left wing only a few feathers are delineated, and on the shoulder of the right wing most detail is gone. Detail in the pine branch is lost and it appears as a clump.

Illustrated coin: 1921-D. VG-8.

G-4, 6 (Good)

Obverse. Miss Liberty is worn flat, with her head, neck, and arms all blended together. Folds can be seen at the bottom of the skirt, but the lines are worn away. The rim is worn done into the tops of some of the letters.

Reverse. All areas show more wear. The rim is worn down into the tops of some of the letters, particularly at the top border.

Illustrated coin: 1917-S, mintmark on obverse. G-4.

AG-3 (About Good)

Obverse. Wear is more extensive. The sun's rays are nearly all gone, the motto is very light and sometimes incomplete, and the rim is worn down into more of the letters.

Reverse. Wear is more extensive, with the eagle essentially worn flat. The rim is worn down into more of the letters.

Illustrated coin: 1918. AG-3.

Proof Liberty Walking Half Dollars, PF-60 to 70

Proofs were made beginning in 1936 and continuing through 1942. The entire die was polished (including the figure of Miss Liberty and the eagle), generating pieces of low contrast. Proofs are usually fairly well struck. Most Proofs of 1941 are from over-polished dies, with the AW monogram of the designer no longer present. Striking sharpness can vary. Seek coins with full head and left hand details.

Illustrated coin: 1939. PF-65.
This example is a brilliant gem Proof.

Obverse and Reverse. Proofs that are extensively cleaned and have many hairlines, or that are dull and grainy, are lower level, such as PF-60 to 62. These are not widely desired, and represent coins that have been mistreated. With medium hairlines and good reflectivity, assigned grades of PF-63 or 64 are appropriate. Tiny horizontal lines on Miss Liberty's leg, known as slide marks, from National and other album slides scuffing the relief of the cheek, are common; coins with such marks should not be graded higher than PF-64, but sometimes are. With relatively few hairlines and no noticeable slide marks, a rating of PF-65 can be given. PF-66 should have hairlines so delicate that magnification is needed to see them. Above that, a Proof should be free of any hairlines or other problems.

1948–1963 FRANKLIN

History. Designed by Chief Engraver John R. Sinnock (after a motif he made for an unadopted *silver half dime* in 1942), the Franklin half dollar was introduced in 1948. It attracted almost no numismatic interest or attention, perhaps as the design was viewed as sub-par in comparison to the elegant Liberty Walking half dollar. Collectors routinely added examples to keep their sets current, and rolls were saved by investors. In 1964 the motif was replaced by John F. Kennedy's portrait. The change was little lamented. Franklin halves disappeared from circulation in the late 1960s as their silver value became greater than their face value. As time went on, the Franklin half dollar grew increasingly popular with numismatists. Today it is widely collected.

Striking and Sharpness. The indistinct details of the obverse make a review of the sharpness of strike difficult, and thus this aspect is usually ignored. On the reverse the bottom lines of the Liberty Bell are often studied. If complete, the coin may be designated as Full Bell Lines (FBL). Certain varieties with FBL are worth a strong premium.

Availability. All dates and mintmarks are easily available in grades from Very Fine upward. Lower-level Mint State coins can be unattractive due to contact marks and abrasion, particularly noticeable on the obverse. High-quality gems are generally inexpensive, although varieties that are rare with FBL can be costly amid much competition in the marketplace. Most numismatists collect Mint State coins. Grades below Extremely Fine are not widely desired.

MS-60 to 70 (Mint State)

Illustrated coin: 1951-S. MS-65.
Satiny brilliance is seen on the obverse of this coin, light golden toning on the reverse.

Note: All coins are shown enlarged, for clarity.

Obverse. At MS-60, some abrasion and contact marks are evident on the cheek, on the hair left of the ear, and the neck. At MS-63, abrasion is slight at best, less so for MS-64. An MS-65 coin should display no abrasion or contact marks except under magnification, and MS-66 and higher coins should have none at all. Luster should be full and rich. As details are shallow on this design, the amount and "depth" of luster is important to grading.

Reverse. General comments apply as for the obverse. The points to check are the bell harness, the words PASS AND STOW on the upper area of the Liberty Bell, and the bottom of the bell.

AU-50, 53, 55, 58 (About Uncirculated)

Obverse. At AU-50, medium wear is evident on the portrait, and most of the luster in the field is gone. At AU-53, wear is less and luster is more extensive. AU-55 and 58 coins show much luster. Wear is noticeable on the portrait and, to a lesser extent, in the field.

Reverse. At AU-50, medium wear is evident on most of the Liberty Bell, and most of the luster in the field is gone. At AU-53, wear is slightly less. AU-55 and 58 coins show much luster. Light wear is seen on the higher areas of the bell.

Illustrated coin: 1949-D. AU-50.

EF-40, 45 (Extremely Fine)

Obverse. Wear is more extensive, and some hair detail (never strong to begin with) is lost. There is no luster.

Reverse. Wear is seen overall. The inscription on the bell is weak, and the highest parts of the bottom horizontal lines are worn away. There is no luster.

Illustrated coin: 1955. EF-40.

The Franklin half dollar is seldom collected in grades lower than EF-40.

Proof Franklin Half Dollars, PF-60 to 70

Proofs were made from 1950 to 1963 and are available today in proportion to their mintages. Those with cameo-frosted devices are in the minority and often sell for strong premiums. Virtually all Proofs are well struck.

Illustrated coin: 1950. PF-65 Cameo.

Obverse and Reverse. Proofs that are extensively cleaned and have many hairlines, or that are dull and grainy, are lower level, such as PF-60 to 62. These are not widely desired, and represent coins that have been mistreated. Fortunately, only a few Proof Franklin half dollars are in this category. With medium hairlines and good reflectivity, assigned grades of PF-63 or 64 are appropriate. PF-66 should have hairlines so delicate that magnification is needed to see them. Above that, a Proof should be free of any hairlines or other problems.

1964 TO DATE KENNEDY

History. Kennedy half dollars, minted from 1964 to date, were struck in 90% silver the first year, then with reduced silver content through 1970, and in later years in copper-nickel (except for special silver issues made for collectors). The obverse, by Chief Engraver Gilroy Roberts, features a pleasing portrait of President John F. Kennedy, while the reverse, by Frank Gasparro, displays a modern version of a heraldic eagle. The 1976 Bicentennial design features a depiction of Independence Hall virtually identical to that shown on the 1926 Sesquicentennial commemorative quarter eagle.

Striking and Sharpness. Nearly all are well struck. Check the highest points of the hair on the obverse and the highest details on the reverse.

Availability. All issues are common in such grades as Extremely Fine, About Uncirculated, and Mint State, including Gems of the latter.

MS-60 to 70 (Mint State)

Illustrated coin: 1964. MS-66.

Note: All coins are shown enlarged, for clarity.

Obverse. At MS-60, some abrasion and contact marks are evident on the cheek, and on the hair to the right of the forehead and temple. At MS-63, abrasion is slight at most, and less so for MS-64. An MS-65 coin should display no abrasion or contact marks except under magnification, and MS-66 and higher coins should have none at all. Luster should be full and rich.

Reverse. Comments apply as for the obverse, except that the highest parts of the eagle at the center are the key places to check.

AU-50, 53, 55, 58 (About Uncirculated)

Obverse. Light wear is seen on the cheek and higher-relief area of the hair below the part, high above the ear. At AU-58, the luster is extensive but incomplete, especially on the higher parts and in the field. At AU-50 and 53, luster is less.

Reverse. Light wear is seen on the higher parts of the eagle. At AU-50 and 53 there still is significant luster.

Illustrated coin: 1964. AU-55.

EF-40, 45 (Extremely Fine)

Obverse. Further wear is seen on the head. More details are gone on the higher parts of the hair.

Reverse. Further wear is seen on the eagle in particular, but also on other areas in high relief (including the leaves, arrowheads, and clouds).

Illustrated coin: 1964. EF-45.

The Kennedy half dollar is seldom collected in grades lower than EF-40.

Proof Kennedy Half Dollars, PF-60 to 70

Proofs of 1964 were struck at the Philadelphia Mint. Those from 1968 to date have been made in San Francisco. All are easily obtained. Most from the 1970s to date have cameo contrast. Special Mint Set (SMS) coins were struck in lieu of Proofs from 1965 to 1967; in some instances, these closely resemble Proofs. Silver Proofs have been struck in recent years, for Silver Proof sets. In 1998, a special Matte Proof silver Kennedy half dollar was struck for inclusion in the Robert F. Kennedy commemorative coin set.

Illustrated coin: 1964. PF-66.

Obverse and Reverse. Proofs that are extensively cleaned and have many hairlines, or that are dull and grainy, are lower level, such as PF-60 to 62. There are not many of these in the marketplace. With medium hairlines and good reflectivity, assigned grades of PF-63 or 64 are appropriate. With relatively few hairlines a rating of PF-65 can be given. PF-66 should have hairlines so delicate that magnification is needed to see them. Above that, a Proof should be free of any hairlines or other problems.

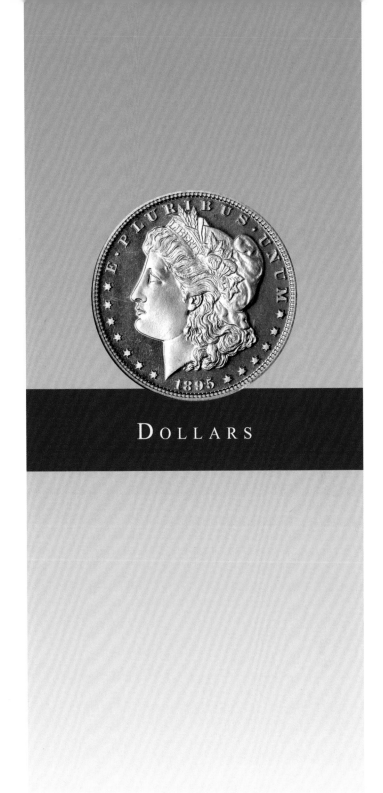

DOLLARS

DOLLARS, 1794 TO DATE

1794–1795 FLOWING HAIR

History. The first silver dollars were of the Flowing Hair design. In 1794 only 1,758 were released (slightly more were struck), and in 1795 an estimated 160,295 or more were made. These were popular in their time and circulated for decades afterward. Many were used in international trade, particularly in the Caribbean.

Striking and Sharpness. On the obverse, check the hair details. It is essential to check the die variety, as certain varieties were struck with very little detail at the center. Accordingly, high-grade examples can appear to be well worn on the hair. Check the star centers as well. On the reverse, check the breast and wings of the eagle. All 1794 dollars are lightly struck at the lower left of the obverse (often at portions of the date) and to a lesser extent the corresponding part of the reverse. Many coins of both dates have planchet adjustment marks, often heavy and sometimes even disfiguring; these are not noted by the certification services. Expect weakness in some areas on dollars of this type. There is hardly such a coin as one with Full Details on each side. Sharp striking and excellent eye appeal will add to the value dramatically. These large and heavy coins are very difficult to find problem-free, even at the Mint State level.

Availability. The 1794 is rare in all grades, with an estimated 125 to 135 known, including a handful of Mint State coins. "Anything goes" with the grading of this date, as can be seen if images are inspected of coins certified at different levels. The 1795 is easily available, although some die varieties range from scarce to rare. Many if not most have been dipped at one time or another, and many have been retoned, often satisfactorily. The existence of *any* luster bespeaks an exceptional coin at any level of sharpness between EF-40 and AU-58. Mint State coins are quite scarce, especially at MS-63 or above. Today's low-level Mint State coins may well have been designated as About Uncirculated generations ago (this statement being generally applicable to 18th-century coins). Connoisseurship is a requisite for buying, if you want good value for the price paid.

MS-60 to 70 (Mint State)

Illustrated coin: 1794, Bowers-Borckardt 1, Bolender 1. MS-64. Fully brilliant and highly lustrous. This coin exhibits the peculiarities of all 1794 dollars and is weak at the left obverse and the corresponding part of the reverse. Planchet flaws are seen at stars 3 and 5. The center obverse is very well struck and presents an elegant appearance. Formerly owned by F.C.C. Boyd, this is among the top handful of finest-known examples.

Note: Abbreviations used in die-variety attributions, along with the reference works on which the attributions are based, are discussed on the first page of this chapter. Mint State images are shown enlarged, for clarity.

Obverse. At MS-60, some abrasion and contact marks are evident, most noticeably on the cheek and in the fields. Luster is present, but may be dull or lifeless, and interrupted in patches. At MS-63, contact marks are very few, and abrasion is light and not obvious. An MS-65 coin has little or, better yet, no abrasion, and contact marks are minute. Luster should be full and rich. Coins graded above MS-65 are more theoretical than actual for this type—but they do exist, and are defined by having fewer marks as perfection is approached.

Reverse. Comments apply as for the obverse, except that abrasion and contact marks are most noticeable on the eagle at the center, although most dollars of this type are lightly struck in the higher points of that area. The field area is small and is protected by lettering and the wreath and in any given grade shows fewer marks than on the obverse.

AU-50, 53, 55, 58 (About Uncirculated)

Obverse. Light wear is seen on the hair area immediately to the left of the face and neck (except that some varieties were flatly struck in this area to begin with), on the cheek, and on the top of the neck truncation, more so at AU-50 than at 53 or 55. An AU-58 coin has minimal traces of wear. An AU-50 coin has luster in protected areas among the stars and letters, with little luster in the open fields or on the portrait. Some certified coins have virtually no luster, but are considered to be of high quality in other aspects. At AU-58, most luster is partially present in the fields. On any high-grade dollar, luster is often a better key to grading than is the appearance of wear.

Illustrated coin: 1795, BB-21, B-1. AU-58.
This coin shows above-average striking sharpness on the obverse.

Reverse. Light wear is seen on the eagle's body and the upper edges of the wings. At AU-50, detail is lost for some of the feathers in this area. However, striking can play a part, and some coins are weak to begin with. Light wear is seen on the wreath and lettering. Again, luster is the best key to actual wear. This ranges from perhaps 20% remaining in protected areas (at AU-50) to two-thirds or more (at AU-58). As a general rule, the reverse will have more luster than the obverse.

EF-40, 45 (Extremely Fine)

Obverse. More wear is evident on the portrait, especially on the hair to the left of the face and neck (again, remember that some varieties were struck with flatness in this area), the cheek, and the tip of the neck truncation. Excellent detail remains in low-relief areas of the hair. The stars show wear, as do the date and letters. Luster, if present at all, is minimal and in protected areas.

Illustrated coin: 1795, BB-26, B-12a. EF-40.
On the obverse, a massive die crack extends upward through the 7 of the date.

Reverse. The eagle shows more wear, this being the focal point to check. Most or nearly all detail is well defined. These aspects should be reviewed in combination with knowledge of the die variety, to determine the sharpness of the coin when it was first struck. Most silver dollars of this type were flat at the highest area of the center at the time they were made, as this was opposite the highest point of the hair in the press when the coins were struck. Additional wear is on the wreath and letters, but many details are present. Some luster may be seen in protected areas, and if present is slightly more abundant than on the obverse.

VF-20, 30 (Very Fine)

Obverse. The hair is well worn at VF-20, less so at VF-30. On well-struck varieties the weakness is in the area left of the temple and cheek. The strands are blended as to be heavy. The cheek shows only slight relief. The stars have more wear, making them appear larger (an optical illusion).

Illustrated coin: 1795, BB-21, B-1. VF-20.
Light rim bumps were described by the cataloger. Note the attractive medium toning.

Reverse. The body of the eagle shows few if any feathers, while the wings have a third to half of the feathers visible, depending on the strike. The leaves lack most detail, but veins can be seen on a few. Scattered, non-disfiguring marks are normal for this and lower grades. Any major defects should be noted separately.

F-12, 15 (Fine)

Obverse. Wear is more extensive than on the preceding, reducing the definition of the thick strands of hair. The cheek has less detail, but the eye is usually well defined. On most coins, the stars appear larger. The rim is distinct in most areas, and many dentils remain visible.

Reverse. Wear is more extensive. Now, feather details are fewer, mostly remaining on the wing to the left and at the extreme tip of the wing on the right. As always, the die variety in question can have an influence on this. The wreath and lettering are worn further. The rim is usually complete, with most dentils visible.

Illustrated coin: 1795, BB-27, B-5. F-12.
This variety is flatly struck on the head, and examples in higher grades show no detail at the center. Note the smooth, even wear with some marks.

VG-8, 10 (Very Good)

Obverse. The portrait is mostly seen in outline form, with most hair strands gone, although some are visible left of the neck, and the tips at the lower left are clear. The eye is distinct. The stars appear larger still, again an illusion. LIBERTY and the date are readable and usually full, although some letters may be weak at their tops. The rim is usually complete, and many dentils can be seen.

Reverse. The eagle is mostly an outline, although some traces of feathers may be seen in the tail and the lower part of the inside of the right wing. The rim is worn, as are the letters, with some weak, but the motto is readable.

Illustrated coin: 1795, BB-11, B-3. VG-10.
This coin shows some microscopic granularity overall. It is an interesting variety with a silver plug inserted at the center of the planchet prior to minting, to slightly increase the weight; this feature can barely be seen in outline form.

G-4, 6 (Good)

Obverse. Wear is more extensive. LIBERTY and the stars are all there, but weak. The head is an outline, although the eye can still be seen. The rim is well worn or even missing. LIBERTY is worn, and parts of some letters may be missing, but elements of all should be readable. The date is readable, but worn.

Reverse. The eagle is flat and discernible in outline form. The wreath is well worn. Some of the letters may be partly missing. At this level some "averaging" can be done. If the letters are stronger than usual in one area, but some are missing in another area, the coin can still qualify as G-4.

Illustrated coin: 1795, BB-11, B-1. G-6.
This is an attractive example with smooth, even wear and a few defects.

AG-3 (About Good)

Obverse. Wear is extensive, but some stars and letters can usually be discerned. The head is in outline form. The date, while readable, may be partially worn away.

Reverse. The reverse is well worn, with parts of the wreath and lettering missing.

Illustrated coin: 1795. AG-3.

1795–1798 DRAPED BUST, SMALL EAGLE

History. Inaugurated in 1795, the Draped Bust silver dollar type, with Small Eagle reverse, represents the first appearance of this popular obverse portrait—a depiction of Miss Liberty that later was extended to other silver denominations as well as copper half cents and cents. The motif was continued into 1798. Such coins circulated widely in their time, as evidenced by extensive wear on most surviving examples.

Striking and Sharpness. On the obverse, check the highest areas of the hair, the bust line, and the centers of the stars. On the reverse, check the feathers on the eagle's breast and wings. Examine the dentils. Planchet adjustment marks are common and should be avoided. Studying die varieties can be helpful. For example, the Small Letters reverse, a long-lived die design used from 1795 to 1798, has shallow relief and is usually seen with a low rim, with the result that its grade is lower than that of the obverse. On some reverse dies the eagle has very little detail. Fairly sharp striking (not necessarily Full Details) and excellent eye appeal will add to the value dramatically.

Availability. Examples are readily available as a type, although certain varieties range from scarce to very rare. Gradeflation is not as prevalent as for the Flowing Hair type. Mint State coins are elusive and when seen are usually of the 1795 date, sometimes with prooflike surfaces. Most coins have been dipped and/or retoned, some successfully. These large and heavy coins acquired marks more readily than did lower denominations, and such are to be expected (but should be separately described if distracting). Careful buying is needed to obtain coins with good eye appeal.

MS-60 to 70 (Mint State)

Illustrated coin: 1796, Small Date, Large Letters; Bowers-Borckardt 61, Bolender 2. MS-60. Note the tiny dig near Miss Liberty's ear. This coin is fairly well struck overall, but with some lightness on the eagle's body and leg on the right. It has excellent eye appeal.

Note: Abbreviations used in die-variety attributions, along with the reference works on which the attributions are based, are discussed on the first page of this chapter. Mint State images are shown enlarged, for clarity.

Obverse. At MS-60, some abrasion and contact marks are evident, most noticeably on the cheek, the drapery at the shoulder, and the right field. Luster is present, but may be dull or lifeless, and interrupted in patches. At MS-63, contact marks are few, and abrasion is harder to detect. Many coins listed as Mint State are deeply toned, making it impossible to evaluate abrasion and even light wear; these are best avoided completely. An MS-65 coin has no abrasion, and contact marks are so minute as to require magnification. Luster should be full and rich. Coins grading above MS-65 are more theoretical than actual for this type—but they do exist, and are defined by having fewer marks as perfection is approached.

Reverse. Comments apply as for the obverse, except that abrasion and contact marks are most noticeable on the eagle at the center, a situation complicated by the fact that this area was often flatly struck, not only on the famous Small Letters dies used from 1795 to 1798, but on some others as well. Grading is best done by the obverse, then verified by the reverse. In the Mint State category the amount of luster is usually a good key to grading. The field area is small and is protected by lettering and the wreath, and in any given grade shows fewer marks than on the obverse.

AU-50, 53, 55, 58 (About Uncirculated)

Obverse. Light wear is seen on the hair area above the ear and extending to left of the forehead, on the ribbon, and on the drapery at the shoulder, more so at AU-50 than at 53 or 55. An AU-58 coin has minimal traces of wear. An AU-50 coin has luster in protected areas among the stars and letters, with little in the open fields or on the portrait. At AU-58, most luster is present in the fields, but is worn away on the highest parts of the motifs. At this level there are many deeply toned and recolored coins, necessitating caution when buying.

Illustrated coin: 1797, Stars 9x7, Large Letters; BB-73, B-1. AU-50.
This coin has some lightness of strike, but is better than average. It has some dings and marks, but these are not immediately obvious; without them, the coin might grade higher. This illustrates the many variables on these large, heavy coins. No single rule fits all.

Reverse. Light wear is seen on the eagle's body (keep in mind this area might be lightly struck) and edges of the wings. Light wear is seen on the wreath and lettering. Luster is the best key to actual wear. This ranges from perhaps 20% remaining in protected areas (at AU-50) to nearly full mint bloom (at AU-58).

EF-40, 45 (Extremely Fine)

Obverse. More wear is evident on the upper hair area and the ribbon, and on the drapery and bosom. Excellent detail remains in low-relief areas of the hair. The stars show wear, as do the date and letters. Luster, if present at all, is minimal and in protected areas. For any and all dollars of this type, knowledge of die variety characteristics is essential to grading. Once again, one rule does not fit all.

Illustrated coin: 1796, Small Date, Large Letters; BB-61, B-4. EF-40.
Some marks are on the neck and a small pit is above the eagle's beak.

Reverse. The eagle, this being the focal point to check, shows more wear. On most strikings, the majority of feathers remain on the interior areas of the wings. Additional wear is on the wreath and letters, but many details are present. Some luster may be seen in protected areas and if present is slightly more abundant than on the obverse.

VF-20, 30 (Very Fine)

Obverse. The higher-relief areas of hair are well worn at VF-20, less so at VF-30. The drapery and bosom show extensive wear, usually resulting in loss of most detail below the neck. The stars have more wear, making them appear larger.

Reverse. The body of the eagle shows few if any feathers, while the wings have about half of the feathers visible, depending on the strike. The leaves lack most detail and are in outline form. Scattered, non-disfiguring marks are normal for this and lower grades. Any major defects should be noted separately.

Illustrated coin: 1797, Stars 9x7, Small Letters; BB-72, B-2. VF-20.

This is the particularly famous Small Letters die (one of three Small Letters dies used for this type) first used in 1795 and last used in 1798. Used on 1795 BB-51, later 1796 BB-62, BB-63, and BB-66 now relapped, 1797 BB-72, and 1798 BB-81. The rims are low, and the eagle is in low relief. For coins struck from this particular reverse die, grading must be done by the obverse only.

F-12, 15 (Fine)

Obverse. Wear is more extensive than on a Very Fine coin, particularly noticeable on the hair, face, and bosom. The stars appear larger. About half the hair detail remains, most noticeably behind the neck and shoulder. The rim shows wear but is complete or nearly so, with most dentils visible.

Reverse. Wear is more extensive. Now, feather details are diminished, with relatively few remaining on the wings. The wreath and lettering are worn further, and the rim is usually weak in areas, although most dentils can be seen.

Illustrated coin: 1796, Large Date, Small Letters; BB-65, B-5. F-12.

This is not the long-lived Small Letters die discussed above; this Small Letters die was used only in 1796. It is distinguished by a piece out of the die at the lower right of the reverse.

VG-8, 10 (Very Good)

Obverse. The portrait is worn further, with much detail lost in the area above the level of the ear, although the curl over the forehead is delineated. There is some definition at the back of the hair and behind the shoulder, with the hair now combined to form thick strands. The ear is discernible, as is the eye. The stars appear larger still, again an illusion. The rim is weak in areas. LIBERTY and the date are readable and usually full. The rim is worn away in areas, although many dentils can still be discerned.

Illustrated coin: 1796, Small Date, Large Letters; BB-61, B-4. VG-10. Note the vertical scratches on the cheek.

Reverse. The eagle is mostly an outline, with parts blending into the field (on lighter strikes). The rim is worn, as are the letters, with some weak, but the motto is readable.

G-4, 6 (Good)

Obverse. Wear is more extensive, and some stars may be partly missing. The head is an outline. The eye is visible only in outline form. The rim is well worn or even missing in areas. LIBERTY is worn, and parts of some letters may be missing, but elements of all should be readable. The date is readable, but worn. Usually the date is rather bold.

Illustrated coin: 1797, Stars 9x7, Large Letters; BB-73, B-1. G-4. This is a well-circulated coin with several edge bumps.

Reverse. The eagle is flat and discernible in outline form, and may be blending into the field. The wreath is well worn. Some of the letters may be partly missing (for some shallow-relief dies with low rims). At this level some "averaging" can be done. If the letters are stronger than usual in one area, but some are missing in another area, the coin can still qualify as G-4. This general rule is applicable to most other series as well.

AG-3 (About Good)

Obverse. Wear is very extensive, but most letters and stars should be discernible. The head is in outline form. The date, while readable, may be partially worn away.

Reverse. The reverse is well worn, with parts of the wreath and lettering missing. At this level, the reverse usually gives much less information than does the obverse.

Illustrated coin: 1796, Large Date, Small Letters; BB-65, B-5a. AG-3.

1798–1804 DRAPED BUST, HERALDIC EAGLE

History. This design closely follows that used on other silver coins of the era. Production continued through early 1804, but the last were from earlier-dated dies. Later, in 1834, new dies were made with the 1804 date, and still later, in 1859, additional 1804-dated dollars were struck. As a class these can be called *novodels,* as no originals were ever made. The 1804 dollars were produced in Proof format.

Striking and Sharpness. Very few coins have Full Details. On the obverse, check the highest points of the hair, the details of the drapery, and the centers of the stars. On the reverse, check the shield, the eagle, the stars above the eagle, and the clouds. Examine the dentils on both sides. Planchet adjustment marks are often seen, but they are usually lighter than on the earlier types. The relief of the dies and the height of the rims can vary, affecting sharpness. Sharp striking and excellent eye appeal will add to the value dramatically. When top-grade Mint State coins are found they are usually dated 1800.

Availability. This is the most readily available type among the early silver dollars. Most often seen are the dates 1798 and 1799. Many varieties are available in any grade desired, although Choice and Gem Mint State coins are elusive. Other die varieties are rare at any level. As with other early dollars, connoisseurship is needed to acquire quality coins. In a word, these large and heavy early dollars usually have *problems*. To evaluate them for the market it is necessary to grade them, determine the quality of striking, and examine the characteristics of the surface. Nearly all have been dipped or cleaned sometime in their lives. This is not necessarily bad, and in any event must be tolerated, or there would be very few coins to collect! Eye appeal comes to the fore as the main answer.

MS-60 to 70 (Mint State)

Illustrated coin: 1798, 10 arrows on reverse; Bowers-Borckardt 108, Bolender 13. MS-63.

This coin is well struck, essentially problem free, and with superb eye appeal. Only a tiny percentage of Mint State dollars are this nice. It is believed to be the finest known example of the die variety.

Note: Abbreviations used in die-variety attributions, along with the reference works on which the attributions are based, are discussed on the first page of this chapter. Mint State images are shown enlarged, for clarity.

Obverse. At MS-60, some abrasion and contact marks are evident, most noticeably on the cheek, the drapery, and the right field. Luster is present, but may be dull or lifeless, and interrupted in patches. At MS-63, contact marks are very few, and abrasion is hard to detect except under magnification. Knowledge of the die variety is desirable, but on balance the portraits on this type are usually quite well struck. An MS-65 coin has no abrasion, and contact marks are so minute as to require magnification. Luster should be full and rich. Coins grading above MS-65 are more theoretical than actual for this type—but they do exist and are defined by having fewer marks as perfection is approached.

Reverse. Comments apply as for the obverse, except that abrasion and contact marks are most noticeable on the eagle's neck, the tips of the wing, and the tail. The field area is complex, without much open space, given the stars above the eagle, the arrows and olive branch, and other features. Accordingly, marks will not be as noticeable as on the obverse.

AU-50, 53, 55, 58 (About Uncirculated)

Obverse. Light wear is seen on the hair area above the ear and extending to left of the forehead, on the ribbon, and on the drapery and bosom, more so at AU-50 than at 53 or 55. An AU-58 coin has minimal traces of wear. An AU-50 coin has luster in protected areas among the stars and letters, with little in the open fields or on the portrait. At AU-58, much luster is present in the fields, but is worn away on the highest parts of the motifs.

Illustrated coin: 1799, BB-152, B-15. AU-50.
This is an attractive and problem-free coin.

Reverse. Comments as preceding, except that the eagle's neck, the tips and top of the wings, the clouds, and the tail now show noticeable wear, as do other features. Luster ranges from perhaps 20% remaining in protected areas (at AU-50) to nearly full mint bloom (at AU-58). Sometimes the reverse of this type retains much more luster than the obverse, this being dependent on the height of the rim and the depth of the strike (particularly at the center).

EF-40, 45 (Extremely Fine)

Obverse. More wear is evident on the upper hair area and the ribbon, and on the drapery and bosom. The shoulder is a key spot to check for wear. Excellent detail remains in low-relief areas of the hair. The stars show wear, as do the date and letters. Luster, if present at all, is minimal and in protected areas.

Reverse. Wear is greater than on an AU coin, overall. The neck has lost its feather detail on the highest points. Feathers have lost some detail near the edges of the wings. Some traces of luster may be seen, more so at EF-45 than at EF-40.

Illustrated coin: 1802, BB-241, B-6. EF-45.
This is an attractive example retaining some mint luster. It has above-average striking sharpness.

VF-20, 30 (Very Fine)

Obverse. The higher-relief areas of hair are well worn at VF-20, less so at VF-30. The drapery at the shoulder and the bosom show extensive wear. The stars have more wear, making them appear larger (an optical illusion seen on most worn silver coins of this era).

Reverse. Wear is greater, including on the shield and the wing feathers. Most of the feathers on the wings are clear. The star centers are flat. Other areas have lost detail as well.

Illustrated coin: 1799, BB-157, B-5. VF-20.
Some scratches appear on the portrait. This coin was cleaned long ago and now is retoned. It is a typical early dollar at this grade.

F-12, 15 (Fine)

Obverse. Wear is more extensive than on a Very Fine coin, particularly on the hair, face, and bosom. The stars appear larger. About half the hair detail remains, most noticeably behind the neck and shoulder. The rim may be partially worn away and blend into the field.

Reverse. Wear is even more extensive, with the shield and wing feathers being points to observe. Half or slightly more of the feathers will remain clear. The incuse E PLURIBUS UNUM may have a few letters worn away. The clouds all seem to be connected except on varieties in which they are spaced apart. The stars are weak. Parts of the border and lettering may be weak.

Illustrated coin: 1798, BB-122, B-14. F-12.
This coin was cleaned long ago; this was noted on the coin's grading-service label. Cleaning and retoning is common on dollars of this era, but often is not noted.

VG-8, 10 (Very Good)

Obverse. The portrait is mostly seen in outline form, with most hair strands gone, although there is some definition at the back of the hair and behind the shoulder. The ear is discernible, as is the eye. The stars appear larger still, again an illusion. The rim is weak in areas. LIBERTY and the date are readable and usually full, although some letters may be weak at their tops.

Illustrated coin: 1799. VG-8.

Reverse. Wear is more extensive. Half or more of the letters in the motto are worn away. Most feathers are worn away, although separation of some of the lower feathers may be seen at the edges of the wings. Some stars are faint or missing. The border blends into the field in areas and some letters are weak. As always, a particular die variety can vary in areas of weakness.

G-4, 6 (Good)

Obverse. Wear is more extensive, and some stars may be partly missing. The head is an outline. The eye is visible only in outline form. The rim is well worn or even missing in areas. LIBERTY is worn, and parts of some letters may be missing, but elements of all should be readable. The date is readable, but worn.

Illustrated coin: 1799, B-169, B-21. G-4.
This coin has some marks, but is respectable for the grade.

Reverse. Wear is more extensive. The upper part of the eagle is flat. The feathers are noticeable only at the lower edge of the wings, sometimes incompletely, and do not have detail. The upper part of the shield is mostly flat. Only a few letters of the motto can be seen, if any at all. The rim is worn extensively, and the letters are well worn, but the inscription should be readable.

AG-3 (About Good)

Obverse. Wear is so extensive that the coin is barely identifiable. The head is in outline form. LIBERTY is mostly gone; same for the stars. The date, while readable, may be partially worn away.

Reverse. Extensive wear is seen overall, with the rim worn away and some areas worn smooth. The eagle can be discerned in outline form, but not necessarily completely. A few stray motto letters may remain.

Illustrated coin: 1799. AG-3.

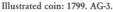

Proof Draped Bust / Heraldic Silver Dollars, PF-60 to 70

There were no Proofs coined in the era this type was issued. Years later, in 1834, the U.S. Mint made up new dies with the 1804 date and struck an unknown number of Proofs, perhaps a dozen or so, for inclusion in presentation Proof sets for foreign dignitaries. Today these are called Class I 1804 dollars. Eight examples are known, one of which shows circulation. The finest by far is the Sultan of Muscat coin, which approaches perfection. Circa 1858 the Mint prepared a new obverse die dated 1804 and struck an unknown number of examples for private sale to collectors and dealers—the Class III dollars. No records were kept. These were artificially worn to give them the appearance of original dollars struck in 1804.

Illustrated coin: 1804, Class I. Proof.

Sometime between circa 1858 and the 1870s, the Mint prepared new obverse dies dated 1801, 1802, and 1803, and struck Proof dollars for secret sale to the numismatic market. Many if not most were distributed through J.W. Haseltine, a Philadelphia dealer who had close connections with Mint officials. Today these are known as "Proof restrikes." All are rare, the 1801 being particularly so.

Class I 1804 dollars typically show hairlines and light abrasion. Grading is usually very liberal, in view of the fame of this rarity (not that this is logical). Circulated examples of Class I and Class III 1804 dollars have been graded using prefixes such as EF and AU. Proof restrikes of 1801 to 1803 generally survive in much higher grades, PF-64 or finer.

Obverse and Reverse. For lower Proof levels, extensive abrasion is seen in the fields, or even evidence of circulation (the Mickley specimen of the 1804 Class I, earlier graded as AU-50, was certified as PF-62 by a leading certification service in 2008). Numbers assigned by grading services have been erratic. No rules are known, and grading has not been consistent.

1836 AND 1839 GOBRECHT

History. The 1836 issue marks the inauguration of the Liberty Seated design in federal coinage. Some 1,600 examples of the 1836-dated Gobrecht dollar were struck in December 1836 and early 1837; most of these were placed into circulation. The 1836 issues have no stars on the obverse and 26 stars on the reverse. Beginning in the 1850s, alert bankers and bullion dealers retrieved many pieces and sold them into numismatic channels. Commencing in the spring of 1859, these were restruck. Several varieties of die alignment exist.

In 1839, Gobrecht dollars were struck to the extent of 300 coins, nearly all of which seem to have been placed into circulation. These have 13 stars on the obverse and none on the reverse. Beginning in the spring of 1859, many restrikes were made.

Striking and Sharpness. Check the details on Miss Liberty's head and the higher parts of the eagle. Striking is usually very good. On Gobrecht dollars the word LIBERTY is raised.

Availability. Examples of the 1836 are available in grades from Very Fine upward. As these were struck as Proofs, they are properly designated as PF-30, PF-40, and so on, for worn examples. Practice varies, and sometimes Fine, Very Fine, and Extremely Fine prefixes are used for grades below PF-50. Most in the marketplace range from PF-50 to 62. Most have contact marks. Truly pristine Gems are very elusive. The demand for these coins is intense. For the 1839, circulated grades are typically PF-50 or higher, often with damage. Pristine Proofs are available, but virtually all are restrikes.

Proofs, PF-60 to 70

Illustrated coin: 1839. PF-65.
This is a restrike made at the Mint in or after spring 1859.

Note: Shown enlarged, for clarity.

Obverse and Reverse. Many Proofs have been extensively cleaned and have many hairlines and dull fields. This is more applicable to 1836 than to 1839. Grades are PF-60 to 61 or 62. With medium hairlines and good reflectivity, an assigned grade of PF-64 is appropriate, and with relatively few hairlines, Gem PF-65. In various grades hairlines are most easily seen in the obverse field. PF-66 should have hairlines so delicate that magnification is needed to see them. Above that, a Proof should be free of such lines.

Proofs, PF-50, 53, 55, 58

Obverse. Light wear is seen on the thighs and knees, bosom, and head. At PF-58, the Proof surface is extensive, but the open fields show abrasion. At PF-50 and 53, most if not all mirror surface is gone and there are scattered marks.

Reverse. Wear is most evident on the eagle's breast and the top of the wings. Mirror surface ranges from perhaps 60% complete (at PF-58) to none (at PF-50).

Illustrated coin: 1836. PF-58.
This original 1836 Gobrecht dollar, of which 1,000 were coined in 1836, is nicely toned and has excellent eye appeal.

Proofs, PF-40 to 45

Obverse. Further wear is seen on all areas, especially the thighs and knees, bosom, and head. The center of LIBERTY, which is in relief, is weak. Most at this level and lower are the 1836 issues.

Reverse. Further wear is evident on the eagle, including the back edge of the closest wing, the top of the farthest wing, and the tail.

Illustrated coin: 1836. PF-45.

Proof Gobrecht Silver Dollars, PF-20, 25, 30, 35

Obverse. Further wear is seen. Many details of the gown are worn away, but the lower-relief areas above and to the right of the shield remain well defined. Hair detail is mostly or completely gone. LIBERTY is weak at the center.

Reverse. Even more wear is evident on the eagle, with only about 60% of the feathers visible.

Illustrated coin: 1836. PF-20.

1840–1873 LIBERTY SEATED

History. The Liberty Seated dollar was minted continuously from 1840 to 1873. The obverse is a modification of that used on the 1839 Gobrecht dollar, now with drapery added to the elbow and a few other adjustments. The reverse depicts a perched eagle similar to that used on the contemporary quarter dollar and half dollar. These were made in modest quantities and circulated domestically through 1850. In that year the price of silver rose on international markets to the point at which these coins cost more than $1 to produce. Mintage continued through 1873, but was for the international market. Depositors of silver bullion requested dollars, paying more than face value to have them made. In China, the destination of most, they were valued on their silver content, such as $1.02, $1.03, or whatever. In 1873 the Liberty Seated dollar was replaced by the trade dollar.

Striking and Sharpness. On the obverse, check the head of Miss Liberty and the centers of the stars. On the reverse, check the feathers of the eagle. The dentils are usually sharp. Dollars of 1857 are usually weakly struck, but have semi-prooflike surfaces. The word LIBERTY is in a high-relief area on the dollar, with the result that it wore away quickly. Accordingly, this feature cannot be used as the only guide to grading an obverse.

Availability. All issues from 1840 to 1850 are available in proportion to their mintages. Issues from 1851 to the late 1860s are all either scarce or rare in circulated grades, and in Mint State they range from rare to extremely rare, despite generous mintages in some instances. The later coins were shipped to China and later melted. Coins of the 1870s are more readily available, although some are scarce to rare. Collecting circulation-strike Liberty Seated dollars by varieties is not for the financially faint of heart, but for those who can afford it, the quest is stimulating.

MS-60 to 70 (Mint State)

Illustrated coin: 1864. MS-65.
The fields show striations from incomplete polishing of the dies, but this does not affect the grade. This is an exceedingly rare coin in Mint State, as few were saved (collectors of the era opted to buy Proofs instead).

Note: Mint State images are shown enlarged, for clarity.

Obverse. At MS-60, some abrasion and contact marks are evident, most noticeably on the bosom and thighs and knees. Luster is present, but may be dull or lifeless. At MS-63, contact marks are very few, and abrasion is minimal. An MS-65 coin has no abrasion in the fields (but may have a hint on the knees), and contact marks are trivial. Check the knees of Liberty and the right field. Luster should be full and rich on later issues, not necessarily so for dates in the 1840s. Most Mint State coins of the 1861 to 1865 years, Philadelphia issues, have extensive die striae (from not completely finishing the die).

Reverse. Comments apply as for the obverse, except that in lower Mint State grades, abrasion and marks are most noticeable on the eagle's head, the neck, the claws, and the top of the wings (harder to see there, however). At MS-65 or higher, there are no marks visible to the unaided eye. The field is mainly protected by design elements and does not show abrasion as much as does the obverse on a given coin.

AU-50, 53, 55, 58 (About Uncirculated)

Obverse. Light wear is seen on the thighs and knees, bosom, and head. At AU-58, the luster is extensive but incomplete, especially in the right field. At AU-50 and 53, luster is less.

Reverse. Wear is visible on the eagle's neck, the claws, and the top of the wings. An AU-58 coin has nearly full luster. At AU-50 and 53, there still are traces of luster.

Illustrated coin: 1842. AU-58.
This is an attractive example with much of the original luster.

EF-40, 45 (Extremely Fine)

Obverse. Further wear is seen on all areas, especially the thighs and knees, bosom, and head. Little or no luster is seen on most coins. From this grade downward, strike sharpness in the stars and the head does not matter to connoisseurs.

Reverse. Further wear is evident on the eagle's neck, claws, and the wings, although on well-struck coins nearly all details are sharp.

Illustrated coin: 1846. EF-40.

VF-20, 30 (Very Fine)

Obverse. Further wear is seen. Many details of the gown are worn away, but the lower-relief areas above and to the right of the shield remain well defined. Hair detail is mostly or completely gone. The word LIBERTY is weak at BE (PCGS allows BER to be missing "on some coins").

Reverse. Wear is more extensive, with some feathers blended together, especially on the neck for a typical coin. Detail remains quite good overall.

Illustrated coin: 1854. VF-20.

F-12, 15 (Fine)

Obverse. The seated figure is well worn, but with some detail above and to the right of the shield. BER in LIBERTY is visible only in part or missing entirely.

Reverse. Wear is extensive, with about a third to half of the feathers flat or blended with others.

Illustrated coin: 1872-CC. F-12.
The reverse is stronger than the obverse on this coin.

VG-8, 10 (Very Good)

Obverse. The seated figure is more worn, but some detail can be seen above and to the right of the shield. The shield is discernible, but the upper-right section may be flat and blended into the seated figure. In LIBERTY two or three letters, or a combination totaling that, are readable.

Reverse. Further wear has flattened half or slightly more of the feathers (depending on the strike). The rim is visible all around, as are the ends of the dentils. A Very Good Liberty Seated dollar usually has more detail overall than a lower-denomination coin of the same design.

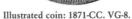

Illustrated coin: 1871-CC. VG-8.

G-4, 6 (Good)

Obverse. The seated figure is worn nearly smooth. The stars and date are complete, but may be weak toward the periphery.

Reverse. The eagle shows only a few details of the shield and feathers. The rim is worn down. The tops of the border letters are weak or worn away, although the inscription can still be read.

Illustrated coin: 1860. G-6.

AG-3 (About Good)

Obverse. The seated figure is visible in outline form. Much or all of the rim is worn away. The stars are weak and some may be missing. The date remains clear.

Reverse. The border letters are partially worn away. The eagle is mostly in outline form, but with a few details discernible. The rim is weak or missing.

Illustrated coin: 1872. AG-3.

Proof Liberty Seated Silver Dollars, PF-60 to 70

Proof coins were made for all dates. All of 1851 and 1853 are restrikes, as are most of 1852. In 1858 only Proofs were struck, to the extent of an estimated 210 pieces, with no related circulation strikes. Most early dates were restruck at the Mint, augmenting the supply of originals. Today, Proofs from 1858 to 1873 are readily available, but high-quality examples with superb eye appeal are in the minority. Most Proofs prior to 1860 survive only in grades below PF-65 if strict grading is applied. Nearly all Proofs are very well struck.

Illustrated coin: 1861. Proof-63. The frosty cameo motifs on this example contrast with the deeply mirrored fields.

Obverse and Reverse. Proofs that are extensively cleaned and have many hairlines, or that are dull and grainy, are lower level, such as PF-60 to 62. These are not widely desired, except for use as fillers for the dates (most circulation-strike dollars are rare after 1849 and before 1870). The rarities of 1851, 1852, and 1858 are in demand no matter what the grade. With medium hairlines and good reflectivity, an assigned grade of PF-64 is appropriate, and with relatively few hairlines, gem PF-65. In various grades hairlines are most easily seen in the obverse field. PF-66 should have hairlines so delicate that magnification is needed to see them. Above that, a Proof should be free of such lines.

1873–1885 TRADE DOLLARS

History. Trade dollars were minted under the Coinage Act of 1873. Containing 420 grains of .900 fine silver, they were heavier than the Liberty Seated dollar (of 412.5 grains). They were made for use in the China export trade and proved to be a great success. Some circulated in America until they were demonetized by the Act of July 22, 1876. The Bland-Allison Act of 1878 provided for the new "Morgan" silver dollar, and trade dollars were discontinued, although Proofs continued to be made through 1885.

Striking and Sharpness. Weakness is often seen. On the obverse, check Miss Liberty's head and the star centers first. On the reverse, check the feathers on the eagle, particularly on the legs. Luster can range from dull to deeply frosty.

Availability. Although the 1878-CC is a rarity, other dates and mintmarks are readily collected in grades from Extremely Fine to Mint State. Lower-grade coins are not often seen, for these did not circulate for a long time. Many used in China have counter-stamps, called "chopmarks," which are of interest to collectors. On a Choice or Gem Mint State coin a chopmark will decrease value, but on Extremely Fine and About Uncirculated coins they are eagerly sought. Mint State coins are mostly in the lower ranges, often with unsatisfactory surfaces. True gems are very scarce. Be aware that in recent years a flood of counterfeit trade dollars, many coming from Asia, has deluged the American market.

MS-60 to 70 (Mint State)

Illustrated coin: 1875-S. MS-61.
Some friction in the fields is seen, but much of the original luster remains.

Note: Mint State images are shown enlarged, for clarity.

Obverse. At MS-60, some abrasion and contact marks are evident, most noticeably on the left breast, left arm, and left knee. Luster is present, but may be dull or lifeless. Many of these coins are light in color or even brilliant, having been repatriated from China, and have been cleaned to remove sediment and discoloration. At MS-63, contact marks are very few, and abrasion is minimal. An MS-65 coin has no abrasion in the fields (but may have a hint on the higher parts of the seated figure), and contact marks are trivial. Luster should be full and rich.

Reverse. Comments apply as for the obverse, except that in lower Mint State grades abrasion and contact marks are most noticeable on the eagle's head, the claws, and the top of the wings. At MS-65 or higher there are no marks visible to the unaided eye. The field is mainly protected by design elements and does not show abrasion as much as does the obverse on a given coin.

AU-50, 53, 55, 58 (About Uncirculated)

Obverse. Light wear is seen on the knees, bosom, and head. At AU-58, the luster is extensive but incomplete. At AU-50 and 53, luster is less.

Reverse. Wear is visible on the eagle's head, the claws, and the top of the wings. An AU-58 coin will have nearly full luster. At AU-50 and 53, there still are traces of luster.

Illustrated coin: 1876. AU-53.
This example shows light, even wear. Most of the luster is gone, except in protected areas, but it has excellent eye appeal for the grade.

EF-40, 45 (Extremely Fine)

Obverse. Further wear is seen on all areas, especially the head, the left breast, the left arm, the left leg, and the bale on which Miss Liberty is seated. Little or no luster is seen on most coins. From this grade downward, strike sharpness on the stars and the head does not matter to connoisseurs.

Reverse. Further wear is evident on the eagle's head, legs, claws, and wings, although on well-struck coins nearly all feather details on the wings are sharp.

Illustrated coin: 1876-CC. EF-40.

VF-20, 30 (Very Fine)

Obverse. Further wear is seen on the seated figure, although more than half the details of her dress are visible. Details of the wheat sheaf are mostly intact. IN GOD WE TRUST and LIBERTY are clear.

Reverse. Wear is more extensive; some feathers are blended together, with two-thirds or more still visible.

Illustrated coin: 1877-S. VF-30.

F-12, 15 (Fine)

Obverse. The seated figure is further worn, with fewer details of the dress visible. Most details in the wheat sheaf are clear. Both mottoes are readable, but some letters may be weak.

Reverse. Wear is extensive, with about half to nearly two-thirds of the feathers flat or blended with others. The eagle's left leg is mostly flat. Wear is seen on the raised E PLURIBUS UNUM, and one or two letters may be missing.

Illustrated coin: 1873-CC. F-12.

The trade dollar is seldom collected in grades lower than F-12.

Proof Trade Dollars, PF-60 to 70

Proofs for collectors were made from 1873 to 1883 in quantity to supply the demand. In addition, a few were secretly made in 1884 and 1885. Most survivors are of high quality today, although gems of the 1873 to 1877 years are much harder to find than are those of 1878 to 1883. Some Proofs are lightly struck on the head and the stars on the obverse and the leg feathers of the eagle on the reverse.

Illustrated coin: 1882. PF-62.
This coin has medium-gray toning overall.

Obverse and Reverse. Proofs that are extensively cleaned and have many hairlines, or that are dull and grainy, are lower level, such as PF-60 to 62. These are not widely desired. With medium hairlines and good reflectivity, an assigned grade of PF-64 is appropriate, and with relatively few hairlines, Gem PF-65. In various grades hairlines are most easily seen in the obverse field. PF-66 may have hairlines so delicate that magnification is needed to see them. Above that, a Proof should be free of such lines.

1878–1921 MORGAN

History. Designed by George T. Morgan, these coins were minted continuously from 1878 to 1904 and again in 1921. Production was a political boondoggle to satisfy Western silver interests by furnishing an artificial market for the metal, the value of which had sharply depreciated by 1878. Hundreds of millions of unwanted coins, stored in cloth bags of 1,000 each, piled up in government vaults. In the 20th century some were melted, but immense quantities were bought by collectors and investors, with the result that today they are the most widely collected of all coins of their era.

Striking and Sharpness. On coins of 1878 to 1900, check the hair above Miss Liberty's ear and, on the reverse, the breast feathers of the eagle. These are weak on many issues, particularly those of the New Orleans Mint. From 1900 to 1904 a new reverse hub was used, and breast feathers, while discernible, are not as sharp. In 1921 new dies were made in lower relief, with certain areas indistinct. Many Morgan dollars have partially or fully prooflike surfaces. These are designated as Prooflike (PL), Deep Prooflike (DPL), or Deep Mirror Prooflike (DMPL). Certification practices can be erratic, and some DMPL coins are not fully mirrored. All prooflike coins tend to emphasize contact marks, with the result that lower Mint State levels can be unattractive. *A Guide Book of Morgan Silver Dollars* and other guides furnish information as to which dates and mintmarks are easily found with Full Details and which are usually weak, as well as the availability of the various levels of prooflike surface. With such knowledge at hand you will know, for example, that the 1881 is nearly always found with Full Details, while the breast feathers on the 1891-O are nearly always poorly struck.

Availability. All dates and mints of Morgan dollars are available in grades from well worn to Mint State. Some issues such as certain Carson City coins are rare if worn and common in Mint State, the 1884-CC being a prime example. Other issues such as the 1901 Philadelphia coins are common if worn and are rarities at MS-65. The 1889-CC and1893-S, and the Proof 1895, are considered to be the key issues. Again, a good book on Morgan dollars is a vital help when you buy.

MS-60 to 70 (Mint State)

Illustrated coin: 1895-O. MS-61.
This is a lustrous and attractive example.

Note: Mint State images are shown enlarged, for clarity.

Obverse. At MS-60, some abrasion and contact marks are evident, most noticeably on the cheek and on the hair above the ear. The left field also shows such marks. Luster is present, but may be dull or lifeless. At MS-63, contact marks are extensive but not distracting. Abrasion still is evident, but less than at lower levels. Indeed, the cheek of Miss Liberty showcases abrasion. An MS-65 coin may have minor abrasion, but contact marks are so minute as to require magnification. Luster should be full and rich. Coins with prooflike surfaces such as PL, DPL, and DMPL display abrasion and contact marks much more noticeably than coins with frosty surfaces; in grades below MS-64 many are unattractive. With today's loose and sometimes contradictory interpretations, many at MS-64 appear to have extensive marks as well.

Reverse. Comments apply as for the obverse, except that in lower Mint State grades abrasion and contact marks are most noticeable on the eagle's breast. At MS-65 or higher there are no marks visible to the unaided eye. The field is mainly protected by design elements, so the reverse often appears to grade a point or two higher than the obverse. A Morgan dollar can have an MS-63 obverse and an MS-65 reverse, as was indeed the nomenclature used prior to the single-number system. A careful cataloger may want to describe each side separately for a particularly valuable or rare Morgan dollar. An example with an MS-63 obverse and an MS-65 reverse should have an overall grade of MS-63, as the obverse is traditionally given prominence.

AU-50, 53, 55, 58 (About Uncirculated)

Obverse. Light wear is seen on the cheek and, to a lesser extent, on the hair below the coronet. Generally, the hair details mask friction and wear and it is not as easy to notice as on the cheek and in the fields. At AU-58, the luster is extensive, but incomplete, especially on the higher parts and in the left field. At AU-50 and 53, luster is less, but still is present. PL, DPL, and DMPL coins are not widely desired at these levels, as the marks are too distracting.

Reverse. Wear is evident on the head, breast, wing tips, and, to a lesser extent, in the field. An AU-58 coin (as determined by the obverse) can have a reverse that appears to be full Mint State. (Incidentally, this is also true of Barber quarter dollars and half dollars.)

Illustrated coin: 1889-CC. AU-58.
This is a lustrous example of the rarest Carson City Morgan dollar. As is typical of AU-58 dollars of this design, the reverse appears to be full Mint State, as the field is protected by the design elements.

EF-40, 45 (Extremely Fine)

Obverse. Further wear is seen on the cheek in particular. The hair near the forehead and temple has flatness in areas, most noticeable above the ear. Some luster can be seen in protected areas on many coins, but is not needed to define the EF-40 and 45 grades.

Reverse. Further wear is seen on the breast of the eagle (most noticeably), the wing tips, and the leaves.

Illustrated coin: 1879-CC. EF-40.

VF-20, 30 (Very Fine)

Obverse. The head shows more wear, now with most of the detail gone in the areas adjacent to the forehead and temple. The lower area has most hair fused into large strands.

Reverse. Wear is more extensive on the breast and on the feathers in the upper area of the wings, especially the right wing, and on the legs. The high area of the leaves has no detail.

Illustrated coin: 1889-CC. VF-20.

F-12, 15 (Fine)

Obverse. The head shows more wear, with most hair detail gone, and with a large flat area above the ear. Less detail is seen in the lower curls.

Reverse. More wear is seen on the reverse, with the eagle's breast and legs flat and about a third of the feather detail gone, mostly near the tops of the wings.

Illustrated coin: 1893-S. F-15.

VG-8, 10 (Very Good)

Obverse. More hair details are gone, especially from the area from the top of the head down to the ear. The details of the lower part of the cap are gone. The rim is weak in areas, and some dentils are worn away.

Reverse. Further wear has smoothed more than half of the feathers in the wing. The leaves are flat except for the lowest areas. The rim is weak in areas.

Illustrated coin: 1892-CC. VG-8.

G-4, 6 (Good)

Obverse. The head is in outline form, with most details gone. LIBERTY still is readable. The eye position and lips are discernible. Most of the rim is worn away.

Reverse. The eagle shows some feathers near the bottom of the wings, but nearly all others are gone. The leaves are seen in outline form. The rim is mostly worn away. Some letters have details toward the border worn away.

Illustrated coin: 1893-S. G-4.
Here is a well-worn example of this key issue.

The Morgan dollar is seldom collected in grades lower than G-4.

Proof Morgan Silver Dollars, PF-60 to 70

Proofs were struck from 1878 to 1904, with 1878–1901 generally having cameo contrast, and 1902–1904 have the portrait lightly polished in the die. Some are lightly struck; check the hair above Liberty's ear (in particular), and the eagle's breast feathers. In 1921 many so-called Zerbe Proofs, with many microscopic die-finish lines, were made. A very few deeply mirrored 1921 coins were made, called "Chapman Proofs." Some "Zerbe Proofs" have been miscertified as "Chapman Proofs."

Illustrated coin: 1898. PF-64.

Obverse and Reverse. Dull, grainy Proofs, or extensively cleaned ones with many hairlines, are lower level (PF-60 to 62). Only the 1895 is desirable at such low grades. Those with medium hairlines and good reflectivity may grade at about PF-64, and with relatively few hairlines, Gem PF-65. Hairlines are most easily seen in the obverse field. Horizontal slide marks on Miss Liberty's cheek, caused by clear slides on some coin albums, are common. PF-66 may have hairlines so delicate that magnification is needed to see them. Above that, a Proof should be free of such lines, including slide marks.

1921–1935 Peace

History. In 1921 the Treasury decided to make more silver dollars, and rushed to coin many of the Morgan type, this despite hundreds of millions of older silver dollars still remaining in storage. In the meantime, Anthony de Francisci was tapped to create the new Peace design. The obverse features Miss Liberty, the face of which is a close copy of that used on Saint-Gaudens's $10 coin of 1907. The reverse shows a perched eagle. Coins of 1921 were struck in high relief. As they were weak at the centers, the design was changed to low relief in 1922. Coins were struck until 1928, then again in 1934 and 1935. Some 1964-dated Peace silver dollars were struck years later, but were not released into circulation.

Striking and Sharpness. Peace dollars of 1921 are always lightly struck at the center of the obverse, with hair detail not showing in an area. The size of this flat spot can vary. For this and other Peace dollars, check the hair detail at the center and, on the reverse, the feathers on the eagle. Many coins are struck from overly used dies, giving a grainy appearance to the fields, particularly the obverse. On many Peace dollars tiny white "milk spots" are seen, left over from when they were struck. These should be avoided.

Availability. All dates and mintmarks are readily available. Although some are well worn, they are generally collected at the Extremely Fine level and higher. Mint State coins are available for each, with the 1934-S considered to be the key date. San Francisco issues of the 1920s, except for 1926-S, are often heavily bagmarked. The appearance of luster varies from issue to issue and can be deeply frosty, or—in the instance of Philadelphia Mint coins of 1928, 1934, and 1935—satiny or "creamy."

MS-60 to 70 (Mint State)

Illustrated coin: 1921. MS-64.
Some scattered marks define the grade. The high relief of this particular year results in light striking at the center; this is normal and not to be mistaken for wear.

Note: Mint State images are shown enlarged, for clarity.

Obverse. At MS-60, some abrasion and contact marks are evident, most noticeably on the cheek and on the hair to the right of the face and forehead. Luster is present, but may be dull or lifeless. At MS-63, contact marks are extensive but not distracting. Abrasion still is evident, but less than at lower levels. MS-64 coins are slightly finer. Some Peace dollars have whitish "milk spots" in the field; while these are not caused by handling, but seem to have been from liquid at the mint or in storage, coins with these spots are rarely graded higher than MS-63 or 64. An MS-65 coin may have minor abrasion, but contact marks are so minute as to require magnification. Luster should be full and rich on earlier issues, and either frosty or satiny on later issues, depending on the date and mint.

Reverse. At MS-60 some abrasion and contact marks are evident, most noticeably on the eagle's shoulder and nearby. Otherwise, comments apply as for the obverse.

AU-50, 53, 55, 58 (About Uncirculated)

Obverse. Light wear is seen on the cheek and the highest-relief areas of the hair. The neck truncation edge also shows wear. At AU-58, the luster is extensive, but incomplete. At AU-50 and 53, luster is less but still present.

Reverse. Wear is evident on the eagle's shoulder and back. Otherwise, comments apply as for the obverse.

Illustrated coin: 1934-S. AU-53.
This coin shows medium and somewhat mottled toning. Luster is still seen in protected areas.

EF-40, 45 (Extremely Fine)

Obverse. Further wear is seen on the highest-relief areas of the hair, with many strands now blended together. Some luster can usually be seen in protected areas on many coins, but is not needed to define the EF-40 and 45 grades.

Reverse. Further wear is seen on the eagle, and the upper 60% of the feathers have most detail gone, except for the delineation of the edges of rows of feathers. PEACE shows light wear.

Illustrated coin: 1928. EF-40.

VF-20, 30 (Very Fine)

Obverse. More wear shows on the hair, with more tiny strands now blended into heavy strands.

Reverse. Further wear has resulted in very little feather detail except on the neck and tail. The rock shows wear. PEACE is slightly weak.

Illustrated coin: 1934-D. VF-30.

F-12, 15 (Fine)

Obverse. Most of the hair is worn flat, with thick strands blended together, interrupted by fewer divisions than on higher grades. The rim is full.

Reverse. Fewer feather details show. Most of the eagle, except for the tail feathers and some traces of feathers at the neck, is in outline only. The rays between the left side of the eagle and PEACE are weak and some details are worn away.

Illustrated coin: 1921. F-12.

The Peace dollar is seldom collected in grades lower than F-12.

Proof Peace Silver Dollars, PF-60 to 70

Some Sandblast Proofs were made in 1921 and a limited issue in 1922 in *high relief.* These are rare today. Seemingly, a few Satin Proofs were also made in 1921. Sandblast Proofs of 1922 have a peculiar whitish surface in most instances, sometimes interrupted by small dark flecks or spots. There are a number of impostors among certified "Proofs."

Obverse and Reverse. Proofs of both types usually display very few handling marks or defects. To qualify as Satin PF-65 or Sandblast PF-65 or finer, contact marks must be microscopic.

Illustrated coin: 1921. Satin Proof.

1971–1978 EISENHOWER

History. Coins of the Eisenhower type, designed by Frank Gasparro, were made from 1971 through 1978, except that none were dated 1975. The obverse features the portrait of President Dwight David Eisenhower, and the reversed depicts an eagle on the surface of the Moon. The 1976 Bicentennial coins have a different reverse, with the Liberty Bell and, in the distance, the Moon. Circulation strikes were produced for use in casinos and elsewhere, while silver clad pieces were sold at a premium to numismatists.

Striking and Sharpness. Striking is generally very good. On the obverse, check the high parts of the portrait, and on the reverse, the details of the eagle.

Availability. Mint State coins are common in the marketplace, although several early varieties are elusive at the Gem level (MS-65 or better). Lower grades are not widely collected.

MS-60 to 70 (Mint State)

Illustrated coin: 1971-S. MS-65.

Note: Mint State images are shown enlarged, for clarity.

Obverse. At MS-60, some abrasion and contact marks are evident, most noticeably on the cheek, jaw, and temple. Luster is present, but may be dull or lifeless. At MS-63, contact marks are extensive but not distracting. Abrasion still is evident, but less than at lower levels. MS-64 coins are slightly finer. An MS-65 coin may have minor abrasion, but contact marks are so minute as to require magnification. Luster should be full and rich.

Reverse. At MS-60, some abrasion and contact marks are evident, most noticeably on the eagle's breast, head, and talons. Otherwise, the same comments apply as for the obverse.

AU-50, 53, 55, 58 (About Uncirculated)

Obverse. Light wear is seen on the higher-relief areas of the portrait. At AU-58, the luster is extensive, but incomplete. At AU-50 and 53, luster is less but still present.

Reverse. Further wear is evident on the eagle, particularly the head, breast, talons, and tops of the wings. Otherwise, the same comments apply as for the obverse.

Illustrated coin: 1972. AU-50.

The Eisenhower dollar is seldom collected in grades lower than AU-50.

Proof Eisenhower Dollars, PF-60 to 70

Proofs were made of the various issues (both copper-nickel clad and silver clad from 1971 to 1976; copper-nickel only in 1977 and 1978). All are readily available in the marketplace today. Nearly all are well struck and of high quality.

Obverse and Reverse. Proofs that are extensively cleaned and have many hairlines, or that are dull and grainy, are lower level, such as PF-60 to 62. There are not many of these in the marketplace. With medium hairlines and good reflectivity, assigned grades of PF-63 or 64 are appropriate. With relatively few hairlines a rating of PF-65 can be given. PF-66 may have hairlines so delicate that magnification is needed to see them. Above that, a Proof should be free of any hairlines or other problems.

Illustrated coin: 1776–1976, Bicentennial. PF-68.

1979–1999 Susan B. Anthony

History. Designed by U.S. Mint Chief Engraver Frank Gasparro, following a mandate by Congress, this coin features the portrait of Susan B. Anthony on the obverse and an eagle-and-Moon motif on the reverse, the latter being a reduced version of the motif used on the Eisenhower dollar. It was hoped that these mini-dollars, as some called them, would be a cost-effective substitute for paper dollars, which lasted only for a short time in circulation. Had the Treasury eliminated the paper dollar (as Canada did when it introduced dollar coins), it might have been a success. However, lobbying interests for the paper supplier prevented this from happening, and coin-operated machines were not adjusted to accept the new issue. After a generous production in 1979, mintages dropped sharply. The coins were discontinued in 1981, but for unclear reasons were revived in 1999.

Striking and Sharpness. Most are well struck, but check the highest areas of both sides.

Availability. Readily available in Mint State, although those of 1981 are scarcer. Circulated coins are not widely sought.

MS-60 to 70 (Mint State)

Illustrated coin: 1980-D. MS-65.

Note: All coins are shown enlarged, for clarity.

Obverse. At MS-60, some abrasion and contact marks are evident, most noticeably on the cheek and upper center of the hair. Luster is present, but may be dull or lifeless. At MS-63, contact marks are extensive but not distracting. Abrasion still is evident, but less than at lower levels. MS-64 coins are slightly finer. An MS-65 coin may have minor abrasion, but contact marks are so minute as to require magnification. Luster should be full and rich.

Reverse. At MS-60, some abrasion and contact marks are evident, most noticeably on the eagle's breast, head, and talons. Otherwise, the same comments apply as for the obverse.

AU-50, 53, 55, 58 (About Uncirculated)

Obverse. Light wear is seen on the higher-relief areas of the portrait. At AU-58, the luster is extensive but incomplete. At AU-50 and 53, luster is less but still present.

Reverse. Further wear is evident on the eagle, particularly the head, breast, talons, and tops of the wings. Otherwise, the same comments apply as for the obverse.

Illustrated coin: 1979-D. AU-50.

The Susan B. Anthony dollar is seldom collected in grades lower than AU-50.

Proof Anthony Dollars, PF-60 to 70

Proofs were made of all issues and are readily available today.

Obverse and Reverse. Proofs that are extensively cleaned and have many hairlines, or that are dull and grainy, are lower level, such as PF-60 to 62. This comment is more theoretical than practical, as nearly all Proofs have been well kept. With medium hairlines and good reflectivity, assigned grades of PF-63 or 64 are appropriate. With

Illustrated coin: 1979-S. PF-69 Cameo.

relatively few hairlines a rating of PF-65 can be given. PF-66 may have hairlines so delicate that magnification is needed to see them. Above that, all the way to PF-70, a Proof should be free of any hairlines or other problems under strong magnification.

2000 TO DATE SACAGAWEA

History. The Sacagawea dollar, called the "Golden Dollar" in U.S. Mint publicity, was launched with much enthusiasm in 2000. The obverse shows an artist's conception of Sacagawea and her baby (no contemporary likeness exists), and the reverse shows an eagle in flight. Additional reverse designs in 2009 honor and memorialize Native Americans. It was hoped that this mini-dollar, made of a special alloy with a golden color, would be widely accepted by the public; so far it hasn't been.

Striking and Sharpness. Most are very well struck. Check the higher points.

Availability. Common in Mint State and usually collected that way.

MS-60 to 70 (Mint State)

Illustrated coin: 2006-D. MS-65.

Note: All coins are shown enlarged, for clarity.

Obverse. At MS-60, some abrasion and contact marks are evident, most noticeably on the cheekbone and the drapery near the baby's head. Luster is present, but may be dull or lifeless. At MS-63, contact marks are extensive but not distracting. Abrasion still is evident, but less than at lower levels. MS-64 coins are slightly finer. An MS-65 coin may have minor abrasion, but contact marks are so minute as to require magnification. Luster should be full and rich.

Reverse. At MS-60, some abrasion and contact marks are evident, most noticeably on the eagle's breast. Otherwise, the same comments apply as for the obverse.

AU-50, 53, 55, 58 (About Uncirculated)

Obverse. Light wear is seen on cheekbone, drapery, and elsewhere. At AU-58, the luster is extensive, but incomplete. At AU-50 and 53, luster is less but still present.

Reverse. Further wear is evident on the eagle. Otherwise, the same comments apply as for the obverse.

Illustrated coin: 2000-P. AU-55.

The Sacagawea dollar is seldom collected in grades lower than AU-50.

Proofs, PF-60 to 70

Proofs have been made each year and are readily available.

Obverse and Reverse. Proofs that are extensively cleaned and have many hairlines, or that are dull and grainy, are lower level, such as PF-60 to 62. This comment is more theoretical than practical, as nearly all Proofs have been well kept. With medium hairlines and good reflectivity, assigned grades of PF-63 or 64 are appropriate. With

Illustrated coin: 2002-S. PF-69.

relatively few hairlines a rating of PF-65 can be given. PF-66 may have hairlines so delicate that magnification is needed to see them. Above that, all the way to PF-70, a Proof should be free of any hairlines or other problems under strong magnification.

2007–2016 PRESIDENTIAL

History. Launched in 2007, these dollars have been issued at the rate of four designs a year, in order, starting with George Washington. Each has a common reverse showing the Statue of Liberty. Similar to the Anthony and Sacagawea mini-dollars, they have not been popular in commerce, but collectors enjoy owning them.

Striking and Sharpness. Usually well struck, but check the higher-relief parts of each side.

Availability. Very common in Mint State. Most have from a few to many bagmarks, with true gems in the minority.

MS-60 to 70 (Mint State)

Illustrated coin: 2007-P, Washington. MS-68.

Note: All coins are shown enlarged, for clarity.

Obverse. At MS-60, some abrasion and contact marks are evident, most noticeably on the highest-relief areas of the portrait, the exact location varying with the president depicted. Luster is present, but may be dull or lifeless. At MS-63, contact marks are extensive but not distracting. Abrasion still is evident, but less than at lower levels. MS-64 coins are slightly finer. An MS-65 coin may have minor abrasion, but contact marks are so minute as to require magnification. Luster should be full and rich.

Reverse. At MS-60, some abrasion and contact marks are evident, most noticeably on the cheek and arm. Otherwise, the same comments apply as for the obverse.

AU-50, 53, 55, 58 (About Uncirculated)

Obverse. Light wear is seen on the portrait, most prominently on the higher-relief areas. At AU-58, the luster is extensive, but incomplete. At AU-50 and 53, luster is less, but still is present.

Reverse. Further wear is evident on statue. Otherwise, the same comments apply as for the obverse.

Illustrated coin: 2007-P, Madison. AU-53.

Presidential dollars are seldom collected in grades lower than AU-50.

Proof Presidential Dollars, PF-60 to 70

Proofs have been struck of each issue and are readily available. All seen have been well struck and of exceptional quality.

Obverse and Reverse. Proofs that are extensively cleaned and have many hairlines, or that are dull and grainy, are lower level, such as PF-60 to 62. This comment is more theoretical than practical, as nearly all Proofs have been well kept. With medium hairlines and good reflectivity, assigned grades of PF-63 or

Illustrated coin: 2007-S, Madison. PF-65

64 are appropriate. With relatively few hairlines a rating of PF-65 can be given. PF-66 may have hairlines so delicate that magnification is needed to see them. Above that, all the way to PF-70, a Proof should be free of any hairlines or other problems under strong magnification.

GOLD DOLLARS

GOLD DOLLARS, 1849–1889

1849–1854 LIBERTY HEAD • TYPE I

History. Gold dollars of this and other types were designed by Chief Engraver James B. Longacre. This type measured 13 mm in diameter, which proved to be inconvenient, and the two later types were enlarged to 15 mm.

Striking and Sharpness. As a rule, Philadelphia coins are sharper than those of the Charlotte and Dahlonega mints. On the obverse, check the highest areas of the hair below the coronet. On the reverse, check the wreath and the central two figures in the date. On both sides check the dentils (the toothlike projections from the rim), which can be mushy or indistinct, particularly on Charlotte and Dahlonega coins; these often have planchet roughness as well.

Availability. All dates and mintmarks are readily collectible, save for the 1849-C Open Wreath variety. Mint State coins are often found for the Philadelphia issues but can be elusive for the branch mints. Charlotte and Dahlonega coins often have striking problems, and "gradeflation" is rampant, so care is needed when buying. The few gold dollars of this type that are less than Very Fine in grade are usually damaged or have problems (and are not studied here).

MS-60 to 70 (Mint State)

Illustrated coin: 1854, Close Wreath. MS-62.
Some friction is visible on the portrait and in the fields.

Note: All coins are shown enlarged, for clarity.

Obverse. At MS-60 to 62, there is abrasion on the hair below the coronet (an area that can be weakly struck as well) and on the cheeks. Marks may be seen. At MS-63, there may be slight abrasion. Luster is irregular. At MS-64, abrasion is less. Luster is rich on most coins, less so on Charlotte and Dahlonega varieties. At MS-65 and above, luster is deep and frosty. At MS-66, and higher, no marks at all are visible without magnification.

Reverse. On MS-60 to 62 coins, there is abrasion on the 1, the highest parts of the leaves, and the ribbon. Otherwise, the same comments apply as for the obverse.

AU-50, 53, 55, 58 (About Uncirculated)

Obverse. Light wear on the hair below the coronet and the cheek is very noticeable at AU-50, and progressively less at higher levels to AU-58. Luster is minimal at AU-50 and scattered and incomplete at AU-58. Some tiny nicks and contact marks are to be expected and should be mentioned if they are distracting.

Reverse. Light wear on the 1, the wreath, and the ribbon characterize an AU-50 coin, progressively less at higher levels to AU-58. Otherwise, the same comments apply as for the obverse.

Illustrated coin: 1853-D. AU-58. Much of the luster remains, especially in protected areas. The coin is a rare Dahlonega Mint issue.

EF-40, 45 (Extremely Fine)

Obverse. Medium wear is seen on the hair below the coronet, extending to near the bun, and on the curls below. Detail is partially gone on the hair to the right of the coronet. Luster is gone on most coins.

Reverse. Light wear is seen overall, and the highest parts of the leaves are flat. Luster is gone.

Illustrated coin: 1849-C, Open Wreath. EF-45.

VF-20, 30 (Very Fine)

Obverse. Most hair detail is gone, except in the lower-relief areas and on the lower curls. Star centers are flat.

Reverse. The wreath and other areas show more wear. Most detail is gone on the higher-relief leaves.

Illustrated coin: 1851-D. VF-25.

The Type I gold dollar is seldom collected in grades lower than VF-20.

Proof Liberty Head Gold Dollars, PF-60 to 70

Although a few Proofs were coined in the early years, they are for all practical purposes unobtainable. Only about a dozen are known.

Obverse and Reverse. PF-60 to 62 coins have extensive hairlines and may have nicks and contact marks. At PF-63, hairlines are prominent, but the mirror surface is very reflective. PF-64 coins have fewer hairlines. At PF-65, hairlines should be minimal and mostly seen only under magnification. One cannot be "choosy" with Proofs of this type, as only a few exist.

Illustrated coin: 1849, Open Wreath. Proof.

1854–1856 INDIAN PRINCESS, SMALL HEAD • TYPE II

History. These coins, with the diameter increased from 13 mm to 15 mm, were first made in 1854. At the outset they proved difficult to strike, leading to the design being modified in 1856.

Striking and Sharpness. On the obverse, check the highest area of the hair below the coronet and the tips of the feathers. Check the letters. On the reverse, check the ribbon bow knot and in particular the two central digits of the dates. Examine the digits on both sides. Nearly all have problems. This type is often softly struck in the centers, with weak hair detail and the numerals 85 in the date sometimes faint—this should not be confused with wear. The 1855-C and 1855-D coins are often poorly struck and on rough planchets.

Availability. All are collectible, but the Charlotte and Dahlonega coins are rare. With patience, Full Details coins are available of 1854, 1855, and 1856-S, but virtually impossible to find for the branch-mint issues of 1855. Overgrading is commonplace. The few gold dollars of this type that are less than Very Fine in grade are usually damaged or have problems (and are not studied here).

MS-60 to 70 (Mint State)

Illustrated coin: 1854. MS-61.
Some loss of luster is evident in the fields, but strong luster remains among the letters and in other protected areas. Good eye appeal is elusive for this type.

Note: All coins are shown enlarged, for clarity.

Obverse. At MS-60 to 62, there is abrasion on the hair below the band lettered LIBERTY (an area that can be weakly struck as well), on the tips of the feather plumes, and throughout the field. Contact marks may also be seen. At MS-63, there should be only slight abrasions. Luster is irregular. At MS-64, abrasions and marks are less. Luster is rich on most coins, less so on Charlotte and Dahlonega issues. At MS-65 and above, luster is deep and frosty, with no marks at all visible without magnification at MS-66 and higher.

Reverse. At MS-60 to 62, there may be abrasions on the 1, on the highest parts of the leaves, on the ribbon knot, and in the field. Otherwise, the same comments apply as for the obverse.

AU-50, 53, 55, 58 (About Uncirculated)

Obverse. Light wear on the hair below the coronet, the cheek, and the tips of the feather plumes is very noticeable at AU-50, progressively less at higher levels to AU-58. Luster is minimal at AU-50 and scattered and incomplete at AU-58. Some tiny nicks and contact marks are to be expected and should be mentioned if they are distracting.

Reverse. Light wear on the 1, the wreath, and the ribbon knot characterize an AU-50 coin, progressively less at higher levels to AU-58. Otherwise, the same comments apply as for the obverse.

Illustrated coin: 1855. AU-55.
This coin was lightly struck at the center. Clash marks appear on both sides, most prominent within the wreath on the reverse.

EF-40, 45 (Extremely Fine)

Obverse. Medium wear is seen on the hair below the coronet and on the feather plume tips. Detail is partially gone on the hair, although the usual light striking may make this moot. Luster is gone on most coins.

Reverse. Light wear is seen overall, and the highest parts of the leaves are flat. Luster is gone on most coins.

Illustrated coin: 1855-C. EF-40.
This coin was lightly struck at the centers, but overall has extraordinary quality for this, the only Charlotte gold dollar of the Type II design.

VF-20, 30 (Very Fine)

Obverse. Most hair detail is gone, except at the back of the lower curls. The feather plume ends are flat.

Reverse. The wreath and other areas show more wear. Most detail is gone on the higher-relief leaves.

Illustrated coin: 1854. VF-25.
This coin is well worn, but has an exceptionally bold date, indicating that it must have been a very sharp strike.

The Type II gold dollar is seldom collected in grades lower than VF-20.

Proof Indian Princess / Small Head Gold Dollars, PF-60 to 70

Proofs exist of the 1854 and 1855 issues, but were made in very small quantities.

Obverse and Reverse. PF-60 to 62 coins have extensive hairlines and may have nicks and contact marks. At PF-63, hairlines are prominent, but the mirror surface is very reflective. PF-64 coins have fewer hairlines. At PF-65, hairlines should be minimal and mostly seen only under magnification. There should be no nicks or marks. PF-66 and higher coins have no marks or hairlines visible to the unaided eye.

Illustrated coin: 1854. PF-66.

1856–1889 INDIAN PRINCESS, LARGE HEAD • TYPE III

History. In 1856 the obverse of the gold dollar was modified to a larger head in shallower relief. After this time, most (but hardly all) coins were produced with excellent details. Gold dollars of this type did not circulate extensively after 1861, except in the West. As they did not see heavy use, today most pieces are Extremely Fine or better. Mint State coins abound, particularly for the dates 1879 through 1889, during which time they were popular among investors and speculators, and many were saved.

Striking and Sharpness. Usually well struck, but with many exceptions. Charlotte and Dahlonega coins are usually weak in areas and can have planchet problems. On all coins, check the hair details on the obverse. The word LIBERTY can be only partially present or missing completely, as the dies were made this way for some issues, particularly in the 1870s; this does not affect their desirability. On the reverse, check the ribbon knot and the two central date numerals. Check the dentils on both sides. Copper stains are sometimes seen on issues of the 1880s due to incomplete mixing of the alloy. Many coins of the 1860s onward have highly prooflike surfaces.

Availability. All are collectible, but many issues are scarce. In Mint State most gems are dated from 1879 to 1889. The few gold dollars of this type that are less than Very Fine in grade are usually damaged or have problems (and are not studied here).

Special note: PCGS and *Photograde* use identical descriptors for Type II and Type III gold dollars, and the ANA grading standards are nearly parallel. We have separated the Type III here to provide for illustrations and comments concerning the pieces showcased.

MS-60 to 70 (Mint State)

Illustrated coin: 1878. MS-67.
This exceptionally high-grade coin has superb eye appeal.
Note: All coins are shown enlarged, for clarity.

Obverse. At MS-60 to 62, there is abrasion on the hair below the band lettered LIBERTY (an area that can be weakly struck as well), on the tips of the feather plumes, and throughout the field. Contact marks may also be seen. At MS-63, there should be only slight abrasions. Luster is irregular. At MS-64, abrasions and marks are less. Luster is rich on most coins, less so on Charlotte and Dahlonega issues. At MS-65 and above, luster is deep and frosty, with no marks at all visible without magnification at MS-66 and higher.

Reverse. At MS-60 to 62, there may be abrasions on the 1, on the highest parts of the leaves, on the ribbon knot, and in the field. Otherwise, the same comments apply as for the obverse.

AU-50, 53, 55, 58 (About Uncirculated)

Obverse. Light wear on the hair below the coronet, the cheek, and the tips of the feather plumes is very noticeable at AU-50, progressively less at higher levels to AU-58. Luster is minimal at AU-50 and scattered and incomplete at AU-58. Some tiny nicks and contact marks are to be expected and should be mentioned if they are distracting.

Reverse. Light wear on the 1, the wreath, and the ribbon knot characterize an AU-50 coin, progressively less at higher levels to AU-58. Otherwise, the same comments apply as for the obverse.

Illustrated coin: 1857-C. AU-58.
The obverse field is slightly bulged. This coin is lightly struck at the center, unusual for most Type III gold dollars, but sometimes seen on Charlotte and Dahlonega varieties. Among 1857-C gold dollars this coin is exceptional. Most have poor striking and/or planchet problems.

EF-40, 45 (Extremely Fine)

Obverse. Medium wear is seen on the hair below the coronet and on the feather plume tips. Detail is partially gone on the hair, although the usual light striking may make this moot. Luster is gone on most coins.

Reverse. Light wear is seen overall, and the highest parts of the leaves are flat. Luster is gone on most coins.

Illustrated coin: 1859-S. EF-40.

VF-20, 30 (Very Fine)

Obverse. Most hair detail is gone, except at the back of the lower curls. The feather plume ends are flat.

Reverse. The wreath and other areas show more wear. Most detail is gone on the higher-relief leaves.

Illustrated coin: 1859-D. VF-20.
This coin is lightly struck at the center obverse, as well as at the U and IC in the border lettering. It is lightly struck at the center of the reverse.

The Type III gold dollar is seldom collected in grades lower than VF-20.

Proof Indian Princess / Large Head Gold Dollars, PF-60 to 70

Proofs were made of all years. Most range from rare to very rare, some dates in the 1880s being exceptions. Some later dates have high Proof mintages, but likely many of these coins were sold to the jewelry trade (as the Mint was reluctant to release circulation strikes to this market sector). Such coins were incorporated into jewelry and no longer exist as collectible coins.

Obverse and Reverse. PF-60 to 62 coins have extensive hairlines and may have nicks and contact marks. At PF-63, hairlines are prominent, but the mirror surface is very reflective. PF-64 coins have fewer hairlines. At PF-65, hairlines should be minimal and mostly seen only under magnification. There should be no nicks or marks. PF-66 and higher coins have no marks or hairlines visible to the unaided eye.

Illustrated coin: 1884. PF-68.
This splendid cameo Proof is one of the finest graded.

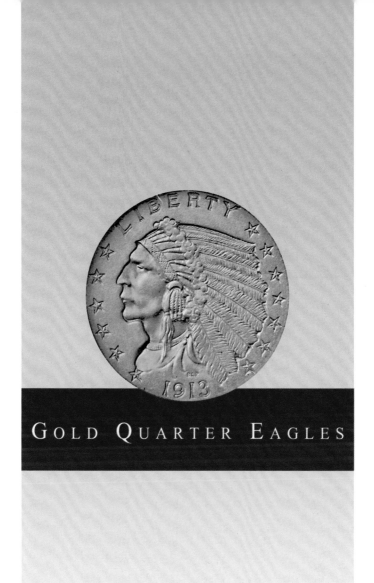

GOLD QUARTER EAGLES

GOLD QUARTER EAGLES, 1796–1929

1796–1807 CAPPED BUST TO RIGHT

History. Coins of this type were struck intermittently during the late 1790s and early 1800s. The earliest issues of 1796 lack obverse stars. Mintages were small. It is likely that most were used domestically, rather than being exported in international trade.

Striking and Sharpness. Most have light striking in one area or another. On the obverse, check the hair details and the stars. On the reverse, check the shield, stars, and clouds. Examine the dentils on both sides. Planchet adjustment marks are seen on many coins and are not noted by the certification services. On high-grade coins the luster is usually very attractive. Certain reverse dies of this type were also used to coin dimes.

Availability. Most in the marketplace are Extremely Fine or About Uncirculated. Mint State coins are elusive, and when seen are apt to be later dates. Apart from some weakness of striking, most quarter eagles of this type are very attractive.

MS-60 to 70 (Mint State)

Illustrated coin: 1802, 2 Over 1. MS-61.
Some friction appears on the higher areas of this example, but the fields retain nearly full luster, and the coin overall has nice eye appeal.

Note: Abbreviations used in die-variety attributions, along with the reference works on which the attributions are based, are discussed on the first page of this chapter. All coins are shown enlarged, for clarity.

Obverse. At MS-60, some abrasion and contact marks are evident, most noticeably on the hair to the left of Miss Liberty's forehead and on the higher-relief areas of the cap. On the No Stars quarter eagles, there is some abrasion in the field—more so than the With Stars coins, on which the field is more protected. Luster is present, but may be dull or lifeless, and interrupted in patches. At MS-63, contact marks are few, and abrasion is very light. An MS-65 coin will have hardly any abrasion, and contact marks are so minute as to require magnification. Luster should be full and rich. Coins grading above MS-65 exist more in theory than in reality for this type—but they do exist, and are defined by having fewer marks as perfection is approached.

Reverse. Comments apply as for the obverse, except that abrasion and contact marks are most noticeable on the upper part of the eagle and the clouds. The field area is complex; there is not much open space, with stars above the eagle, the arrows and olive branch, and other features. Accordingly, marks are not as noticeable as on the obverse.

AU-50, 53, 55, 58 (About Uncirculated)

Obverse. Light wear is seen on the cheek, the hair immediately to the left of the face, and the cap, more so at AU-50 than at 53 or 55. An AU-58 coin has minimal traces of wear. An AU-50 coin has luster in protected areas among the stars and letters, with little in the open fields or on the portrait. At AU-58 most luster is present in the fields, but is worn away on the highest parts of the motifs. The 1796 No Stars type has less luster in any given grade.

Illustrated coin: 1796, No Stars, BD-2. AU-58.

Reverse. Comments as for Mint State, except that the eagle's neck, the tips and top of the wings, the clouds, and the tail now show noticeable wear, as do other features. Luster ranges from perhaps 40% remaining in protected areas at AU-50 to nearly full mint bloom at AU-58. Often the reverse of this type retains much more luster than does the obverse.

EF-40, 45 (Extremely Fine)

Obverse. Wear is evident all over the portrait, with some loss of detail in the hair to the left of Miss Liberty's face. Excellent detail remains in low-relief areas of the hair, such as the front curl and the back of the head. The stars show wear, as do the date and letters. Luster, if present at all, is minimal and in protected areas.

Illustrated coin: 1802, BD-1. EF-45.

Reverse. Wear is greater than at the About Uncirculated level. The neck lacks feather detail on its highest points. Feathers have lost some detail near the edges of the wings, and some areas of the horizontal lines in the shield may be blended together. Some traces of luster may be seen, more so at EF-45 than at EF-40. Overall, the reverse appears to be in a slightly higher grade than the obverse.

VF-20, 30 (Very Fine)

Obverse. The higher-relief areas of hair are well worn at VF-20, less so at VF-30. The stars are flat at their centers.

Reverse. Wear is greater, including on the shield and wing feathers. The star centers are flat. Other areas have lost detail as well. E PLURIBUS UNUM is easy to read.

Illustrated coin: 1796, With Stars, BD-3. VF-30.

The Capped Bust to Right quarter eagle is seldom collected in grades lower than VF-20.

1808 CAPPED BUST TO LEFT

History. This single-year type features the Capped Bust Left design by John Reich, an adaptation of the design introduced in 1807 on the half dollar. Just 2,710 were struck. This is the rarest of the major gold types.

Striking and Sharpness. All examples are lightly struck on one area or another, particularly the stars and rims. The rims are low and sometimes missing or nearly so (on the obverse), causing quarter eagles of this date and type to wear more quickly than otherwise might be the case.

Availability. Examples are rare in any grade. Typical grades are Extremely Fine and About Uncirculated. Mint State coins are rare. Lower grades are rarely seen, as these did not circulate to any great extent. Gold coins of this era were not seen in circulation after 1821, so they did not get a chance to acquire significant wear.

MS-60 to 70 (Mint State)

Illustrated coin: 1808, Bass-Dannreuther 1. MS-63.
This is the only die combination of this year. Superbly struck, this coin is a "poster example" with few peers. Curiously, sharpness of strike is overlooked by most buyers.

Note: Abbreviations used in die-variety attributions, along with the reference works on which the attributions are based, are discussed on the first page of this chapter. All coins are shown enlarged, for clarity.

Obverse. At MS-60, some abrasion and contact marks are seen on the cheek, on the hair below the LIBERTY inscription, and on the highest-relief folds of the cap. Luster is present, but may be dull or lifeless, and interrupted in patches. At MS-63, contact marks are few, and abrasion is very light. Abrasion is even less at MS-64. (Discussion of such high grades in these early coins starts to enter the realm of theory.) Quarter eagles of this type are almost, but not quite, non-existent in a combination of high grade and nice eye appeal.

Reverse. Comments apply as for the obverse, except that abrasion is most noticeable on the eagle's neck and highest area of the wings.

AU-50, 53, 55, 58 (About Uncirculated)

Obverse. Light wear is seen on the cheek and higher-relief areas of the hair and cap. Friction and scattered marks are in the field, ranging from extensive at AU-50 to minimal at AU-58. The low rim affords little protection to the field of this coin, but the stars in relief help. Luster may be seen in protected areas, minimal at AU-50, but less so at AU-58. At AU-58 the field retains some luster as well.

Illustrated coin: 1808. AU-50.
Note some lightness of strike.

Reverse. Comments are as for a Mint State coin, except that the eagle's neck, the top of the wings, the leaves, and the arrowheads now show noticeable wear, as do other features. Luster ranges from perhaps 40% remaining in protected areas at AU-50 to nearly full mint bloom at AU-58. Often the reverse of this type retains much more luster than does the obverse, as on this type the motto, eagle, and lettering protect the surrounding flat areas.

EF-40, 45 (Extremely Fine)

Obverse. More wear is seen on the portrait, the hair, the cap, and the drapery near the clasp. Luster is likely to be absent on the obverse due to the low rim.

Reverse. Wear is more extensive on the eagle, including the top of the wings, the head, the top of the shield, and the claws. Some traces of luster may be seen in protected areas, more so at EF-45 than at EF-40.

Illustrated coin: 1808. EF-40.

VF-20, 30 (Very Fine)

Obverse. Wear on the portrait has reduced the hair detail, especially to the right of the face and the top of the head, but much can still be seen.

Reverse. Wear on the eagle is greater, and details of feathers near the shield and near the top of the wings are weak or missing. All other features show wear, but most are fairly sharp. Generally, Capped Bust gold coins at this grade level lack eye appeal.

Illustrated coin: 1808. VF-20.
This is a nice, problem-free example of a lower but very desirable grade for this rare issue.

The Capped Bust to Left quarter eagle is seldom collected in grades lower than VF-20.

1821–1834 CAPPED HEAD TO LEFT

History. Quarter eagles of this era have stars surrounding the head, except for the date. Those dated 1821 through 1827 have a larger diameter—18.5 mm—and can be considered a separate type from those of 1829 to 1834, with 18.2 mm diameter. However, grading rules apply to both. Gold coins of this type did not circulate in commerce, because their face value was lower than their bullion value. Most wear was due to use as pocket pieces, or minor handling.

Striking and Sharpness. Most are well struck. On the obverse, check the hair details (which on the 1829 to 1834 style can be light in areas) and the stars. On the reverse, check the eagle. On both sides inspect the dentils. Fields are often semi-prooflike on higher grades.

Availability. All are rare. Grades are from Extremely Fine to Mint State, with choice examples in the latter category being scarce, and gems being very rare. Liberal grading by today's collectors, dealers, and grading services has resulted in many About Uncirculated coins of a generation ago being called Mint State today.

Special note: PCGS and *Photograde* use identical descriptors for all Capped Bust quarter eagles 1808 to 1834, and the ANA grading standards are parallel. We have separated the later issues here to provide for illustrations and comments concerning the pieces showcased.

MS-60 to 70 (Mint State)

Illustrated coin: 1827, Bass-Dannreuther 1. MS-65.
Here is a well-struck lustrous gem.

Note: Abbreviations used in die-variety attributions, along with the reference works on which the attributions are based, are discussed on the first page of this chapter. All coins are shown enlarged, for clarity.

Obverse. At MS-60, some abrasion and contact marks are seen on the cheek, on the hair below the LIBERTY inscription, and on the highest-relief folds of the cap. Luster is present, but may be dull or lifeless, and interrupted in patches. At MS-63, contact marks are few, and abrasion is very light. Abrasion is even less at MS-64. (Discussion of such high grades in these early coins starts to enter the realm of theory.) Quarter eagles of this type are almost, but not quite, non-existent in a combination of high grade and nice eye appeal.

Reverse. Comments apply as for the obverse, except that abrasion is most noticeable on the eagle's neck and highest area of the wings.

AU-50, 53, 55, 58 (About Uncirculated)

Obverse. Light wear is seen on the cheek and higher-relief areas of the hair and cap. Friction and scattered marks are in the field, ranging from extensive at AU-50 to minimal at AU-58. The low rim affords little protection to the field of this coin, but the stars in relief help. Luster may be seen in protected areas, minimal at AU-50, but less so at AU-58. At AU-58 the field retains some luster as well.

Illustrated coin: 1833, BD-1. AU-53.

Reverse. Comments are as for a Mint State coin, except that the eagle's neck, the top of the wings, the leaves, and the arrowheads now show noticeable wear, as do other features. Luster ranges from perhaps 40% remaining in protected areas at AU-50 to nearly full mint bloom at AU-58. Often the reverse of this type retains much more luster than does the obverse, as on this type the motto, eagle, and lettering protect the surrounding flat areas.

EF-40, 45 (Extremely Fine)

Obverse. More wear is seen on the portrait, the hair, the cap, and the drapery near the clasp. Luster is likely to be absent on the obverse due to the low rim.

Reverse. Wear is more extensive on the eagle, including the top of the wings, the head, the top of the shield, and the claws. Some traces of luster may be seen in protected areas, more so at EF-45 than at EF-40.

Illustrated coin: 1831, BD-1. EF-45.

The Capped Head quarter eagle is seldom collected in grades lower than EF-40.

Proof Capped Head Quarter Eagles, PF-60 to 70

Proof coins were made on a limited basis for presentation and for distribution to numismatists. All examples are exceedingly rare today, and are usually encountered only when great collections are dispersed.

Obverse and Reverse. PF-60 to 62 coins have extensive hairlines and may have nicks and contact marks. At PF-63, hairlines are prominent, but the mirror surface is very reflective. PF-64 coins have fewer hairlines. At PF-65, hairlines should be minimal and mostly seen only under magnification. There should be no nicks or marks. PF-66 and higher coins should have no marks or hairlines visible to the unaided eye.

Illustrated coin: 1824, 4 Over 1. Proof.
This coin resides in the National Numismatic Collection, Smithsonian Institution.

1834–1839 CLASSIC HEAD

History. Gold quarter eagles had not circulated at par in the United States since 1821, as the price of bullion necessitated more than $2.50 worth of gold to produce a single coin. Accordingly, they traded at their bullion value. The Act of June 28, 1834, provided lower weights for gold coins, after which the issues, of new designs to differentiate them from the old, circulated effectively. The Classic Head design by William Kneass is an adaptation of the head created by John Reich for the cent of 1808. The reverse illustrates a perched eagle. The motto E PLURIBUS UNUM, seen on earlier gold coins, is no longer present. These coins circulated widely until mid-1861, after which hoarding took place because of the Civil War. For this reason, many show extensive wear.

Striking and Sharpness. Weakness is often seen on the higher areas of the hair curls. Also check the star centers. On the reverse, check the rims. The dentils are usually well struck.

Availability. Most coins range from Very Fine to About Uncirculated or lower ranges of Mint State. Most Mint State coins are of the first three years. Choice and Gem Mint State examples are rare. Eye appeal can be a problem, and connoisseurship is recommended.

MS-60 to 70 (Mint State)

Illustrated coin: 1834. MS-65.
This coin is especially well struck.

Note: All coins are shown enlarged, for clarity.

Obverse. At MS-60, some abrasion and contact marks are seen on the portrait, most noticeably on the cheek, as the hair details are complex on this type. Luster is present, but may be dull or lifeless, and interrupted in patches. Many low-level Mint State coins have grainy surfaces. At MS-63, contact marks are few, and abrasion is very light. Abrasion is even less at MS-64. An MS-65 coin has hardly any abrasion, and contact marks are minute. Luster should be full and rich and is often more intense on the obverse. Grades above MS-65 are defined by having fewer marks as perfection is approached.

Reverse. Comments apply as for the obverse, except that abrasion is most noticeable on the eagle's neck and the highest area of the wings.

AU-50, 53, 55, 58 (About Uncirculated)

Obverse. Friction is seen on the higher parts, particularly the cheek and hair (under magnification) of Miss Liberty. Friction and scattered marks are in the field, ranging from extensive at AU-50 to minimal at AU-58. Luster may be seen in protected areas, minimal at AU-50 but more visible at AU-58. On an AU-58 coin the field retains some luster as well.

Illustrated coin: 1837. AU-55.
The coin has light wear overall, but traces of luster can be seen here and there.

Reverse. Comments as for Mint State, except that the eagle's neck, the top of the wings, the leaves, and the arrowheads now show noticeable wear, as do other features. Luster ranges from perhaps 40% remaining in protected areas at AU-50 to nearly full mint bloom at AU-58. Often the reverse of this type retains much more luster than does the obverse.

EF-40, 45 (Extremely Fine)

Obverse. Wear is seen on the portrait overall, with reduction or elimination of some separation of hair strands, especially in the area close to the face. The cheek shows light wear. Luster is minimal or nonexistent at EF-40, and may survive in among the letters of LIBERTY at EF-45.

Reverse. Wear is greater than on an About Uncirculated coin. On most (but not all) coins the eagle's neck lacks some feather detail on its highest points. Feathers have lost some detail near the edges and tips of the wings. Some areas of the horizontal lines in the shield may be blended together. Some traces of luster may be seen, more so at EF-45 than at EF-40.

Illustrated coin: 1834. EF-45.
This coin is well struck.

VF-20, 30 (Very Fine)

Obverse. Wear on the portrait has reduced the hair detail, especially to the right of the face and the top of the head, but much can still be seen.

Reverse. Wear is greater, including on the shield and wing feathers. Generally, Classic Head gold at this grade level lacks eye appeal.

Illustrated coin: 1836. VF-30.
This coin was lightly cleaned. It is lightly struck at the centers, although at this grade level that is not important.

The Classic Head quarter eagle is seldom collected in grades lower than VF-20.

Proof Classic Head Quarter Eagles, PF-60 to 70

Proofs were made in small quantities, and today probably only a couple dozen or so survive, most bearing the 1834 date.

Obverse and Reverse. PF-60 to 62 coins have extensive hairlines and may have nicks and contact marks. At PF-63, hairlines are prominent, but the mirror surface is very reflective. PF-64 coins have fewer hairlines. At PF-65, hairlines should be minimal and mostly seen only under magnification. There should be no nicks or marks. PF-66 and higher coins should have no marks or hairlines visible to the unaided eye.

Illustrated coin: 1836. PF-65 Cameo.

1840–1907 LIBERTY HEAD

History. Introduced in 1840, the Liberty Head quarter eagle remained in use with essentially the same design until 1907—one of the longest such spans in American coinage history. Designed by Christian Gobrecht, the motifs with the Liberty Head obverse and perched eagle reverse closely follow those used on $5 coins from 1839 to 1908 and $10 coins from 1838 to 1907.

Striking and Sharpness. On the obverse, check the highest points of the hair and the star centers. On the reverse, check the eagle's neck, and the area to the lower left of the shield and the lower part of the eagle. Examine the dentils on both sides. Branch-mint coins struck before the Civil War are often lightly struck in areas and have weak dentils. Often, a certified Extremely Fine coin from the Dahlonega or Charlotte mints will not appear any sharper than a Very Fine coin from Philadelphia. There are exceptions, and some C and D coins are sharp. The careful study of photographs, including those on the Internet, is useful in acquainting you with the peculiarities of a given date or mint. Most quarter eagles from the 1880s to 1907 are sharp in all areas. Tiny copper staining spots can be a problem.

Availability. Early dates and mintmarks are generally scarce to rare in Mint State and very rare in Choice or Gem Mint State, with only a few exceptions. Coins of Charlotte and Dahlonega (all of which are especially avidly collected) are usually Extremely Fine or About Uncirculated, or overgraded low Mint State. Rarities for the type include 1841, 1854-S, and 1875. Coins of the 1860s onward are generally seen with sharper striking and in higher average grades. Typically, San Francisco quarter eagles are in lower average grades than are those from the Philadelphia Mint, as Philadelphia coins did not circulate at par in the East and Midwest from late December 1861 until December 1878, and thus did not acquire as much wear. Mint State coins are readily available for the early-20th century years, and usually have outstanding eye appeal.

MS-60 to 70 (Mint State)

Illustrated coin: 1859-S. MS-65.
Sharply struck, bright, and with abundant luster and great eye appeal, this is a "just right" coin for the connoisseur.

Note: All coins are shown enlarged, for clarity.

Obverse. At MS-60, some abrasion and contact marks are evident, most noticeably on the hair to the right of Miss Liberty's forehead, and on the jaw. Luster is present, but may be dull or lifeless, and interrupted in patches. At MS-63, contact marks are few, and abrasion is very light. An MS-65 coin has hardly any abrasion, and contact marks are so minute as to require magnification. Luster should be full and rich. Grades above MS-65 are usually found late in the series and are defined by having fewer marks as perfection is approached.

Reverse. Comments apply as for the obverse, except that abrasion and contact marks are most noticeable on the eagle's neck and to the lower left of the shield.

AU-50, 53, 55, 58 (About Uncirculated)

Obverse. Light wear is seen on the face, the hair to the right of the face, and the highest area of the hair bun, more so at AU-50 than at 53 or 55. An AU-58 coin has minimal traces of wear. An AU-50 coin has luster in protected areas among the stars and letters, with little in the open fields or on the portrait. At AU-58, most luster is present in the fields, but is worn away on the highest parts of the motifs.

Reverse. Comments apply as for the preceding, except that the eagle shows wear in all of the higher areas, as well as the leaves and arrowheads. Luster ranges from perhaps 40% remaining in protected areas at AU-50 to nearly full mint bloom at AU-58. Often the reverse of this type retains more luster than the obverse.

Illustrated coin: 1855-D. AU-55.
The example has the bold rims often seen on Dahlonega Mint coins of this denomination.

EF-40, 45 (Extremely Fine)

Obverse. Wear is evident on all high areas of the portrait, including the hair to the right of the forehead, the tip of the coronet, and the hair bun. The stars show light wear at their centers. Luster, if present at all, is minimal and in protected areas such as between the star points.

Reverse. Wear is greater than on an AU coin. The eagle's neck is nearly smooth, much detail is lost on the right wing, and there is flatness at the lower left of the shield, and on the leaves and arrowheads. Traces of luster may be seen, more so at EF-45 than at EF-40. Overall, the reverse appears to be in a slightly higher grade than the obverse.

Illustrated coin: 1860-C. EF-40.
This is an attractive coin with medium wear.

VF-20, 30 (Very Fine)

Obverse. The higher-relief areas of hair are worn flat at VF-20, less so at VF-30. The hair to the right of the coronet is merged into heavy strands. The stars are flat at their centers.

Reverse. Much of the eagle is flat, with less than 50% of the feather detail remaining. The vertical shield stripes, being deeply recessed, remain bold.

Illustrated coin: 1843-O, Small Date, Crosslet 4. VF-20.

The Liberty Head quarter eagle is seldom collected in grades lower than VF-20.

Proof Liberty Head Quarter Eagles, PF-60 to 70

Proofs exist relative to their original mintages; all prior to the 1890s are rare. Cameo contrast is the rule prior to 1902, when the portrait was polished in the die (a few years later cameo-contrast coins were again made).

Obverse and Reverse. PF-60 to 62 coins have extensive hairlines and may have nicks and contact marks. At PF-63, hairlines are prominent, but the mirror surface is very reflective. PF-64 coins have fewer hairlines; PF-65, minimal hairlines mostly seen only under magnification, and no nicks or marks. PF-66 and higher coins should have no marks or hairlines visible to the unaided eye.

Illustrated coin: 1895. PF-66.
This is an exceptional gem in rich yellow-orange gold.

1908–1929 INDIAN HEAD

History. Introduced in 1908 and minted continuously to 1915 and again from 1925 to 1929, the Indian Head quarter eagle and the related half eagle are unusual in that the lettering and motifs are *incuse* or recessed in the fields. These coins circulated as money in the West, but not elsewhere. As the lowest gold denomination at the time, they were popular for use as souvenirs and gifts. Many were saved in this manner.

Striking and Sharpness. Striking varies. On many early issues the rims are flat, while on others, including most of the 1920s, they are slightly raised. Some have traces of a wire rim, usually on the reverse. Look for weakness on the high parts of the Indian's bonnet (particularly the garland of flowers) and in the feather details in the headdress. On the reverse, check the feathers on the highest area of the wing, the top of the shoulder. On some issues of the 1911-D, the D mintmark can be weak.

Availability. This design was not popular with collectors, and they specifically saved relatively few of the coins. However, many gift coins were preserved. The survival of Choice and Gem Mint State coins is a matter of chance, especially for the issues dated from 1909 to 1915. The only scarce issue is 1911-D. Luster can range from deeply frosty to grainy. As the fields are the highest areas of the coin, luster diminished quickly as examples were circulated or jostled with others in bags. The Indian Head $2.50 and $5 coins are two of the most challenging series for professional graders, and opinions can vary widely.

MS-60 to 70 (Mint State)

Illustrated coin: 1911-D. MS-64.
This lustrous example has excellent eye appeal.
Note: All coins are shown enlarged, for clarity.

Obverse. On MS-60 to 62 coins there is abrasion in the field, this representing the highest part of the coin. Abrasion is also evident on the headdress. Marks and, occasionally, a microscopic pin scratch may be seen. At MS-63, there may be some abrasion and some tiny marks. Luster is irregular. At MS-64, abrasion is less. Luster is rich. At MS-65 and above, luster is deep and frosty. No marks at all are visible without magnification at MS-66 and higher.

Reverse. At MS-60 to 62, there is abrasion in the field, this representing the highest part of the coin. Abrasion is also evident on the eagle's wing. Otherwise, the same comments apply as for the obverse.

AU-50, 53, 55, 58 (About Uncirculated)

Obverse. Friction on the cheek is very noticeable at AU-50, progressively less at higher levels to AU-58. The headdress shows light wear, most evident on the ribbon above the forehead and on the garland. Luster is minimal at AU-50 and scattered and incomplete at AU-58. Nicks and contact marks are to be expected.

Reverse. Friction on the wing and neck is very noticeable at AU-50, increasingly less at higher levels to AU-58. Otherwise, the same comments apply as for the obverse.

Illustrated coin: 1911-D. AU-55.
Much of the original luster remains in the incuse areas but not in the fields, which are the highest points on this design.

EF-40, 45 (Extremely Fine)

Obverse. Light wear characterizes the portrait and headdress. Luster is gone. Marks and tiny scratches are to be expected, but not distracting.

Reverse. Light wear is most evident on the eagle's head and wing, although other areas are lightly worn as well. Luster is gone. Marks and tiny scratches are to be expected, but not distracting.

Illustrated coin: 1911-D. EF-40.

VF-20, 30 (Very Fine)

Obverse. Many details of the ribbon above the forehead and the garland are worn away. Many feather vanes are blended together. The field is dull and has contact marks.

Reverse. The neck and the upper part of the wing show extensive wear, other areas less so. The field is dull and has contact marks.

Illustrated coin: 1912-D. VF-30.

Proof Indian Head Quarter Eagles, PF-60 to 70

Sandblast (also called Matte) Proofs were made in 1908 and 1911 to 1915, while Satin (also called Roman Finish) Proofs were made in 1909 and 1910. The Sandblast issues are usually somewhat dull, while the Satin Proofs are usually of a light-yellow gold. In their time the Proofs of both styles, made for all gold series, were not popular with numismatists. Today, they are in strong demand. As a class these are significantly more readily available than half eagles of the same date and style of finish. Most are in grades from PF-63 upward. At lower levels coins can show light contact marks. Some microscopic bright flecks may be caused by the sandblasting process and, although they do not represent handling, usually result in a coin being assigned a slightly lower grade.

Illustrated coin: 1913. PF-66.
Here is a Sandblast Proof of exceptionally high quality.

Obverse and Reverse. At PF-60 to 63, there is light abrasion and some contact marks; the lower the grade, the higher the quantity. On Sandblast Proofs these show up as visually unappealing bright spots. At PF-64 and higher levels, marks are fewer, with magnification needed to see any at PF-65. At PF-66, there should be none at all.

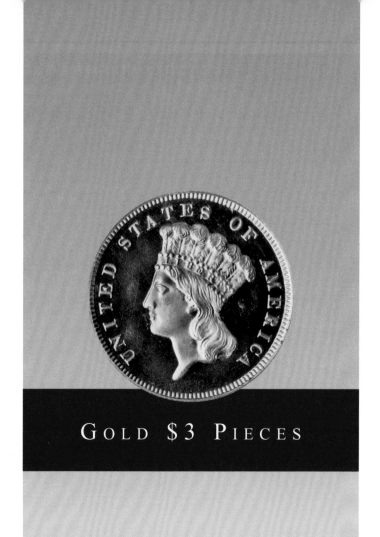

GOLD $3 PIECES

GOLD $3 PIECES, 1854–1889

History. The $3 gold coin, designed by Chief Engraver James B. Longacre, was introduced in 1854. The obverse and reverse designs were the same as used on the gold dollar type of 1856 to 1889. After 1854 the mintage declined. Production continued until 1889, with the mintages being small for most years.

Striking and Sharpness. Points to observe on the obverse include the tips of the ostrich feathers in the headdress, and the hair details below the band inscribed LIBERTY. On the reverse: the wreath details (especially the vertical division in the ribbon knot), and the two central date numerals. Many of the later issues are prooflike, this being particularly true of the dates in the early 1880s.

Availability. In circulated grades the issues of 1854 to 1860 survive in approximate proportion to their mintages. Mint State coins are plentiful for the first-year Philadelphia issue, 1854, but are scarce to rare for other years and all branch-mint issues. For the 1860s and 1870s most are in grades such as Extremely Fine, About Uncirculated, and low Mint State, except for 1874 and in particular 1878, easily found in Mint State. Dates from 1879 to 1889 have a higher survival ratio and are mostly in Mint State, often at the Gem level.

MS-60 to 70 (Mint State)

Illustrated coin: 1879. MS-64.
Satiny luster and partial mirror surfaces yield excellent eye appeal.
Note: All coins are shown enlarged, for clarity.

Obverse. On MS-60 to 62 coins there is abrasion on the hair below the band lettered LIBERTY (an area that can be weakly struck as well) and on tips of the feather plumes. At MS-63, there may be slight abrasion. Luster can be irregular. At MS-64, abrasion is less. Luster is rich on most coins, less so on the 1854-D (which is often overgraded). At MS-65 and above, luster is deep and frosty, with no marks at all visible without magnification at MS-66 and higher.

Reverse. On MS-60 to 62 coins there is abrasion on the 1, the highest parts of the leaves, and the ribbon knot. Otherwise, the same comments apply as for the obverse.

AU-50, 53, 55, 58 (About Uncirculated)

Obverse. Light wear on the hair below the coronet, the cheek, and the tips of the feather plumes is very noticeable at AU-50, increasingly less at higher levels to AU-58. Luster is minimal at AU-50 and scattered and incomplete at AU-58. Some tiny nicks and contact marks are to be expected and should be mentioned if they are distracting.

Reverse. Light wear on the 1, the wreath, and the ribbon knot characterize an AU-50 coin, increasingly less at higher levels to 58. Otherwise, the same comments apply as for the obverse.

Illustrated coin: 1854. AU-55.
Most of the original luster is gone, but perhaps 15% remains in the protected areas.

EF-40, 45 (Extremely Fine)

Obverse. Medium wear is seen on the hair below the coronet and on the feather plume tips. Detail is partially gone on the hair. Luster is gone on most coins.

Reverse. Light wear is seen overall, and the highest parts of the leaves are flat, but detail remains elsewhere. Luster is gone on most coins.

Illustrated coin: 1854-D. EF-40.
Note the mushy dentils (as seen on all but one specimen of this, the only Dahlonega variety in the series).

VF-20, 30 (Very Fine)

Obverse. Most hair detail is gone, except at the back of the lower curls. The feather plume ends are flat.

Reverse. The wreath and other areas show more wear. Most detail is gone on the higher-relief leaves.

Illustrated coin: 1874. VF-20.

Three-dollar gold pieces are seldom collected in grades lower than VF-20.

Proof $3 Pieces, PF-60 to 70

Proofs were struck of all years. All prior to the 1880s are very rare today, with issues of the 1850s being exceedingly so. Coins of 1875 and 1876 were made only in Proof format, with no related circulation strikes. Most often seen in the marketplace are the higher-mintage Proofs of the 1880s. Some have patches of graininess or hints of non-Proof surface on the obverse, or an aura or "ghosting" near the portrait, an artifact of striking.

Illustrated coin: 1876. PF-61.
Extensive friction is visible in the fields, but the mirror surface can be seen in protected areas. This is still a desirable example of a date of which only 45 were minted.

Obverse and Reverse. PF-60 to 62 coins have extensive hairlines and may have nicks and contact marks. At PF-63, hairlines are prominent, but the mirror surface is very reflective. PF-64 coins have fewer hairlines. At PF-65, hairlines should be minimal and mostly seen only under magnification. There should be no nicks or marks. PF-66 and higher coins should have no marks or hairlines visible to the unaided eye.

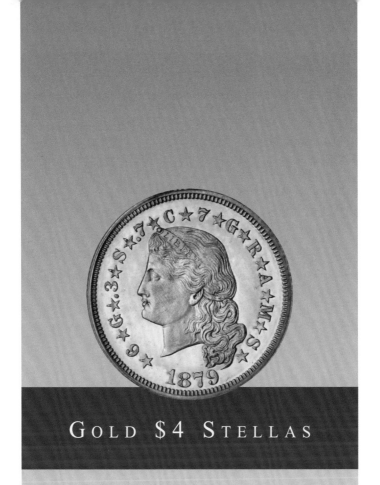

GOLD $4 STELLAS

GOLD $4 STELLAS, 1879–1880

1879–1880 FLOWING HAIR

History. The $4 gold Stellas of 1879 and 1880 are Proof-only patterns, not regular issues. However, as they have been listed in popular references for a long time, collectors with the means have adopted them into their collections. The obverse inscription gives the metallic content in proportions of gold, silver, and copper in the metric system, intended to facilitate the coin's use in foreign countries, where its value could be quickly ascertained. The coin was proposed by John A. Kasson (former chairman of the congressional Committee of Coinage, Weights, and Measures; in 1879 serving as envoy extraordinary and minister plenipotentiary to Austria-Hungary). Charles E. Barber designed the Flowing Hair type, as here, and George T. Morgan created the Coiled Hair style. The only issue produced in quantity, to the extent of more than 425 coins, was the 1879 Flowing Hair. The others were made in secret and privately sold by Mint officers and employees. Stellas are cataloged by their Judd numbers, assigned in the standard reference, *United States Pattern Coins*.

Striking and Sharpness. On nearly all examples the high parts of the hair are flat, often with striations. The other areas of the coin are typically well struck. Tiny planchet irregularities are common.

Availability. The 1879 Flowing Hair is often available on the market—usually in PF-61 to 64, although higher-condition examples come on the market with regularity (as do lightly handled and impaired coins). The 1880 Flowing Hair is typically found in PF-63 or higher.

Proof Flowing Hair $4 Stellas, PF-60 to 70

Illustrated coin: 1879. PF-62.
A nick above the head and some light friction define the grade, but the coin has nice eye appeal overall.

Note: Abbreviations used in die-variety attributions, along with the reference works on which the attributions are based, are discussed on the first page of this chapter. All coins are shown enlarged, for clarity.

Obverse and Reverse. PF-60 to 62 coins have extensive hairlines and may have nicks and contact marks. At PF-63, hairlines are prominent, but the mirror surface is very reflective. PF-64 coins have fewer hairlines. At PF-65, hairlines should be minimal and mostly seen only under magnification. There should be no nicks or marks. PF-66 and higher coins should have no marks or hairlines visible to the unaided eye.

1879–1880 COILED HAIR

History. The Coiled Hair Stella was created by George T. Morgan. These were made in small quantities and sold by Mint employees. They were not generally known to the numismatic community until they were illustrated in *The Numismatist* in the early 20th century.

Striking and Sharpness. On nearly all examples the high parts of the hair are flat, often with striations. The other areas of the coin are typically well struck. Tiny planchet irregularities are common, from debris adhering to the dies, particularly on the 1880 version.

Availability. Both years are great rarities. Typical grades are PF-63 to 65, with flat strike on the head and with some tiny planchet flaws.

Proof Coiled Hair $4 Stellas, PF-60 to 70

Illustrated coin: 1879, Coiled Hair, J-1660. PF-65.

Obverse and Reverse. PF-60 to 62 coins have extensive hairlines and may have nicks and contact marks. At PF-63, hairlines are prominent, but the mirror surface is very reflective. PF-64 coins have fewer hairlines. At PF-65, hairlines should be minimal and mostly seen only under magnification. There should be no nicks or marks. PF-66 and higher coins should have no marks or hairlines visible to the unaided eye.

GOLD HALF EAGLES

GOLD HALF EAGLES, 1795–1929

1795–1798 CAPPED BUST TO RIGHT / SMALL EAGLE REVERSE

History. Half eagles of this style, the first federal gold coins, were introduced in July 1795. The obverse features Miss Liberty wearing a conical cap, and is generally called Capped Bust to Right. The reverse depicts a "small" eagle perched on a palm branch. The same motif was used on contemporary $10 gold coins.

Striking and Sharpness. On the obverse, check the star centers and the hair details. On the reverse, check the feathers of the eagle, particularly on the breast. Examine the dentils on both sides. Adjustment marks often are visible, but are not noted by the grading services.

Availability. Typical grades range from Extremely Fine to About Uncirculated and low Mint State. MS-63 and higher coins are rare and when seen are usually of the 1795 date (of which many different die varieties exist). Certain varieties are rare, most famously the 1798 with Small Eagle reverse.

MS-60 to 70 (Mint State)

Illustrated coin: 1795, Bass-Dannreuther 6.
MS-63.

This is the error die with the second S over an erroneous D in STATES (which originally read as STATED).

Note: Abbreviations used in die-variety attributions, along with the reference works on which the attributions are based, are discussed on the first page of this chapter. All coins are shown enlarged, for clarity.

Obverse. At MS-60, some abrasion and contact marks are evident, most noticeably on the hair to the left of Miss Liberty's forehead and on the higher-relief areas of the cap. Luster is present, but may be dull or lifeless, and interrupted in patches. At MS-63, contact marks are few, and abrasion is very light. An MS-65 coin has hardly any abrasion, and contact marks are so minute as to require magnification. Luster should be full and rich. Grades above MS-65 for this type are more often theoretical than actual—but they do exist and are defined by having fewer marks as perfection is approached.

Reverse. Comments apply as for the obverse, except that abrasion and contact marks are most noticeable on the breast and head of the eagle. The field area is mainly protected by the eagle, branch, and lettering.

AU-50, 53, 55, 58 (About Uncirculated)

Obverse. Light wear is seen on the cheek, the hair immediately to the left of the face, and the cap, more at AU-50 than at 53 or 55. An AU-58 coin has minimal traces of wear. An AU-50 coin has luster in protected areas among the stars and letters, with little in the open fields or on the portrait. At AU-58, most luster is present in the fields but is worn away on the highest parts of the motifs.

Illustrated coin: 1795, BD-7. AU-58.

Reverse. Comments as preceding, except that the eagle shows light wear on the breast and head in particular, but also at the tip of the wing on the left and elsewhere. Luster ranges from perhaps 40% remaining in protected areas (at AU-50) to nearly full mint bloom (at AU-58).

EF-40, 45 (Extremely Fine)

Obverse. Wear is evident all over the portrait, with some loss of detail in the hair to the left of Miss Liberty's face. Excellent detail remains in low-relief areas of the hair, such as the front curl and at the back of her head. The stars show wear, as do the date and letters. Luster, if present at all, is minimal and in protected areas.

Illustrated coin: 1795, BD-4. EF-40.

Reverse. Wear is greater than on an About Uncirculated coin. The breast, neck, and legs of the eagle lack nearly all feather detail. More wear is seen on the edges of the wing. Some traces of luster may be seen, more so at EF-45 than at EF-40.

VF-20, 30 (Very Fine)

Obverse. The higher-relief areas of hair are well worn at VF-20, less so at VF-30. The stars are flat at their centers.

Reverse. Wear is greater, the eagle is flat in most areas, and about 40% to 60% of the wing feathers can be seen.

Illustrated coin: 1795. VF-30.

The Capped Bust to Right half eagle with Small Eagle reverse is seldom collected in grades lower than VF-20.

1795–1807 CAPPED BUST TO RIGHT / HERALDIC EAGLE REVERSE

History. Half eagles of this type were probably not struck until about 1798. The rare 1795 with this reverse was made from a leftover die on hand at that later time. The obverse is the same design as the preceding. The reverse depicts the Heraldic Eagle as used on other silver and gold coins of the era.

Striking and Sharpness. On the obverse, check the star centers and the hair details. On the reverse, check the upper part of the shield, the lower part of the eagle's neck, the eagle's wing, the stars above the eagle, and the clouds. Inspect the dentils on both sides. Adjustment marks can be a problem and are not identified by the grading services.

Availability. Although there are many rare die varieties, as a type this half eagle is plentiful. Typical grades are Extremely Fine to lower Mint State ranges. MS-63 and higher coins are seen with some frequency and are usually dated from 1802 to 1807. Sharply struck coins without adjustment marks are in the minority, but can be cherrypicked, as most other buyers are not aware of *quality* considerations and think only of the assigned grade.

MS-60 to 70 (Mint State)

Illustrated coin: 1802, 2 Over 1. MS-62.
This is an attractive coin with rich luster. Some friction is visible on the higher points and in the obverse field.

Note: Abbreviations used in die-variety attributions, along with the reference works on which the attributions are based, are discussed on the first page of this chapter. All coins are shown enlarged, for clarity.

Obverse. At MS-60, some abrasion and contact marks are evident, most noticeably on the hair to the left of Miss Liberty's forehead and on the higher-relief areas of the cap. Luster is present, but may be dull or lifeless, and interrupted in patches. At MS-63, contact marks are few, and abrasion is very light. An MS-65 coin has hardly any abrasion, and contact marks are so minute as to require magnification. Luster should be full and rich. Grades above MS-65 are not often seen but are defined by having fewer marks as perfection is approached.

Reverse. Comments apply as for the obverse, except that abrasion and contact marks are most noticeable on the upper part of the eagle and the clouds. The field area is complex, with not much open space, given the stars above the eagle, the arrows and olive branch, and other features. Accordingly, marks are not as noticeable as on the obverse.

AU-50, 53, 55, 58 (About Uncirculated)

Obverse. Light wear is seen on the cheek, the hair immediately to the left of the face, and the cap, more at AU-50 than at 53 or 55. An AU-58 coin has minimal traces of wear. An AU-50 coin has luster in protected areas among the stars and letters, with little in the open fields or on the portrait. At AU-58, most luster is present in the fields, but is worn away on the highest parts of the motifs.

Reverse. Comments as preceding, except that the eagle's neck, the tips and top of the wings, the clouds, and the tail now show noticeable wear, as do other features. Luster ranges from perhaps 40% remaining in protected areas (at AU-50) to nearly full mint bloom (at AU-58). Often the reverse of this type retains much more luster than the obverse.

Illustrated coin: 1804. AU-58.
An abrasion in the left obverse field keeps this otherwise lustrous and attractive coin below the Mint State level.

EF-40, 45 (Extremely Fine)

Obverse. Wear is evident all over the portrait, with some loss of detail in the hair to the left of Miss Liberty's face. Excellent detail remains in low-relief areas of the hair, such as the front curl and at the back of her head. The stars show wear, as do the date and letters. Luster, if present at all, is minimal and in protected areas.

Reverse. Wear is greater than on an About Uncirculated coin. The neck lacks feather detail on its highest points. Feathers have lost some detail near the edges of the wings, and some areas of the horizontal lines in the shield may be blended together. Some traces of luster may be seen, more so at EF-45 than at EF-40. Overall, the reverse appears to be in a slightly higher grade than the obverse.

Illustrated coin: 1799, BD-5. EF-45.

VF-20, 30 (Very Fine)

Obverse. The higher-relief areas of hair are well worn at VF-20, less so at VF-30. The stars are flat at their centers.

Reverse. Wear is greater, including on the shield and wing feathers. The star centers are flat. Other areas have lost detail as well. E PLURIBUS UNUM may be light or worn away in areas.

Illustrated coin: 1798, BD-4. VF-20.

The Capped Bust to Right half eagle with Heraldic Eagle reverse is seldom collected in grades lower than VF-20.

1807–1812 Capped Bust to Left

History. Designed by John Reich and loosely similar to his Capped Bust half dollar of 1807, this style was used only for a short time in the half eagle series. Large quantities were produced, and they were widely used in their time.

Striking and Sharpness. The striking is usually quite good and is significantly better than on earlier half eagle types. Adjustment marks are seen only occasionally. On the obverse, check the star centers and the hair details. On the reverse, check the eagle, particularity at the shield and the lower left. Examine the dentils on both sides.

Availability. After 1821 gold coins of this standard no longer circulated, as the melted-down value was more than the face value. Accordingly, coins of this type never sustained extensive wear, and nearly all examples are in Extremely Fine or higher grades (coins used as pocket pieces or jewelry are exceptions). As a type this issue is readily available in grades up to MS-63, although MS-64 and 65 coins are seen on occasion. Most have excellent eye appeal.

MS-60 to 70 (Mint State)

Illustrated coin: 1808. MS-60.
This attractive Capped Bust Left half eagle has nice luster.

Note: Abbreviations used in die-variety attributions, along with the reference works on which the attributions are based, are discussed on the first page of this chapter. All coins are shown enlarged, for clarity.

Obverse. At MS-60, some abrasion and contact marks are seen on the cheek, the hair below the LIBERTY inscription, and the highest-relief folds of the cap. Luster is present, but may be dull or lifeless, and interrupted in patches. At MS-63, contact marks are few, and abrasion is very light. At MS-64, abrasion is even less. An MS-65 coin has hardly any abrasion, and contact marks are minute. Luster should be full and rich and is often more intense on the obverse. Grades above MS-65 are defined by having fewer marks as perfection is approached.

Reverse. Comments apply as for the obverse, except that abrasion is most noticeable on the eagle's neck and the highest area of the wings.

AU-50, 53, 55, 58 (About Uncirculated)

Obverse. Light wear is seen on the cheek and the higher-relief areas of the hair and cap. Friction and scattered marks are in the field, ranging from extensive at AU-50 to minimal at AU-58. Luster may be seen in protected areas, minimal at AU-50 but more evident at AU-58. On an AU-58 coin the field retains some luster as well.

Reverse. Comments as preceding, except that the eagle's neck, the top of the wings, the leaves, and the arrowheads now show noticeable wear, as do other features. Luster ranges from perhaps 40% remaining in protected areas (at AU-50) to nearly full mint bloom (at AU-58). Often the reverse of this type retains much more luster than the obverse, as the motto, eagle, and lettering protect the surrounding flat areas.

Illustrated coin: 1811. AU-58.
This lustrous example is well struck.

EF-40, 45 (Extremely Fine)

Obverse. More wear is seen on the portrait, the hair, the cap, and the drapery near the clasp. Luster is minimal or nonexistent at EF-40, and may be slight at EF-45.

Reverse. Wear is more extensive on the eagle, including the top of the wings, the head, the top of the shield, and the claws. Some traces of luster may be seen, more so at EF-45 than at EF-40.

Illustrated coin: 1807, BD-8. EF-40.

VF-20, 30 (Very Fine)

Obverse. Wear on the portrait has reduced the hair detail, especially to the right of the face and the top of the head, but much can still be seen.

Reverse. Wear on the eagle is greater, and details of feathers near the shield and near the top of the wings are weak or missing. All other features show wear, but most are fairly sharp. Generally, Capped Bust gold coins at this grade level lack eye appeal.

Illustrated coin: 1807, BD-8. VF-35.

The Capped Bust to Left half eagle is seldom collected in grades lower than VF-20.

1813–1834 CAPPED HEAD TO LEFT

History. Half eagles of this design are divided into issues of 1813 to 1829 (with a larger diameter), and the slightly restyled smaller-diameter issues of 1829 to 1834.

Striking and Sharpness. On the obverse, check the star centers and the hair details (these details are usually less distinct on the 1829–1834 smaller-diameter coins). On the reverse, check the eagle. Most examples are well struck. Adjustment marks are not often encountered.

Availability. The 1813 and 1814, 4 Over 3, are seen with some frequency and constitute the main supply available for assembling type sets. Other dates range from very rare to extremely rare, with the 1822 topping the list (just three are known, two of which are in the Smithsonian Institution). As gold coins did not circulate after 1821, issues of 1813 to 1820 are usually seen in high-level About Uncirculated or in Mint State, and those of the 1820s in Mint State. The half eagles of the early 1830s are exceptions; these usually show light wear and are much rarer in high-level Mint State.

Special note: PCGS and *Photograde* use identical descriptors for all Capped Bust half eagles of 1807 to 1834, and the ANA grading standards are parallel. We have separated the later issues here to provide for illustrations and comments concerning the pieces showcased.

MS-60 to 70 (Mint State)

Illustrated coin: 1832, 13 obverse stars, Bass-Dannreuther 1. MS-63.

Note: Abbreviations used in die-variety attributions, along with the reference works on which the attributions are based, are discussed on the first page of this chapter. All coins are shown enlarged, for clarity.

Obverse. At MS-60, some abrasion and contact marks are seen on the cheek, the hair below the LIBERTY inscription, and the highest-relief folds of the cap. Luster is present, but may be dull or lifeless, and interrupted in patches. At MS-63, contact marks are few, and abrasion is very light. At MS-64, abrasion is even less. An MS-65 coin has hardly any abrasion, and contact marks are minute. Luster should be full and rich and is often more intense on the obverse. Grades above MS-65 are defined by having fewer marks as perfection is approached.

Reverse. Comments apply as for the obverse, except that abrasion is most noticeable on the eagle's neck and the highest area of the wings.

AU-50, 53, 55, 58 (About Uncirculated)

Obverse. Light wear is seen on the cheek and the higher-relief areas of the hair and cap. Friction and scattered marks are in the field, ranging from extensive at AU-50 to minimal at AU-58. Luster may be seen in protected areas, minimal at AU-50 but more evident at AU-58. On an AU-58 coin the field retains some luster as well.

Illustrated coin: 1813, BD-1. AU-50.

Reverse. Comments as preceding, except that the eagle's neck, the top of the wings, the leaves, and the arrowheads now show noticeable wear, as do other features. Luster ranges from perhaps 40% remaining in protected areas (at AU-50) to nearly full mint bloom (at AU-58). Often the reverse of this type retains much more luster than the obverse, as the motto, eagle, and lettering protect the surrounding flat areas.

EF-40, 45 (Extremely Fine)

Obverse. More wear is seen on the portrait, the hair, the cap, and the drapery near the clasp. Luster is minimal or nonexistent at EF-40, and may be slight at EF-45.

Reverse. Wear is more extensive on the eagle, including the top of the wings, the head, the top of the shield, and the claws. Some traces of luster may be seen, more so at EF-45 than at EF-40.

Illustrated coin: 1813, BD-1. EF-45.

The Capped Head half eagle is seldom collected in grades lower than EF-40.

Proof Capped Head Half Eagles, PF-60 to 70

Proof coins were struck on a limited basis for inclusion in sets and for numismatists. All are exceedingly rare. Over the years some prooflike Mint State pieces have been classified as Proofs.

Illustrated coin: 1829, Small Diameter, BD-2. Proof.

Obverse and Reverse. PF-60 to 62 coins have extensive hairlines and may have nicks and contact marks. At PF-63, hairlines are prominent, but the mirror surface is very reflective. PF-64 coins have fewer hairlines. At PF-65, hairlines should be minimal and mostly seen only under magnification. There should be no nicks or marks. PF-66 and higher coins should have no marks or hairlines visible to the unaided eye.

1834–1838 Classic Head

History. The obverse of half eagles of this design was copied by Chief Engraver William Kneass from John Reich's cent of 1808. The Classic Head quarter eagle is related, but the imitation is not as close. Minted under the Act of June 28, 1834, their lighter weight permitted them to circulate widely, which they did until hoarding took place in the Civil War. Accordingly, many show extensive wear.

Striking and Sharpness. On the obverse, weakness is often seen on the higher areas of the hair curls. Also check the star centers. On the reverse, check the rims. The dentils are usually well struck.

Availability. Most coins range from Very Fine to About Uncirculated or lower grades of Mint State. Most Mint State coins are dated 1834. Choice and Gem Mint State examples are rare. Eye appeal can be a problem, and connoisseurship is recommended.

MS-60 to 70 (Mint State)

Illustrated coin: 1834, Plain 4. MS-65.
This well-struck coin has some light abrasion, most evident in the reverse field.

Note: All coins are shown enlarged, for clarity.

Obverse. At MS-60, some abrasion and contact marks are seen on the portrait, most noticeably on the cheek, as the hair details are complex on this type. Luster is present, but may be dull or lifeless, and interrupted in patches. Many low-level Mint State coins have grainy surfaces. At MS-63, contact marks are few, and abrasion is very light. Abrasion is even less at MS-64. An MS-65 coin will have hardly any abrasion, and contact marks are minute. Luster should be full and rich and is often more intense on the obverse. Grades above MS-65 are defined by having fewer marks as perfection is approached.

Reverse. Comments apply as for the obverse, except that abrasion is most noticeable in the field, on the eagle's neck, and on the highest area of the wings. Most Mint State coins in the marketplace are graded liberally, with slight abrasion on both sides of MS-65 coins.

AU-50, 53, 55, 58 (About Uncirculated)

Obverse. Friction is seen on the higher parts, particularly the cheek and the hair (under magnification) of Miss Liberty. Friction and scattered marks are in the field, ranging from extensive at AU-50 to minimal at AU-58. Luster may be seen in protected areas, minimal at AU-50, more evident at AU-58. On an AU-58 coin the field retains some luster as well.

Reverse. Comments as preceding, except that the eagle's neck, the top of the wings, the leaves,

Illustrated coin: 1834, Crosslet 4. AU-50.

and the arrowheads now show noticeable wear, as do other features. Luster ranges from perhaps 40% remaining in protected areas (at AU-50) to nearly full mint bloom (at AU-58). Often the reverse of this type retains much more luster than the obverse.

EF-40, 45 (Extremely Fine)

Obverse. Wear is seen on the portrait overall, with reduction or elimination of some separation of hair strands, especially in the area close to the face. The cheek shows light wear. Luster is minimal or nonexistent at EF-40, and may survive in among the letters of LIBERTY at EF-45.

Reverse. Wear is greater than on an About Uncirculated coin. On most (but not all) coins the neck lacks some feather detail on its highest points. Feathers have lost some detail near the edges and tips of the wings, and some areas of the horizontal lines in the shield may be blended together. Some traces of luster may be seen, more so at EF-45 than at EF-40.

Illustrated coin: 1837. EF-40.

VF-20, 30 (Very Fine)

Obverse. Wear on the portrait has reduced the hair detail, especially to the right of the face and the top of the head, but much can still be seen.

Reverse. Wear is greater, including on the shield and the wing feathers. Generally, Classic Head gold at this grade level lacks eye appeal.

Illustrated coin: 1835. VF-30.

The Classic Head half eagle is seldom collected in grades lower than VF-20.

Proof Classic Head Half Eagles, PF-60 to 70

Proofs of the Classic Head type were made in small quantities, and today probably only a couple dozen or so survive, most bearing the 1834 date.

Obverse and Reverse. PF-60 to 62 coins have extensive hairlines and may have nicks and contact marks. At PF-63, hairlines are prominent, but the mirror surface is very reflective. PF-64 coins have fewer hairlines. At PF-65, hairlines should be minimal and mostly seen only under magnification. There should be no nicks or marks. PF-66 and higher coins should have no marks or hairlines visible to the unaided eye.

Illustrated coin: 1834, Plain 4. PF-65.

1839–1908 LIBERTY HEAD

History. The Liberty Head half eagle designed by Christian Gobrecht made its debut in 1839. Branch-mint coins of this year had the mintmark on the obverse; it was relocated to the reverse for all later issues. The motifs with the Liberty Head obverse and perched eagle reverse closely follow those used on $2.50 coins of 1840 to 1907 and $10 coins of 1838 to 1907. The motto IN GOD WE TRUST was added to the reverse in 1866.

Striking and Sharpness. On the obverse, check the highest points of the hair and the star centers. On the reverse, check the eagle's neck, and the area to the lower left of the shield and the lower part of the eagle. Generally, the eagle on the $5 coins is better struck than on those of the $2.50 denomination. Examine the dentils on both sides. Branch-mint coins struck before the Civil War are often lightly struck in areas. San Francisco half eagles are in lower average grades than are those from the Philadelphia Mint, as Philadelphia coins did not circulate at par in the East and Midwest from late December 1861 until December 1878, and thus did not acquire as much wear. Most late 19th- and early 20th-century coins are sharp in all areas; for these issues, tiny copper staining spots can be a problem.

Availability. Early dates and mintmarks are generally scarce to rare in Mint State and very rare in choice or gem Mint State, with only a few exceptions. Charlotte and Dahlonega coins are usually Extremely Fine or About Uncirculated, or overgraded as low Mint State, this situation paralleling that seen with quarter eagles. C and D mint coins are everlastingly popular. Rarities include 1854-S and several varieties in the 1860s and 1870s. Coins of the 1880s onward are generally seen in higher average grades.

MS-60 to 70 (Mint State)

Illustrated coin: 1848-C. MS-63.
This is a high-level example of the Charlotte Mint half eagle. Friction is seen in the obverse fields amid luster; on the reverse the luster is nearly complete.

Note: All coins are shown enlarged, for clarity.

Obverse. At MS-60, some abrasion and contact marks are evident, most noticeably on the hair to the right of Miss Liberty's forehead and on the jaw. Luster is present, but may be dull or lifeless, and interrupted in patches. At MS-63, contact marks are few, and abrasion is very light. An MS-65 coin has only slight abrasion, and contact marks are so minute as to require magnification. Luster should be full and rich. Grades above MS-65 are defined by having fewer marks as perfection is approached.

Reverse. Comments apply as for the obverse, except that abrasion and contact marks are most noticeable on the eagle's neck and to the lower left of the shield.

AU-50, 53, 55, 58 (About Uncirculated)

Obverse. Light wear is seen on the face, the hair to the right of the face, and the highest area of the hair bun, more so at AU-50 than at 53 or 55. An AU-58 coin has minimal traces of wear. An AU-50 coin has luster in protected areas among the stars and letters, with little in the open fields or on the portrait. At AU-58, most luster is present in the fields, but is worn away on the highest parts of the motifs. Striking must be taken into consideration, for a lightly struck coin can be About Uncirculated, but be weak in the central areas.

Illustrated coin: 1840. AU-55.

Reverse. Comments as preceding, except that the eagle shows wear in all of the higher areas, as well as the leaves and arrowheads. From 1866 to 1908 the motto IN GOD WE TRUST helped protect the field, with the result that luster is more extensive on this side in comparison to the obverse. Luster ranges from perhaps 50% remaining in protected areas (at AU-50) to nearly full mint bloom (at AU-58).

EF-40, 45 (Extremely Fine)

Obverse. Wear is evident on all high areas of the portrait, including the hair to the right of the forehead, the tip of the coronet, the back of the head, and the hair bun. The stars show light wear at their centers (unless protected 1by a high rim). Luster, if present at all, is minimal and in protected areas such as between the star points.

Illustrated coin: 1844. EF-40.
This coin is well struck on both sides, now exhibiting the wear characteristic of the assigned grade.

Reverse. Wear is greater than on an About Uncirculated coin, and flatness is seen on the feather ends, the leaves, and elsewhere. Some traces of luster may be seen, more so at EF-45 than at EF-40. Overall, the reverse appears to be in a slightly higher grade than the obverse on coins from 1866 to 1908 (With Motto).

VF-20, 30 (Very Fine)

Obverse. The higher-relief areas of hair are worn flat at VF-20, less so at VF-30. The hair to the right of the coronet is merged into heavy strands. The stars are flat at their centers.

Reverse. Feather detail is mostly worn away on the neck and legs, less so on the wings. The vertical shield stripes, being deeply recessed, remain bold.

Illustrated coin: 1858-C. VF-20.

The Liberty Head half eagle is seldom collected in grades lower than VF-20.

Proof Liberty Head Half Eagles, PF-60 to 70

Proof coins exist in relation to their original mintages, with all issues prior to the 1890s being rare. Cameo contrast is the rule for Proofs prior to 1902. Beginning that year the portrait was polished in the die, although a few years later cameo-contrast coins were again made.

Obverse and Reverse. PF-60 to 62 coins have extensive hairlines and may have nicks and contact marks. At PF-63, hairlines are prominent, but the mirror surface is very reflective. PF-64 coins have fewer hairlines. At PF-65, hairlines A should be minimal and mostly seen only under magnification. There should be no nicks or marks. PF-66 and higher coins should have no marks or hairlines visible to the unaided eye.

Illustrated coin: 1872. PF-55.

1908–1929 INDIAN HEAD

History. Introduced in 1908 and minted continuously through 1916 and again in 1929, the Indian Head half eagle is similar in appearance to the quarter eagle of the same design. All features are *incuse* or recessed in the fields, except for mintmarks, which are raised. On most coins the rims are flat, while on others they are slightly raised. These coins saw limited use in circulation in the West, but were hardly seen elsewhere.

Striking and Sharpness. Striking varies. Look for weakness on the high parts of the Indian's bonnet and in the feather details in the headdress. On the reverse, check the feathers on the highest area of the wing.

Availability. These were not popular with numismatists of the time, who saved very few. The survival of Choice and Gem Mint State coins is a matter of chance. Rare issues include those of 1909-O, which is usually seen with evidence of circulation, often extensive, and 1929, most of which are in Mint State. Luster can range from deeply frosty to grainy. Because the fields are the highest areas of the coin, luster diminished quickly as the coins were circulated or jostled with others in bags.

MS-60 to 70 (Mint State)

Illustrated coin: 1911-D. MS-62.
This example is lustrous and attractive. Most of the luster in the fields (the highest-relief area of this unusual design) is still intact.

Note: All coins are shown enlarged, for clarity.

Obverse. At MS-60 to 62, there is abrasion in the field, this representing the highest part of the coin. Abrasion is also evident on the headdress. Marks and, occasionally, a microscopic pin scratch may be seen. At MS-63, there may be some abrasion and some tiny marks. Luster is irregular. At MS-64, abrasion is less. Luster is rich. At MS-65 and above, luster is deep and frosty, with no marks at all visible without magnification at MS-66 and higher.

Reverse. At MS-60 to 62 there is abrasion in the field, this representing the highest part of the coin. Abrasion is also evident on the eagle's wing. Otherwise, the same comments apply as for the obverse.

AU-50, 53, 55, 58 (About Uncirculated)

Obverse. Friction on the cheek is very noticeable at AU-50, increasingly less at higher levels to AU-58. The headdress shows light wear, most evident on the ribbon above the forehead and on the garland. Luster is minimal at AU-50 and scattered and incomplete at AU-58. Nicks and contact marks are to be expected.

Reverse. Friction on the wing and neck is very noticeable at AU-50, increasingly less noticeable at higher levels to 58. Otherwise, the same comments apply as for the obverse.

Illustrated coin: 1911. AU-50.

EF-40, 45 (Extremely Fine)

Obverse. Light wear will characterize the portrait and headdress. Luster is gone. Marks and tiny scratches are to be expected, but not distracting.

Reverse. Light wear is most evident on the eagle's head and wing, although other areas are lightly worn as well. Luster is gone. Marks and tiny scratches are to be expected, but not distracting.

Illustrated coin: 1909-O. EF-40.

VF-20, 30 (Very Fine)

Obverse. Many details of the garland and of the ribbon above the forehead are worn away. Many feather vanes are blended together. The field is dull and has contact marks.

Reverse. The neck and the upper part of the wing show extensive wear, other areas less so. The field is dull and has contact marks.

Illustrated coin: 1909. VF-25.
Some bumps are seen on the top obverse rim and should be mentioned in a description.

The Indian Head half eagle is seldom collected in grades lower than VF-20.

Proof Indian Head Half Eagles, PF-60 to 70

Sandblast (also called Matte) Proofs were made in 1908 and from 1911 to 1915, while Satin (also called Roman Finish) Proofs were made in 1909 and 1910. When seen, these are usually in higher Proof grades, PF-64 and above. As a class these are rarer than quarter eagles of the same date and style of finish. Most are in grades from PF-63 upward. At lower levels, coins can show light contact marks. Some microscopic bright flecks may be caused by the sandblasting process and, although they do not represent handling, usually result in a coin being assigned a slightly lower grade.

Illustrated coin: 1911. PF-67.
This is a particularly nice example.

Obverse and Reverse. At PF-60 to 63, there is light abrasion and some contact marks (the lower the grade, the higher the quantity). On Sandblast Proofs these show up as visually unappealing bright spots. At PF-64 and higher levels, marks are fewer, with magnification needed to see any at PF-65. At PF-66, there should be none at all.

GOLD EAGLES

GOLD EAGLES, 1795–1933

1795–1797 CAPPED BUST TO RIGHT / SMALL EAGLE REVERSE

History. Eagles of this style were introduced in the autumn of 1795. The obverse features Miss Liberty wearing a conical cap, generally called Capped Bust to Right. The reverse depicts a "small" eagle perched on a palm branch. The same motif was used on contemporary $5 gold coins.

Striking and Sharpness. On the obverse, check the star centers and the hair details. On the reverse, check the feathers of the eagle. In particular, the breast feathers are often weakly struck (cherrypickers will hunt for the minority of specimens that exhibit strong breast feathers; these are normally found at the same price as for a weak strike). Examine the dentils on both sides. Planchet adjustment marks are often visible, but are not noted by the grading services.

Availability. Typical grades range from Extremely Fine to About Uncirculated and low Mint State. MS-63 and higher coins are rare, and when seen are usually of the 1795 or 1796 dates. Certain varieties are rare. Certain eagles of 1796 have prooflike surfaces and are particularly attractive if in high grades.

MS-60 to 70 (Mint State)

Illustrated coin: 1795, Bass-Dannreuther 5. MS-63.
This coin is of the style with 13 leaves in the palm branch, as usually seen.

Note: Abbreviations used in die-variety attributions, along with the reference works on which the attributions are based, are discussed on the first page of this chapter. All coins are shown enlarged, for clarity.

Obverse. At MS-60, some abrasion and contact marks are evident, most noticeably on the hair to the left of Miss Liberty's forehead and on the higher-relief areas of the cap. Luster is present, but may be dull or lifeless, and interrupted in patches. At MS-63, contact marks are few, and abrasion is very light. An MS-65 coin has hardly any abrasion, and contact marks are so minute as to require magnification. Luster should be full and rich. On prooflike coins in any Mint State grade, abrasion and surface marks are much more noticeable. Coins above MS-65 exist more in theory than in reality for this type—but they do exist, and are defined by having fewer marks as perfection is approached.

Reverse. Comments apply as for the obverse, except that abrasion and contact marks are most noticeable on the breast and head of the eagle. The field area is mainly protected by the eagle, branch, and lettering.

AU-50, 53, 55, 58 (About Uncirculated)

Obverse. Light wear is seen on the cheek, the hair immediately to the left of the face, and the cap, more so at AU-50 than at 53 or 55. An AU-58 coin has minimal traces of wear. An AU-50 coin has luster in protected areas among the stars and letters, with little in the open fields or on the portrait. At AU-58, most luster is present in the fields, but is worn away on the highest parts of the motifs.

Illustrated coin: 1796. AU-58.
This example shows light wear overall, with hints of original luster in protected areas.

Reverse. Comments as preceding, except that the eagle shows light wear on the breast and head in particular, but also at the tip of the wing on the left and elsewhere. Luster ranges from perhaps 40% remaining in protected areas (at AU-50) to nearly full mint bloom (at AU-58).

EF-40, 45 (Extremely Fine)

Obverse. Wear is evident all over the portrait, with some loss of detail in the hair to the left of Miss Liberty's face. Excellent detail remains in low-relief areas of the hair, such as the front curl and at the back of her head. The stars show wear, as do the date and letters. Luster, if present at all, is minimal and in protected areas.

Reverse. Wear is greater than on an About Uncirculated coin. The breast, neck, and legs of the eagle lack nearly all feather detail. More wear is seen on the edges of the wing. Some traces of luster may be seen, more so at EF-45 than at EF-40.

Illustrated coin: 1795, BD-3. EF-45.

VF-20, 30 (Very Fine)

Obverse. The higher-relief areas of hair are well worn at VF-20, less so at VF-30. The stars are flat at their centers.

Reverse. Wear is greater, the eagle is flat in most areas, and about 40% to 60% of the wing feathers can be seen.

Illustrated coin: 1795, BD-2. VF-30.

The Capped Bust to Right eagle coin with Small Eagle reverse is seldom collected in grades lower than VF-20.

1797–1804 CAPPED BUST TO RIGHT / HERALDIC EAGLE REVERSE

History. Eagles of this type combine the previous obverse style with the Heraldic Eagle as used on other silver and gold coins of the era.

Striking and Sharpness. On the obverse, check the star centers and the hair details. On the reverse, check the upper part of the shield, the lower part of the eagle's neck, the eagle's wing, the stars above the eagle, and the clouds. Inspect the dentils on both sides. Planchet adjustment marks can be a problem and are not identified by the grading services.

Availability. The eagles of 1797 turn up with some regularity. Those of 1798 are rare. Usually seen are the 1799 through 1803 issues. Typical grades are Extremely Fine to lower Mint State ranges. MS-62 and higher coins are seen with some frequency and are usually dated 1799 and later. The 1804 is rare in true Mint State. Sharply struck coins without planchet adjustment marks are in the minority.

MS-60 to 70 (Mint State)

Illustrated coin: 1799, Large Stars, Bass-Dannreuther 10. MS-65.

This coin has an exceptionally sharp strike overall, but with some lightness on the eagle's dexter (viewer's left) talon. Note some trivial abrasion in the right obverse field.

Note: Abbreviations used in die-variety attributions, along with the reference works on which the attributions are based, are discussed on the first page of this chapter. All coins are shown enlarged, for clarity.

Obverse. At MS-60, some abrasion and contact marks are evident, most noticeably on the hair to the left of Miss Liberty's forehead and on the higher-relief areas of the cap. Luster is present, but may be dull or lifeless, and interrupted in patches. At MS-63, contact marks are few, and abrasion is very light. An MS-65 coin has even less abrasion (most observable in the right field), and contact marks are so minute as to require magnification. Luster should be full and rich. Coins graded above MS-65 are more theoretical than actual for this type—but they do exist, and are defined by having fewer marks as perfection is approached. Large-size eagles are usually graded with slightly less strictness than the lower gold denominations of this type.

Reverse. Comments apply as for the obverse, except that abrasion and contact marks are most noticeable on the upper part of the eagle and the clouds. The field area is complex, without much open space, given the stars above the eagle, the arrows and olive branch, and other features. Accordingly, marks are not as noticeable as on the obverse.

AU-50, 53, 55, 58 (About Uncirculated)

Obverse. Light wear is seen on the cheek, the hair immediately to the left of the face, and the cap, more so at AU-50 than at 53 or 55. An AU-58 coin has minimal traces of wear. An AU-50 coin has luster in protected areas among the stars and letters, with little in the open fields or on the portrait. At AU-58, most luster is present in the fields, but is worn away on the highest parts of the motifs.

Illustrated coin: 1799, Small Stars, BD-7. AU-50.
Note some lightness of strike at the center of the obverse. Significant luster remains.

Reverse. Comments as preceding, except that the eagle's neck, the tips and top of the wings, the clouds, and the tail now show noticeable wear, as do other features. Luster ranges from perhaps 40% remaining in protected areas (at AU-50) to nearly full mint bloom (at AU-58). Often the reverse of this type retains much more luster than the obverse.

EF-40, 45 (Extremely Fine)

Obverse. Wear is evident all over the portrait, with some loss of detail in the hair to the left of Miss Liberty's face. Excellent detail remains in low-relief areas of the hair, such as the front curl and at the back of her head. The stars show wear as do the date and letters. Luster, if present at all, is minimal and in protected areas.

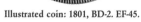

Illustrated coin: 1801, BD-2. EF-45.

Reverse. Wear is greater than on the preceding. The neck lacks some feather detail on its highest points. Feathers have lost some detail near the edges of the wings, and some areas of the horizontal lines in the shield may be blended together. Some traces of luster may be seen, more so at EF-45 than at EF-40. Overall, the reverse appears to be in a slightly higher grade than the obverse.

VF-20, 30 (Very Fine)

Obverse. The higher-relief areas of hair are well worn at VF-20, less so at VF-30.

Reverse. Wear is greater, including on the shield and wing feathers. The star centers are flat. Other areas have lost detail as well. E PLURIBUS UNUM may be faint in areas, but is usually sharp.

Illustrated coin: 1799, Small Stars, BD-7. VF-30.

The Capped Bust to Right eagle coin with Heraldic Eagle reverse is seldom collected in grades lower than VF-20.

Proof Capped Bust / Heraldic Eagle Reverse, PF-60 to 70

There were no Proofs coined in the era in which this type was issued. Years later, in 1834, the Mint made up new dies with the 1804 date and struck an unknown number of Proofs, perhaps a dozen or so, for inclusion in presentation Proof sets for foreign dignitaries. A handful of these survive today.

Obverse and Reverse. PF-60 to 62 coins have extensive hairlines and may have nicks and contact marks. At PF-63, hairlines are prominent, but the mirror surface is very reflective. PF-64 coins have fewer hairlines. At PF-65, hairlines should be minimal and mostly seen only under magnification. There should be no nicks or marks.

Illustrated coin: 1804, Plain 4. Proof.

1838–1907 LIBERTY HEAD

History. The Liberty Head eagle designed by Christian Gobrecht was first issued in 1838, after a suspension of this denomination since 1804. In mid-1839 the design was modified slightly (in such details as its lettering and Liberty's portrait). The obverse features the head of Miss Liberty with stars around and the date below. The reverse has a perched eagle. The same motif was later used on quarter eagles (1840) and half eagles (1839). The motto IN GOD WE TRUST was added to the reverse in 1866.

Striking and Sharpness. On the obverse, check the highest points of the hair and the star centers. On the reverse, check the eagle's neck, and the area to the lower left of the shield and the lower part of the eagle. Examine the dentils on both sides. Branch-mint coins issued before the Civil War are often lightly struck in areas, and some Carson City coins of the early 1870s can have areas of lightness. Most late 19th-century and early 20th-century coins are sharp in all areas. Tiny copper staining spots can be a problem for those issues.

Availability. Early dates and mintmarks are generally scarce to rare in Mint State and very rare in Choice or Gem Mint State, with only a few exceptions. These were work-horse coins in commerce; Very Fine and Extremely Fine grades are the rule for dates through the 1870s, and for some dates the finest known grade can be About Uncirculated. In Mint State, Liberty Head eagles as a class are rarer than either quarter eagles or half eagles. Some varieties are not known to exist at this level. Eagles of the 1880s onward are generally seen in higher average grades.

MS-60 to 70 (Mint State)

Illustrated coin: 1880. MS-63.
Brilliant and lustrous with scattered marks in the field as is typical for this grade.

Note: All coins are shown enlarged, for clarity.

Obverse. At MS-60, some abrasion and contact marks are evident, most noticeably on the hair to the right of Miss Liberty's forehead and on the jaw. Luster is present, but may be dull or lifeless, and interrupted in patches. At MS-63, contact marks are few, and abrasion is very light. An MS-65 coin has hardly any abrasion, and contact marks are so minute as to require magnification. Luster should be full and rich. For most dates, coins graded above MS-65 exist more in theory than in actuality—but they do exist, and are defined by having fewer marks as perfection is approached.

Reverse. Comments apply as for the obverse, except that abrasion and contact marks are most noticeable on the eagle's neck and to the lower left of the shield.

AU-50, 53, 55, 58 (About Uncirculated)

Obverse. Light wear is seen on the face, the hair to the right of the face, and the highest area of the hair bun, more so at AU-50 than at 53 or 55. An AU-58 coin has minimal traces of wear. An AU-50 coin has luster in protected areas among the stars and letters, with little in the open fields or on the portrait. At AU-58 most luster is present in the fields, but is worn away on the highest parts of the motifs.

Illustrated coin: 1839, 9 Over 8. AU-53.

Reverse. Comments as preceding, except that the eagle shows wear in all of the higher areas, as well as the leaves and arrowheads. Luster ranges from perhaps 40% remaining in protected areas (at AU-50) to nearly full mint bloom (at AU-58). Often the reverse of this type retains more luster than the obverse.

EF-40, 45 (Extremely Fine)

Obverse. Wear is evident on all high areas of the portrait, including the hair to the right of the forehead, the tip of the coronet, and the hair bun. The stars show light wear at their centers. Luster, if present at all, is minimal and in protected areas such as between the star points.

Illustrated coin: 1868. EF-40.
Note the many contact marks on both sides—enough that a careful cataloger would do well to mention them.

Reverse. Wear is greater than on an About Uncirculated coin. On the $10 coins (in contrast to the $2.50 and $5 of the same design), most of the details on the eagle are sharp. There is flatness on the leaves and arrowheads. Some traces of luster may be seen, more so at EF-45 than at EF-40.

VF-20, 30 (Very Fine)

Obverse. The higher-relief areas of hair are worn flat at VF-20, less so at VF-30. The hair to the right of the coronet is merged into heavy strands. The stars are flat at their centers.

Reverse. The eagle is worn further, with most neck feathers gone and with the feathers in the wing having flat tips. The branch leaves have little or no detail. The vertical shield stripes, being deeply recessed, remain bold.

Illustrated coin: 1838. VF-25.

The Liberty Head eagle is seldom collected in grades lower than VF-20.

Proof Liberty Head Eagles, PF-60 to 70

Proof coins exist in relation to their original mintages, with all issues prior to the 1890s being very rare. Cameo contrast is the rule for Proofs prior to 1902. Beginning that year the portrait was polished in the die, although a few years later, cameo contrast coins were again made.

Obverse and Reverse. PF-60 to 62 coins have extensive hairlines and may have nicks and contact marks. At PF-63, hairlines are prominent, but the mirror surface is very reflective. PF-64 coins have fewer hairlines. At PF-65, hairlines should be minimal and mostly seen only under magnification. There should be no nicks or marks. PF-66 and higher coins should have no marks or hairlines visible to the unaided eye.

Illustrated coin: 1862. PF-65.
This is a museum-quality gem, with cameo-contrast motifs and mirror fields.

1907–1933 INDIAN HEAD

History. Designed by famous sculptor Augustus Saint-Gaudens, this type was minted from 1907 to 1916 and again in the issues of 1920-S, 1926, 1930-S, 1932, and 1933. Beginning in July 1908 the motto IN GOD WE TRUST was added to the reverse. These coins were widely used in their time in the American West (until 1918) and for export.

Striking and Sharpness. On the obverse, check the hair details and the vanes in the feathers. On the reverse, check the shoulder of the eagle. As well-struck coins are available for all varieties, avoid those that are weakly struck. Luster varies, but is often deeply frosty. On other coins, particularly from 1910 to 1916, it may be grainy.

Availability. The rolled (or round) rim and wire rim 1907 coins, the 1920-S, 1930-S, and the 1933 are the key rarities. Others are generally available. MS-63 and higher coins are generally scarce to rare for the mintmarked issues. This is a very popular series, and a collection makes a fine display. Most in collectors' hands are coins that were exported in their time, then brought back to America after World War II.

MS-60 to 70 (Mint State)

Illustrated coin: 1907. MS-62.
This is a brilliant and lustrous example.

Note: All coins are shown enlarged, for clarity.

Obverse. At MS-60, some abrasion and contact marks are evident, most noticeably on the hair to the left of Miss Liberty's forehead and in the left field. Luster is present, but may be dull or lifeless, and interrupted in patches. At MS-63, contact marks are few, and abrasion is very light. An MS-65 coin has hardly any abrasion, and contact marks are minute. Luster should be full and rich. Grades above MS-65 are defined by having fewer marks as perfection is approached.

Reverse. Comments apply as for the obverse, except that abrasion and contact marks are most noticeable on the front of the left wing and in the left field.

AU-50, 53, 55, 58 (About Uncirculated)

Obverse. Light wear is seen on the cheek, the hair to the right of the face, and the headdress, more so at AU-50 coin than at 53 or 55. An AU-58 coin has minimal traces of wear. An AU-50 coin has luster in protected areas among the stars and in the small field area to the right. At AU-58, most luster is present in the fields but is worn away on the highest parts of the Indian.

Reverse. Comments as preceding, except that the eagle's left wing, left leg, neck, and leg show light wear. Luster ranges from perhaps 40% (at AU-50) to nearly full mint bloom (at AU-58).

Illustrated coin: 1908-D. AU-58.
With nearly full original luster, this coin has great eye appeal.

EF-40, 45 (Extremely Fine)

Obverse. More wear is evident on the hair to the right of the face, and the feather vanes lack some details, although most are present. Luster, if present at all, is minimal.

Reverse. Wear is greater than on the preceding. The front edge of the left wing is worn and blends into the top of the left leg. Some traces of luster may be seen, more so at EF-45 than at EF-40.

Illustrated coin: 1907. EF-40.

VF-20, 30 (Very Fine)

Obverse. The Indian's forehead blends into the hair to the right. Feather-vane detail is gone except in the lower areas.

Reverse. Wear is greater on the eagle, with only a few details remaining on the back of the left wing and the tail.

Illustrated coin: 1908-S. VF-25.

The Indian Head eagle is seldom collected in grades lower than VF-20.

Proof Indian Head Eagles, PF-60 to 70

Sandblast (also called Matte) Proofs were made each year from 1907 through 1915. These have dull surfaces, much like fine-grained sandpaper. Satin (also called Roman Finish) Proofs were made in 1908, 1909, and 1910; they have satiny surfaces and are bright yellow. All are rare today.

Illustrated coin: 1915. Sandblast PF-65.

Obverse and Reverse. At PF-60 to 63, there is light abrasion and some contact marks (the lower the grade, the higher the quantity). On Sandblast Proofs these show up as visually unappealing bright spots. At PF-64 and higher levels, marks are fewer, with magnification needed to see any at PF-65. At PF-66, there should be none at all.

GOLD DOUBLE EAGLES

GOLD DOUBLE EAGLES, 1850–1933

1850–1907 LIBERTY HEAD

History. Double eagles were introduced in 1850 as a convenient denomination to convert quantities of Gold Rush metal into coins. The Liberty Head style was created by James B. Longacre, chief engraver at the U.S. Mint. In 1866, IN GOD WE TRUST was added to the reverse, and in 1877 the denomination on the reverse, formerly given as TWENTY D., was changed to TWENTY DOLLARS. Double eagles proved to be very popular, especially for export. By 1933, more than 75% of the gold used to strike coins from the early days onward had been used to coin pieces of this denomination.

Striking and Sharpness. On the obverse, check the star centers and the hair details. As made, the hair details are less distinct on many coins of 1859 (when a slight modification was made) through the 1890s, and knowledge of this is important. Later issues usually have exquisite detail. The reverse is usually well struck, but check the eagle and other features. The dentils are sharp on nearly all coins, but should be checked.

Availability. Basic dates and mintmarks are available in proportion to their mintages. The 1854-O, 1856-O, 1861 and 1861-S Paquet Reverse, 1866 No Motto, 1870-CC, 1879-O, and several Philadelphia Mint dates of the 1880s are key issues, but the vast majority of others are readily collectible. Among early coins, Mint State examples from about 1854 to 1857 are available, most notably the 1857-S (of which more than 5,000 Mint State coins, many of which were choice and gem quality, were recovered from the wreck of the SS *Central America*) and certain varieties of the 1860s (recovered from the 1865 wrecks of the SS *Brother Jonathan* and SS *Republic*). Most varieties of the 1880s onward, and particularly the 1890s and 1900s, are easily available in Mint State, due to the repatriation of millions of coins that were exported.

MS-60 to 70 (Mint State)

Illustrated coin: 1876-S. MS-64.
A common date and mint, the 1876-S (like many double eagles) becomes elusive in this high Mint State grade.

Note: All coins are shown enlarged, for clarity.

Obverse. At MS-60, some abrasion and contact marks are evident, most noticeably on the hair to the right of Miss Liberty's forehead and on the cheek. Luster is present, but may be dull or lifeless, and interrupted in patches. At MS-63, contact marks are few, and abrasion is light. An MS-65 coin has little abrasion, and contact marks are minute. Luster should be full and rich. Grades above MS-65 are defined by having fewer marks as perfection is approached.

Reverse. Comments apply as for the obverse, except that abrasion and contact marks are most noticeable on eagle's neck, wingtips, and tail.

AU-50, 53, 55, 58 (About Uncirculated)

Obverse. Light wear is seen on the face, the hair to the right of the face, and the highest area of the hair behind the coronet, more so at AU-50 than at 53 or 55. An AU-58 coin has minimal traces of wear. An AU-50 coin has luster in protected areas among the stars and letters, with little in the open fields or on the portrait. At AU-58 most luster is present in the fields, but is worn away on the highest parts of the motifs.

Reverse. Comments as preceding, except that the eagle and ornaments show wear in all of the higher areas. Luster ranges from perhaps 40% remaining in protected areas (at AU-50) to nearly full mint bloom (at AU-58). Often the reverse of this type retains more luster than the obverse.

Illustrated coin: 1856-S. AU-53.
Much of the original luster still remains at this grade level, especially on the reverse.

EF-40, 45 (Extremely Fine)

Obverse. Wear is evident on all high areas of the portrait, including the hair to the right of the forehead, the tip of the coronet, and hair behind the coronet. The curl to the right of the neck is flat on its highest-relief area. Luster, if present at all, is minimal and in protected areas such as between the star points.

Reverse. Wear is greater than on an About Uncirculated coin. The eagle's neck and wingtips show wear, as do the ornaments and rays. Some traces of luster may be seen, more so at EF-45 than at EF-40. Overall, the reverse appears to be in a slightly higher grade than the obverse.

Illustrated coin: 1855-S. EF-45.

VF-20, 30 (Very Fine)

Obverse. The higher-relief areas of hair are worn flat at VF-20, less so at VF-30. The hair to the right of the coronet is merged into heavy strands and is flat at the back, as is part of the bow. The curl to the right of the neck is flat.

Reverse. The eagle shows further wear on the head, the tops of the wings, and the tail. The ornament has flat spots.

Illustrated coin: 1857-S. VF-20.
Note the small test cut or mark on the top rim.

The Liberty Head double eagle is seldom collected in grades lower than VF-20.

Proof Liberty Head Double Eagles, PF-60 to 70

Proofs were struck in all years from 1858 to 1907, and a few were made before then. Those dated through the 1870s are all very rare today; those of the 1880s are less so; and those of the 1890s and 1900s are scarce. Many have been mishandled. Dates that are Proof-only (and those that are very rare in circulation-strike form) are in demand even if in impaired Proof condition. These include 1883, 1884, 1885, 1886, and 1887. Proofs of 1902 onward, particularly 1903, have the portrait polished in the die and lack the cameo contrast of earlier dates.

Illustrated coin: 1903. PF-64.
A beautiful Proof, this is just a few hairlines away from a higher level. Beginning in this year and continuing for a short time afterward, the Mint polished the portrait in the Proof die.

Obverse and Reverse. PF-60 to 62 coins have extensive hairlines and may have nicks and contact marks. At PF-63, hairlines are prominent, but the mirror surface is very reflective. PF-64 coins have fewer hairlines. At PF-65, hairlines should be relatively few. These large and heavy coins reveal hairlines more readily than do the lower denominations, mostly seen only under magnification. PF-66 and higher coins should have no marks or hairlines visible to the unaided eye.

MCMVII (1907) HIGH RELIEF

History. Created by noted sculptor Augustus Saint-Gaudens under a commission arranged by President Theodore Roosevelt, this double eagle was first made (in pattern form) with sculptured-effect ultra high relief on both sides and the date in Roman numerals. The story of its production is well known and has been described in several books, notably *Renaissance of American Coinage, 1905–1908* (Burdette, 2006) and *Striking Change: The Great Artistic Collaboration of Theodore Roosevelt and Augustus Saint-Gaudens* (Moran, 2008). After the Ultra High Relief patterns of 1907, a modified High Relief version was developed to facilitate production. Each coin required three blows of the press to strike up properly. They were made on a medal press in December 1907 and January 1908, to the extent of fewer than 13,000 pieces. In the meantime, production was under way for low-relief coins, easier to mint in quantities sufficient for commerce–these dated 1907 rather than MCMVII. Today, the MCMVII double eagle is a favorite, and when surveys are taken of beautiful and popular designs (as in *100 Greatest U.S. Coins*, by Garrett and Guth), it usually ranks at the top.

Striking and Sharpness. The striking is usually good. Check the left knee of the standing figure, which sometimes shows lightness of strike and, most often, shows flatness or wear (sometimes concealed by etching or clever tooling). Check the Capitol at the lower left. On the reverse, check the high points at the top of the eagle. The surface on all is a delicate matte texture, grainy rather than deeply frosty. Under examination the fields show myriad tiny raised curlicues and other die-finish marks. There is no record of any being made as *Proofs,* nor is there any early numismatic record of any being sold as Proofs. Walter Breen in the 1960s made up some "guidelines" for Proofs, which some graders have adopted. PCGS, for one, does not recognize the Proof category, nor did the late Harry W. Bass Jr. (the foremost student of gold coins in the late-20th century). Some homemade "Proofs" have been made by pickling or sandblasting the surface of regular coins. *Caveat emptor.*

Availability. Half or more of the original mintage still exist today, as many were saved, and these grade mostly from AU-50 to MS-62. Circulated examples have often been cleaned, polished, or used in jewelry. Higher-grade coins are seen with some frequency, through MS-65. Overgrading is a common practice.

MS-60 to 70 (Mint State)

Illustrated coin: MCMVII (1907), High Relief. MS-65.
This is a splendid gem striking of one of America's most beautiful coins.

Note: All coins are shown enlarged, for clarity.

Obverse. At MS-60, some abrasion and contact marks are seen on Liberty's chest. The left knee is flat on lower Mint State coins and all circulated coins. Scattered marks and abrasion are in the field. Satiny luster is present, but may be dull or lifeless, and interrupted in patches. Many coins at this level have been cleaned. At MS-63, contact marks are fewer, and abrasion is light, but the knee still has a flat spot. An MS-65 coin has little abrasion and few marks. Grades above MS-65 are defined by having fewer marks as perfection is approached.

Reverse. Comments apply as for the obverse, except that abrasion and contact marks are most noticeable on the side of the eagle's body and the top of the left wing.

AU-50, 53, 55, 58 (About Uncirculated)

Obverse. Light wear is seen on the chest, the left leg, and the field, more so at AU-50 than at 53 or 55. An AU-58 coin has fewer traces of wear. An AU-50 coin has satiny luster in protected areas among the rays, with little in the open field above. At AU-58, most luster is present.

Reverse. Comments as preceding, except that the side of the eagle below the front of the wing, the top of the wing, and the field show light wear. Satiny luster ranges from perhaps 40% (at AU-50) to nearly full mint bloom (at AU-58).

Illustrated coin: MCMVII (1907), High Relief. AU-55.

EF-40, 45 (Extremely Fine)

Obverse. Wear is seen on all the higher-relief areas of the standing figure and on the rock at the lower right. Luster is minimal, if present at all. Eye appeal is apt to be lacking. Nearly all Extremely Fine coins have been cleaned.

Reverse. The eagle shows more wear overall, especially at the bottom and on the tops of the wings.

Illustrated coin: MCMVII (1907), High Relief. EF-45.

VF-20, 30 (Very Fine)

Obverse. Most details of the standing figure are flat, her face is incomplete, and the tips of the rays are weak. Eye appeal is usually poor. As these coins did not circulate to any extent, a Very Fine coin was likely carried as a pocket piece.

Reverse. Wear is greater overall, but most evident on the eagle. Detail is good at the center of the left wing, but worn away in most other areas of the bird.

Illustrated coin: MCMVII (1907), High Relief. VF-30.

The MCMVII (1907) High Relief double eagle is seldom collected in grades lower than VF-20.

1907–1933 Saint-Gaudens

History. In autumn 1907 Chief Engraver Charles E. Barber modified Saint-Gaudens's design by lowering the relief and using arabic (not roman) numerals. Coins of this type were struck in large quantities from 1907 to 1916 and again from 1920 to 1933. In July 1908 the motto IN GOD WE TRUST was added to the reverse. The vast majority of these coins were exported. Since World War II millions have been repatriated, supplying most of those in numismatic hands today.

Striking and Sharpness. The details are often light on the obverse. Check the bosom of Miss Liberty, the covering of which is apt to be weak on 1907 and, especially, 1908 No Motto coins. Check the Capitol building and its immediate area at the lower left. The reverse is usually well struck, but check the feathers on the eagle and the top of the wings.

Availability. Most dates and mintmarks range from very common to slightly scarce, punctuated with scarce to very rare issues such as 1908-S, 1920-S, 1921, mintmarks from 1924 to 1927, and all issues of 1929 to 1933. A million or more Mint State coins probably exist of certain dates, most notably 1908 No Motto, 1924, and 1927. (Although 1928 has by far the highest mintage, most were exported or melted, and 1928 is the least frequently seen of those three dates mentioned.) Quality varies, as many have contact marks. "Gradeflation" has taken place in recent years, and many nicked and marked coins certified as MS-63 in the 1980s are now sold as MS-64 or 65. Philadelphia Mint coins from 1922 onward are usually seen with excellent eye appeal. Common varieties are not usually collected in grades below Mint State. Connoisseurship will pay dividends.

MS-60 to 70 (Mint State)

Illustrated coin: 1924. MS-65.
This is one of the most common dates in gem Mint State.

Note: All coins are shown enlarged, for clarity.

Obverse. At MS-60, some abrasion and contact marks are seen on Liberty's chest and left knee, and scattered marks and abrasion are in the field. Luster is present, but may be dull or lifeless, and interrupted in patches. At MS-63, contact marks are fewer, and abrasion is light. An MS-65 coin has little abrasion and few marks, although quality among certified coins can vary. On a conservatively graded coin the luster should be full and rich. Grades above MS-65 are defined by having fewer marks as perfection is approached. Generally, Mint State coins of 1922 onward are choicer and more attractive than the earlier issues.

Reverse. Comments apply as for the obverse, except that abrasion and contact marks are most noticeable on the eagle's left wing.

AU-50, 53, 55, 58 (About Uncirculated)

Obverse. Light wear is seen on the chest, the left knee, the midriff, and across the field, more so at AU-50 than at 53 or 55. An AU-58 coin has minimal traces of wear. An AU-50 coin has luster in protected areas among the rays, with little in the open field above. At AU-58, most luster is present.

Reverse. Comments as preceding, except that the side of the eagle below the front of the wing, the top of the wing, and the field show light wear. Luster ranges from perhaps 40% (at AU-50) to nearly full mint bloom (at AU-58).

Illustrated coin: 1909, 9 Over 8. AU-50.

EF-40, 45 (Extremely Fine)

Obverse. Wear is seen on all the higher-relief areas of the standing figure and on the rock at the lower right. Luster is minimal, if present at all. Eye appeal is apt to be lacking.

Reverse. The eagle shows more wear overall, especially at the bottom and on the tops of the wings.

Illustrated coin: 1908-S. EF-40.

VF-20, 30 (Very Fine)

Obverse. Most details of the standing figure are flat, her face is incomplete, and the tips of the rays are weak. Eye appeal is usually poor.

Reverse. Wear is greater overall, but most evident on the eagle. Detail is good at the center of the left wing, but worn away in most other areas of the bird.

Illustrated coin: 1914. VF-20.

The Saint-Gaudens double eagle is seldom collected in grades lower than VF-20.

Proof Saint-Gaudens Double Eagles, PF-60 to 70

Sandblast (also called Matte) Proofs were made in 1908 and from 1911 to 1915. These have dull surfaces, much like fine-grained sandpaper. Satin (also called Roman Finish) Proofs were made in 1909 and 1910. They have satiny surfaces and are bright yellow. All are rare today.

Obverse and Reverse. At PF-60 to 63, there is light abrasion and some contact marks (the lower the grade, the higher the quantity). On Sandblast Proofs these show up as visually unappealing bright spots. At PF-64 and higher levels, marks are fewer, with magnification needed to see any at PF-65. At PF-66, there should be none at all.

Illustrated coin: 1909. Satin Finish PF-66.
This coin's certified-grade holder was marked simply "Proof-66."

The Expert's Guide
to
COLLECTING & INVESTING IN RARE COINS

Coin collecting—the "Hobby of Kings"—pays rich dividends in fun and enjoyment. But it can also pay the old-fashioned way: with a huge return on your investment. Now you can learn how to be a smart collector and investor, straight from the expert: award-winning author and numismatist Q. David Bowers.

With hands-on advice, real-life examples, and entertaining storytelling, the "dean of American numismatics" shares 50 years of experience buying and selling rare coins, tokens, medals, and paper money.

Want to know how to evaluate a coin's potential? Use the four-step process in chapter 2. What's the best way to predict the rare-coin market? It doesn't take a crystal ball; find out in chapter 13. To avoid getting burned in online auctions, read chapter 15. And if you want to be a smart seller, you can learn the ropes in chapter 34. All of these expert secrets, and more, are waiting inside. . . .

THE AUTHORITATIVE RESOURCE FOR INVESTING IN RARE COINS
From the Publisher of the Best-Selling Official Red Book of U.S. Coins

The Expert's Guide
to
COLLECTING & INVESTING IN RARE COINS

Invest Hundreds
Make Thousands!
Eliasberg, Pittman, and Ford did it—and you can too.
LEARN HOW INSIDE!

Q. DAVID BOWERS

688 pages, illustrated.
Softcover $19.95,
hardcover $29.95

Whitman
Publishing, LLC
PUBLISHING SINCE 1934
www.whitman.com

"[Bowers brings] proper balance to the interplay of collecting and investing in our hobby community."
—Clifford Mishler, numismatic author and researcher

"Are there really 'secrets' to successful coin buying? You bet! And Dave Bowers reveals them here. His style is entertaining, informative, and motivating. . . ."
—Kenneth Bressett, editor of the *Guide Book of United States Coins*

Order online at www.whitman.com
Call 1-800-546-2995 • Email info@whitman.com

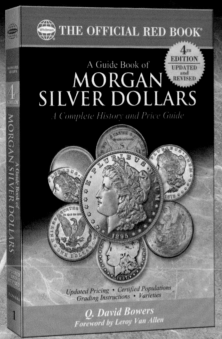

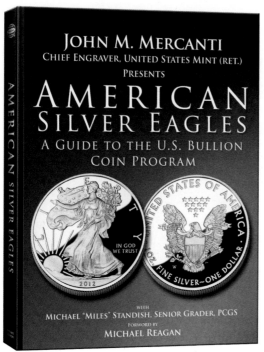